"Matthieu Richelle's introduction to exegesis is a real gem. Many primers on method lose sight of the biblical text amidst the various technicalities. In contrast, Richelle's guide is packed full of examples. Not only will readers come away with an outstanding knowledge about how to read the biblical text, but they will also acquire a deeper appreciation of the richness and subtlety of the Hebrew Bible."

—**Nathan MacDonald, Professor of the Interpretation of the Old Testament, University of Cambridge (UK)**

"Matthieu Richelle has written a much-needed primer that unlocks the key ideas and methods of biblical exegesis through concrete examples, useful resources, and practical exercises. He takes readers on an incredible journey into the historical and literary worlds of the Hebrew Bible, and also reveals the fascinating afterlives of its texts. I can't wait to share this book with the students in my classroom!"

—**Lydia Lee, Assistant Professor of Biblical Studies, Fudan University (China)**

"*Interpreting Israel's Scriptures* is a detailed and accessible introduction, but what really sets it apart is its comprehensive nature. Matthieu Richelle covers a diverse array of approaches, from textual to literary-historical to reader-oriented. The chapters are filled with helpful examples and annotated bibliographies that effectively illustrate and expand upon the various approaches described therein. Richelle's expert collection of material results in an invaluable resource for all who teach biblical literature."

—**Matthew J. Suriano, Associate Professor, The Joseph and Rebecca Meyerhoff Center for Jewish Studies, University of Maryland (USA)**

"*Interpreting Israel's Scriptures* proves that Matthieu Richelle is not only an excellent scholar but also a dedicated and enthusiastic educator. Capably covering everything from translation and textual criticism to feminist criticism and postcolonial studies, Richelle pulls back the veil to offer a behind-the-scenes look at how biblical scholars work: what resources they consult, how they reason their way through problems, and how they make decisions in the face of incomplete data. With concrete examples and helpful practice exercises, this book is the perfect resource for professors who want to transform their students from passive observers into active scholars in their own right."

—**Sara J. Milstein, Associate Professor of Hebrew Bible and Ancient Near Eastern Studies, The University of British Columbia (Canada)**

"With impressive range and knowledge, Richelle offers a clear, accessible, and up-to-date guide to interpreting biblical texts. An indispensable resource for the classroom."

—**Jacqueline Vayntrub, Associate Professor of Hebrew Bible Yale Divinity School (Connecticut, USA)**

"This impressive volume displays the broad range of skills professional biblical scholars use when they analyze the Hebrew Bible / Old Testament. If this activity is mapped as 'behind, within, and beyond' the text, Matthieu Richelle does it all, with clear explanations, copious examples, and annotated bibliographies—plus exercises that invite readers to cultivate the skills for themselves. Now translated and developed from the original French, here you will learn from a clear, balanced, and reliable teacher of the interpretation of the largest part of the world's most widely distributed canon of religious literature."

**—Hywel Clifford, Lecturer in Old Testament
Ripon College Cuddesdon, University of Oxford (UK)**

"Peppered with vivid examples and practical exercises, *Interpreting Israel's Scriptures* is an invaluable guide for students learning to apply the exegetical method to the Hebrew Bible. The book fruitfully combines traditional approaches to biblical exegesis with more recent modes of interpretation that emphasize the power dynamics behind biblical texts and their later reception, including gender analysis and postcolonial theory."

**—Julia Rhyder, Assistant Professor of Near Eastern Languages
and Civilizations, Harvard University (Massachusetts, USA)**

"Richelle's handbook is exactly the sort of practical introduction that many students need. The step-by-step guides, full of sage advice and top tips, encourage students to try their hand at a range of historical, literary, and ideological approaches to the Bible. Richelle introduces the theory and often arcane terminology in an accessible way, provides pertinent examples from the biblical text, and directs readers to the standard reference works. His aim is not to be prescriptive nor to offer the 'final word' on any given methodology, but to equip students with the basic tools they need to begin to develop their own informed judgments about the biblical text."

**—Hector M. Patmore, Associate Professor in Biblical Studies
Katholieke Universiteit Leuven (Belgium)**

"*Interpreting Israel's Scriptures* is a comprehensive guide to biblical exegesis, one that informs without overwhelming and fosters creativity and love of exegesis without imposing a specific method or agenda. Richelle's authentic and engaging style, his openness to a diversity of perspectives, and his impressive breadth of knowledge of the field invite students and seasoned scholars alike to explore the rich tapestry of biblical interpretation."

**—Mahri Leonard-Fleckman, Assistant Professor of Hebrew Bible
College of the Holy Cross (Massachusetts, USA)**

"The English edition of Matthieu Richelle's guide for interpreting the Hebrew Bible is a very welcome and comprehensive working tool for biblical scholars. It offers philological, historical, and hermeneutical perspectives and is replete with illustrative textual examples. I have no doubt that this book will be used and read widely."

—Konrad Schmid, Professor of Hebrew Bible and Ancient Judaism
University of Zurich (Switzerland)

"Matthieu Richelle deserves great thanks from all of us who study the Hebrew Bible—both students and teachers—for *Interpreting Israel's Scriptures*. This practical guide is tuned into the needs of students, who are often mystified by the novelty and complexity of how their professors interpret the Bible. Not only does *Interpreting Israel's Scriptures* rival other introductory textbooks in coverage of the concepts foundational to twenty-first-century exegesis, but Richelle's book stands out for having copious, illuminating examples and exercises for students to refine their developing skills in exegesis. I eagerly look forward to teaching with this book in my courses."

—Justin Reed, Assistant Professor of Old Testament / Hebrew Bible
Louisville Presbyterian Theological Seminary (Kentucky, USA)

"This is an extraordinary volume, with respect to both its contents and its pedagogical approach. It is enjoyable to read, with many practical examples and exercises to help students acquire concrete skills. A highly recommended work for all students who are beginning study of the Old Testament, for teachers, and for other readers as well."

—Jean Koulagna, Professor of Old Testament, Philology, and Biblical
Hermeneutics, Institut Œcuménique de Théologie Al Mowafaqa (Morocco)

"Perceiving the need for a different kind of introduction to biblical exegesis, Matthieu Richelle has given us a wonderful treatment of the topic focused on practical aspects of methodology. Each section of *Interpreting Israel's Scriptures* succinctly articulates the theoretical bases of a methodology, and then spends significant time on the 'how to' of biblical interpretation. The book is packed with real examples and covers an impressive range of both traditional and more recent methodologies. Richelle has thought hard and well about how to present this material in an accessible way. *Interpreting Israel's Scriptures* is pedagogically astute and student-focused. In my Introduction to Old Testament course, where students are assigned an exegetical paper for a large part of their grade, *Interpreting Israel's Scriptures* will be required reading."

—John Screnock, Tutor in Old Testament
Wycliffe Hall, University of Oxford (UK)

"I just loved this book! Using great examples, Matthieu Richelle shows how to handle the text of the Hebrew Bible in all its variety, complexity, and plurality. This is a book that needs to be studied in a seminar—I could work with it for years in a row."

—**Kristin De Troyer, Professor of Old Testament**
University of Salzburg (Austria)

"Richelle leaves no stone unturned in this sophisticated yet practical introduction to biblical interpretation. From textual criticism to historical geography, from poetic analysis to postcolonial criticism, this book illustrates the many possible dimensions of examination of the biblical text through the use of copious examples. Richelle's erudition, attention to detail, and judicious approach are evident on every page, and the up-to-date lists of bibliographical resources will be useful even for the most advanced of students. I can't think of a better one-volume guide to the world of biblical exegesis."

—**Joseph Lam, Associate Professor of Religious Studies**
University of North Carolina at Chapel Hill (USA)

"This is a very useful book that Matthieu Richelle offers to all who want to practice biblical exegesis seriously. Its value lies in its approach, which is not only to provide the theoretical foundations of the various existing methods but also to present the steps by which one can apply each of these methods and to illustrate these steps with numerous and detailed examples. In this very pedagogical guide, Richelle is a companion for beginners, showing them ways to examine various biblical texts and pointing them to the right resources. In this respect, it is valuable that electronic resources are mentioned, as it is difficult to find one's way through the abundance of what is published on the Internet. In addition, we can be grateful to the author for refusing to favor one exegetical method over another and for highlighting the value of each of them as well as the interaction that exists between methods or approaches that at first sight seem very different. This book will undoubtedly be useful to many students and will even give them an idea of how fun exegesis can be!"

—**Sophie Ramond, Professor of Biblical Exegesis**
Institut Catholique de Paris (France)

"Some reference works, though useful, are not user-friendly. This is not the case with Matthieu Richelle's *Interpreting Israel's Scriptures*. Orienting the reader toward all aspects of exegesis, Richelle demystifies the process of academic biblical interpretation. He succeeds admirably in making the implicit explicit. A wealth of sidebars containing worked examples and up-to-date bibliographies makes the book an exceedingly valuable reference work. Yet it is the book's clear and winsome presentation that makes it such a welcome companion for students at various levels and for teachers who, until now, have had to piece together what Richelle has expertly gathered in a single, indispensable volume."

—**Michael C. Legaspi, Associate Professor of Scripture**
St. Vladimir's Orthodox Theological Seminary (New York, USA)

"The uniqueness of this handbook is the author's consistently practical approach to the exegetical enterprise, always with the student in mind, which immediately sets it apart from other such resources currently available. And his practicality leads to another unique feature: the numerous and detailed examples and exercises, illustrating for the student how the theoretical discussion finds real-world application when interpreting an Old Testament text. This volume will quickly become the standard handbook for students learning to interpret the Hebrew Bible responsibly."

—**Bill T. Arnold, Paul S. Amos Professor of Old Testament Interpretation Asbury Theological Seminary (Kentucky, USA)**

"Matthieu Richelle has masterfully crafted a guide to exegesis that is sure to develop and sharpen the exegetical skills of those who use it. Especially unique is Richelle's integrated approach that invites the reader to join the dialectic between the 'three worlds' of interpretation: the world *behind* the text, the world *of* the text, and the world *in front of* the text. Whether at a college, university, or seminary, all students who desire to effectively plumb the depths of the Hebrew Bible would do well to acquire Richelle's exegetical guide, which is both expansive yet practical, erudite yet accessible."

—**Julian C. Chike, Assistant Professor of Hebrew Bible / Old Testament Baylor University (Texas, USA)**

"This handbook is sorely needed for introductory courses in theological/biblical studies today because of the way in which it bridges traditional exegesis and more recent interpretive approaches. Richelle lays out step-by-step the process of textual analysis, with plenty of examples that illustrate the importance of doing it well. He then moves to reader-centered interpretive methods, showing how they build on careful exegesis. Highly recommended for seminaries, graduate schools, and upper-division undergraduate courses."

—**Steven L. McKenzie, Professor of Hebrew Bible / Old Testament and Spence L. Wilson Senior Research Fellow, Rhodes College (Tennessee, USA)**

"This book will be highly appreciated by teachers and students. Matthieu Richelle addresses the complexity of biblical exegetical methodologies in a language that is accessible to beginners while taking into consideration the latest developments in the field. Through well-chosen examples, the book presents fourteen exegetical methods, among which are classic ones, such as textual and compositional criticism, as well as more current approaches, such as postcolonial criticism and feminist studies. Thank you, Prof. Richelle, for giving us a manual that, I believe, will be indispensable for professors and students of the Bible."

—**Peter Dubovský, Professor of Old Testament Exegesis Pontifical Biblical Institute (Italy)**

INTERPRETING ISRAEL'S SCRIPTURES

INTERPRETING ISRAEL'S SCRIPTURES

A **PRACTICAL GUIDE**
to the **EXEGESIS** of the
HEBREW BIBLE / OLD TESTAMENT

MATTHIEU RICHELLE
translated by Sarah E. Richelle

an imprint of Hendrickson Publishing Group

Interpreting Israel's Scriptures: A Practical Guide to the Exegesis of the Hebrew Bible / Old Testament

© 2022 by Matthieu Richelle

Published by Hendrickson Academic
an imprint of Hendrickson Publishing Group
Hendrickson Publishers, LLC
P. O. Box 3473
Peabody, Massachusetts 01961-3473
www.hendricksonpublishinggroup.com

ISBN 978-1-61970-958-4

Originally published in French under the title:
Guide pour l'exégèse de l'Ancien Testament: Méthodes, exemples et instruments de travail
Copyright © 2012 by Matthieu Richelle
Published by permission of Excelsis, 26450 Charols, France
Internet: www.XL6.com

All rights reserved. No part of this book may be reproduced or transmitted in any form or by any means, electronic or mechanical, including photocopying, recording, or by any information storage and retrieval system, without permission in writing from the publisher.

Neither the publisher nor the author is responsible for, nor do they have any control over, the content of any third-party websites referenced in this book, whether at the time of the book's publication or in the future.

Unless otherwise noted, the Scripture quotations contained herein are from the *New Revised Standard Version Updated Edition*, copyright © 2021 National Council of the Churches of Christ in the United States of America. Used by permission. All rights reserved worldwide.

Scripture quotations marked (NRSV) are taken from the New Revised Standard Version of the Bible, copyright © 1989 by the Division of Christian Education of the National Council of the Churches of Christ in the United States of America, and are used by permission.

Quotations marked NETS are taken from *A New English Translation of the Septuagint*, ©2007 by the International Organization for Septuagint and Cognate Studies, Inc. Used by permission of Oxford University Press. All rights reserved.

Scripture quotations marked NJPS are taken from *Tanakh: The Holy Scriptures*, copyright ©1985 by The Jewish Publication Society. Used by permission. All rights reserved.

Quotations designated (NET) are from the NET Bible® copyright ©1996-2016 by Biblical Studies Press, L.L.C. All rights reserved.

Scripture quotations marked (NIV) are taken from the Holy Bible, New International Version®, NIV®. Copyright © 1973, 1978, 1984, 2011 by Biblica, Inc.™ Used by permission of Zondervan. All rights reserved worldwide. www.zondervan.com. The "NIV" and "New International Version" are trademarks registered in the United States Patent and Trademark Office by Biblica, Inc.™

Scripture quotations marked (ESV) are taken from the Holy Bible, English Standard Version (ESV®), copyright © 2001 by Crossway, a publishing ministry of Good News Publishers. Used by permission. All rights reserved.

Printed in the United States of America

First Printing — December 2022

Library of Congress Control Number: 2022938735

ABBREVIATED CONTENTS

List of Tables xxvii

List of Abbreviations xxix

Introduction 1

Part One: The Making of the Text
    1   Translation 9
    2   Textual Criticism 38
    3   Compositional Criticism: Analysis 74
    4   Compositional Criticism: Synthesis 95

Part Two: The Various Facets of the Text
    5   Literary Genre 127
    6   Literary Context 154
    7   Historical Geography 167
    8   History 178
    9   Literary Structure 206
    10   Poetry 224
    11   Narrative Criticism 250
    12   Intertextuality 272

Part Three: The Reader in Front of the Text
    13   Reception 297
    14   Feminist and Gender Studies 319
    15   Postcolonial Criticism 346

Bibliography 359

Index of Biblical References 383

DETAILED CONTENTS

List of Tables. xxvii

List of Abbreviations. xxix

Introduction. 1
    A Practical Approach for a Student-Friendly Guide. 1
    Organization of the Book 2
    A Final Word 5

PART ONE: THE MAKING OF THE TEXT

1 TRANSLATION

    Overview. 9

1.1 How to Deal with Difficult Grammatical Forms 10
        Example 1.1 ▸ *Psalm 16:2*   11
        SIDEBAR: GRAMMARS OF BIBLICAL HEBREW AND ARAMAIC   12

1.2 What to Do When You Suddenly Discover Rare or Obscure Meanings for Common Words. 13
    A. Do Not Neglect Rare Meanings of Common Words 14
        Example 1.2a ▸ *Isaiah 29:16*   14
        Example 1.2b ▸ *Psalm 7:12 [13]*   14
        SIDEBAR: HELP FOR READING THE HEBREW TEXT   15
    B. Choose the Most Pertinent Meaning for the Context 16
        Example 1.2c ▸ *The Word* בַּיִת   16
        SIDEBAR: LEXICONS OF BIBLICAL HEBREW AND ARAMAIC   17

    C. Do Not Import a Nuance from One Context into Another. 18
        Example 1.2d ▸   *The Word* עָבַד   18
    D. Recognize Idiomatic Expressions 19
        Example 1.2e ▸   *Isaiah 22:15*   19

1.3 How to Deal with Rare Words and Unexpected Meanings **20**
    A. Check the Context. 21
    B. Examine the Other Occurrences. 22
    C. Consult the Ancient Versions 22
    D. Consult the Other Hebrew Corpora 22
        SIDEBAR: WHERE CAN YOU CONSULT OTHER HEBREW AND
        ARAMAIC TEXTS?   23
    E. Look for Cognates in Other Semitic Languages 24
        Example 1.3a ▸   *Isaiah 52:15*   25
        Example 1.3b ▸   *Exodus 15:2*   27
        SIDEBAR: LEXICONS OF OTHER SEMITIC LANGUAGES   29

1.4 How to Tackle Difficult Syntactic Constructions **30**
        Example 1.4 ▸   *1 Samuel 3:14*   31

**1.5 Take Advantage of the Translation Process to Detect Soundplay and
Double Entendres** **32**
    A. Soundplay. 32
        Example 1.5a ▸   *Genesis 11:3*   33
        Example 1.5b ▸   *Job 7:17; 15:14*   33
    B. Double Entendres 34
        Example 1.5c ▸   *Amos 6:12b–13*   35
        Example 1.5d ▸   *2 Kings 1:9–16*   35
        Example 1.5e ▸   *Isaiah 28:16*   36

EXERCISES FOR CHAPTER 1 36

2 TEXTUAL CRITICISM

Overview **38**
    A. Theoretical Considerations 38
        SIDEBAR: TWO MODELS FOR THE ORIGINS OF
        BIBLICAL BOOKS   40
    B. Practical Considerations. 42
        SIDEBAR: HANDBOOKS AND REFERENCE WORKS ON
        TEXTUAL CRITICISM   44

2.1	Collect the Evidence	44
	A. Hebrew and Aramaic Witnesses	45
	(i) The Masoretic Text	45
	SIDEBAR: THE MASORAH	45
	(ii) The Samaritan Pentateuch	46
	(iii) The Dead Sea Scrolls	46
	B. Ancient Versions	47
	(i) The Septuagint	47
	SIDEBAR: HELP FOR READING THE SEPTUAGINT	49
	(ii) The Revisions of the Septuagint	50
	(iii) Other Ancient Versions	50
	C. The Usual Editions, at a Glance	51
2.2	Compare the Textual Witnesses	52
	Example 2.2 ▸ 1 Kings 14:24	55
2.3	Explain Scribal Mistakes	56
	Example 2.3a ▸ Zechariah 4:2	57
	Example 2.3b ▸ Isaiah 40:7–8	58
2.4	Explain Intentional Changes	59
	Example 2.4a ▸ Genesis 11:8	60
	Example 2.4b ▸ Deuteronomy 17:14	62
	Example 2.4c ▸ Isaiah 19:25	63
	Example 2.4d ▸ Song of Songs 2:12–14, 17	64
2.5	Explain Large-Scale Differences	66
	Example 2.5a ▸ 1 Kings 8:1–6	66
	Example 2.5b ▸ Judges 6:8–10	69
2.6	Explore the Impact of the Variants	70
	Example 2.6 ▸ Ezekiel 28:11–19	70
EXERCISES FOR CHAPTER 2		72

3 COMPOSITIONAL CRITICISM: ANALYSIS

Overview	74
SIDEBAR: LOST IN TERMINOLOGY?	77
3.1 How to Detect Scribal Activity	78
SIDEBAR: LINGUISTIC DATING	79

3.2	Examples			82
	Example 3.2a	▸	*Genesis 1 and 2*	82
	Example 3.2b	▸	*Judean Updates in Hosea*	82
	Example 3.2c	▸	*Job 32–37*	83
	Example 3.2d	▸	*Isaiah 19:16–25*	85
	Example 3.2e	▸	*Isaiah 17:7–8*	87
	Example 3.2f	▸	*Genesis 24*	88
	Example 3.2g	▸	*Numbers 22:22–35*	89
	Example 3.2h	▸	*Exodus 3:1–4:18 and 6:2–7:7*	90
	Example 3.2i	▸	*Exodus 6:14–25*	90
	Example 3.2j	▸	*2 Kings 17:34–40*	91
	Example 3.2k	▸	*2 Kings 18:13–19:37*	92

EXERCISES FOR CHAPTER 3 93

4 COMPOSITIONAL CRITICISM: SYNTHESIS

Overview 95

4.1 How to Determine If Several Scribal Interventions Belong to the Same Compositional Layer 96

	Example 4.1a	▸	*Judean Updates in Hosea*	96
	Example 4.1b	▸	*Isaiah 19:16–25 and Other Positive Statements about the Nations*	97

4.2 How Certain Scribal Activity Can Be Correlated with a Known Composition or Compositional Layer 97

	Example 4.2a	▸	*Genesis 1 and 2*	98
	SIDEBAR: CURRENT MODELS FOR THE FORMATION OF THE PENTATEUCH			98
	Example 4.2b	▸	*Exodus 3:1–4:18 and 6:2–7:7*	100
	Example 4.2c	▸	*Exodus 12:15–20*	102
	SIDEBAR: JUXTAPOSITION, CONFLATION, AND SUPPLEMENTATION			103

4.3 How to Date a Text 104

A. Attestation in the Dead Sea Scrolls or the Septuagint 105

	Example 4.3a	▸	*Genesis 14:18–20*	105

B. Linguistic Profile 106

	Example 4.3b	▸	*2 Kings 17:24–34*	107

    C. Texts Written for an Audience Living in a Specific Period 107
        Example 4.3c ▸   *Genesis 11:28, 31; 15:7*   108
        Example 4.3d ▸   *Genesis 37–50*   109
    D. Links to Datable Events or Realities 110
        Example 4.3e ▸   *Nahum 3:8*   110
        Example 4.3f ▸   *"Until This Day" in Judges and Kings*   111
        Example 4.3g ▸   *Jeremiah 50–51*   111
        Example 4.3h ▸   *2 Kings 18:13–19:37*   112
    E. Literary Dependence. 112
        Example 4.3i ▸   *Isaiah 17:7–8*   113
        SIDEBAR: MODELS FOR THE FORMATION OF THE
        DEUTERONOMISTIC HISTORY   113
        Example 4.3j ▸   *Exodus 34:11–26*   115
        SIDEBAR: P AS A BENCHMARK   117
    F. The Text Shows Awareness (or Lack Thereof) about a
    Tradition or Idea 117
        Example 4.3k ▸   *Amos 5:25; Jeremiah 7:22*   118
        Example 4.3l ▸   *2 Kings 5:1–19*   119

4.4 Synthesis **120**
        Example 4.4 ▸   *2 Kings 3*   120

EXERCISES FOR CHAPTER 4 123

PART TWO:
THE VARIOUS FACETS OF THE TEXT

5 LITERARY GENRE

Overview 127
5.1 Identify the Literary Genre of the Text. **128**
5.2 Compare the Text with Biblical Texts of the Same Literary Genre **131**
        Example 5.2 ▸   *1 Kings 19*   131

5.3	Take Note of the Literary Genre's Conventions		133
	A. Figurative Language		133
	Example 5.3a ▸	Psalm 18 and Exodus 15	133
	Example 5.3b ▸	Metaphors in the Prophetic Books	134
	B. The Conditionality of Prophetic Announcements		134
	Example 5.3c ▸	Jonah and Micah 3	134
	C. Illocutionary Stance		135
	Example 5.3d ▸	Esther	135
5.4	Determine the Text's Function and *Sitz im Leben*		136
	Example 5.4a ▸	Genesis 19:3–38; Kings	137
	Example 5.4b ▸	The Oracles against the Nations	137
	Example 5.4c ▸	Chronicles	138
5.5	Compare with Extrabiblical Texts Whose Genre Is Similar		139
	A. Consult an Anthology		140
	B. Consult an Edition		141
	C. Consult a Comparative Study		145
	Example 5.5a ▸	Exodus 22:2–3 [1–2]	148
	Example 5.5b ▸	Job	149
	Example 5.5c ▸	Genesis 5 and 11	150
EXERCISES FOR CHAPTER 5			153

6 LITERARY CONTEXT

Overview			154
6.1	How to Identify Useful Information in the Context		155
	Example 6.1a ▸	Genesis 12:10–20	155
	Example 6.1b ▸	Genesis 23	155
	Example 6.1c ▸	Ezekiel 40–48	156
	Example 6.1d ▸	Psalms 1 and 2	156
6.2	How to Locate the Passage within a Possible Literary Progression		157
	Example 6.2a ▸	Passages about Women in Judges	157
	Example 6.2b ▸	Genesis 4:1–16	159
	Example 6.2c ▸	Exodus 15:22–17:7	161
	Example 6.2d ▸	Psalms 111 and 112	163
	SIDEBAR: LITERARY CONTEXT, SYNCHRONIC AND DIACHRONIC APPROACHES		164
EXERCISES FOR CHAPTER 6			165

7 HISTORICAL GEOGRAPHY

Overview	167
7.1 Situate Places on a Map	168
SIDEBAR: ATLASES	168
Example 7.1 ▸ Tyre in Ezekiel 26–28	169
SIDEBAR: FOR FURTHER READING ON HISTORICAL GEOGRAPHY	170
7.2 Assess the Distance between Places	171
Example 7.2 ▸ 2 Chronicles 20:2	172
7.3 Identify an Itinerary and Interpret It as Such	172
Example 7.3 ▸ Isaiah 15	172
7.4 Explore a Place's History	173
Example 7.4 ▸ Tel Dan	173
SIDEBAR: WHERE TO FIND OUT ABOUT AN ARCHAEOLOGICAL SITE	174
7.5 Detect Allusions to the Possible Overtones of a Place Name	175
Example 7.5a ▸ Micah 1:10–15	175
Example 7.5b ▸ Micah 5:2 [1]	176
Example 7.5c ▸ Amos 6:14	176
EXERCISES FOR CHAPTER 7	177

8 HISTORY

Overview	178
8.1 Determine Exactly What Your Research Question Is	180
Example 8.1a ▸ 2 Chronicles 33	182
Example 8.1b ▸ Leviticus 18	183
Example 8.1c ▸ Hezekiah's Reform in 2 Kings 18:4, 22	184
8.2 Obtain Relevant Historical Information from Extrabiblical Sources	185
SIDEBAR: WHERE TO FIND OUT ABOUT DAILY LIFE IN ANCIENT ISRAEL	186
Example 8.2a ▸ Judges	187
SIDEBAR: WHERE TO FIND OUT ABOUT THE HISTORY OF ISRAEL AND JUDAH	188

Example 8.2b ▸	Multiple Places of Worship	190
Example 8.2c ▸	Hezekiah's Reform	192

SIDEBAR: WHERE TO FIND OUT ABOUT THE HISTORY OF OTHER ANCIENT NEAR EASTERN COUNTRIES ... 193

Example 8.2d ▸	Tyre in Ezekiel 26:7–12	195

SIDEBAR: WHERE TO FIND OUT ABOUT ICONOGRAPHY ... 196

Example 8.2e ▸	Cherubim	197

8.3 Compare the Biblical and Extrabiblical Sources 198

Example 8.3 ▸ The Murder of Joram and Ahaziah
 (2 Kings 9:14–28) ... 199

8.4 Synthesis: Reconstruct the Sequence of Events 201

Example 8.4 ▸ The Assyrian Siege of Jerusalem
 (2 Kings 18:13–19:37) ... 201

SIDEBAR: COMMUNICATIVE MEMORY AND CULTURAL MEMORY ... 203

EXERCISES FOR CHAPTER 8 204

9 LITERARY STRUCTURE

Overview 206

9.1 Look for Inclusios 207

Example 9.1a ▸	Psalms 1 and 2	207
Example 9.1b ▸	Psalm 8 and Psalm 103	208

9.2 Note Structural Markers 208

Example 9.2a ▸	Habakkuk	209
Example 9.2b ▸	Micah 3	209

SIDEBAR: ACROSTIC POEMS ... 210

9.3 Distinguish Different Sections in the Text 211

Example 9.3 ▸	Song of Songs 2:8–17	211

9.4 Identify a Repeated Pattern 213

Example 9.4a ▸	Amos 1:3–2:16	213
Example 9.4b ▸	Malachi	214

9.5 Recognize a Standard Symmetrical Structure 215

A. Regular Parallelism 215

Example 9.5a ▸	Psalm 132	216

    B. Inverse Parallelism (Concentric Structure, Chiasmus) 217
        Example 9.5b ▸ *Leviticus 6:8–13 [1–6]*   217
        Example 9.5c ▸ *Daniel 2–7*   218
        Example 9.5d ▸ *Psalm 1*   219
        SIDEBAR: CHIASMO-MANIA AND CHIASMO-PHOBIA   220
        Example 9.5e ▸ *Psalms 26–32*   221
        Example 9.5f ▸ *Proverbs 1:22–33*   221
EXERCISES FOR CHAPTER 9 223

10 POETRY

Overview 224
        SIDEBAR: APPROACHES TO BIBLICAL POETRY   225

10.1 Analyze the Microstructure 225
        SIDEBAR: WHERE TO FIND THE BIBLICAL TEXT
            ALREADY LAID OUT IN COLA   226
        Example 10.1a ▸ *Psalm 29*   231
        SIDEBAR: WHAT ABOUT METER?   233
        Example 10.1b ▸ *Song of Songs 2:8–17*   234

10.2 Analyze the Macrostructure 236
        Example 10.2a ▸ *Psalm 29*   237
        Example 10.2b ▸ *Psalm 93*   238
        SIDEBAR: WHERE TO FIND DETAILED ANALYSIS
            OF POETIC TEXTS   240

10.3 Study Figures of Speech and Other Poetic Devices 241
        SIDEBAR: THE ABC OF CMT, AND MORE   242
        Example 10.3a ▸ *Song of Songs 2:8–17*   243
        Example 10.3b ▸ *Song of Songs 2:8–17*   244
        Example 10.3c ▸ *Song of Songs 2:8–17*   244

10.4 Determine the Rhetorical Function of the Text 244
        Example 10.4a ▸ *Micah 3:2–3*   245
        Example 10.4b ▸ *Haggai*   246
        Example 10.4c ▸ *Song of Songs 2:8–17*   248
EXERCISES FOR CHAPTER 10 249

11 NARRATIVE CRITICISM

Overview 250
        SIDEBAR: CLASSIC STUDIES   252

11.1 Identify the Plot(s) 253
    A. Identify the Type of Plot 253
        Example 11.1a ▸   Judges 13   253
    B. Identify the Plot Structure 255
        Example 11.1b ▸   2 Kings 6:8–23   255
        Example 11.1c ▸   Judges 13   255

11.2 Study the Characters 256
    A. Study the Characterization 256
        Example 11.2a ▸   Job 1:8   257
        Example 11.2b ▸   1 Kings 17   257
    B. Round or Flat Character? 259
        Example 11.2c ▸   Eli (1 Samuel 2)   259
    C. Identify the Levels of Knowledge 259
        Example 11.2d ▸   Genesis 42   259
        Example 11.2e ▸   Job   260
        Example 11.2f ▸   Judges 13   260
        Example 11.2g ▸   2 Kings 6:8–23   260

11.3 Identify Any *Mise En Abyme* 262
        Example 11.3 ▸   2 Kings 6:8–23   262

11.4 Study Type-Scenes 263
        Example 11.4 ▸   Judges 13   263

11.5 Identify Discrepancies or Anomalies 265
        Example 11.5a ▸   Judges 13   265
        Example 11.5b ▸   2 Kings 6:8–23   267

11.6 Study the Focalizations 267
        Example 11.6 ▸   2 Kings 6:8–23   268

11.7 Identify the Presence of Irony, Double Meanings, and Misunderstandings 268
        Example 11.7a ▸   Esther   268
        Example 11.7b ▸   Jonah   269

11.8 Listen to the Narrative Voice 269
        Example 11.8a ▸   *Eli (1 Samuel 2)*   269
        Example 11.8b ▸   *The Schism between Israel and*
                             Judah (1 Kings 12)   270
        Example 11.8c ▸   *The Murder of Uriah (2 Samuel 11)*   270
EXERCISES FOR CHAPTER 11 270

12 INTERTEXTUALITY

Overview 272
              SIDEBAR: INNER-BIBLICAL EXEGESIS   273

12.1 The Author-Oriented Approach: Method 275
    A. Detect an Intertextual Link (or Several Such Links) 275
    B. Determine the Direction of Dependence 277
    C. Determine the Purpose of the Intertextual Link and the Diachronic
       and Synchronic Consequences 279
    D. Examples 279
        Example 12.1a ▸   *Zechariah 2:1–13 [5–17]*   279
              SIDEBAR: INVERTED QUOTATIONS, OR SEIDEL'S LAW   281
        Example 12.1b ▸   *Lamentations and Isaiah 40–55*   281
        Example 12.1c ▸   *Hosea 10:1–8, Isaiah 5:2–7, and*
                         Ezekiel 15:1–6; 17; 19:10–14   282
        Example 12.1d ▸   *Isaiah 4:2–6 and Exodus*   283
        Example 12.1e ▸   *Isaiah 42 and 49*   283
        Example 12.1f ▸   *1 Kings 19 and Exodus 32–34*   284
        Example 12.1g ▸   *Genesis 1 and 8–9*   286
        Example 12.1h ▸   *Genesis 3–4 and 9*   287
        Example 12.1i ▸   *Isaiah 2:1–4 and 4:2–6*   288
        Example 12.1j ▸   *Exodus 20:24 and Deuteronomy 12:13–14*   289

12.2 The Reader-Oriented Approach: Method and Examples 290
        Example 12.2a ▸   *Nahum and Jonah*   291
        Example 12.2b ▸   *Deuteronomy 23:3 [4] and Nehemiah 9–10*   292
        Example 12.2c ▸   *Ruth*   293
EXERCISES FOR CHAPTER 12 293

PART THREE: THE READER IN FRONT OF THE TEXT

13 RECEPTION

Overview 297

13.1 Consult Overviews of the Reception History 300
       A. Chapter-by-Chapter Surveys 300
       B. Studies of the Use of the Hebrew Bible in New Testament Books 301
       C. Anthologies 301
       D. Survey the Reception History of a Passage or Figure 301
       E. Encyclopedia 302
       F. Study Bible 302
       G. Others 302

13.2 Consult the Scriptural Index of a Corpus 302
       A. Second Temple Literature 303
       B. New Testament 303
       C. Church Fathers 303
       D. Apocryphal Literature 304
       E. Rabbinic Literature 304

13.3 Read the Texts and Check Whether the Hebrew Bible Passage Is Really Used in Them 304
       A. Second Temple Literature as a Whole 305
       B. The (Nonbiblical) Dead Sea Scrolls in Particular 305
       C. Rabbinic Literature and Medieval Jewish Interpreters 306
       D. Church Fathers 306

13.4 Check the Form of the Hebrew Bible Passage That the Interpreting Text Has Used 307

13.5 Determine What Kind of Use the Interpreting Text Has Made of the Hebrew Bible Passage 307

13.6 Consider the Use against the Backdrop of Past and Contemporary Interpretations 308

13.7 Examples **309**

        Example 13.7a ▸ Some Jewish and Christian Interpretations of
                                      Song of Songs 2:8–17   309

        Example 13.7b ▸ The Fate of the Tower of Babel in
                                      Ancient Jewish Reception   314

EXERCISES FOR CHAPTER 13 318

14 FEMINIST AND GENDER STUDIES

Overview **319**
            SIDEBAR: FOR FURTHER READING   323
            SIDEBAR: A TYPOLOGY OF FEMINIST VIEWS ON BIBLICAL
                AUTHORITY   326

14.1 Scrutinize the Text for Gender Ideology **327**
        Example 14.1a ▸ Isaiah 3:12   328
        Example 14.1b ▸ Mothers in the Hebrew Bible   330
        Example 14.1c ▸ Jeremiah 13:22, 26   331

14.2 Scrutinize the Text for Deconstruction of Gender Ideology **332**
        Example 14.2a ▸ Proverbs 31   333
        Example 14.2b ▸ Isaiah 42:14; 49:15   334
        Example 14.2c ▸ Judges   335

14.3 Scrutinize the Interpretation History **337**
        Example 14.3a ▸ 2 Samuel 11   337
        Example 14.3b ▸ Genesis 4:1   339
        Example 14.3c ▸ Cosmetics in Esther and Ruth   340

14.4 Engage in Reconstructive Reading **341**
        Example 14.4a ▸ 2 Kings 11   341
        Example 14.4b ▸ 2 Samuel 11   343
        Example 14.4c ▸ Isaiah 40–55   343

EXERCISES FOR CHAPTER 14 344

15 POSTCOLONIAL CRITICISM

Overview	346
15.1 Scrutinize the Text for Colonial Entanglements	**348**
Example 15.1a ▸ Royal Psalms	349
Example 15.1b ▸ Deuteronomy	349
SIDEBAR: RESOURCES ON POSTCOLONIAL READINGS OF THE HEBREW BIBLE	350
15.2 Engage in Reconstructive Reading	**351**
Example 15.2a ▸ Isaiah 10:5–34	351
Example 15.2b ▸ Deuteronomy	354
Example 15.2c ▸ Esther	354
SIDEBAR: ENCULTURED AND CROSS-TEXTUAL READINGS	356
15.3 Scrutinize the Reception History	**357**
Example 15.3 ▸ Genesis 9:23–26	357
EXERCISES FOR CHAPTER 15	358

✶ ✶ ✶ ✶ ✶

Bibliography	359
Index of Biblical References	383

LIST OF TABLES

Chapter 2: Textual Criticism
Table 2.1	The Most Important Ancient Versions	47
Table 2.2	Ancient Versions other than the Septuagint	50
Table 2.3	Overview of Editions of Textual Witnesses	51
Table 2.4	1 Kings 14:24 in the MT and in the LXX	55
Table 2.5	Definitions for the Most Common Scribal Errors	56
Table 2.6	Isaiah 40:7–8 in the MT, 1QIsaiah^a, and in the LXX	58
Table 2.7	Isaiah 19:25 in the MT and in the LXX	63
Table 2.8	1 Kings 8:1–6 in the MT and in the LXX	67
Table 2.9	Ezekiel 28:14–16 in the MT and in the LXX	71

Chapter 3: Compositional Criticism: Analysis
Table 3.1	Different Periods in the History of Biblical Hebrew	80

Chapter 5: Literary Genre
Table 5.1	The Main Literary Genres in the Hebrew Bible	129
Table 5.2	Ancient Near Eastern Parallels and Where to Read Them	142
Table 5.3	Examples of Comparative Studies for Most Genres	146

Chapter 6: Literary Context
Table 6.1	Passages about Women in Judges	158
Table 6.2	Comparison of Genesis 3 and Genesis 4	159
Table 6.3	Exodus 15, 16, and 17	162
Table 6.4	Psalms 111 and 112	163

Chapter 9: Literary Structure
Table 9.1	First and Third Oracles in Micah 3	210
Table 9.2	Song of Songs 2:8–9, 17	212
Table 9.3	Structure of Psalm 132	216
Table 9.4	Psalms 26–32	221

Chapter 10: Poetry

    Table 10.1   Song of Songs 2:12, 14 236

    Table 10.2   Chiastic Structure of Psalm 29 237

    Table 10.3   Oracles in Haggai 247

Chapter 11: Narrative Criticism

    Table 11.1   Birth Announcements in the Hebrew Bible 263

Chapter 12: Intertextuality

    Table 12.1   Monographs on Intertextuality in Isaiah. 276

    Table 12.2   Habakkuk 2 and Zechariah 2 280

    Table 12.3   The Servant in Isaiah 42 and 49 284

    Table 12.4   Creation and Its Renewal in Genesis 1 and 8–9 286

    Table 12.5   Adam and His Sons, Noah and His Sons 287

Chapter 15: Postcolonial Criticism

    Table 15.1   Selected Echoes of Neo-Assyrian texts in Isaiah 10:5–15 352

LIST OF ABBREVIATIONS

General

*	online resource
§	section
ABH	Archaic Biblical Hebrew
BCE	before the Common Era
ca.	circa
CBH	Classical Biblical Hebrew
CE	Common Era
cf.	confer, compare
CMT	Conceptual Metaphor Theory
DH	Deuteronomistic History
DSS	Dead Sea Scrolls
ed.	edited by; edition
e.g.	exempli gratia, for example
etc.	et cetera, and so on
esp.	especially
HB	Hebrew Bible
i.e.	id est, that is
LBH	Late Biblical Hebrew
LXX	Septuagint
LXX^A	Codex Alexandrinus
LXX^B	Codex Vaticanus
LXX.D	Septuaginta Deutsch
LXX^L	Lucianic Recension
LXX^S	Codex Sinaiticus
MT	Masoretic Text
NET	New English Translation
NIV	New International Version
NJPS	Tanakh: The Holy Scriptures: The New JPS Translation according to the Traditional Hebrew Text
NRSV	New Revised Standard Version
OG	Old Greek
SKL	Sumerian King List

Smr   Samaritan Pentateuch
TBH   Transitional Biblical Hebrew
trans.   translated by
v(v.)   verse(s)

Journals, Series, and Reference Works

AB   Anchor Bible
ABS   Archaeology and Biblical Studies
ACCS   Ancient Christian Commentary on Scripture
ADPV   Abhandlungen des Deutschen Palästina-Vereins
AHw   *Akkadisches Handwörterbuch*. Edited by Wolfram von Soden. 3 vols. Wiesbaden: Harrassowitz, 1965–81.
AIL   Ancient Israel and its Literature
ANEP   *The Ancient Near East in Pictures Relating to the Old Testament*. 2nd ed. Edited by James B. Pritchard. Princeton: Princeton University Press, 1994.
ANET   *Ancient Near Eastern Texts Relating to the Old Testament*. Edited by James B. Pritchard. 3rd ed. Princeton: Princeton University Press, 1969.
ANEM   Ancient Near East Monographs
ArchBib   Archaeology and Bible
Archibab   *Archives babyloniennes*
ATD   Das Alte Testament Deutsch
AYBRL   Anchor Yale Bible Reference Library
BAR   *Biblical Archaeology Review*
BASOR   *Bulletin of the American Society of Oriental Research*
BBC   Blackwell Bible Commentaries
BDB   Brown, Francis, S. R. Driver, and Charles A. Briggs. *A Hebrew and English Lexicon of the Old Testament*. Boston: Houghton Mifflin, 1906.
*BEST   The Bible in Its Traditions
BETL   Bibliotheca Ephemeridum Theologicarum Lovaniensium
BHAW   Blackwell History of the Ancient World
BHQ   *Biblia Hebraica Quinta*
BHS   *Biblia Hebraica Stuttgartensia*
Bib   *Biblica*
BIS   Biblical Interpretation Series
BJS   Brown Judaic Studies
BMT   The Bible in Medieval Tradition
BRP   Brill Research Perspectives in Biblical Interpretation
BS   Biblical Seminar
BZAW   Beihefte zur Zeitschrift für die alttestamentliche Wissenschaft
*CAD   *The Assyrian Dictionary of the Oriental Institute of the University of Chicago*. Chicago: The Oriental Institute of the University of Chicago, 1956–2010.

CahRB	Cahiers de la Revue biblique
*CAL	Comprehensive Aramaic Lexicon
CBET	Contributions to Biblical Exegesis and Theology
CBQ	*Catholic Biblical Quarterly*
CBQMS	Catholic Biblical Quarterly Monograph Series
CDA	*A Concise Dictionary of Akkadian*. Edited by Jeremy A. Black, Andrew George, and J. Nicholas Postgate. 2nd ed. SANTAG 5. Wiesbaden: Harrassowitz, 2000.
CDCH	*A Concise Dictionary of Classical Hebrew*. Edited by David J. A. Clines. Sheffield: Sheffield Academic, 2009.
CHANE	Culture and History of the Ancient Near East
CIPOA	Cahiers de l'Institut du Proche-Orient Ancien
COS	*The Context of Scripture*. Edited by William W. Hallo and K. Lawson Younger. 3 vols. Leiden: Brill, 2003.
CSHB	Critical Studies in the Hebrew Bible
*CTIJ	Cuneiform Texts mentioning Israelites, Judeans, and Related People
CurBR	*Currents in Biblical Research*
DCH	*Dictionary of Classical Hebrew*. Edited by David J. A. Clines. 9 vols. Sheffield: Sheffield Phoenix Press, 1993–2014.
DJD	Discoveries in the Judaean Desert
DNWSI	*Dictionary of the North-West Semitic Inscriptions*. Jacob Hoftijzer and Karel Jongeling. HdO. Leiden: Brill, 1995.
Ebib	Études bibliques
EBR	*Encyclopedia of the Bible and Its Reception*. Edited by Hans-Josef Klauck et al. Berlin: de Gruyter, 2009–.
EBS	Essentials of Biblical Studies
*eTACT	Electronic Translations of Akkadian Cuneiform Texts
*ETCSL	Electronic Text Corpus of Sumerian Literature
FAT	Forschungen zum Alten Testament
FCB	Feminist Companion to the Bible
FOTL	Forms of the Old Testament Literature
FRLANT	Forschungen zur Religion und Literatur des Alten und Neuen Testaments
FSBP	Fontes et Subsidia ad Bibliam Pertinentes
EHLL	*Encyclopedia of Hebrew Language and Linguistics*. Edited by Geoffrey Khan. Leiden: Brill, 2013.
GKC	Kautzsch, Arthur Ernest, and Emil Cowley. *Gesenius' Hebrew Grammar*. Oxford: Clarendon, 1960.
GPBS	Global Perspectives on Biblical Scholarship
HALOT	*The Hebrew and Aramaic Lexicon of the Old Testament*. Ludwig Koehler, Walter Baumgartner, and Johann J. Stamm. Translated and edited under the supervision of Mervyn E. J. Richardson. 4 vols. Leiden, Brill: 1994–99.
HeBAI	*Hebrew Bible and Ancient Israel*

HBCE	*The Hebrew Bible: A Critical Edition*. Edited by Ronald S. Hendel. Atlanta: SBL Press, 2015–.
HCOT	Historical Commentary on the Old Testament
HdO	Handbuch der Orientalistik
HSS	Harvard Semitic Studies
HTLS	*Historical and Theological Lexicon of the Septuagint*. Edited by Eberhard Bons. Tübingen: Mohr Siebeck, 2021–.
HUB	*The Hebrew University Bible*. Jerusalem: Magnes, 1981–.
IBHS	Waltke, Bruce K., and Michael P. O'Connor. *An Introduction to Biblical Hebrew Syntax*. Winona Lake, IN: Eisenbrauns, 1990.
ICC	International Critical Commentary
IECOT	International Exegetical Commentary on the Old Testament
IEJ	*Israel Exploration Journal*
JAOS	*Journal of the American Oriental Society*
JAJ	*Journal of Ancient Judaism*
JAJSup	Journal of Ancient Judaism Supplements
JBL	*Journal of Biblical Literature*
JCI	Jewish and Christian Interpretation
JCP	Jewish and Christian Perspectives
JETS	*Journal of the Evangelical Theological Society*
JJAR	*Journal of Jerusalem Archaeology*
JNES	*Journal of Near Eastern Studies*
JNSL	*Journal of Northwest Semitic Languages*
JM	Joüon, Paul, and Takamitsu Muraoka. *A Grammar of Biblical Hebrew: Translated and Revised*. SubBi 14.1. Rome: Editrice Pontificio Istituto Biblico, 1991.
JSJSup	Supplements to the Journal for the Study of Judaism
JSOT	*Journal for the Study of the Old Testament*
JSOTSup	Journal for the Study of the Old Testament Supplement Series
LAI	Library of Ancient Israel
LHBOTS	Library of Hebrew Bible/Old Testament Studies
LSTS	Library of Second Temple Studies
MC	Mesopotamian Civilizations
MdB	Le Monde de la Bible
NEA	*Near Eastern Archaeology* (formerly *Biblical Archaeologist*)
NEAEHL	*The New Encyclopedia of Archaeological Excavations in the Holy Land*. Edited by Ephraim Stern. 4 vols. Jerusalem: Israel Exploration Society & Carta; New York: Simon & Schuster, 1993; vol. 5 (update), 2008.
NETS	New English Translation of the Septuagint and the Other Greek Translations Traditionally Included under That Title
NSBT	New Studies in Biblical Theology
NTSI	New Testament and the Scriptures of Israel
OBO	Orbis Biblicus et Orientalis

OEANE	*The Oxford Encyclopedia of Archaeology in the Ancient Near East.* Edited by Eric M. Meyers. 5 vols. New York: Oxford University Press, 1997.
OLA	Orientalia Lovaniensia Analecta
OLP	*Orientalia Lovaniensia Periodica*
OPA	Les œuvres de Philon d'Alexandrie
ORA	Orientalische Religionen in der Antike
OSHT	Oxford Studies in Historical Theology
OTL	Old Testament Library
OTRM	Oxford Theology and Religion Monographs
OTS	Old Testament Studies
PLO	Porta Linguarum Orientalium
RB	*Revue biblique*
RBS	Resources for Biblical Study
RCS	Reformation Commentary on Scripture
RHAW	Routledge History of the Ancient World
*RINAP	Royal Inscriptions of the Neo-Assyrian Period
RW	Routledge Worlds
SAA	State Archives of Assyria
SAACT	State Archives of Assyria Cuneiform Texts
SAAS	State Archives of Assyria Studies
*SAAo	State Archives of Assyria Online
SANTAG	Santag – Arbeiten und Untersuchungen zur Keilschriftkunde
SBL	Society of Biblical Literature
SBLDS	Society of Biblical Literature Dissertation Series
SBLSBS	Society of Biblical Literature Sources for Biblical Study
SBR	Studies of the Bible and Its Reception
SHCANE	Studies in the History and Culture of the Ancient Near East
SJOT	*Scandinavian Journal of the Old Testament*
SSN	Studia Semitica Neerlandica
StPohl	Studia Pohl
SubBi	Subsidia Biblica
SVTG	Septuaginta: Vetus Testamentum Graecum Auctoritate Academiae Scientiarum Gottingensis editum
TA	*Tel Aviv: Journal of the Institute of Archaeology of Tel Aviv University*
TBN	Themes in Biblical Narrative
TCSt	Text-Critical Studies
TDOT	*Theological Dictionary of the Old Testament.* Edited by G. Johannes Botterweck and Helmer Ringgren. Translated by John T. Willis et al. 8 vols. Grand Rapids: Eerdmans, 1974–2006.
TECC	Textos y Estudios "Cardenal Cisneros" de la Biblia Políglota Matritense
ThEv	*Théologie évangélique*
THB	*Textual History of the Bible.* Edited by Armin Lange. 2 vols. Leiden: Brill, 2016–19.

TLOT	*Theological Lexicon of the Old Testament*. Edited by Ernst Jenni, with assistance from Claus Westermann. Translated by Mark E. Biddle. 3 vols. Peabody, MA: Hendrickson, 1997.
TS	*Theological Studies*
VT	*Vetus Testamentum*
VTSup	Supplements to Vetus Testamentum
VWGT	Veröffentlichungen der Wissenschaftlichen Gesellschaft für Theologie
WANEM	Worlds of the Ancient Near East and Mediterranean
WAW	Writings from the Ancient World
WAWSup	Writings from the Ancient World Supplement Series
WBC	Word Biblical Commentary
WGRW	Writings from the Greco-Roman World
WMANT	Wissenschaftliche Monographien zum Alten und Neuen Testament
ZAW	*Zeitschrift für die alttestamentliche Wissenschaft*
ZDPV	*Zeitschrift des Deutschen Palästina-Vereins*
ZIBBC	*Zondervan Illustrated Bible Backgrounds Commentary*. Edited by John Walton. 5 vols. Grand Rapids: Zondervan, 2009.

INTRODUCTION

A PRACTICAL APPROACH FOR A STUDENT-FRIENDLY GUIDE

"What should I do, in practical terms, when my professor assigns me a paper instructing me to 'exegete' a biblical passage? What steps should I follow? Are there resources that could help me? In fact, what does it look like behind the scenes when a biblical scholar studies a text before publishing the polished 'finished product' that we end up reading in an exegetical commentary?" These are the kinds of questions that many students ask themselves. This book is designed to answer them, and to do so in the most student-friendly way possible.

A number of exegetical handbooks already exist, but they often focus on the theoretical foundations of the various existing methods. While this is very helpful, the consequence is that these books provide only a few illustrations of the concrete manner in which one might proceed when studying a text. In this book, I take the opposite, practical approach: after providing the necessary foundational ideas and underlining the relevance of a method, I focus on the actual steps that can be followed to apply it, and I illustrate these with numerous and detailed examples. In addition, each chapter ends with a section of exercises that gives readers a chance to practice on their own. When I was writing these chapters, I constantly tried to put myself in a student's shoes. I can also imagine that some scholars will secretly leaf through the book, because it is not the norm to be trained in all the methods I discuss.

Exegesis is like cooking—good cooking. The methods I outline are like recipes, correctly understood: it's helpful to have them when you learn how to cook or when you try a dish for the first time; with experience, however, you can take some liberties with them. But if you don't have a recipe in the first place, well . . . good luck! Thus, these methods and the corresponding steps are not presented as models to be rigidly followed over the long term, but rather as practical suggestions for beginners. Quite often, when I offer a list of steps, the subtext is not "you must do this," but "why don't you try this?"

Moreover, in some chapters we are dealing with a series of "tasks" rather than a series of "steps." In some cases—such as for feminist and gender studies—it is more accurate to speak of an orientation toward the text rather than of a unique method.

Professional exegetes intuitively know how to sensibly approach a particular text and know what are the most relevant ways in which to examine it in light of its specific characteristics. This is probably one of the reasons why exegetes don't always bother to explain, on a practical level, how they proceed with their work. Students, by contrast, face the risk of the blank page, or of lacking a method. This is precisely why I have written this book—for the students in my classroom. There are various ways of presenting each topic, and I certainly don't claim that the ones I have chosen are the only possible ones, or even the best ones, although I am convinced that they are helpful.

Throughout the book, I mention books and articles that are valuable resources for the exegete. I often hear my students ask excellent questions like, "Could you please advise me about a good lexicon I can use when working on the Greek translation of the Bible?" or, "Could you please point me to a good handbook on the history of ancient Israel?" I found it more helpful to mention these kinds of resources in the course of my discussions or in sidebars set off from the main text rather than in endless bibliographical lists that hardly anyone would read. Plenty of resources can also, of course, be found online,[1] as well as in very helpful software packages such as Accordance or Logos. I also mention a number of publications in footnotes, notably when an example is based on a specific article or book; however, as a rule, I have tried to resist the temptation to multiply such references. In many cases, I have refrained from mentioning counterarguments and additional hypotheses I know of, because my goal has simply been to illustrate a task or a step in a method. In such cases, the best interests of the reader demanded that I keep the scholarly addiction to exhaustivity and references on a leash.

ORGANIZATION OF THE BOOK

There is nothing absolute about the order in which I have presented the exegetical methods found in this book or about the order in which one might read about them

---

1. I mention a number of websites in this book, but—at the request of my publisher—I have done so by using their names (with an asterisk) rather than by providing their URLs, because, in addition to occasionally going out-of-date, URLs are, alas, sometimes hijacked. For example, a reader in search of a website on, say, West-Semitic toponyms in the ancient Levant might unfortunately happen upon a site containing indecent images instead, which would indeed create cognitive dissonance. Brave new world. A simple Google search with the name of a website should immediately lead the reader to the relevant location; in addition, a regularly updated list of the relevant URLs is available at my academia.edu page.

or engage with them in practice. With the exception of chapters 3 and 4 (which constitute a sequence), each chapter in this book can be read independently of the others, and I have included cross-references to other chapters (whether earlier or later ones) when I found this to be helpful or necessary. Moreover, Part One (on which see immediately below) assumes a knowledge of Hebrew, so readers who have not yet studied Hebrew may wish to skim or initially skip these chapters (and hopefully return to them at a later time). These caveats notwithstanding, however, there is an overall logic to how the book is organized, as follows.

Part One ("The Making of the Text") concerns what the text actually says (in technical terms, this is called "establishing" the text) and the process by which the text came to be (i.e., its formation). First, before studying a text, it's important to translate it, and this is the subject of chapter 1 ("Translation"). This chapter does not explain how to translate Hebrew, however (that is a matter for other books); rather, it explains how to move from the basic skills one learns in introductory language courses to tackling more advanced situations that are relevant for exegesis, such as how to deal with rare Hebrew words and surprising constructions. Chapter 2 ("Textual Criticism") discusses the fact that there are textual differences among ancient manuscripts and highlights the necessity of examining the most important of them, which will enable you to be sure of exactly what text it is that you are considering before you study it further. Because the changes we observe in the transmission of the text are similar to the changes that scholars assume occurred when the biblical books were being composed (often, presumably, in several stages), our discussion of textual criticism naturally leads next to the question of how the text was formed ("Compositional Criticism"), which is the subject of chapters 3 and 4. Working on this topic is equivalent to discovering the "making of" a movie. It's more than a matter of curiosity, however: studying a text's compositional history can shed light on the motivations and the ideas lying behind the text, as well as on the dating of the text and its origins. It's important to note that this is not a matter of "dissecting" the text or deconstructing it, however, but of understanding its formation. Because this method is relatively demanding, I have gone out of my way to unpack it as clearly as I could. With this goal in mind, I have divided this material on compositional history into two chapters, one devoted to "analysis" (how you discern traces of redaction), the other devoted to "synthesis" (what you make of these observations in order to try to reconstruct the formation of a biblical book).

Part Two ("The Various Facets of the Text") constitutes the heart of this book. Its chapters are designed to introduce you to the various ways in which you can explore the features of the text, akin to how you might observe a single physical object from different angles in order to see and understand it as clearly as possible. It has taken centuries for scholars to develop and refine these methods, which are complementary to one other and most of which belong to what is often called "the world of the text." Here we approach the text more and more closely, by successively zooming in. To begin with, what kind of text are we talking about in any given instance? This means determining the text's literary genre and the implications of this for interpretation (chapter 5). The next three chapters are devoted to examining the text's contexts, whether these be literary (chapter 6), geographical (chapter 7), or historical (chapter 8). Then, we move to the study of literary features: the text's structure (chapter 9), and—depending on the kind of text—its poetic (chapter 10) or narrative (chapter 11) features, respectively. Finally, we examine the possible links a text may have with other texts (chapter 12).

The book's final section, Part Three ("The Reader in Front of the Text") rests on the observation that the story does not end when the text is completed; it starts when people read it. The notes on the score of a symphony need to be interpreted in order to become alive and for music to "happen." The same is true for a text—with as much potential for variation as for musical interpretation. For this reason, we learn a great deal when studying how a passage has been read, interpreted, and used throughout the centuries, and how it has influenced people; this is called the text's "reception history" (the subject of chapter 13). But historical, cultural, and ideological factors influence every reader, and scholars have become more aware in recent times of how this constitutes both an opportunity and a danger for the interpretation and use of the Bible in society. A large array of methods have been developed in the last few decades to help facilitate discussion around this point: postcolonial interpretation, feminist interpretation, womanist interpretation, gender studies, queer studies, disability studies, ecological studies, and so on. It is obviously not possible to devote a chapter to each of these; otherwise this book would be as long as the Mahabharata. But these approaches share some core features: they focus on the perspective of a category of persons (e.g., colonized people or women) or a topic (e.g., ecology), they address a problem (e.g., imperialism, in postcolonial studies; patriarchalism, in feminist studies; pollution, in ecological studies), and they imagine how the Bible can be read in constructive ways from the corresponding perspective. I have chosen to discuss the well-established fields of feminist and gender studies (chapter 14) and postcolonial interpretation (chapter 15) as illustrative examples of such methods of interpretation. As its title indicates, chapter 14 actually deals with two topics; they are interrelated and so it is natural to treat them together, although this results in a lengthier chapter.

In a way, this final section of the book is meant to be open-ended, because—in contrast to the methods presented in the first two sections—reader-oriented approaches are in a robust, continual state of expansion and new such approaches are created every year. Therefore, this final section can be read both as a first introduction to reader-oriented approaches in the context of one's initial training (which, like a class, has to end at some point!) and as an invitation to continue the conversation (which does not need to end).

Individual biblical scholars often prefer a limited set of methods. Some believe that the historical-critical methods (which roughly correspond to the ones presented in Part One, as well as, in a way, to the material in chapter 8) constitute the most important and the most "serious" tasks of biblical scholarship. Others, by contrast, think that studying the various facets of the text (see Part Two) must be the focus of exegesis. And still others regard the most recently developed methods (the kind discussed in Part Three) as the only ones that are exciting today. I must confess that this situation plunges me into an abyss of perplexity, akin to when I must choose between two appetizing dishes in a restaurant or two excellent novels in a bookstore. Of course, nobody can be a specialist in all these fields, and in some seasons of life one's own scholarship may end up focusing on just one or a few areas (for example, for the past few years I have found myself publishing mostly on textual criticism). But I find valuable insights in every single method that is presented in this book. Moreover, we should not underestimate the interplay that exists between methods or approaches that look very different at first sight. For example, feminist and gender studies have recourse to a large array of historical-critical and literary methods; conversely, we will see that studying a text from a feminist perspective can lead to results that are directly apposite to a historical-critical perspective on the text.

A FINAL WORD

I have written this book in an irenic, ecumenical, and interreligious spirit. My hope is that it can serve people of all convictions, whether they are religious or not, and whether they are Jewish, Christian, or something else. Of course I have my own convictions, but they teach me to respect and love others; moreover, I naively believe that the study of the texts composing the Hebrew Bible has the potential to bring people together rather than to separate them, even when people interpret them differently. The original, French version of this guide (published in 2012) is used by teachers and students in universities and colleges of various confessions and denominations in the French-speaking world, and I am delighted about this.

The present, English version of this book is entitled *Interpreting Israel's Scriptures: A Practical Guide to the Exegesis of the Hebrew Bible / Old Testament*. This reflects the fact that the literary corpus that is the subject of this book is called by different names: most prominently, the Hebrew Bible (or Tanakh), in Judaism, and the Old Testament, in Christianity. (It should also be noted that the Catholic and Orthodox canons of the Old Testament include several books in addition to those found in the Hebrew Bible.) Throughout this book, I have chosen to use the term "Hebrew Bible" because it does not offend anybody and because it is the standard expression used in academic works.

Since it is important to some readers to know a bit about the author of a book, let me just say that I am French, am married to an Englishwoman, and live in Belgium; I am a Protestant who teaches in a Catholic university. (Go figure.) I am also well aware, from my own experience, of the challenges encountered by many students of biblical studies or theology who come from a conservative religious background when they discover biblical criticism. It is often difficult for them to square the latter with their view of the Scriptures, to hear that some texts were composed by redactors who held different views, or to learn that some inspired narratives they have taken at face value since their youth were actually written as fictions. I myself have come to see the variegated aspects of the biblical texts as perfectly compatible with faith, but I completely understand that they can be challenging. Therefore, when in this book I unpack the range of reasoning that exists in the fields of compositional criticism and historical criticism, for example, I have tried to carefully explain why scholars reach conclusions that may sound counterintuitive. For those who might say of these methods, "These are not my cup of tea," I would encourage reading these chapters with patience and curiosity (as I try to do, with varying degrees of success, when my kids teach me about Minecraft and Pokémon); in any case, the methods they describe are widely used in biblical scholarship, so at the very least reading them will help you understand the way in which many scholars reason and will aid your use of exegetical commentaries whose authors practice these methods.

I warmly thank Laura Quick, Régis Burnet, and Pierre-Edouard Detal for reading drafts of chapters in this book and helping me to improve them. Translating this book into English and revising it at the same time was a challenge for which I found a practical solution: being married to the translator, and marrying an Englishwoman in the first place. I am thus very grateful to my wife, Sarah, for translating the French version and checking the many changes I made, in a way that gave me all the liberty I needed to thoroughly improve the text. (And no, I did not marry her for that reason; but you did not really believe that, did you?) I entirely revised the original version, finding new examples, refining the methods, listing new resources that are better adapted to an English-speaking readership, replacing examples with better ones, adding exercises, and writing two new chapters. My thanks also go to the members of the Hendrickson team who worked on this book: Arley Kangas (updating of the biblical quotations to the NRSVue, and making of the index), Sarah Welch (proofreading), and Phil Frank (typesetting). Last but not least, this book owes a lot to Jonathan Kline, a wonderful and skilled editor who is also a scholar himself. I thank him for his patience, his help, and his many encouragements, as well as for improving the book in many ways and making it much clearer.

Finally, I hope that this book, in giving you a taste of the amazing variety of methods that have been developed over the centuries to exegete the Hebrew Bible, whets your appetite for more. Most biblical scholars are simply fascinated by the texts, and their work springs from their passion. I hope that you, too, will get a sense of how fun exegesis can be. Welcome to the party!

PART ONE

THE MAKING OF THE TEXT

CHAPTER 1

TRANSLATION

OVERVIEW

As I stated in the Introduction, the object of the present chapter is not to provide you with the basic skills in Biblical Hebrew (and Aramaic) that are necessary for translating the Hebrew Bible; numerous textbooks exist for that purpose, of course. My assumption here is that you have already taken an introductory course in Hebrew, that you are able to parse most verbs, and that, with the help of a lexicon, you can translate a text of medium difficulty (e.g., a narrative from Genesis or Samuel) into English. You might be thinking, "Well, I am able to do that, but it takes me hours." This is perfectly normal. And happily, it gets better: with more experience, you will expand your vocabulary and become faster at finding a root or a word in a lexicon. The aim of this chapter is to help you take the next step: to replace your textbook, which was sufficient and appropriate for an initiation into the Hebrew language, with *standard reference tools*, which are the works that you must refer to in academic essays. And, more importantly, in this chapter you will learn how to *tackle difficult cases*, whether these involve obscure Hebrew words or unexpected syntactical constructions that are unrecognizable at first sight.

When speaking about "the Hebrew text," I am referring to the standard text of the Hebrew Bible, that is, the Masoretic Text (henceforth "the MT"). This is the text shared, with only slight variations, by all the extant medieval manuscripts. The Masoretes were Jewish scholars who, between the seventh and tenth centuries CE, prepared an outstanding edition of the Hebrew text, furnishing it with additional information to facilitate the continued transmission of the traditions of reading and study that they had inherited: the vowel points, the cantillation signs (for ritual chanting), indications for dividing the text into sections, and marginal notes. The oldest Masoretic manuscripts date from the ninth and tenth centuries, and the most important of these are the Aleppo Codex and the Leningrad Codex. The latter, also designated as manuscript L or B 19[A], is the oldest manuscript containing the entire text of the Hebrew Bible; it dates from 1008/1009 CE. It serves as the main text in the most widely used editions of the Hebrew Bible, which are:

- *BHS* = Karl Elliger and Wilhelm Rudolph, eds., *Biblia Hebraica Stuttgartensia*, 5th ed., ed. Adrian Schenker (Stuttgart: Deutsche Bibelgesellschaft, 1997).
- *BHQ* = Adrian Schenker, ed., *Biblia Hebraica Quinta* (Stuttgart: Deutsche Bibelgesellschaft, 2004–).

The MT can also be found in many other printed editions, however, as well as online (for instance, on the website of the Deutsche Bibelgesellschaft) or in software such as Accordance or Logos.

Rather than being exhaustive, this chapter provides advice, suggests tools and resources, and gives examples to illustrate how one can deal with the following situations:

1. DIFFICULT GRAMMATICAL FORMS (MORPHOLOGY)
2. RARE OR OBSCURE MEANINGS OF COMMON WORDS (SEMANTICS)
3. RARE WORDS AND UNEXPECTED MEANINGS (SEMANTICS)
4. DIFFICULT CONSTRUCTIONS (SYNTAX)

In addition, since the translation process facilitates a close encounter with the Hebrew text that can provide an opportunity to spot literary devices often not detectable in English translation, the final section of this chapter deals with:

5. SOUNDPLAY AND DOUBLE ENTENDRES

1.1 HOW TO DEAL WITH DIFFICULT GRAMMATICAL FORMS

Compared with the orderly paradigms that one finds in Hebrew textbooks, the reality of the actual text can produce some surprises: for example, we sometimes come across grammatical forms that seem to be anomalies or that seem not to fit the context. In such instances, it is helpful to think of two possibilities (though these do not cover every case):

- It may be that the grammatical form in question is rare but not an anomaly. Every language has exceptions to rules and exceptional forms. If you have come upon a genuine case of this kind, the form may be noted in reference grammars that include a section on morphology (see the sidebar "Grammars of Biblical Hebrew and Aramaic" below), and it is even possible that the verse you are reading will be cited among the relevant occurrences. The simplest method is thus to look for the verse in the index of biblical references at the end of a grammar. Otherwise, you can look at the index of subjects, or at the table of contents, provided that you have identified the pertinent grammatical category.

- It may be that the grammatical form is an anomaly and that the vocalization of the Masoretic Text needs to be corrected. It should be remembered that, although the vowels transmit an ancient reading tradition, they were added centuries after the consonantal text was written. Furthermore, the Masoretic vocalization corresponds to only one way of reading the text; it is often the best one, but not always. That being said, the Masoretes were experts whose work is characterized by precision and rigor, so you should assume that their vocalization had a meaning for them; it is therefore important to understand it before trying to do better yourself.

EXAMPLE 1.1   ▸   **Psalm 16:2**

Let us consider Ps 16:2:[1]

אָמַרְתְּ לַיהוָה אֲדֹנָי אָתָּה טוֹבָתִי בַּל־עָלֶיךָ:

Here, the Masoretic Text literally means, "you [fem.] said to Yhwh my Lord . . ." Who is the subject of the verb אָמַרְתְּ "you said," which is in the 2nd-person feminine singular? Some think that the psalmist is speaking to his soul (the noun נֶפֶשׁ "soul" is feminine), as when he says, "my soul [fem.], bless [fem.] Yhwh" (Ps 103:1). The Masoretes may have understood Ps 16:2 this way. However, this mode of expressing oneself seems surprising, all the more so because, unlike in Ps 103, the psalmist's "soul" is not explicitly mentioned in the immediate context of Ps 16:2. It could also be imagined that the psalmist is talking to an unnamed person, but that would seem quite cryptic. A more natural reading suggests that the whole of the psalm is about the psalmist. In short, we would expect to find a 1st-person singular verb in v. 2 ("*I said to Yhwh . . .*"), since that would fit the context perfectly. But in that case, the expected form would be אָמַרְתִּי.

By consulting the index of biblical references in the reference grammar *GKC* (see the sidebar "Grammars of Biblical Hebrew and Aramaic"), you can see that Ps 16:2 is discussed in §44i. This paragraph indicates that, in a few rare cases, the 1st-person singular of the Qal appears without a final *yod*, thus ending in תְּ (e.g., אָמַרְתְּ "I said") rather than in תִּי (e.g., אָמַרְתִּי "I said"). (In nearly all such cases—Ps 140:12 [13]; Job 42:2; 1 Kgs 8:48; Ezek 16:59—the

---

1. All biblical verse references in this book are to the English (as represented, for example, in the NRSVue). Whenever the English and Hebrew versification differ, the Hebrew will be indicated, in square brackets, following the English (e.g., 59:4 [5]).

verbal ending תְּ is the *qere* reading.²) *GKC* considers that these forms without the final *yod* could preserve an early spelling of the 1st-person singular ending. Thus, coming back to Ps 16:2, it may be that the consonantal text אמרת there was vocalized אָמַרְתְּ by the Masoretes because they understood the psalmist to be speaking to his own "soul," or perhaps to another (female) person. As we have seen, however, the word אמרת here could also have been vocalized אָמַרְתִּ—that is, equivalent to the normal 1st-personal singular form אָמַרְתִּי but with an ancient form of the 1st-person singular ending. This second reading seems to fit the text better, and it is adopted by various modern translations (notably NRSVue and NJPS).

Grammars of Biblical Hebrew and Aramaic

Here are the most important grammars of Biblical Hebrew:

- *JM* = Paul Jouön and Takamitsu Muraoka, *A Grammar of Biblical Hebrew*, rev. ed., SubBi 27 (Rome: Pontifical Biblical Institute, 2006; original English edition published, in 2 vols., in 1991). The most recent complete grammar.

- *GKC* = Arthur E. Kautzsch and Emil Cowley, *Gesenius' Hebrew Grammar*, 2nd ed. (Oxford: Clarendon, 1910; with numerous reprintings since). Advantages: the best grammar alongside *JM*. Disadvantages: this book does not integrate recent data, such as Ugaritic texts. However, a thoroughly revised version is in preparation: Geoffrey Khan et al., *The Oxford Grammar of Biblical Hebrew (based on Gesenius' Hebrew Grammar)*. Oxford: Oxford University Press, forthcoming.

- *IBHS* = Bruce K. Waltke and Michael P. O'Connor, *An Introduction to Biblical Hebrew Syntax* (Winona Lake, IN: Eisenbrauns, 1990). Advantages: dedicated to syntax, the area that generally receives the least coverage in grammars; recent; clear; provides helpful examples. Disadvantages: only treats syntax; table of contents not detailed enough.

Scholars refer to these publications not by page numbers but by paragraph or section numbers; for example, *JM* §111d or *GKC* §36c (the small letters designate the subdivisions indicated in the margins of the books). This reference system has the advantage of remaining the same throughout successive editions.

---

2. A *qere* is an indication in the margin of a Masoretic manuscript suggesting that what should be read is different from what is written.

The following intermediate-level works are also very helpful:

- Christo H. J. van der Merwe, Jacobus A. Naudé, and Jan H. Kroeze, *A Biblical Hebrew Reference Grammar*, 2nd ed. (London: Bloomsbury, 2017).
- Eric D. Reymond, *Intermediate Biblical Hebrew Grammar: A Student's Guide to Phonology and Morphology*, RBS 89 (Atlanta: SBL Press, 2018).
- Bill T. Arnold and John H. Choi, *A Guide to Biblical Hebrew Syntax*, 2nd ed. (Cambridge: Cambridge University Press, 2018).
- Benjamin J. Noonan, *Advances in the Study of Biblical Hebrew and Aramaic: New Insights for Reading the Old Testament* (Grand Rapids: Zondervan Academic, 2020).

If you are looking for an up-to-date synthesis on a particular grammatical issue, you can consult:

- Geoffrey Khan, ed., *Encyclopedia of Hebrew Language and Linguistics*, 4 vols. (Leiden: Brill, 2013).

A number of resources are available for Biblical Aramaic, including:

- Franz Rosenthal, *A Grammar of Biblical Aramaic*, 7th ed. (Wiesbaden: Harrassowitz, 2006). The classic work, both concise and reliable.
- Takamitsu Muraoka, *A Biblical Aramaic Reader: With an Outline Grammar*, 2nd ed. (Leuven: Peeters, 2020). Includes a concise description of the most important grammatical features of Aramaic.

1.2 WHAT TO DO WHEN YOU SUDDENLY DISCOVER RARE OR OBSCURE MEANINGS FOR COMMON WORDS

An intuitive approach to this problem would be to look in a lexicon! Yes, but that is not always enough if you want to discern precisely what the meaning of a word is in a particular context. The examples discussed below will illustrate the following points:

- **Ⓐ** the risk of neglecting rare meanings of common words
- **Ⓑ** the importance of choosing the most pertinent meaning for the context
- **Ⓒ** the risk of "importing" a nuance from one context into another
- **Ⓓ** the importance of recognizing idiomatic expressions

A. Do Not Neglect Rare Meanings of Common Words

When learning Biblical Hebrew, you acquire knowledge of a base of vocabulary for which, quite soon, you no longer feel the need to consult a lexicon. Yet introductory textbooks typically give only one or perhaps a couple of meanings for each word, leaving aside other, rarer meanings. This is the case not only for many substantives and verbs but also for prepositions: for example, student generally know that אִם can mean "if," but they do not necessarily learn that the same preposition sometimes means "when," "or," and even "if," or that it can indicate a question. By the same token, students do not always learn the meanings of combinations of particles. For example, כִּי אִם does not mean "because if," as you might assume by translating it word-for-word; it means "but rather," "except," or "unless." The point is that even common words can have surprises in store for you, but because you think you know them well it may not occur to you to consult a lexicon to see what they mean in a given context.

EXAMPLE 1.2a ▸ Isaiah 29:16

In Isa 29:16, a word-for-word rendering of the clause אִם־כְּחֹמֶר הַיֹּצֵר יֵחָשֵׁב, based on the most frequent meanings of the terms it contains, would be: "If like the clay the potter is considered." This hardly makes sense in the context. In reality, this phrase is only understandable if we know that אִם can introduce a question. So it should be translated: "Shall the potter be regarded as the clay?" (NRSVue).

EXAMPLE 1.2b ▸ Psalm 7:12 [13]

Let us consider Ps 7:12 [13]:

אִם־לֹא יָשׁוּב חַרְבּוֹ יִלְטוֹשׁ קַשְׁתּוֹ דָרַךְ וַיְכוֹנְנֶהָ׃

Here again, a word-for-word translation, based on the most frequent meanings of the words found here, does not make sense: "If he does not come back, his sword he sharpens, his bow *he walks* and gets it ready." In this verse, the verb דרך cannot have the usual meaning of "to walk"; rather, it means "to bend (a bow)" (as many dictionaries indicate). This corresponds perfectly to the immediate context, and so the phrase can be translated, "If one does not repent, God [lit., he] will whet his sword; *he has bent* and strung his bow" (NRSVue; italics added).

Help for Reading the Hebrew Text

Three types of resources may help you to read the text of the Hebrew Bible:

(1) Interlinear Bibles, with the English equivalent below each Hebrew word. These should be used wisely, so as not to rely on the translation as a "crutch" and look at it systematically. For example:

- John R. Kohlenberger III, *The Interlinear NIV Hebrew-English Old Testament* (Grand Rapids: Zondervan, 1993).
- Thom Blair, ed., *Hebrew-English Interlinear ESV Old Testament: Biblia Hebraica Stuttgartensia (BHS) and English Standard Version (ESV)* (Wheaton, IL: Crossway, 2014).

(2) Bilingual editions. For example:

- *The JPS Hebrew-English Tanakh* (Philadelphia: Jewish Publication Society of America, 2003).

(3) Reader's editions, with notes indicating vocabulary and the parsing of weak verbs. This is probably the best kind of resource: such volumes give you the necessary information, but you interrupt your reading only for words you do not yet know or for verbs you find difficult to parse:

- A. Philip Brown II and Bryan W. Smith, *A Reader's Hebrew Bible* (Grand Rapids: Zondervan, 2008).
- Donald R. Vance, George Athas, and Yael Avrahami, *Biblia Hebraica Stuttgartensia: A Reader's Edition* (Peabody, MA: Hendrickson; Stuttgart: Deutsche Bibelgesellschaft, 2014).
- Drayton C. Benner, Andrew Zulker, James R. Covington, and H. H. Hardy II, *The Hebrew Old Testament, Reader's Edition* (Wheaton, IL: Crossway, 2020).
- Donald R. Vance, George Athas, Yael Avrahami, and Jonathan G. Kline, *Biblical Aramaic: A Reader & Handbook* (Peabody, MA: Hendrickson, 2016).

See also the following book (already mentioned above), which includes a verse-by-verse grammatical commentary on the Aramaic passages in Daniel and Ezra:

- Takamitsu Muraoka, *A Biblical Aramaic Reader: With an Outline Grammar*, 2nd ed. (Leuven: Peeters, 2020).

B. Choose the Most Pertinent Meaning for the Context

When you consult a lexicon for a Hebrew word you do not know, you may be confronted with a choice of many possible meanings, and it may seem difficult at first to choose among them. You will also sometimes encounter homographic roots—that is, roots that are distinct despite being written with exactly the same consonants—and not know which of these is the one you are looking for. In such situations, the most useful point to remember is that the immediate context of the word you are studying must guide your decision about which meaning to choose.

> **EXAMPLE 1.2c** ▸ **The Word** בַּיִת
>
> The most common meaning of the word בַּיִת is "house." But the same term is used to speak of a "palace," a "temple," or even a "dynasty"! The text of 2 Sam 7 plays on these three meanings, in fact:
>
> - David notes that he is living in a "house of cedar" (meaning his palace) (v. 2).
>
> - He wishes to build a "house" (that is, a temple) for the Lord, but the Lord refuses this desire by announcing that it is David's son who will do so (vv. 6–7, 13).
>
> - The Lord turns around the situation by promising that *he* will give a "house" (in the sense of a dynastic line) to David (v. 11).
>
> As observed above, it is context that determines the appropriate meaning of a word. In a case like 2 Sam 7, a translator has two options: either (1) to write "house" in each instance (which has the advantage of allowing the reader to see that the term "house" is repeated and, by comparing the repeated instances, to understand how the passage is playing on this word), or (2) to translate "house" in this passage as "palace," "temple," and "dynasty," as relevant (which adds more precision in the target language but which hides the wordplay). Neither solution is perfect: the second obscures the literary artistry of the original text, whereas the first presumes that the reader already knows about the polysemy of the term or that the context is sufficiently clear for the reader to infer the correct meaning of each of its occurrences.

Lexicons of Biblical Hebrew and Aramaic

The standard lexicons of Biblical Hebrew and Aramaic are as follows:

- Wilhelm Gesenius, *Hebräisches und Aramäisches Handwörterbuch über das Alte Testament*, 18th ed., 6 vols (Berlin: Springer, 1987–2010). The latest version of Gesenius's lexicon, an earlier edition of which served as the basis for the following lexicon:

- BDB = Francis Brown, Samuel R. Driver, and Charles A. Briggs, *A Hebrew and English Lexicon of the Old Testament* (Oxford: Clarendon, 1906; with numerous reprintings since). Advantages: fairly rich in examples; gives the gender of substantives; lists parallels in other Semitic languages. Disadvantages: classes substantives by their root (a more "scientific" approach but one that sometimes complicates research); old (the original edition dates from the beginning of the twentieth century); does not take into account certain more recent discoveries, such as the texts from Ugarit and from Qumran.

- *HALOT* = Ludwig Koehler and Walter Baumgartner, *The Hebrew and Aramaic Lexicon of the Old Testament*, 5 vols. (Leiden: Brill, 1994–99). This is a translation of a German work. Advantages: relatively recent (integrates Ugaritic); gives parallel words from other Semitic languages; in the case of words with a difficult etymology, sometimes refers to articles on the subject. Disadvantages: does not integrate all the data from the Dead Sea Scrolls; provides fewer examples than BDB (see above) and *DCH* (see below). An abridged version exists: William L. Holladay, *A Concise Hebrew and Aramaic Lexicon of the Old Testament* (Leiden: Brill, 1971). In addition, a concise and updated version of the German original exists: Walter Dietrich and Samuel Arnet, eds., *Konzise und aktualisierte Ausgabe des Hebräischen und Aramäischen Lexikons zum Alten Testament* (Leiden: Brill, 2013).

- *DCH* = David J. A. Clines, ed., *The Dictionary of Classical Hebrew*, 9 vols. (Sheffield: Sheffield Academic, 1993–2012). Advantages: recent; integrates Ugaritic, the Dead Sea Scrolls, and other epigraphic texts; indicates the gender of substantives; provides numerous examples and aims to be exhaustive in the lists of meanings and uses of a word in various syntactical functions. Disadvantages: does not indicate parallels from other Semitic languages. An abridged version exists in one volume: *CDCH* = David J. A. Clines, ed., *The Concise Dictionary of Classical Hebrew* (Sheffield: Sheffield Academic, 2009).

> Alongside these purely philological dictionaries, there are lexicons that aim to show the *theological usage* of different terms. For instance:
>
> - *TDOT* = G. Johannes Botterweck and Helmer Ringgren, eds., *Theological Dictionary of the Old Testament*, trans. John T. Willis et al., 15 vols. (Grand Rapids: Eerdmans, 1974–2006; original German edition, 1970–2000).
>
> - *TLOT* = Ernst Jenni and Claus Westermann, eds., *Theological Lexicon of the Old Testament*, trans. Mark E. Biddle, 3 vols. (Peabody, MA: Hendrickson, 1997; original German edition, 1971–76).
>
> These last two tools can help students go further in research but can never replace the "purely philological" lexicons cited above. Indeed, they do not aim to be exhaustive and do not treat every root. What is more, these volumes include semantic analyses tied to theological interpretations that are subject to debate.
>
> BDB and *HALOT* include sections dedicated to Biblical Aramaic. Another very helpful resource is:
>
> - Ernst Vogt, ed., *A Lexicon of Biblical Aramaic: Clarified by Ancient Documents*, trans. and rev. by James A. Fitzmyer (Rome: Gregorian and Biblical Press, 2011). In addition to citing the biblical occurrences of words, this volume also provides occurrences from ancient Aramaic texts (inscriptions, Egyptian papyri, and others).

C. Do Not Import a Nuance from One Context into Another

Context often colors the meaning of a word, giving it a particular nuance. For instance, a verb that in general means "to reply" could take on the specific nuance of "to retort" in the context of a discussion involving conflict. Yet this does not necessarily allow us to translate this verb as "to retort" in any other text. By doing so, we would run the risk of making an *illegitimate totality transfer* (an expression coined by James Barr), importing a specific nuance or overtone from one context into a passage where it is not pertinent. For example, it would be absurd to infer from the fact that בַּיִת means "dynasty" in certain contexts (as discussed in the preceding example) that this Hebrew word can be translated in this way *in any passage whatsoever*.

A practical consequence of this is that you must take care not to just pick one meaning from among all those that are mentioned for a given word in a Hebrew lexicon and apply it to any particular verse. Rather, it is crucial to carefully consider the context of the specific verse you are reading.

> **EXAMPLE 1.2d** ▸ **The Word עֶבֶד**
>
> The word עֶבֶד generally means "servant." In certain contexts (e.g., 2 Kgs 5:6; 22:9), it seems clear that this word designates (in the plural) senior "civil

servants," "officials," even "ministers." This is confirmed by seals from the royal period that are inscribed in Hebrew, on which the word serves as a title for persons who were sufficiently powerful to have possessed such a seal and where the word is frequently followed by the name of a king. This is the case, for example, on the famous seal of "Shema, servant of Jeroboam," which would perhaps be more correctly rendered as "Shema, minister of Jeroboam." At the same time, just because עֶבֶד *can* carry the meaning "official" or "minister" in certain contexts, this does not mean that the word *must* convey this meaning in any other verse. Translating the word with this meaning in any given text could therefore involve an "illegitimate totality transfer," which would lead to an erroneous, or even an absurd, translation (that would clearly be the case, for example, in Exod 13:3, where the expression בֵּית עֲבָדִים means "house of slaves," i.e., "house of slavery").

D. Recognize Idiomatic Expressions

Finally, you may well stumble on an idiomatic expression (i.e., an expression that is particular to the source language [Hebrew] and thus does not exist in the target language [e.g., English]). What can alert you to this is when a more or less literal translation does not make sense. In such a situation, you can choose a significant word from the expression in question and look it up in a detailed lexicon; if you are in fact dealing with an idiomatic expression, there is a good chance that the lexicon will mention it.

EXAMPLE 1.2e ▸ Isaiah 22:15

In Isa 22:15, God orders the prophet Isaiah to go and find a certain Shebna:

כֹּה אָמַר אֲדֹנָי יְהוִה צְבָאוֹת לֶךְ־בֹּא אֶל־הַסֹּכֵן הַזֶּה
עַל־שֶׁבְנָא אֲשֶׁר עַל־הַבָּיִת:

A word-for-word translation of this verse would be: "Thus says the Lord GOD of hosts: 'Come, go to this official, to Shebna, *who is over the house*.'" Understood literally, the expression in italics does not make sense in context: certainly, the text does not mean that this man is hovering above the roof! It is not difficult to guess, therefore, that the formula designates someone who is *metaphorically* "above" the house, that is, who has authority over it. Since the same verse indicates that Shebna is an "official" (סֹכֵן), "house" here is easily understood to mean "palace household." The phrase "who is over the house" is in fact a Hebrew expression indicating a "steward," and, indeed, this is often how it is translated.

> As it happens, this same formula is used as a title on seals from the royal period that are inscribed in Hebrew. It even appears in an inscription from around 700 BCE decorating the tomb of a certain "[. . .]-yahu who is over the house," which was dug out of a hillside located in the present-day village of Silwan (in Jerusalem, opposite the city of David).[3] It is possible that this is precisely the person whom Isaiah was talking about, since Shebna is an abbreviated form of Shebnayahu, and the biblical text reproaches him for having had a tomb dug for himself "on the height . . . in the rock" (v. 16). Unfortunately, however, this cannot be known for certain, because the beginning of the name is missing on the inscription.

1.3 HOW TO DEAL WITH RARE WORDS AND UNEXPECTED MEANINGS

Dealing with rare words can be difficult, but it is important to discuss this since the Hebrew Bible contains many of them, including hundreds of terms that only appear once! (Collectively, the words that appear only one time are called *hapax legomena* [Greek for "said only once"]; any particular such word is called a *hapax legomenon* [or a *hapax*, for short].) An intuitive approach to determining the meaning of rare words (for example, those occurring once or only a few times) would be to look in a lexicon. Yet this should not be done uncritically. You may very well think: "Who am I, a mere student, to second-guess the views of erudite scholars?" I applaud your humility: lexicons are indeed the fruit of a considerable amount of philological work. That said, the meanings they provide are not always certain. Sometimes, they are just . . . educated guesswork. So, a mature student should not trust the lexicons implicitly but should use them critically and be able to make up his or her own mind.

A related situation occurs when you are translating a text in which a more common word occurs and you notice that a modern translation renders the word in a way that you find unexpected or that you do not understand (perhaps because the word's typical meaning makes sense to you in the context). In such a case, you want to understand why the translator(s) chose a rare meaning over a common meaning in this context.

These two situations (rare words or unexpected meanings) require the same kind of inquiry. Five different but complementary approaches can be followed in order to try to discover the meaning of a rare word or to check if a rare meaning of a word is the most contextually appropriate one. Before looking at each of these points in more detail, it is worth mentioning four resources that can be very helpful for these tasks:

---

3. Shmuel Aḥituv, *Echoes from the Past: Hebrew and Cognate Inscriptions from the Biblical Period* (Jerusalem: Carta, 2008), 44–47.

- Ernest Klein, *A Comprehensive Etymological Dictionary of the Hebrew Language for Readers of English* (Jerusalem: Carta, 1987). An etymological dictionary based on all the periods of Hebrew (from ancient to modern); indicates parallels in other Semitic languages.

- Eliezer Ben-Yehuda, *Dictionary and Thesaurus of the Hebrew Language*, 8 vols. (New York: Yoseloff, 1960) [Hebrew]. This covers all the periods of Hebrew (from ancient to modern). It is the ancestor of the following project:

- **The Historical Dictionary Project* ("Maagarim") of the Academy of the Hebrew Language, which is the most complete dictionary of Hebrew. Using it requires some knowledge of Modern Hebrew.

- **Semantics of Ancient Hebrew Database*, an international project involving several universities. This excellent resource summarizes the available data for a given lexeme and indicates the state of research on this subject. Work on this project is ongoing, but a number of entries have been completed.

A. Check the Context

The golden rule (again!) is that the meaning of a word must fit the context in which it appears. The most convincing suggestions produced by erudite philological reasoning can only be accepted provided that they meet this condition.[4] But the context is not just an external control for hypotheses about what a word means; it is often the factor that prompts such hypotheses, since it reduces the range of options. And in the best-case scenario, the context requires a relatively precise meaning.

Most interesting is the case of poetic texts because, chances are, the word under study has a parallel in another poetic line. Indeed, most poetic sentences in the Hebrew Bible contain (at least) two lines that echo each other thanks to, for instance, the presence of synonyms or antonyms. (We will learn more about this subject in chapter 10.) For example:

> *Praise* the Lord, **all you nations**!
> *Extol* him, **all you peoples!**

Depending on the type of parallelism that is present in the verse you are studying, you may find a synonym or an antonym of the word whose meaning you are trying to determine. The trouble, of course, is that in many cases you can only determine what kind of echo ("parallelism," in technical terms) you are dealing with once you know the meaning of all the words that are in the sentence in question—hence, there is the risk of circular reasoning.

---

4. Note, however, that although this is a necessary condition, it is not a sufficient one. That is, just because a particular meaning *can* fit a context does not mean that it is *actually* the correct meaning in that context.

B. Examine the Other Occurrences

An extension of the preceding approach (i.e., one that involves multiple texts, not just one) entails examining most or all of the passages where a word appears, a process that should not take long when you are studying a word that is rare. (If the word is a *hapax*, you can check if other words derived from the same root occur.) An exhaustive concordance will provide a list of all the occurrences of a word; and in the case of rare words, lexicons will often indicate all the occurrences as well. It should be noted, however, that examining the other places where a word occurs can often merely shift the problem, since the same difficulty of determining what a (rare) word means is frequently applicable for the other occurrences of the word as well. What is important to look for are (if they exist) occurrences for which the context *requires* a relatively precise meaning or range of possible meanings.

Several concordances exist in printed format, notably:

- Abraham Even-Shoshan, ed., *A New Concordance of the Bible* (Jerusalem: Kiryat Sefer, 1989).

- Gerhard Lisowsky, *Konkordanz zum Hebräischen Alten Testament*, 2nd ed. (Stuttgart: Württembergische Bibelanstalt, 1958).

Although these printed concordances are valuable, software such as Accordance or Logos is both easier to use and more powerful, since you can search not only for all the occurrences of a single term, but also for all the occurrences of two words together and the like.

C. Consult the Ancient Versions

The ancient versions of the Hebrew Bible show us how translators in antiquity understood the words of the Hebrew text. (In the next chapter, we will learn more about where these versions can be consulted.) When the translation techniques of these ancient translators are fairly "literal," they provide a sort of mirror (in the target language, such as Greek or Syriac) of the Hebrew text they were reading. That said, the ancient translators were sometimes in the same position as we are (e.g., not knowing the precise meaning of certain Hebrew words in some contexts), so some of their renderings are educated guesswork, that is, *ad hoc* hypotheses. In addition, not all of these translations were made directly from the Hebrew text: the versions in Greek (the Septuagint), Aramaic (the Targumim), and Syriac (the Peshitta) were, but by contrast, the Old Latin, the Ethiopic version, the Armenian version, and others are translations of various forms of the Septuagint.

D. Consult the Other Hebrew Corpora

The books of the Hebrew Bible are not the only texts from antiquity that were written in Hebrew; this was also the case for a number of Jewish texts written during the

Hellenistic and Roman periods. Some of these have been found among the Dead Sea Scrolls, albeit often in a fragmentary state. An important case is Ben Sira (also called Ecclesiasticus or Sirach), which belongs to the Catholic and Orthodox canons. In addition, Hebrew inscriptions (epigraphic texts) from the first millennium BCE date from the same time that some biblical texts were redacted. The dictionary *DCH* (mentioned above) integrates most of these data. However, it should be noted that studying inscriptions is often more difficult than studying the biblical text, so deeper study can require verification of the details concerning the decipherment and the interpretation of the relevant inscriptions. Lastly, one can also consult the range of meanings a Hebrew word has in rabbinic literature, although since this literature was written at a later stage of the history of the language than Biblical Hebrew, it is important to remember that the meanings of a given word may have evolved in the meantime.

Where Can You Consult Other Hebrew and Aramaic Texts?

Epigraphic Hebrew

- Graham I. Davies, *Ancient Hebrew Inscriptions: Corpus and Concordance*, 2 vols. (Cambridge: Cambridge University Press, 1991–2004). Includes transcriptions and a concordance.

- F. W. Dobbs-Allsopp, J. J. M. Roberts, Choon-Leong Seow, and Richard E. Whitaker, *Hebrew Inscriptions: Texts from the Biblical Period of the Monarchy with Concordance* (New Haven: Yale University Press, 2005). Includes transcriptions, translations, philological analysis, and concordances for proper nouns and for substantives.

- Johannes Renz and Wolfgang Röllig, *Handbuch der althebräischen Epigraphik*, 3 vols. (Darmstadt: Wissenschaftliche Buchgesellschaft, 1995). Includes transcriptions, translations, philological analysis, drawings, and paleographic tables.

- Shmuel Aḥituv, *Echoes from the Past: Hebrew and Cognate Inscriptions from the Biblical World* (Jerusalem: Carta, 2008). Not exhaustive, but contains many photos and drawings, which may help when checking a reading.

- Peter Bekins, *Inscriptions from the World of the Bible: A Reader and Introduction to Old Northwest Semitic* (Peabody, MA: Hendrickson Academic, 2020). Includes transcriptions, translations, and philological notes for a nice selection of Northwest Semitic inscriptions, including in Hebrew (chapter 6).

> It should be noted that there is a grammar of epigraphic texts in Hebrew:
>
> - Sandra Gogel, *A Grammar of Epigraphic Hebrew*, RBS 23 (Atlanta: Scholars Press, 1998).
>
> In addition, Peter Bekins's book, cited above, provides a concise and helpful survey of the grammatical features of epigraphic texts in Hebrew and other Northwest Semitic languages.
>
> **Qumran Hebrew and Aramaic**
>
> - Martin G. Abegg Jr., with James E. Bowley and Edward Cook, *The Dead Sea Scrolls Concordance*, 3 vols. (Leiden: Brill, 2003–10).
>
> **Hebrew and Aramaic in Rabbinic Literature**
>
> - Marcus Jastrow, *A Dictionary of the Targumim, the Talmud Babli and Yerushalmi, and the Midrashic Literature*, 2 vols. (New York: Title Publishing, 1943; with various reprints, in one volume, by Judaica Press).
>
> **Aramaic (general)**
>
> - *CAL = Comprehensive Aramaic Lexicon. Aims to cover all the periods and all the dialects of Aramaic.

E. Look for Cognates in Other Semitic Languages

This is the most technical method of trying to determine the meaning of a Hebrew word. The Semitic languages (i.e., the languages that belong to the same family as Hebrew) constitute a reservoir of information for lexicography. A rare word in Hebrew may have a corresponding (a.k.a. cognate) term that is more widely attested in Aramaic, Ugaritic, Akkadian, or the like. As noted above, these languages are one source of data that the authors of modern dictionaries have used in their work. For example, at the beginning of each entry in *HALOT*, there is a list of the known (or supposed) parallels in other Semitic languages. These can be a good starting point for comparison, but it should be noted that any given list of cognate terms is not necessarily exhaustive, nor are the correspondences in meaning across the languages always precise.

One should take several precautions when using lexicons of other Semitic languages (see the sidebar "Lexicons of Other Semitic Languages" below for a list). The main problem is that of being misled by false cognates (sometimes colloquially called "false friends"); for example, in Hebrew the root שכח means "to forget," whereas in Aramaic the same root means "to find"! In the following book, James Barr brilliantly describes the abuses that can occur in comparing languages:

- James Barr, *Comparative Philology and the Text of the Old Testament*, 2nd ed. (Winona Lake, IN: Eisenbrauns, 1987).

Another problem is that—due to the phonological changes each Semitic language underwent when it evolved from Proto-Semitic (the supposed common ancestor of all the Semitic languages)—certain phonemes in Hebrew are equivalent to *different* phonemes in other Semitic languages. For example, the Arabic equivalent of Hebrew *š* is *s*; thus, the Hebrew greeting *šālôm* corresponds to Arabic *salām*. For tables giving the correspondences, see, for example:

- Sabatino Moscati, *An Introduction to the Comparative Grammar of the Semitic Languages: Phonology and Morphology*, PLO 6 (Wiesbaden: Harrassowitz, 1980), 43–45.

EXAMPLE 1.3a ▸ **Isaiah 52:15**

The famous passage on the "suffering servant" in Isa 53 actually begins in 52:13. At the beginning of the third verse of this passage, 52:15 (the last verse of ch. 52), we read in the NIV that the servant "will sprinkle many nations," but in the NRSVue we read that the servant "shall startle many nations." The underlying Hebrew sentence is:

כֵּן יַזֶּה גּוֹיִם רַבִּים

The difference concerns how one understands the verb יַזֶּה here (a Hiphil form of the root נזה). All the lexicons list the meaning "to sprinkle" for the Hiphil and indicate that this meaning is well attested (Lev 4:6; etc.). But BDB and *DCH* also mention "to startle" (or "to cause to leap"), albeit only for Isa 52:15. Where does this meaning come from, and is it justified here? Let us review the five approaches mentioned above:

Context. A look at the immediate context shows that "to startle" makes sense:

> Just as there were many who were astonished at him
> —so marred was his appearance, beyond human semblance,
> and his form beyond that of mortals—
> so he shall *startle* many nations;
> kings shall shut their mouths because of him,
> for that which had not been told them they shall see,
> and that which they had not heard they shall contemplate.
>
> (Isa 52:14–15 NRSVue; italics added)

Indeed, the clause we are considering (כֵּן יַזֶּה גּוֹיִם רַבִּים) constitutes the continuation of a sentence that starts at the beginning of v. 14 ("Just as . . .")

and is interrupted by a parenthesis ("—so marred was . . ."). Grammatically speaking, the main statement here is: "Just as there were many who were astonished at him . . . so he shall startle many nations." This statement would make little sense, however, if we were to translate it, "Just as there were many who were astonished at him . . . so he shall sprinkle many nations." Why and how would the servant "sprinkle" these people? While some Christian interpreters through the centuries have read an allusion here to the cleansing of people by the blood of Christ, that is a rereading, or reinterpretation, of the text: it is not possible to use a later idea to find out what the text of Isaiah originally meant. Indeed, the next sentence (v. 15) confirms that it is the surprise of the nations that is being described in the context.

Other occurrences. In all the other occurrences of the root נזה, the meaning "to sprinkle" is the most relevant. This does not, however, imply that the meaning "to startle" is impossible, only that it is rare in the Bible (indeed, unique to this passage).

Ancient versions. While some ancient versions favor the meaning "to sprinkle," the Greek version says that "many nations will be astonished [θαυμάσονται] at him" (with the sentence having been reformulated from the active to the passive voice, perhaps to make it more similar to the beginning of v. 14). This seems to be another way of saying that these nations will be *startled* by the servant. That said, we cannot rule out the possibility that the translator made a contextual guess here, translating the verb in light of the immediate context.

Other corpora. The usual lexicons are not very helpful here. A look at a concordance of the Dead Sea Scrolls shows that the verb נזה is attested twenty-one times there, always with the meaning "to sprinkle."

Cognates. BDB mentions an Arabic verb meaning "leap, leap up, upon" as a support to the translation "*so shall he cause to leap* (i.e. in joyful surprise, or=*startle*) *many nations.*" This may sound like a tenuous support, because Arabic is relatively remote from Biblical Hebrew in the genealogy of Semitic languages, and because going from "leap" to "cause to leap" and from there to the meaning "startle" requires something of a . . . leap of faith. However, this is no different from the kinds of indirect relationships that do in fact exist between many other cognates that are well established.

In the end, the "external" evidence (i.e., the evidence from ancient versions and cognates) for the translation "to startle" may not be as strong as one might wish, but it is real. The decisive factor that makes this a plausible translation here in the eyes of a number of exegetes is the fact that it fits the context very well, whereas the alternative, "to sprinkle," strikes them as meaningless. Nevertheless, some scholars do opt for the latter understanding.⁵

EXAMPLE 1.3b ▸ **Exodus 15:2**

Let us consider the beginning of Exod 15:2:

עָזִּי וְזִמְרָת יָהּ וַיְהִי־לִי לִישׁוּעָה

The King James Version renders this sentence as: "The LORD is my strength and song, he is become my salvation," and some modern versions (e.g., the NET Bible) translate similarly. In the NRSVue and many other modern versions, however, we read: "The LORD is my strength and my *might*, and he has become my salvation." Why the difference?

Let's first note briefly that the absence of a personal pronoun before the noun in question (e.g., "*my* song" or "*my* might") is not the real problem here. The context makes it clear that the personal pronoun is implied. The absence of the expected suffix -*î* ("my") from the end of וְזִמְרָת may be due to the presence of the following יָהּ (see *GKC* §80g, a reference you would have found thanks to the index of biblical references at the end of that grammar, since this index mentions Exod 15:2).

The most important difference concerns the semantics of the word זִמְרָה (the lexical form of זִמְרָת). While the meaning "song" is well known and acknowledged in all the lexicons, the meaning "might" is less evident. Let us review the five approaches described above:

Context. In Exod 15:2, "might" fits the immediate context very well, since it is synonymous with "strength," which appears just before it. The whole constitutes a good parallel to "my salvation" (or "my deliverance") in the next poetic line. By contrast, "my song" is surprising within this verse, although it does make sense in the wider context: the Lord (or, more precisely, his deeds) is the subject of the entire song.

Other occurrences. HALOT has two relevant entries here: I זִמְרָה ("melody, sound") and II זִמְרָה ("strength"). For the former, this lexicon lists Isa 53:3; Amos 5:23, and Pss 81:2 [3]; 98:5. For the latter, it mentions Exod 15:2 as well as Isa 12:2, Ps 118:4, and Gen 43:11. Isaiah 12:2 and Ps 118:4 involve the same phrase as Exod 15:2. As for Gen 43:11, *HALOT* provides the translation "strength (i.e. the best products) of the land." Since the reference in context

---

5. See, e.g., John Goldingay and David Payne, *A Critical and Exegetical Commentary on Isaiah 40–55*, vol. 2, *Commentary on Isaiah 44:24–55:13*, ICC (London: T&T Clark, 2006), 294–95; they translate "to spatter," though they do not really provide an explanation of what it means here.

is to the products described in the rest of the verse (balm, honey, aromatic spices, etc.), understanding "the strength of the land" in the sense of "best products" seems reasonable.

Ancient versions. In Exod 15:2, while the word זִמְרָה is rendered "praise" in various versions, including the Latin (Vulgate: *laus*), it is translated σκεπαστής ("protector, defender") in the Greek version (Septuagint).

Other corpora. DCH mentions some occurrences in the Dead Sea Scrolls where the word means "song."

Cognates. As parallels to "strength," HALOT mentions the Amorite word *zmr* ("to protect"), Ugaritic *ḏmr* ("to protect, protection"), and Arabic *ḏamir*, *ḏamīr* ("brave"). This is one of those situations where a consonant in one language corresponds to another one elsewhere: that is, in this instance Hebrew and Amorite *z* and Ugaritic and Arabic *ḏ* ultimately derive from the same phoneme.

In sum, the context of our verse and the contexts of the other verses in which the word occurs support the meaning "might," while at least one ancient version as well as a pair of Semitic cognates support the meaning "protector." These meanings seem related: it is because the Lord is strong that he is able to protect. Yet two considerations may tilt the balance toward "might" rather than "protector" in Exod 15:2: *(a)* "might," which is an abstract noun, seems to form a pair with the abstract noun עָזִּי ("my strength") in a more fitting way than "protector," which is not abstract; for the same reason, "might" forms a better parallel to the abstract "salvation" in the next poetic line than "protector" does; *(b)* the meaning "might" (or "strength") fits Gen 43:11, which cannot be said of "protector."

The alternative meaning, "song," is less plausible in Exod 15:2 due to the inner parallelism of the verse. That said, it does echo the wider context, inasmuch as this word appears at the beginning of a poem that is explicitly described as a song (שִׁירָה, Exod 15:1). So perhaps we should not exclude the possibility that a double entendre is intended.

Lexicons of Other Semitic Languages

General Semitic Lexicon

- David Cohen, *Dictionnaire des racines sémitiques ou attestées dans les langues sémitiques* (Paris: Mouton, 1970–). A prodigious work; however, only some of the fascicles have been published.

Ugaritic

- Gregorio del Olmo Lete and Joaquín Sanmartín, *A Dictionary of the Ugaritic Language in the Alphabetic Tradition*, trans. and ed. by Wilfred G. E. Watson, 3rd ed., 2 vols., HdO 112 (Leiden: Brill, 2015).

Phoenician

- Charles R. Krahmalkov, *Phoenician-Punic Dictionary* (Leuven: Peeters, 2000).

Syriac

- Jessie Payne Smith, ed., *A Compendious Syriac Dictionary: Founded upon the Thesaurus Syriacus of R. Payne Smith* (Oxford: Clarendon, 1903; repr., Eugene, OR: Wipf & Stock, 1999).

- Michael Sokoloff, *A Syriac Lexicon: A Translation from Latin; Correction, Expansion, and Update of C. Brockelmann's Lexicon Syriacum* (Winona Lake, IN: Eisenbrauns; Piscataway, NJ: Gorgias, 2009).

Akkadian

- CAD = *The Assyrian Dictionary of the Oriental Institute of the University of Chicago* (Chicago: The Oriental Institute of the University of Chicago, 1956–2010). Also available online.

- AHw = Wolfram von Soden, ed., *Akkadisches Handwörterbuch* (Wiesbaden: Harrassowitz, 1965–81).

- CDA = Jeremy A. Black, Andrew George, and J. Nicholas Postgate, eds., *A Concise Dictionary of Akkadian*, 2nd ed., SANTAG 5 (Wiesbaden: Harrassowitz, 2000). Abridged English version of *AHw*.

Arabic

- Edward William Lane, *An Arabic-English Lexicon*, 8 vols. (London: Williams & Norgate, 1863–93). Also available online.

South Arabic

- Joan Copeland Biella, *Dictionary of Old South Arabic: Sabaean Dialect*, HSS 25 (Chico, CA: Scholars Press, 1982).
- Alfred Felix Landon Beeston, Mahmud Ali Ghul, and Walter W. Müller, *Dictionnaire sabéen (anglais – français – arabe)* (Louvain-la-Neuve: Peeters; Beyrouth: Librairie du Liban, 1982).
- Stephen D. Ricks, *Lexicon of Inscriptional Qatabanian*, StPohl 14 (Rome: Pontifical Biblical Institute, 1989).

Old Ethiopic (Ge'ez)

- Wolf Leslau, *Comparative Dictionary of Ge'ez (Classical Ethiopic): Ge'ez-English/English-Ge'ez; With an Index of Semitic Roots* (Wiesbaden: Harrassowitz, 1987). Very useful because the entries are transliterated into Latin characters and because it lists cognates in other Semitic languages.
- Wolf Leslau, *Concise Dictionary of Ge'ez (Classical Ethiopic)* (Wiesbaden: Harrassowitz, 1989). Abridged version of the previous entry, with Ethiopic characters and without the Semitic cognates.

West Semitic Inscriptions

- DNWSI = Jacob Hoftijzer and Karel Jongeling, *Dictionary of the North-West Semitic Inscriptions*, HdO (Leiden: Brill, 1995).

1.4 HOW TO TACKLE DIFFICULT SYNTACTIC CONSTRUCTIONS

The last type of difficulty that will be discussed here concerns syntax. As with any other language, Hebrew writers use special syntactic constructions that do not make much sense when you encounter them for the first time and try to render them word for word or according to the most frequent meanings of the words they contain. The good news is that (most of) these constructions are listed in grammars. The bad news is that it is not always easy to know where to search if you do not know the syntactic construction in the first place. Here are a few tips:

- You can consult the index of biblical references at the end of a reference grammar (*JM*, *GKC*, *IBHS*) to see if the particular verse you are studying appears there. Indeed, an impressive number of passages are used as examples in these books. It may be that the verse in question serves to illustrate a different grammatical point (e.g., a morphological feature), but it is still worth trying to look it up. Note that syntax is treated in *JM* only from §111 onward, and in *GKC* from §106 onward.

- If you have a sense of which grammatical category is (or might be) involved, you can consult a reference grammar's table of contents—or its index of subjects (which will contain entries that do not necessarily appear in the table of contents, such as "relative clause")—and look for the section that is most likely to treat the problem in question.

- Even more pragmatically, you can consult an exegetical commentary in the hope that it deals with the issue or refers to a specific place in a grammar (see, e.g., the textual notes in the series WBC).

In the long run, the more texts you translate, the more you will encounter and learn new syntactic constructions, so dealing with these gets easier over time.

EXAMPLE 1.4 ▸ **1 Samuel 3:14**

Let us consider 1 Sam 3:14:

וְלָכֵן נִשְׁבַּעְתִּי לְבֵית עֵלִי אִם־יִתְכַּפֵּר עֲוֹן בֵּית־עֵלִי בְּזֶבַח וּבְמִנְחָה עַד־עוֹלָם׃

A word-for-word translation of this verse produces something like this: "And therefore I swear to the house of Eli, if the sin of the house of Eli is expiated by sacrifice or by offering forever." Since the topic changes in the following verse ("Samuel stayed lying down until the morning"), something seems to be missing in v. 14: that is, after the "if," a "then" is expected. How do we explain this?

Let us consult a grammar—*JM*, for example. As it happens, 1 Sam 3:14 is mentioned in the index of biblical passages, which refers to §165d. This (short) paragraph cannot be understood on its own, so we need to read from the beginning of §165 ("clause of curse and oath") and continue for a little bit, up to §165h, in order to understand what §165d is about. It turns out that, in the Hebrew Bible, negative oaths can be formulated without explicitly mentioning any associated "curse." Thus, "I swear that, *if X happens*" is a way of implying something like, "I swear that, *if X happens, may God do this and that to me*." What this means is, in fact, "I swear that *this will not happen*."

Returning to 1 Sam 3:14, we can translate: "And therefore I swear to the house of Eli that the sin of the house of Eli will never be expiated, neither by sacrifice nor by offering."

We were lucky that this verse was mentioned in the index of biblical passages. What if it had not been? Because the problematic sentence is introduced by "I swear that," we could also have looked for "oath" in *JM*'s table of contents or index of subjects. It so happens that there is an entry on oaths in both places.

> ## 1.5 TAKE ADVANTAGE OF THE TRANSLATION PROCESS TO DETECT SOUNDPLAY AND DOUBLE ENTENDRES

Direct interaction with the Hebrew text provides the opportunity for identifying literary devices that translations often obscure, such as soundplay (or wordplay) and double entendres. The importance of identifying these elements varies from simple aesthetic satisfaction to the identification of nuances and messages in the text that are otherwise veiled.

A. Soundplay

Soundplay is common in Semitic texts from the ancient Near East, and in the Hebrew Bible in particular. (This seems to be a reflection, on the level of sound, of a general penchant for repetition as a literary technique.) The following words designate the most typical situations:

- *Assonance:* similarity of sound on the level of vowels.
- *Alliteration:* similarity of sound on the level of consonants.
- *Paronomasia:* similarity of sound due to assonance, alliteration, or both.

In addition, three common situations naturally entail paronomasia:

- *Homonyms*, that is, words that are spelled the same and sound the same, although they do not have the same meaning; for example, there are two distinct words spelled ראש, but they come from different roots and mean, respectively, "head" and "poison."

- *Figura etymologica (a.k.a. cognate accusative):* a verb and a complement that have the same root; for instance, וַיִּזְבַּח יַעֲקֹב זֶבַח ("And Jacob sacrificed [i.e., made] a sacrifice," Gen 31:54).

- *Paronomastic infinitive:* an infinitive absolute that precedes or follows a finite form of the same verb; for instance: מוֹת תָּמוּת (Gen 2:17), often translated as "you shall surely die." Scholars traditionally regard this device as a mark of emphasis or a way to "intensify" the meaning of the verb, but this is debated and it is often difficult to determine what precise nuance this device entails, if any.

Many other situations involving soundplay occur in the Hebrew Bible. The most interesting and subtle use of soundplay occurs when it is combined with an allusion to another text. On this subject, see:

- Jonathan G. Kline, *Allusive Soundplay in the Hebrew Bible*, AIL 28 (Atlanta: SBL Press, 2016).

Readers interested in delving into wordplay and related subjects can consult the following book:

- Scott B. Noegel, *"Wordplay" in Ancient Near Eastern Texts*, ANEM 26 (Atlanta: SBL Press, 2021).

EXAMPLE 1.5a ▸ **Genesis 11:3**

The narrative of the tower of Babel (Gen 11:1–9), which culminates in the famous play between בָּבֶל "Babel" and בָּלַל "he confused" in v. 9, abounds in soundplay. Let us consider, for instance, v. 3:

וַיֹּאמְר֞וּ אִ֣ישׁ אֶל־רֵעֵ֗הוּ הָ֚בָה נִלְבְּנָ֣ה לְבֵנִ֔ים וְנִשְׂרְפָ֖ה לִשְׂרֵפָ֑ה
וַתְּהִ֨י לָהֶ֤ם הַלְּבֵנָה֙ לְאָ֔בֶן וְהַ֣חֵמָ֔ר הָיָ֥ה לָהֶ֖ם לַחֹֽמֶר׃

And they said to one another, "Come, let us make
bricks and fire them thoroughly." And they had brick
for stone, and they had bitumen for mortar.

Several sequences of words here contain paronomasia:

הָבָה נִלְבְּנָה לְבֵנִים contains alliteration (repetition of the consonants ב, נ, and ל) and assonance (the repetition of *â* and *i*). The alliteration here is mainly due to a *figura etymologica* based on the root לבן.

וְנִשְׂרְפָה לִשְׂרֵפָה contains alliteration (repetition of the consonants שׂ, ר, and פ) and assonance (repetition of the vowel *i*, and the same ending -*â* for the two words). The expression is not a *figura etymologica*, but still involves two words from the same root שׂרף.

הַלְּבֵנָה לְאָבֶן contains alliteration (repetition of the consonants ל, ב, and נ) and assonance (the sounds *a* and *e*).

חֵמָר and חֹמֶר contain alliteration (repetition of the same three consonants) and assonance (the sound *e*).

EXAMPLE 1.5b ▸ **Job 7:17; 15:14**

The book of Job twice alludes to the famous assertion found in Ps 8:4 [5]:

מָה־אֱנ֥וֹשׁ כִּֽי־תִזְכְּרֶ֑נּוּ וּבֶן־אָ֝דָ֗ם כִּ֣י תִפְקְדֶֽנּוּ׃

What are humans, that you are mindful of them,
mortals that you care for them?

The first allusion occurs in Job 7:17, where Job is speaking:

מָה־אֱנוֹשׁ כִּי תְגַדְּלֶנּוּ וְכִי־תָשִׁית אֵלָיו לִבֶּךָ׃

*What are humans, that you make so much of them,
that you set your mind on them?*

It is certain that there is an allusion here, because the beginning of the sentence is the same as in Ps 8:4 [5] (מָה־אֱנוֹשׁ כִּי followed by a 2nd-person singular verb). Together with Job 15:14 (see below), these are the only occurrences of מָה־אֱנוֹשׁ כִּי in the Hebrew Bible. In Job 7:17, the immediate context makes it clear that Job is *parodying* the psalmist's statement; that is, Job is turning it into a sarcastic comment on the fact that the Lord is constantly putting humans to the test. This is particularly evident in what immediately follows: "visit them every morning, test them every moment?" (v. 18).

The second allusion occurs in Job 15:14, where Eliphaz is speaking:

מָה־אֱנוֹשׁ כִּי־יִזְכֶּה וְכִי־יִצְדַּק יְלוּד אִשָּׁה׃

*What are mortals, that they can be clean?
Or those born of woman, that they can be righteous?*

Here, Eliphaz counters Job's stance by turning the focus from God to humans, who are flawed. But this verse is not just alluding to Job 7:17. Its use of the verb יִזְכֶּה, right after מָה־אֱנוֹשׁ כִּי, is an intentional echo of the verb used in the source text, Ps 8:4 [5] (תִזְכְּרֶנּוּ), not the verb in Job 7:17 (where the original verb is replaced by תְגַדְּלֶנּוּ). The allusive paronomasia is based on a subtle replacement of the root זכר ("to remember") by the root זכה ("to be clean"): it can hardly be coincidental that the verbs occupying the same place in the same construction share two consonants out of three. There is just enough here to create an allusion, and just enough to transform the substance. Jonathan Kline comments: "Eliphaz in effect tells Job that the reason he has not found Ps 8:5 to dovetail with his experience (as Job complained in 7:17) is that Job is a sinner."[6] Job's use of Ps 8:4 [5] to accuse God is subverted by Eliphaz into an accusation of Job. The sin of the latter explains why God does not take care of Job as he would expect. The prologue and the epilogue of the book show that Eliphaz is wrong, but he expresses his error in a delightful way!

B. Double Entendres

The use of double entendre is based on polysemy; it corresponds to a situation where a writer deliberately uses a word that, in addition to its expected or standard meaning, has another meaning that, in context, is ironic.

---

6. Jonathan G. Kline, *Allusive Soundplay in the Hebrew Bible*, AIL 28 (Atlanta: SBL Press, 2016), 49.

| EXAMPLE 1.5c | ▶ | Amos 6:12b–13 |

In Amos 6:12b–13, the prophet declares: "But you have turned justice into poison and the fruit of righteousness into wormwood, you who rejoice in Lo-debar, who say, 'Have we not by our own strength taken Karnaim for ourselves?'" This sentence mentions two towns situated east of the Jordan; they had formerly belonged to the kingdom of Aram-Damascus but had been conquered by Jeroboam II during Amos's lifetime, victories of which Israel was apparently quite proud. It is likely that the prophet chose to mention these two particular towns, rather than others, in order to pun on their names:

- *Lo-Debar* is also mentioned in 2 Sam 9:4–5 and 17:27, where it is written לוֹ דְבָר. However, in Amos 6:13 the MT has לֹא דָבָר, which literally means "not a thing." This is not a mistake: the verse contains a sarcastic double entendre, since the sentence could be translated: "you are rejoicing for nothing"!

- *Karnaim* means "two horns," and the horn is a symbol of strength in the Hebrew Bible. In this way, Amos accuses the inhabitants of the Northern Kingdom—specifically its elite— of rejoicing in their (military) "strength" while ignoring the consequences of their ethical behavior (see v. 12).

| EXAMPLE 1.5d | ▶ | 2 Kings 1:9–16 |

In 2 Kgs 1:9–16, King Ahaziah sends several groups of soldiers to arrest Elijah, who is sitting on a mountain. Twice, the leader of the contingent calls Elijah "man of God" (אִישׁ הָאֱלֹהִים) and tells him that the king has said, "Come down!" But Elijah systematically replies, "If I am a man of God, let fire [אֵשׁ] come down from heaven and consume you, you and your fifty"— and this is indeed what happens. Elijah is using a play on words here: the soldiers demand that an אִישׁ of God come down from the mountain, but instead it is an אֵשׁ that comes down from heaven.

What is the point of this wordplay? One might conclude that this is a tasteless joke on the part of Elijah or, rather, on the part of the person who wrote this story. But does the redactor implicitly approve of Elijah's attitude in this episode?

> **EXAMPLE 1.5e** ▸ **Isaiah 28:16**
>
> In Isa 28:16, the Lord promises: "See, I am laying in Zion a foundation stone, a tested stone, a precious cornerstone, a sure foundation" (הִנְנִי יִסַּד בְּצִיּוֹן אֶבֶן אֶבֶן בֹּחַן פִּנַּת יִקְרַת מוּסָד מוּסָּד). The relevance of this announcement has puzzled commentators, since the immediate context is a criticism of the rulers in Jerusalem who have made a treaty with Egypt. Scholars have come up with many interpretations of this stone: that it is a symbol for the messiah, the law, the temple, Mount Zion, the community of believers, the relationship between God and his people, etc. Notably, the New Testament applies this passage, alongside others that mention a cornerstone (Zech 10:4; Ps 118:22), to Jesus (Mark 12:10; Acts 4:11; Eph 2:20; 1 Pet 2:6).
>
> Actually, the Hebrew term here meaning "cornerstone" (פִּנָּה) can also mean "chief" or "leader," as it does in several passages (Judg 20:2; 1 Sam 14:38; Zech 10:4; Zeph 3:6). (An English analogy would be to describe someone as the "pillar" of a family, which means that his or her role is crucial for supporting the family.) In another passage in Isaiah, the same Hebrew term designates Egyptian "princes" who are depicted as drunkards (Isa 19:14). It is therefore likely that here in ch. 28, in the middle of a criticism of *leaders* who are collaborating with Egypt and who are also described as being drunk (vv. 7–13), God is promising to send a *leader* who will be reliable. At the same time, the text elaborates on the polysemy of the word with a series of terms that describe the "stone." This is a case of a double meaning.[7]
>
> Interestingly, Targum Jonathan interprets the "cornerstone" as a "powerful king," which—in light of the fact that what seems to be in view is a leader whom God will install in the capital, Jerusalem—is a logical interpretation.

EXERCISES FOR CHAPTER 1

Exercise A

Translate 1 Kgs 17:1. Here you will encounter two syntactic difficulties mentioned in this chapter!

Exercise B

Translate Ps 1:4.

---

7. See Matthieu Richelle, "La pierre angulaire d'Ésaïe 28 à la lumière de l'oracle contre l'Égypte," *ZAW* 123 (2011): 437–40.

Exercise C

In 1 Kgs 19, Elijah witnesses a series of frightening phenomena, including, finally, קוֹל דְּמָמָה דַקָּה, which is rendered in various ways in modern translations (for instance, "a sound of sheer silence" [NRSVue] or "a soft murmuring sound" [NJPS]). What would be your own translation of this expression, and why?

Exercise D

In Gen 1:6, God makes a רָקִיעַ "in the midst of the waters," and it "separates the waters from the waters." This Hebrew word is rendered as "dome" in the NRSVue, but as "expanse" in the NJPS and in the ESV. What is the best translation in your view, and why?

Exercise E

In the NRSV translation of Ps 16:10, the psalmist tells the Lord: "you will not abandon my soul to Sheol, or let your holy one see corruption [שָׁחַת]." By contrast, in the NRSVue (see already the NJPS), the last word here is rendered as "the Pit." The first meaning is adopted by the Greek translation (Septuagint), which has διαφθοράν ("decay"), and this reading is followed in the quotations of this verse in the New Testament (Acts 2:27; 13:35). What is the correct translation in Ps 16:10?

CHAPTER 2

TEXTUAL CRITICISM

OVERVIEW

A. Theoretical Considerations

Whether we are considering the books of the Hebrew Bible or any other literary work from antiquity, the original manuscripts are lost. In fact, the earliest preserved manuscripts of biblical books date from the third century BCE. This is because literary works in Israel and Judah were written on perishable media: papyri and parchment scrolls. In other words, only copies (of copies) are available. And as is the case for any other text transmitted by a handwritten process, the copyists inevitably made mistakes; moreover, they sometimes modified the text intentionally. As a result, differences exist between the *textual witnesses*, that is, the manuscripts.[1] When two manuscripts contain different words (called *readings*), these different readings are called *variants*. When a manuscript contains words, phrases, or clauses that are absent from another manuscript, they are called *plusses* (or we say that the manuscript lacking these elements has *minuses*).

The comparison of manuscripts, as well as the study of the transmission of the text, is the main task of *textual criticism*. Scholars do not consider it sufficient, however, only to compare manuscripts written in the text's original languages (Hebrew, or Aramaic for a few passages; henceforth I will often write "Hebrew" for the sake of simplicity). To the extent that the ancient versions (i.e., those in Greek, Latin, etc.) constitute a reflection of the Hebrew manuscripts they have translated, they too provide important information. The versions often confirm readings already found in Hebrew manuscripts, but they also often hint at the presence of variant readings, or of plusses or minuses. These differences may be due either to liberties taken by the translators

---

1. Note that the expression "textual witness" also sometimes designates a text—such as "the Masoretic text"—that is shared by a family of manuscripts.

or to the fact that the differences were already present in their Hebrew model (which scholars often refer to using the German word *Vorlage*). Quotations in Second Temple literature and rabbinic writings can also be helpful, although these quotations do not cover the entirety of the text of the Hebrew Bible, and they are more difficult to locate and to check than manuscripts of biblical books.

The extent of variations among the manuscripts is itself variable, both across manuscripts and across biblical books; variations can range from isolated, small differences (e.g., a gloss on—i.e., brief explanation of—a word) to more significant divergences (e.g., entire sentences that have been added or that appear in different places in different manuscripts) to the entire revision of a text (when a biblical book appears in a revised edition).

Against this backdrop, textual criticism can be practiced with at least two different, albeit complementary, aims in mind:

- **A genetic approach:** The idea here is to reconstruct the earliest attainable text, by emending the text in light of what analysis shows to be secondary alterations. In popular thinking, the objective is to reconstruct the "original text," but strictly speaking, the best that one can attempt is to reconstruct the *archetype*. While the original would be the *earliest common ancestor* (i.e., a text separated from the extant manuscripts by an unknown number of generations of copies), the archetype is the *latest common ancestor*. In a family tree of manuscripts, the archetype is situated immediately before the first bifurcation that we can detect between the witnesses. This is the earliest inferable text, in the best-case scenario. The genetic approach to textual criticism is followed in the most common editions of the New Testament (the Nestle-Aland edition and the UBS *Greek New Testament*), in which the text has been reconstituted word for word by selecting from the range of available manuscripts the wording that the editors regard, with some degree of probability, as the earliest. That said, whether each biblical book stems from one original text is a matter of debate (see the sidebar "Two Models for the Origins of Biblical Books").

- **A historical approach:** In this perspective, the ways in which the text has changed over time are regarded as a *mirror of the interpretation history* of the text. Two points are particularly relevant here. First, some variants were intentional and reflect a perceived need on the part of copyists to improve the text, with the changes reflecting their underlying motives and their ideas. This is especially interesting when theological convictions led a copyist to correct a text. This may also open a window into the hermeneutics of those who transmitted the text. Second, variants—whether accidental or intentional—may have had an effect on the ways in which the text was received. It is interesting to see, for instance, whether two significantly different forms of the same passage have led to distinct interpretations in Judaism or Christianity.

In a sense, the genetic approach proceeds backward in time and focuses on how the text may have looked in, say, the Persian period (if scholars believe the final redaction of the biblical book in question was written at that time), whereas the historical approach proceeds forward in time and is interested in the interpretation of the text in the Hellenistic and Roman periods. Since one cannot understand the motives behind a textual change without having an idea of what the earlier reading was, however, the historical approach relies, at least in part, on the genetic approach. Thus, these two approaches are complementary, rather than opposite.

Two Models for the Origins of Biblical Books

Although many scholars simply take for granted the existence of one original text for each biblical book, this presupposes the correctness of the first of the following two models:

The *Urtext* model. Many exegetes today still accept the idea that the extant manuscripts of any given biblical book all derive from an archetype, and ultimately from one original text (*Urtext*). Emanuel Tov defines this view as follows: "at the end of the composition process of a biblical book stood a text that was finished at a literary level and subsequently was considered authoritative, even if only by a limited group of people."[2] When a book existed in several literary editions, Tov considers that these editions constitute several original texts. Other scholars, however, would prefer to reserve the expression "original text" for the earliest edition only. For defenses of the *Urtext* model, see:

- Emanuel Tov and Eugene Ulrich, "(1.1.1) The Search for an Original Text," in vol. 1A of *Textual History of the Bible*, ed. Armin Lange and Emanuel Tov (Leiden: Brill, 2016), 15–19.
- Ronald S. Hendel, *Steps to a New Edition of the Hebrew Bible*, TCSt 10 (Atlanta: SBL Press, 2016), 42–46.

The early parallel texts model. This model postulates that there existed *from the start* parallel forms of the same biblical book; that is, these did not derive from each other or from one original version. The reason for this would be that the same story or poem (for instance) was first composed orally and was then subjected to changes during its oral transmission in various circles; it was only later put into writing, by several scribes working independently in different places. The resulting documents may have had the same general outline but already bore many divergences. This model is often preferred by scholars who

---

2. Emanuel Tov, *Textual Criticism of the Hebrew Bible*, 3rd ed. (Minneapolis: Fortress, 2012), 167.

specialize in the Dead Sea Scrolls because these documents bear witness to a great deal of textual fluidity. For defenses of the early parallel texts model, see:

- Shemaryahu Talmon, "Textual Criticism: The Ancient Versions," in *Text and Canon of the Hebrew Bible: Collected Studies* (Winona Lake, IN: Eisenbrauns, 2010), 383–418.

The early parallel texts model presents a challenge to the *Urtext* model by calling into question the very legitimacy of searching for an archetype on the basis of variant readings. If from the start there existed parallel texts, then it does not make sense to correct one in light of the other, nor to look for the earliest reading, as has traditionally been done in textual criticism.

It is theoretically possible, however, that one model is correct for some biblical books and the other model is correct for other books. In particular, the *Urtext* model gains plausibility when the differences between textual witnesses are limited in number. To explain a high degree of verbal agreement, the early parallel texts model needs to hypothesize a rather drastic process of assimilation that erased many divergences between the manuscripts. On the other hand, the early parallel texts model gains plausibility when the level of textual fluidity among manuscripts is high and when it seems likely that a book ultimately originated as an oral composition. For a detailed discussion of these issues, see:

- Matthieu Richelle, "Reflections on the Model of Early Parallel Texts," in *Urtext – Fluidity – Convergence? The Quest for the Texts of the Hebrew Bible*, ed. Jean-Sébastien Rey and Stefan Schorch, CBET (Leuven: Peeters, forthcoming).

The *Urtext* model remains the default model in most publications on textual criticism. Nearly all the examples in this chapter come from biblical books for which this model is plausible; the one exception is from Song of Songs, where the early parallel texts model is worth considering.

One of the practical results of textual criticism is the creation of critical editions of the biblical text:

- **Diplomatic editions** print the text of an important manuscript as the main text and indicate the variants appearing in the other textual witnesses in a critical apparatus (typically in the form of footnotes). They also often provide explanations for the origins of the variants. The most widely used editions are the following:
    - BHS = Karl Elliger and Wilhelm Rudolph, eds., *Biblia Hebraica Stuttgartensia*, 5th ed., ed. Adrian Schenker (Stuttgart: Deutsche Bibelgesellschaft, 1997).

- BHQ = Adrian Schenker, ed., *Biblia Hebraica Quinta* (Stuttgart: Deutsche Bibelgesellschaft, 2004–).

- HUB = *The Hebrew University Bible* (Jerusalem: Magnes, 1981–). Only a few volumes have been published to date.

While BHS and BHQ are based on the Leningrad Codex, HUB is based on the Aleppo Codex, which is regarded as the best Masoretic manuscript, though unfortunately some parts of it are now missing. Note that the critical apparatus of HUB contains four parts: (1) ancient versions and variants in the MT, (2) quotations in the Dead Sea Scrolls or in rabbinic texts, (3) the consonantal text of the medieval manuscripts, and (4) the vocalization and accentuation of the medieval manuscripts.

- **Eclectic editions** attempt to reconstruct the archetype. Apart from an attempt made in the late nineteenth and early twentieth centuries,[3] the sole edition of this kind is the following new series, which is under the general editorship of Ronald S. Hendel:

  - HBCE = The Hebrew Bible: A Critical Edition (Atlanta: SBL Press, 2015–).

At the present time, only one volume (Proverbs) has been published.

B. Practical Considerations

Most students (and, I am afraid, many biblical scholars) believe that the basic task of textual criticism consists merely of "deciphering" the critical apparatus of BHS or BHQ. These editions describe the most important variants and (often) provide explanations for them; since they describe their results with abbreviations and cryptic sigla, it is not uncommon to translate these into plain English and to consider one's job done! As a member of the team of scholars involved in the making of BHQ as well as HBCE, I will certainly not minimize the value of these resources. But they are not meant to be used in the way just described. Rather, they are designed to save you time by presenting the evidence in a concise manner and to show you what the editor of a particular book regards as the most plausible explanation for each variant. Yet these kinds of suggestions are just that: suggestions that are not put forward as "confirmed results" but as hypotheses to be critically assessed. Quite often, the editors also considered other possible explanations, and sometimes these are mentioned in a textual commentary that accompanies the apparatus. You are invited to develop your own view; indeed, this is your job. You can feel free to disagree with the proposals offered and to find other explanations that you deem more likely.

---

3. Paul Haupt, ed., *The Sacred Books of the Old Testament: A Critical Edition of the Hebrew Text Printed in Colors, with Notes* (Leipzig: Hinrichs, 1893–1904), also called the "Polychrome Bible."

In addition, BHS is sometimes very selective in the variants it records, and while BHQ attempts to record all the significant variants, only some volumes in the series have been published up to this point. Likewise, only a few books are available in the HUB edition, and (as noted above) only one in the HBCE. Furthermore, the editors of BHS, BHQ, and HUB do not systematically provide explanations for the variants they provide (often because they think that doing so would be too hypothetical). In practice, therefore, you often need to investigate the data yourself. Other resources, such as exegetical commentaries, may help you in this task. And even when you want to rely on a particular edition and are able to do so, it is important that you know how it was made.

Given the need to do much of the work of textual criticism oneself, I will now explain in detail what this involves, and I will explain how the critical editions can help you skip some steps if you have only limited time to devote to this work. The following steps may be followed:

❶ **COLLECT** THE EVIDENCE: FIND THE RELEVANT EDITIONS OF THE TEXTUAL WITNESSES.

❷ **COMPARE** THE TEXTUAL WITNESSES IN ORDER TO **DETECT VARIANTS** AND **DESCRIBE** THEM.

❸ **EXPLAIN** THE VARIANTS, WHICH CAN INVOLVE THREE SITUATIONS:

- **scribal mistakes**

- **intentional, local changes**

- **large-scale differences:** either a network of variants that are interconnected, or the addition, omission, or transposition of a long passage. If we already know that a book existed in several literary editions, you may seek to determine if the variants can be correlated with one of them.

❹ FIND OUT ABOUT THE **IMPACT** OF THE VARIANTS ON **RECEPTION HISTORY**.

With regard to the three main aims of textual criticism, steps 1 to 3 correspond to the genetic approach, while 3 (in the case of intentional changes) and 4 are relevant to the historical approach. Critical editions such as BHQ concisely summarize the results of steps 1 to 3.

In some difficult cases, none of the preserved readings represent the archetype because all the textual witnesses contain secondary features. Even in such cases, it may be possible to attempt to reconstruct the reading of the archetype if all the readings can be explained as modifications of it. Such a reading is called a **conjecture**; by definition, it is hypothetical, since the proposed text is not attested in any witness. For this reason, proposing a conjectural reading is a last-resort solution. Nevertheless, since it would be unrealistic to expect that the archetype is always preserved in at least one witness, conjecture is sometimes useful.

> **Handbooks and Reference Works on Textual Criticism**
>
> Before discussing each step of the text-critical method that I will present, it will be helpful to list some handbooks of textual criticism that go into much more detail than is possible here:
>
> - Emanuel Tov, *Textual Criticism of the Hebrew Bible*, 3rd ed. (Minneapolis: Fortress, 2012). The best and most complete one-volume introduction.
>
> - Ernst Würthwein, *The Text of the Old Testament: An Introduction to the* Biblia Hebraica, trans. Erroll F. Rhodes, revised and expanded by Alexander Achilles Fischer, 3rd ed. (Grand Rapids: Eerdmans, 2014).
>
> - Ellis R. Brotzman, *Old Testament Textual Criticism: A Practical Introduction* (Grand Rapids: Baker, 1994).
>
> In addition, the following voluminous work includes both overview chapters on the textual witnesses and chapters on every book in the Hebrew Bible as well as on the deuterocanonical books:
>
> - THB = Armin Lange, ed., *Textual History of the Bible*, 2 vols. (Leiden: Brill, 2016–19). Two more volumes are forthcoming.
>
> The following work contains very detailed and informative analysis of a selection of variants:
>
> - Dominique Barthélemy, *Critique textuelle de l'Ancien Testament*, 4 vols., OBO 50 (Fribourg: Éditions Universitaires; Göttingen: Vandenhoeck & Ruprecht, 1982–2005). Created by a committee of specialists gathered by Barthélemy, these volumes treat selected variants that occur throughout the biblical text, commenting and rendering decisions on them.

2.1 COLLECT THE EVIDENCE

The first thing to do is to find the textual witnesses you want to compare. Effectively, what this means is that you need to find the relevant edition of the Masoretic text; the Dead Sea Scrolls (DSS), when available; the Samaritan Pentateuch; and the main versions (Septuagint, Vulgate, Peshitta, and Targum). Below, I will briefly present each of these witnesses, indicating the pertinent reference editions and suggesting some helpful resources; I also end this section with a table that summarizes the main resources. Thus, although this may look complicated, in practice you just need to grab a few books; and if you use software such as Accordance or Logos and these relevant editions are part of your package, most of these resources are just a click away.

If you are doing an in-depth study, you may also want to check images of the manuscripts themselves, especially for key Masoretic manuscripts (the Leningrad Codex and the Aleppo Codex), for the Dead Sea Scrolls, and for important Septuagint manuscripts (e.g., Vaticanus).

A. Hebrew and Aramaic Witnesses

(i) The Masoretic Text

The main editions of the MT have been mentioned above: BHS, BHQ, HUB. Note that the MT proper, including its vocalization, does not predate the sixth century CE. The parent consonantal text is technically referred to as the "proto-MT," though scholars often use "MT" as shorthand when they are actually talking about the proto-MT.

> **The Masorah**
>
> ───────◆───────
>
> The Masorah is an apparatus found in the margins, and at the end of biblical books, in Masoretic codices; it contains a variety of data, most notably notes on how often forms in the text occur with specific orthographies. These data reflect extremely impressive work done by the Masoretes, but today they prove to be of limited interest for most purposes in textual criticism. For an excellent introduction to the Masorah, see:
>
> - Yosef Ofer, *The Masorah on Scripture and Its Methods*, FSBP 7 (Berlin: de Gruyter, 2019).
>
> To "decipher" the information found in the Masorah, the following guide is very helpful:
>
> - Page H. Kelley, Daniel S. Mynatt, and Timothy G. Crawford, *The Masorah of* Biblia Hebraica Stuttgartensia: *Introduction and Annotated Glossary* (Grand Rapids: Eerdmans, 1998).
>
> Note also that each volume in the BHQ series includes very helpful notes on the Masorah in the commentary section.
>
> In the case of the Former Prophets (Joshua, Judges, Samuel, Kings), a projected six-volume set provides a complete transcription, translation, and annotation of the Masorah of the Leningrad Codex. At present, five volumes are available; for instance:
>
> - David Marcus, *The Masorah of the Former Prophets in the Leningrad Codex*, vol. 5, *1 Kings*, Text and Studies 14 (Piscataway, NJ: Gorgias, 2021).

(ii) The Samaritan Pentateuch

The Samaritan community possesses its own text of the Pentateuch, which is based on a text already in use during the Second Temple period, as some Dead Sea scrolls show. The so-called Samaritan Pentateuch contains a handful of late theological differences compared to the MT. For an edition, see:

- Abraham Tal and Moshe Florentin, *The Pentateuch: The Samaritan Version and the Masoretic Version* (Tel Aviv: Haim Rubin Tel Aviv University Press, 2010). [Hebrew]

A new, critical edition is currently being published:

- Stefan Schorch, ed., *The Samaritan Pentateuch: A Critical Editio Maior* (Berlin: de Gruyter, 2018–).

(iii) The Dead Sea Scrolls

The following series presents the official edition of these texts (both the biblical and the extrabiblical documents):

- DJD = Discoveries in the Judaean Desert, 40 vols. (Oxford: Clarendon, 1955–2009).

All the biblical texts from DJD are gathered in the following book, where they are presented in transcription and with textual variants; this allows you to immediately see which biblical passages are attested among the Dead Sea Scrolls and how their readings differ from those of other textual witnesses:

- Eugene Ulrich, *The Biblical Qumran Scrolls: Transcriptions and Textual Variants*, VTSup 134 (Leiden: Brill, 2010).

The decipherments and reconstructions found in the DJD volumes are not necessarily perfect, and it can be helpful to also consult other editions of the Hebrew text. See, for instance:

- Beate Ego, Armin Lange, Hermann Lichtenberger, and Kristin De Troyer, *Biblia Qumranica*, vol. 3B, *Minor Prophets* (Leiden: Brill, 2005). This is the only volume yet published in this series.

Images of the Dead Sea Scrolls are available online (see *The Leon Levy Dead Sea Scrolls Digital Library; *The Digital Dead Sea Scrolls, developed by the Israel Musem).

For an English translation that briefly indicates the differences between the Dead Sea Scrolls and the MT, see:

- Martin Abegg Jr., Peter Flint, and Eugene Ulrich, *The Dead Sea Scrolls Bible* (New York: HarperCollins, 1999).

To refer to a document, scholars use abbreviations such as 4Q106, which means that the scroll in question is scroll number 106 among those from cave 4 of Qumran. Another possible format consists in using a descriptive title, such as 1QIsaiah^a, which designates manuscript "a" of Isaiah found in cave 1 of Qumran.

B. Ancient Versions

Table 2.1 lists the most important versions. While some were made from Hebrew manuscripts, others are translations of translations, such as the Old Latin, which renders a form of the Septuagint (this is also the case for other versions, such as the Armenian, Georgian, and Ethiopic versions). The most informative witness, by far, is the Septuagint.

Table 2.1: The Most Important Ancient Versions

Language of the Translation	Name	Basis
Aramaic	Targum	Hebrew text close to MT
Syriac	Peshitta	Hebrew text close to MT
Greek	Septuagint	Hebrew text
Latin	Old Latin (*Vetus Latina*)	Septuagint
Latin	Vulgate	Hebrew text close to MT

(i) The Septuagint

The Septuagint is the fruit of a long process of translation of many books into Greek that stretched from the third century BCE (beginning with the Pentateuch) to the first century CE. The original translation of any given book, called the Old Greek (OG), is lost. The most important manuscripts date from the fourth and fifth centuries CE (Codex Sinaiticus [= LXX^S], Codex Vaticanus [= LXX^B], and Codex Alexandrinus [= LXX^A]). Also noteworthy is the Antiochian text (often called the Lucianic recension [= LXX^L]), which appears in a few medieval manuscripts. Like the Hebrew text, the Greek version underwent changes during its transmission over several centuries, hence the need for a critical edition. The Göttingen edition (or SVTG) offers a reconstruction of the OG and a very detailed apparatus; when available for the biblical book you are studying, this is the authoritative reference edition:

- SVTG = *Septuaginta: Vetus Testamentum Graecum auctoritate Academiae Scientiarum Gottingensis editum* (Göttingen: Vandenhoeck & Ruprecht, 1931–).

For books for which the SVTG volume does not yet exist, the Cambridge edition is helpful because, in addition to presenting the text of Vaticanus, it contains a detailed apparatus:

- Alan England Brooke, Norman McLean, and Henry St. John Thackeray, *The Old Testament in Greek*, 9 vols. (Cambridge: Cambridge University Press, 1906–40).

The handiest (and most widely distributed) edition is the one prepared by Rahlfs, which is available in one volume. For each book, Rahlfs chose a manuscript and edited it in the light of other witnesses; his edition contains a limited apparatus:

- Alfred Rahlfs, *Septuaginta: Id est Vetus Testamentum graece iuxta LXX interpretes*, 2nd ed., rev. Robert Hanhart (Stuttgart: Deutsche Bibelgesellschaft, 2006).

An edition of the Antiochian text exists for some of the historical books, where it is especially important, notably for 1–4 Kingdoms (= 1–2 Samuel and 1–2 Kings):

- Natalio Fernández Marcos and José Ramón Busto Saiz, *El texto antioqueno de la Biblia griega*, vol. 1, *1–2 Samuel*, TECC (Madrid: Instituto de Filología del Consejo Superior de Investigaciones Científicas, 1989).

- Natalio Fernández Marcos and José Ramón Busto Saiz, *El texto antioqueno de la Biblia griega*, vol. 2, *1–2 Reyes*, TECC (Madrid: Instituto de Filología del Consejo Superior de Investigaciones Científicas, 1992).

As mentioned above, if the SVTG edition exists for the biblical book you are studying, this is the text you should use. Otherwise, scholars often use Rahlfs as a default edition and consult the Cambridge edition for the information contained in its apparatus. However, in order to know which are the most important manuscripts for the book you are studying (i.e., those whose text is closest to the Old Greek), the best solution is to consult the introduction to the NETS translation (see the sidebar "Help for Reading the Septuagint" below) or a handbook on the Septuagint. These resources will tell you about the book's translation technique, which often varies from one book to another (from very literal to free renderings). Useful handbooks are as follows:

- James T. Aitken, ed., *The T&T Clark Companion to the Septuagint* (London: T&T Clark, 2015).

- Alison Salvesen and T. Michael Law, eds., *The Oxford Handbook of the Septuagint* (Oxford: Oxford University Press, 2021).

- William A. Ross and W. Edward Glenny, eds., *The T&T Clark Handbook of Septuagint Research* (New York: T&T Clark, 2020).

Help for Reading the Septuagint

Lexicons

- Takamitsu Muraoka, *A Greek-English Lexicon of the Septuagint* (Leuven: Peeters, 2009).

- Johan Lust, Erik Eynikel, and Katrin Hauspie, *A Greek-English Lexicon of the Septuagint*, 2nd ed. (Stuttgart: Deutsche Bibelgesellschaft, 2003).

- HTLS = Eberhard Bons, ed., *Historical and Theological Lexicon of the Septuagint* (Tübingen: Mohr Siebeck, 2021–). Very informative articles on selected words; one volume has appeared to date.

Grammar

- Takamitsu Muraoka, *A Syntax of Septuagint Greek* (Leuven: Peeters, 2016).

If you have difficulty analyzing a word in the text, you can check the grammatical tags in Accordance or Logos or consult the following book:

- Bernard A. Taylor, *Analytical Lexicon to the Septuagint* (Peabody, MA: Hendrickson; Stuttgart: Deutsche Bibelgesellschaft, 2009). An alphabetical list of all the words in Rahlfs's edition, followed by parsing for each one.

Reader

The following work provides the text of the Rahlfs edition with an apparatus containing glosses and parsing for a number of words:

- Gregory R. Lanier and William A. Ross, eds., *Septuaginta: A Reader's Edition*, 2 vols. (Peabody, MA: Hendrickson; Stuttgart: Deutsche Bibelgesellschaft, 2018).

Translations of the Septuagint into Modern Languages

- *English:* NETS = Albert Pietersma and Benjamin G. Wright, *A New English Translation of the Septuagint* (New York: Oxford University Press, 2007). Also made available in an open-access electronic edition by the University of Pennsylvania. Translates the SVTG edition when available, otherwise Rahlfs's edition.

- *French:* the series La Bible d'Alexandrie (Paris: Cerf, 1986–). Generally translates Rahlfs's edition; contains valuable introductions and detailed notes on philological matters and on the text's reception in the church fathers.

> - *German:* LXX.D = Wolfgang Kraus and Martin Karrer, *Septuaginta Deutsch: Das griechische Alte Testament in deutscher Übersetzung* (Stuttgart: Deutsche Bibelgesellschaft, 2009). Translates the SVTG edition when available, otherwise Rahlfs's edition; in the historical books, it sometimes provides two columns, one with the Rahlfs text and the other with the Antiochian text.

(ii) The Revisions of the Septuagint

Since the Christians of antiquity "adopted" the Septuagint very early on, new Greek translations (or, more precisely, revisions) were produced by the Jewish community in the first and second centuries CE. The most important are those of Aquila, Symmachus, and Theodotion, though they are preserved only in fragmentary form. For these texts, see the following book, which, despite its age, is still useful:

- Frederick Field, *Origenis Hexaplorum quae supersunt sive veterum interpretum graecorum in totum Vetus Testamentum fragmenta*, 2 vols. (London: Clarendon, 1875).

(iii) Other Ancient Versions

Table 2.2 below indicates where you can find reference editions and English translations for the Peshitta, Vulgate, and Targums. The interest of the Old Latin lies in the fact that it sometimes reflects a form of the Septuagint that existed before it was changed to harmonize it toward the MT. Unfortunately, the Old Latin is preserved only in some fragmentary manuscripts, in quotations by some church fathers (references for each passage are listed in the *Vetus Latina Database), and in marginal glosses in some copies of the Vulgate. For the Targums, printed editions could be mentioned, but it is easier to use the online *CAL (Comprehensive Aramaic Lexicon) database.

Table 2.2: Ancient Versions other than the Septuagint

Version	Edition	English translation
Peshitta (Syriac)	*The Old Testament in Syriac according to the Peshitta Version* (Leiden: Peshitta Institute, 1972–).	*The Antioch Bible* (Piscataway, NJ: Gorgias, 2018). Syriac/English edition.

| Vulgate (Latin) | Robert Weber, *Biblia Sacra Vulgata = Biblia Sacra iuxta vulgatam versionem*, 5th ed. (Stuttgart: Deutsche Bibelgesellschaft, 2007).

Francis Aidan Gasquet et al., *Biblia Sacra iuxta Latinam Vulgatam versionem*, 18 vols. (Rome: Libreria Editrice Vaticana, 1926–96). | Swift Edgar, ed., *The Vulgate Bible: Douay-Rheims Translation*, 5 vols. (Cambridge: Harvard University Press, 2010–12). |
| Targums | *CAL = Comprehensive Aramaic Lexicon | Martin McNamara, ed., *The Aramaic Bible*, 19 vols. (Edinburgh: T&T Clark; Collegeville, MN: Liturgical Press, 1987–2008). |

C. The Usual Editions, at a Glance

Table 2.3 contains a brief overview of the most widely used editions of the main textual witnesses.

Table 2.3: Overview of Editions of Textual Witnesses

Witness	Reference Edition	Other Important Editions
MT	BHS or, better, BHQ	HUB, HBCE
DSS	DJD	
Sam Pent	Schorch	Tal and Florentin
LXX	SVTG	Cambridge edition, Rahlfs
V	San Geronimo (= Gasquet et al.), Weber	
S	Leiden edition	
T	CAL	

2.2 COMPARE THE TEXTUAL WITNESSES

Once you have found the text of each textual witnesses, the next step is to compare them and identify the variants.

The critical editions summarize the results of such a comparison by sorting out the textual witnesses according to their readings. In BHQ, each entry in the critical apparatus begins with a Hebrew word from the MT and then presents a list of witnesses agreeing with it; next, after a vertical stroke, the variants are presented. For instance, in Gen 11:8, the critical apparatus in BHQ reads:

הָעִיר V S T | את העיר ואת המגדל Smr G (assim-v 5)

This entry begins with the "lemma" (here, הָעִיר), which is always a word or phrase taken from the main text, which reproduces the MT. As mentioned, the sigla that immediately follow the lemma indicate the witnesses that agree with the MT here; in the present example, the Vulgate (V), the Syriac version (S), and the Targum (T) all have the equivalent of הָעִיר ("the city"). However, the Samaritan Pentateuch (Smr) has את העיר ואת המגדל ("the city and the tower"), and the Septuagint (G) has the Greek equivalent of this. This is all the information the BHQ apparatus provides here by way of comparing the witnesses; the rest of the entry—that is, "(assim-v 5)," which we will deal with below—is a possible explanation for the variant.

Each volume of BHQ provides a list of abbreviations and definitions of the most important terms that occur in its apparatus. BHS also contains a list of abbreviations, but is less user-friendly for today's readers because the definitions it provides are in Latin. For help, you can consult:

- William R. Scott, *A Simplified Guide to BHS: Critical Apparatus, Masora, Accents, Unusual Letters & Other Markings*, 4th ed. (Richlands Hills, TX: BIBAL Press, 2007).

If you are making your own comparison of the witnesses, you may find it helpful—especially if you are comparing more than one verse—to make a **synoptic table** of the texts (i.e., the MT and the witnesses), highlighting the differences among them by using italics, bold characters, or blank lines; this can help you see the quantitative and qualitative differences among the texts.

At this juncture, it is important to be mindful of **variants that are merely apparent**—in other words, variations of meaning between an ancient version and the MT that do not stem from the version's having translated a Hebrew consonantal text different from the MT. That is, you need to check whether apparent semantic differences in the versions likely reflect differences in the Hebrew text(s) that underlie them or whether these apparent differences are merely due to the following:

- **a different vocalization:** the translators sometimes vocalized the underlying Hebrew text (which was unvocalized) differently from how the Masoretes vocalized it in the MT.

- **a different division of words:** the translator had the same consonantal Hebrew text as the MT but divided the words differently.

- **the freedom of the translator:** the translator took some liberties in translating the Hebrew, either on account of the dictates of style or usage in the target language or in order to produce a rendering whose language was more elegant or elevated than the Hebrew original. Hence, you may want to learn about the **translation technique** of the versions (especially the Septuagint). At the very least, you will want to know if the translation was a more "literal" or a more "free" one. This is noted in the introductions of the NETS translation and in handbooks on the Septuagint (see the sidebar "Help for Reading the Septuagint" above). The ideal situation is when the translation was made in an isomorphic manner, which means that the translation contains an element (a word, a suffix, etc.) that corresponds to each element in the source text.

Let's consider an illustration of the first situation mentioned above (different vocalization). In Amos 1:6, the Lord reproaches the Philistines for having exiled:

- "a whole people" (lit., "a whole deported-population"), according to the MT (גָּלוּת שְׁלֵמָה).

- "a deported-population of Solomon" (αἰχμαλωσίαν τοῦ Σαλωμων), according to the LXX.

The LXX reading does not make sense in context, whereas the MT—which comments on the *extent* of the deportation—presents a credible reason for reproaching the Philistines. It seems clear that the LXX translator was reading the same consonantal text as is found in the MT, שלמה, but vocalized this word as שְׁלֹמֹה ("Solomon") instead of the MT's שְׁלֵמָה ("entire").

When examining a Greek word whose meaning seems to deviate from that of its Hebrew counterpart, you may find it helpful to consult a lexicon of the Septuagint (see the sidebar "Help for Reading the Septuagint") to learn about the range of meanings this Greek word has. Then, you can search for all the occurrences of the Hebrew word and identify what the Greek counterpart in the LXX is in each case. Conversely, you can search for the occurrences of the Greek word and see what the Hebrew counterpart in the MT is in each case. The priority is to find out how the Hebrew word in question is typically rendered in the biblical book you are studying, since other books in the LXX were probably translated by other people, who may have had other translation habits. Fortunately, this work has already been done for every word in the Old Testament, in the following two books:

- Edwin Hatch and Henry A. Redpath, *A Concordance to the Septuagint and the Other Greek Versions of the Old Testament (including the Apocryphal Books)*, 2nd ed., 2 vols. (Grand Rapids: Baker, 1998). This edition contains an appendix consisting of a Hebrew/Aramaic index: for each Hebrew word, it provides a list of the Greek counterparts in the LXX and the relevant page and column in Hatch and Redpath's concordance.

- Takamitsu Muraoka, *A Greek-Hebrew/Aramaic Two-Way Index to the Septuagint* (Leuven: Peeters, 2010). This book reproduces, with slight changes and updates, the index found as an appendix in the book just cited. It adds to it a Greek index that provides, for each Greek word in the LXX, a list of the counterparts in the MT. Muraoka has checked and updated the work done by Hatch and Redpath, so, ideally, you should consult Muraoka's index first. In particular, Muraoka has integrated readings found in the Antiochian text (LXX^L) for books where it is important (Judges, Samuel, and parts of Kingdoms), whereas Hatch and Redpath had done so only occasionally.

It may be that the rendering you find surprising turns out to be well attested. On the other hand, it may be that it is not attested anywhere else. In the latter case, this does not necessarily mean that the underlying Hebrew text was different from the MT; perhaps, for some reason, the translator made an unusual translation choice in this instance. This is more likely if the Hebrew word in question is relatively rare. If, by contrast, it is a frequent word that has well-attested translation equivalents in Greek, and if you cannot determine a reason why the translator would have deviated from these standard renderings, then the hypothesis of a different *Vorlage* becomes more probable. Because the Hatch and Redpath *Concordance* provides a list of all the Hebrew words that were translated by the Greek word in question, its list of such words contains the candidates for the word that was used in your verse in the Hebrew text that the LXX was translating.

Now, it often happens that this list contains a Hebrew word or root that is the same as the word that occurs in the MT of your verse but that differs with respect to one letter. If this is the case, it is likely that a mistake was made by a copyist of the Hebrew text, or that the translator misread the word. It also often happens that the list contains a word that has the same consonants of the word in the MT but not in the same order. Such cases are likely due to a mistake called "metathesis," whereby a copyist accidentally switched two letters or the translator misread the word by switching the letters in his mind. In these kinds of situations, you need to determine whether the error occurred in Hebrew or when the translator was translating the Hebrew into Greek. In the former case, the next question is whether it is the MT or the *Vorlage* of the LXX that is secondary.

EXAMPLE 2.2 ▸ 1 Kings 14:24

Let us consider the beginning of 1 Kgs 14:24; this sentence appears in the section devoted to the reign of Rehoboam (see Table 2.4).

Table 2.4: 1 Kings 14:24 in the MT and in the LXX

LXX	MT
καὶ σύνδεσμος ἐγενήθη ἐν τῇ γῇ	וְגַם־קָדֵשׁ הָיָה בָאָרֶץ
and there was a *conspiracy* in the land	there were also *male temple prostitutes* in the land

How could σύνδεσμος ("conspiracy") be a translation of קָדֵשׁ ("male temple prostitutes")? Let's consult Muraoka's index at the entry σύνδεσμος to see what Hebrew words it usually renders. Interestingly, the sixth item in the list provided is קֶשֶׁר, and Muraoka adds: "[5: + 3K 14.24 MT קדש]." In other words, σύνδεσμος renders קֶשֶׁר in five places, plus our verse ("3K" means 3 Kingdoms, that is 1 Kgs, because in the LXX, the books corresponding to 1–2 Samuel and 1–2 Kings are called 1–4 Kingdoms). A look at a Hebrew lexicon shows that קֶשֶׁר means . . . "conspiracy"! Thus, it seems that the translator read קֶשֶׁר in his Hebrew text, and quite naturally rendered it σύνδεσμος.

Now, let us compare קשר and קדש. They share two consonants, and the difference between the third is due to the resemblance between ר and ד. So, basically, the three consonants were, or looked, the same in the manuscripts when the Greek translation was made. The only remaining difference is that the last two consonants of the words appear in reverse order, a typical example of metathesis.

Who made the mistake? In other words, what was the original word? Let's look at the immediate context: "For they also built for themselves high places, pillars, and sacred poles on every high hill and under every green tree; there were also *X* in the land. They committed all the abominations of the nations that the LORD drove out before the people of Israel." Clearly, the passage is about ethical and religious behavior, not political struggle. If we look at the other passages of Kings that mention a conspiracy (קֶשֶׁר: 1 Kgs 15:27; 16:9–16, 20; 2 Kgs 9:14; 10:9; 11:14; 12:20 [21]; 14:19; 15:10, 15, 25, 30; 17:4; 21:23), it turns out that they always tell what its outcome is (usually the death of the king). This is not the case in 14:24, however. Therefore, it seems highly probable that the text originally read קדש, which is generally understood to refer to "male temple prostitute(s)" (though there are debates about the exact role of the people designated by this expression). The same category of persons appears in other passages in Kings (1 Kgs 15:12; 22:46 [47]; 2 Kgs 23:7).

> While this reading is preserved in the MT, the LXX reflects a mistake. Either its *Vorlage* contained קדש but the translator misread it as קשר (perhaps because he had in his memory other occurrences of this word in Kings, a book that he had presumably read before translating it), or the erroneous word קשר was already present in the *Vorlage*, which means that the mistake had been made by a copyist of the Hebrew text. It is very difficult to decide.

2.3 EXPLAIN SCRIBAL MISTAKES

The main task of textual criticism is to explain the origins of the variants we find in the Hebrew manuscripts and in the versions. This is a subjective task that requires judgment on the part of scholars. The critical apparatus of BHQ (often) and that of HBCE (always) include a **"characterization"** at the end of an entry, in parentheses, that indicates the reason for the variant when it is deemed secondary. This is done in a less systematic way in BHS and in HUB.

For each variant, you need to determine first if it is probably due to a **scribal mistake**. For a complete inventory of standard scribal mistakes, you can consult:

- Emanuel Tov, *Textual Criticism of the Hebrew Bible*, 3rd ed. (Minneapolis: Fortress, 2012), 221–39.

Most scribal mistakes can be explained in terms of a few sets of frequent errors. Table 2.5 provides definitions for the most common errors.

Table 2.5: Definitions for the Most Common Scribal Errors

Error	Definition
Haplography	The accidental omission of a letter, syllable, or word (for example, in the context of repetition that is unnoticed by the copyist)
Dittography	The accidental repetition of a letter, syllable, or word
Graphical confusion	The confusion of letters that look alike (for instance, ר and ד were very similar in the "square Aramaic script" that was used to write Hebrew in the Hellenistic and Roman periods)
Metathesis	The change in position of two letters

Homoioarcton	The disappearance of a phrase, clause, or larger portion of text because of the resemblance between its beginning and that of the text that follows (the scribe's eye jumped from one to the other)
Homoioteleuton	The disappearance of a phrase, clause, or larger portion of text because of the resemblance between its ending and that of the text that precedes it (the scribe's eye jumped from one to the other)
Assimilation	The replacement of a word or phrase by another word or phrase that appears in a similar context and that the copyist still had in mind. (Such a change may have been made unconsciously or intentionally.)

EXAMPLE 2.3a ▸ **Zechariah 4:2**

Let us consider Zech 4:2:

וַיֹּאמֶר אֵלַי מָה אַתָּה רֹאֶה וָאֹמַר רָאִיתִי ׀ וְהִנֵּה מְנוֹרַת
זָהָב כֻּלָּהּ וְגֻלָּהּ עַל־רֹאשָׁהּ וְשִׁבְעָה נֵרֹתֶיהָ עָלֶיהָ שִׁבְעָה
וְשִׁבְעָה מוּצָקוֹת לַנֵּרוֹת אֲשֶׁר עַל־רֹאשָׁהּ׃

He said to me, "What do you see?" And I said, "I see a lampstand all of gold, with a bowl on the top of it; there are seven lamps on it, with seven lips on each of the lamps that are on the top of it."

Here the apparatus of the BHQ reads:

שִׁבְעָה <α'-σ'-θ'> V (S) T | > G (hapl)

Description of the difference: Aquila (α'), Symmachus (σ'), Theodotion (θ'), the Vulgate (V), the Syriac version (S) (with a slight difference since it appears in parentheses), and the Targum (T) attest the same reading as the MT, that is, שִׁבְעָה. However, this word is absent from (>) the Septuagint (G).

Explanation of the variant: The characterization "hapl" means "haplography." Looking back at the text, we can easily see what prompted the loss of the word: it is immediately followed by the same word (plus the conjunction וְ): וְשִׁבְעָה. Because the text contained two occurrences of the same word in immediate succession (i.e., שִׁבְעָה וְשִׁבְעָה), the eye of a copyist simply skipped the first.

> **EXAMPLE 2.3b** ▸ Isaiah 40:7–8

Let us compare Isa 40:7–8 in the MT, in 1QIsaiah^a, and in the LXX:

Table 2.6: Isaiah 40:7–8 in the MT, in 1QIsaiah^a, and in the LXX

LXX		1QIsaiah^a		MT	
ἐξηράνθη ὁ χόρτος, καὶ τὸ ἄνθος ἐξέπεσεν	The grass withers, and the flower fades,	יבש חציר נבל ציץ	The grass withers, the flower fades,	יָבֵ֤שׁ חָצִיר֙ נָ֣בֵֽל צִ֔יץ	The grass withers, the flower fades;
				כִּ֛י ר֥וּחַ יְהוָ֖ה נָ֣שְׁבָה בּ֑וֹ	when the breath of the Lord blows upon it;
				אָכֵ֥ן חָצִ֖יר הָעָֽם׃	surely the people are grass.
				יָבֵ֥שׁ חָצִ֖יר נָ֣בֵֽל צִ֑יץ	The grass withers; the flower fades,
τὸ δὲ ῥῆμα τοῦ θεοῦ ἡμῶν μένει εἰς τὸν αἰῶνα	but the word of our God will stand forever	ודבר אלהינו יקום לעולם	but the word of our God will stand forever	וּדְבַר־אֱלֹהֵ֖ינוּ יָק֥וּם לְעוֹלָֽם׃	but the word of our God will stand forever

Here the texts of the Qumran scroll and of the LXX are much shorter than that of the MT. What happened? The MT contains a repetition of יָבֵשׁ חָצִיר נָבֵל צִיץ. The difference between this and the other two texts may be the result of *homoioteleuton*. That is, after having copied the first occurrence of this expression, the eye of a copyist went back to the scroll but stopped at the second occurrence, and the copyist resumed his task by copying the words following this second occurrence: ודבר אלהינו יקום לעולם. Thus he or she[4] skipped the words that are absent from 1QIsaiah^a. The LXX translator probably had in front of him a Hebrew text that at this spot was similar to 1QIsaiah^a. Interestingly, if you consult images of the Qumran scroll, you can see that a later copyist, one with different handwriting, tried to correct this mistake by adding (in the same scroll) the missing words above the line.

---

4. Although there is not much evidence, it is quite possible that female scribes existed in ancient Israel; on this and other aspects of scribalism, see Matthieu Richelle, "Literacy and Scribalism in Israel during the Iron Age (ca. 1200–586 BCE)," in *The Ancient Israelite World*, ed. Kyle Keimer and George A. Pierce, RW (London: Routledge, forthcoming).

> That said, the opposite scenario can also be defended—namely, that the earlier text is represented here by 1QIsaiah[a]. In this case, the plus attested in the MT would be an interpolation, with the scribe responsible for it framing the interpolated text by repeating, after it, the expression that immediately precedes it. This is in fact a well-known technique that was used by scribes to mark insertions. It serves to resume the main line of argumentation, or the main storyline, after the interruption by reminding the reader what was mentioned right before it. (We will see more instances of this technique in the next chapter.) In this scenario, the supralinear correction in 1QIsaiah[a] would be interpreted as the work of a later copyist who knew the MT and corrected 1QIsaiah[a] in light of it. In favor of this scenario, it can be noted that the repetition of "the grass withers, the flower fades" is not necessary to the logic of the text or to its poetic structure. (While it is possible to explain this repetition as a rhetorical feature intended to emphasize this statement, such an argument does not seem very compelling.)
>
> There is no consensus among scholars about this particular case. It is therefore an interesting illustration of how two opposite text-critical explanations can sometimes both be plausible for a particular passage.

2.4 EXPLAIN INTENTIONAL CHANGES

When no accidental error seems capable of explaining a textual difference, chances are that the difference is the result of an **intentional change**. Once we recognize this, the next step is to try to **find the motive** behind the change. Among the most frequent reasons why a copyist or a translator decided to make a change in the text was the desire to:

- **harmonize**, that is, to remove a perceived tension or contradiction between the reading in question and another passage
- **interpret**, that is, to ensure that the correct meaning of the text (according to the copyist's interpretation, which he may have received from a tradition) is clear; this may have led the copyist to modify or add a word
- **explain**, which generally involves the copyist adding a gloss that makes explicit what in his understanding is implicit in the text
- **elaborate**, that is, to expand on information provided in the text
- **correct** a theological problem

The BHQ and HBCE editions indicate such motives by means of various characterizations.

Based on experience, text critics have formulated a number of "rules" that can aid in discovering what might lie behind a variant (although it must immediately be noted that none of these rules should be applied mechanically, since textual criticism is a matter of judgment, not of mathematical deduction). Thus, when looking for the earliest reading, scholars tend to prefer:

- the **shorter reading** (*lectio brevior*), because copyists tended to expand, elaborate, or make explicit what is implicit; that said, the opposite phenomenon (intentional omission) did occur,[5] albeit less frequently

- the **most difficult reading** (*lectio difficilior*), because copyists tended to replace difficult words by terms that are more easily understandable; that said, a mechanical application of this would lead us to adopt some absurd readings that stem from errors

- the **most dissimilar reading**, because copyists tended to assimilate expressions under the influence of similar passages, or harmonize tensions between passages

- a **reading from which all the others may stem**, thus favoring the scenario that has the greatest explanatory power

- the **most economical scenario** (Occam's razor), preferring sober explanations to far-fetched theories

In addition, when we are trying to understand why there are, say, two readings (A and B), it is important to explore not only one scenario (A was transformed into B) but also the opposite (B was transformed into A). Quite often (as noted in the example of Isa 40:7–8 above), there are good arguments in both directions, so both scenarios are **equally plausible** and it is impossible to decide between them. While this may be frustrating, the need to be responsible in our scholarship requires that we acknowledge this reality.

EXAMPLE 2.4a ▸ Genesis 11:8

Genesis 11:8, which comes near the end of the story of the tower of Babel, tells about how God intervenes in this building project and how this impacts the humans involved in it:

וַיָּפֶץ יְהוָה אֹתָם מִשָּׁם עַל־פְּנֵי כָל־הָאָרֶץ וַיַּחְדְּלוּ לִבְנֹת הָעִיר:

So the LORD scattered them abroad from there over the face of all the earth, and they left off building the city.

---

5. On this subject, see Juha Pakkala, *God's Word Omitted: Omissions in the Transmission of the Hebrew Bible*, FRLANT 251 (Göttingen: Vandenhoeck & Ruprecht, 2013).

As seen above, the critical apparatus in BHQ is as follows:

הָעִיר׃ V S T | את העיר ואת המגדל Smr G (assim-v 5) ⸆

Description of the difference: The Vulgate (V), the Syriac version (S), and the Targum (T) have or translate the same reading as the MT; that is, the last word of the sentence in these versions is the equivalent of הָעִיר ("the city"). However, the Samaritan Pentateuch (Smr) has את העיר ואת המגדל ("the city and the tower"), and this is the phrase that the Septuagint (G) translates.

Explanation of the variant: BHQ has the characterization "assim-v 5," which means that the reading found in Smr and G is explained as the result of an assimilation to a phrase found in Gen 11:5. That verse reads as follows:

וַיֵּרֶד יְהוָה לִרְאֹת אֶת־הָעִיר וְאֶת־הַמִּגְדָּל אֲשֶׁר בָּנוּ בְּנֵי הָאָדָם׃

The Lord came down to see the city and the tower, which mortals had built.

We see that the expression found in the Samaritan Pentateuch and reflected in the Septuagint (את העיר ואת המגדל) appears here. In the judgment of the BHQ editor, the earliest text in v. 8 was simply הָעִיר, and this was expanded in some textual witnesses under the influence of v. 5. To put it another way, a copyist still had in mind the expression "the city and the tower" because he had written it in v. 5, so when he arrived at v. 8, instead of simply writing "the city," he wrote "the city and the tower." (Note, in addition, that v. 4 had also already mentioned עִיר וּמִגְדָּל, "a city and a tower.") This copyist may have made the change intentionally, because he felt that something was missing in v. 8. That said, we cannot exclude the possibility that he made this change spontaneously, without realizing that he was transforming the text under the influence of v. 5.

BHQ also contains, later in the volume, a brief textual commentary on this verse (indicated in BHQ by the presence of a cross [⸆] at the end of the apparatus entry); this commentary states that "Jubilees 10:24 also mentions the tower with the city." In chapter 13 of our book (on the Bible's reception), we will see that this difference that is shared by Smr, G, and Jubilees has a significant impact on the interpretation of the text: it clarifies that the tower was left unfinished, but this view has not historically been adopted by all interpreters of this passage.

> **EXAMPLE 2.4b** ▸ **Deuteronomy 17:14**

Let us consider Deut 17:14:

> כִּי־תָבֹא אֶל־הָאָרֶץ אֲשֶׁר יְהוָה אֱלֹהֶיךָ נֹתֵן לָךְ וִירִשְׁתָּהּ וְיָשַׁבְתָּה בָּהּ
> וְאָמַרְתָּ אָשִׂימָה עָלַי מֶלֶךְ כְּכָל־הַגּוֹיִם אֲשֶׁר סְבִיבֹתָי׃

> "When you have come into the land that the LORD your God is giving you and have taken possession of it and settled in it, and you say, 'I will set a king over me, like all the nations that are around me,' . . ."

The critical apparatus on this verse reads:

> מֶלֶךְ Smr V S T | ἄρχοντα G (theol)

The first part of this entry (before the vertical stroke) lists the textual witnesses that agree with the reading of the MT (מֶלֶךְ): the Samaritan Pentateuch (Smr), the Vulgate (V), the Syriac version (S), and the Targum (T). These either contain the same Hebrew word (in the case of Smr) or a word in another language that has the same meaning ("king"). After the vertical stroke we learn that a variant, ἄρχοντα, appears in the Septuagint, that is, the Greek translation (G). This word means "prince," not "king." Next, the editor's characterization is provided in parentheses: "theol," meaning that the motive behind the change is deemed to have been a theological one. Finally, in BHQ, the entire entry is followed by a cross (✣), which indicates that there is a textual commentary on this case later in this BHQ volume. This commentary explains that:

> Recurring frequently in Deuteronomy, the term מלך is consistently rendered as βασιλεύς, except on the four occasions when it refers to the king of Israel (17:14, 15 [twice], 28:36). . . . Clearly G reflects an interpretation by which the term βασιλεύς is intentionally denied to Israelite kings, since, according to this perspective, only God can be Israel's king. It is perhaps unnecessary to argue, with Rofé ("Qumranic Paraphrases," 169–74), that G was translating from a Hebrew *Vorlage* that read נשיא. Rather, for G's translator, other nations may have kings, but only rulers are permitted for Israel.[6]

This explanation provides a plausible reason why the translator of the Septuagint—assuming he was reading a text that, like the MT, had the word מלך—would have chosen to avoid translating this Hebrew word with a Greek word meaning "king." In the commentary just quoted, Carmel McCarthy, the editor of the BHQ Deuteronomy volume, also mentions an alternative hypothesis that has been put forward by Alexandre Rofé: namely, that the Hebrew text underlying the Septuagint differed from the MT in that it had

---

6. Carmel McCarthy, ed., *Deuteronomy*, BHQ 5 (Stuttgart: Deutsche Bibelgesellschaft, 2007), 103*.

a word meaning "prince" (נשיא) here rather than the word "king" (מלך). However, McCarthy regards this hypothesis as "unnecessary." Another way to put this would be to say that Rofé's theory is less economical since it requires postulating a Hebrew reading that is unattested in the extant textual witnesses; that is, the principle of Occam's razor favors the hypothesis that the translator of the Septuagint made a deliberate decision to translate Hebrew מלך ("king") with a word meaning "prince."

EXAMPLE 2.4c › Isaiah 19:25

The end of the oracle about Egypt in Isa 19 contains a series of positive pronouncements, culminating in a declaration of the Lord in v. 25. However, this declaration reads differently in the MT and in the LXX (see Table 2.7):

Table 2.7: Isaiah 19:25 in the MT and in the LXX

LXX	MT
Εὐλογημένος ὁ λαός μου ὁ ἐν Αἰγύπτῳ καὶ ὁ ἐν Ἀσσυρίοις καὶ ἡ κληρονομία μου Ισραηλ.	בָּרוּךְ עַמִּי מִצְרַיִם וּמַעֲשֵׂה יָדַי אַשּׁוּר וְנַחֲלָתִי יִשְׂרָאֵל׃
Blessed be my people *that are in* Egypt and *among* the Assyrians, even Israel my heritage. (NETS)	Blessed be Egypt my people and Assyria the work of my hands and Israel my heritage. (NRSVue)

In the first line here, "Egypt" (מִצְרַיִם) is in apposition to "my people" (עַמִּי) in the MT, but in the LXX the equivalent words are separated by ὁ ἐν, "that is/are in." As a result, in the LXX the beneficiary of the blessing is not Egypt but the people of the Lord who are in Egypt—that is, Judean people living in diaspora in that country.

In the second line, "Assyria" (אַשּׁוּר) is in apposition to "the work of my hands" (מַעֲשֵׂה יָדַי) in the MT. But the latter expression is absent from the LXX; instead, we find the same construction as in the first line, with ὁ ἐν. As a result, Assyria is not mentioned as the handiwork of the Lord and the beneficiary of a blessing, but, again, as a place where some Judeans live.

These differences cannot be explained by scribal mistakes, as nothing in the text could have prompted an accidental change in one direction or the other. Rather, the text has been deliberately modified, and it is clear that in both the MT and the LXX the variants in the first and second lines are interconnected. The text has been slightly rewritten in one of the textual witnesses—but which one? It is clear that the MT here contains a daring statement that may have surprised, even shocked, a copyist. It is unusual to read in the Hebrew Bible that Egypt is the people of God, or that Assyria was "handmade" by him. For theological reasons, therefore, a copyist may well have chosen to correct this puzzling assertion. He may have decided to "improve" the text (in his eyes), or to "correct" it (if he considered that a preceding copyist had made some mistakes and that the text needed to be restored to its original state). Another reason a copyist may have corrected v. 25 to make it speak of the Lord's people living in Egypt and in Assyria is that the context pictures people who are living in Egypt speaking Hebrew (v. 18) and worshiping the God of Israel (vv. 19–21), which could have led this copyist to think that v. 25 is about the Judean diaspora in Egypt. In contrast to all this, hypothesizing that a copyist changed a text about the diaspora to a more theologically challenging statement about Egypt being God's people and Assyria his handiwork is far less probable.

EXAMPLE 2.4d ▸ **Song of Songs 2:12–14, 17**

Let us consider several verses in Song of Songs 2. First, we will look at vv. 12–14 in the MT:

¹²הַנִּצָּנִים֙ נִרְא֣וּ בָאָ֔רֶץ עֵ֥ת הַזָּמִ֖יר הִגִּ֑יעַ וְק֥וֹל הַתּ֖וֹר נִשְׁמַ֥ע בְּאַרְצֵֽנוּ׃
¹³הַתְּאֵנָה֙ חָֽנְטָ֣ה פַגֶּ֔יהָ וְהַגְּפָנִ֥ים ׀ סְמָדַ֖ר נָ֣תְנוּ רֵ֑יחַ ק֥וּמִי לָ֛ךְ רַעְיָתִ֥י
יָפָתִ֖י וּלְכִי־לָֽךְ׃ ¹⁴יוֹנָתִ֞י בְּחַגְוֵ֣י הַסֶּ֗לַע בְּסֵ֙תֶר֙ הַמַּדְרֵגָ֔ה הַרְאִ֙ינִי֙ אֶת־
מַרְאַ֔יִךְ הַשְׁמִיעִ֖ינִי אֶת־קוֹלֵ֑ךְ כִּי־קוֹלֵ֥ךְ עָרֵ֖ב וּמַרְאֵ֥יךְ נָאוֶֽה׃

¹²*The flowers appear on the earth; the time of singing has come, and the voice of the turtledove is heard in our land.* ¹³*The fig tree puts forth its figs, and the vines are in blossom; they give forth fragrance. Arise, my love, my fair one, and come away.* ¹⁴*O my dove, in the clefts of the rock, in the covert of the cliff, let me see your face; let me hear your voice, for your voice is sweet, and your face is lovely.*

This passage is also attested in the Dead Sea Scrolls, in 4Q107. When comparing this text and the MT, we encounter a few small additions and synonymous readings that are easy to explain if the two texts come from variant oral forms of the same poem.

First, 4Q107 has a plus (הִנֵּה, "behold") at the beginning of both v. 12 and v. 13, compared to the MT. This echoes the beginning of v. 11 (כִּי־הִנֵּה), so in this scroll we read three consecutive verses (vv. 11, 12, 13) that begin the same way ("behold . . ."). Perhaps a scribe made two additions in vv. 12 and 13 because he was influenced by v. 11. But these small differences may just as well reflect fluctuations that are due to the choices of oral performers; in this case, it is difficult to decide whether additions or omissions occurred, since both forms of the text make sense.

Second, v. 14 contains a symmetrical structure in the MT:

   A let me see *your face* (הַרְאִינִי אֶת־מַרְאַיִךְ)

      B let me hear **your voice** (הַשְׁמִיעִנִי אֶת־קוֹלֵךְ)

      B′ for **your voice** is sweet (כִּי־קוֹלֵךְ עָרֵב)

   A′ and *your face* is lovely (וּמַרְאֵיךְ נָאוֶה)

The fourth line (A′) echoes the first (A), while the third (B′) echoes the second (B).

In its equivalent of the B line here, 4Q107 reads שמעך ("your sound," that is, "the sound you make") in place of the MT's קוֹלֵךְ ("your voice"). The symmetrical structure, while not as exact as in the MT, is still present here, since B′ still echoes B. Traditional textual criticism would consider two opposite scenarios. On the one hand, it may be that a scribe behind the MT assimilated B (שמעך) to B′ (קולך). On the other hand, it may be that a scribe behind 4Q107 preferred to write a *figura etymologica* in B, that is, with the verb (השמיעני) and the object (שמעך) being from the same root. However, if we allow for Song of Songs having oral origins, it is quite probable that the two readings simply reflect two variant oral forms of the poem.

Another interesting variant occurs in v. 17. Here the MT reads:

עַד שֶׁיָּפוּחַ הַיּוֹם וְנָסוּ הַצְּלָלִים סֹב דְּמֵה־לְךָ דוֹדִי
לִצְבִי אוֹ לְעֹפֶר הָאַיָּלִים עַל־הָרֵי בָתֶר׃

Until the day breathes and the shadows flee, turn, my beloved,
be like a gazelle, or a young stag on rugged mountains.

The clause "My beloved, be like a gazelle or like a young stag" (דְּמֵה־לְךָ דוֹדִי לִצְבִי אוֹ לְעֹפֶר הָאַיָּלִים) is virtually a repetition of part of v. 9: "My beloved is like a gazelle or a young stag" (דּוֹמֶה דוֹדִי לִצְבִי אוֹ לְעֹפֶר הָאַיָּלִים). Verse 17 is fragmentary in 4Q107, and the size of the gaps indicates that there was not enough space on the scroll for אוֹ לְעֹפֶר הָאַיָּלִים.[7] This suggest that perhaps v. 17 has been assimilated to v. 9 in the MT. However, the addition or omission of the expression "or a young stag" is typical of the kind of change that occurs in oral performances of poems. Thus, as with the variants in vv. 12–14, the variant in v. 17 could be explained either by scribal changes or by variations stemming from oral performances.

---

7. Emile Puech, "Le *Cantique des Cantiques* dans les manuscrits de Qumrân: 4Q106, 4Q107, 4Q108 et 6Q6," *RB* 123 (2016): 29–53, esp. 38–39.

2.5 EXPLAIN LARGE-SCALE DIFFERENCES

Many exegetes habitually consider variants one by one. Yet sometimes we can observe modifications that are linked to one another—for example, when a copyist has made an ideological or theological correction that implies that others also have been made in order for the text to be consistent.

When seeking to identify networks of correlated variants and to get an overview of each witness, it is often worth laying out the textual forms (for example, the MT and the LXX) in a synoptic table that indicates the differences and the plusses in bold or italics, for instance.

Networks of variants are sometimes limited to a pericope, but they can also result from the process of creating a reedition of a book. Eugene Ulrich has pointed out that a number of biblical books existed in distinct literary editions in antiquity. The classic example of a book that existed in different editions is Jeremiah, of which we know of two:[8]

- A shorter edition, which was the Hebrew basis for the LXX; here, the oracles against the nations appear in the middle of the book (right after 25:12). Two Hebrew Dead Sea scroll fragments (4QJer[b] and 4QJer[d]) contain a text close to what would have been the Hebrew model of the LXX.

- A longer edition, attested in the MT and in a few Dead Sea scroll fragments (2QJer, 4QJer[a], and 4QJer[c]); it contains many plusses compared to the shorter edition (the longest plus is Jer 33:14–26), and the oracles against the nations appear at the end of the book.

According to a broad scholarly consensus, the longer form of Jeremiah is a revised and augmented edition of the shorter one.

EXAMPLE 2.5a ▸ 1 Kings 8:1–6

First Kings 8:1–6 is shorter in the LXX than it is in the MT. For the sake of simplicity, I will present these two main witnesses in English translation (NRSVue for the MT, NETS for the LXX): this will suffice to give you an idea of their differences. In the left-hand column of Table 2.8, I have divided the text into numerated segments (note that these do not correspond to the verse numbers).

---

8. Matthieu Richelle, "Jeremiah and Baruch," in *The Oxford Handbook of the Septuagint*, ed. T. Michael Law and Alison Salvesen (Oxford: Oxford University Press, 2021), 259–74.

Table 2.8: 1 Kings 8:1–6 in the MT and in the LXX

	MT	LXX
1	Then Solomon assembled the elders of Israel	Then King Solomon assembled all the elders of Israel
2	and all the heads of the tribes, the leaders of the ancestral houses of the Israelites, before King Solomon	
3	in *Jerusalem*,	in *Sion*
4	to bring up the ark of the covenant of the LORD	to bring up the ark of the covenant of the Lord
	out of the city of David, which is Zion.	out of the city of Dauid (this is Sion)
5	All the people of Israel assembled to King Solomon at the festival	
6	in the month Ethanim,	in the month Athanin.
7	which is the seventh month.	
8	And all the elders of Israel came,	
9	and the priests carried the ark.	And the priests carried the ark
10	So they brought up the ark of the LORD,	
11	the tent of meeting, and all the holy vessels that were in the tent;	and the covert of witness and all the holy vessels that were in the tent of witness,
12	the priests and the Levites brought them up.	
13	King Solomon and all the congregation of Israel,	and the king and all Israel
14	who had assembled before him,	
15	were with him before the ark, sacrificing so many sheep and oxen that they could not be counted or numbered.	were before the ark sacrificing countless sheep and oxen.
16	Then the priests brought the ark of the covenant of the LORD to its place, in the inner sanctuary of the house, in the most holy place, underneath the wings of the cherubim.	And the priests brought the ark into its place in the dabir of the house, into the holy of holies, underneath the wings of the cherubin.

A simple look at the table shows that many expressions from the MT are absent in the LXX. A detailed scrutiny of the texts in Hebrew and in Greek shows that there are no instances of *homoioteleuton* or similar mistakes that could explain the loss of these phrases. Verse 1 contains an exception, since "Sion" in the LXX appears instead of "Jerusalem" in the MT. Because "Sion" appears again at the end of the same verse, it is likely that the first occurrence in the LXX stems from an assimilation. Apart from that, most of the divergences seem intentional.

On closer inspection, a number of plusses (notably in segments 2, 5, 8, and 14) all have the same effect: they insist on the fact that all the chiefs of Israel were united behind Solomon and were following his lead. Thus, it seems that these plusses form a network. It seems unlikely that a scribe would have intentionally deleted all these expressions, since they do not create any theological or ideological difficulty. Rather, it seems likely that a scribe has added them in order to stress Solomon's leadership and the communal participation of all the people (represented by their chiefs) in the inauguration of the temple.

In addition, segment 12 is a very interesting plus, since it involves the Levites. They are never mentioned elsewhere in Kings, but, by contrast, they play a prominent role in Chronicles. It is therefore likely that 1 Kgs 8 was rewritten by a scribe who was interested in stressing the role of the Levites in the inauguration of the temple, which would fit well with the Persian or early Hellenistic periods, perhaps even the time of the Chronicler.

Indeed, the parallel passage in 2 Chr 5 contains all the plusses noted above. Hence, a possible scenario is as follows:[9]

- The earliest form of Kings was shorter, and is reflected by the LXX.
- When composing his own work, the Chronicler used the Kings narrative of the inauguration of the temple as a source, but augmented it by interpolating expressions that stress the unanimous participation of the people in this crucial religious event and that indicate that the Levites joined the priests in bringing the ark.
- Later, during the transmission of Kings, a scribe assimilated 1 Kgs 8 toward 2 Chr 5.[10]

---

9. Matthieu Richelle, "Quel rôle a joué l'époque perse dans la diversification textuelle issue des livres des Rois?" *Transeuphratène* 50 (2018): 164–66.

10. Alternatively, it may be that the expansions were made first in 1 Kgs 8 by a scribe concerned with Priestly matters (on which, see chapter 4) and that the Chronicler inherited the augmented version. This hypothesis is argued brilliantly by Julian Chike, "The Literary Development of MT 1Kgs

| EXAMPLE 2.5b ▸ Judges 6:8–10 |

The stories at the heart of the book of Judges follow, more or less closely, a cyclical pattern comprising four stages: (1) the people do what displeases God; (2) God is angry and delivers Israel into the hand of foreigners; (3) the people endure oppression and, often, call out to God; (4) God sends a judge to deliver them. In Judg 6, we find stage (1) in v. 1a, stage (2) in vv. 1b–6a, stage (3) in vv. 6b–7, and stage (4) in vv. 11–16. But in between stages (3) and (4), there is an unexpected element about an unnamed prophet (vv. 8–10):

> The Lord sent a prophet to the Israelites, and he said to them, "Thus says the Lord, the God of Israel: I led you up from Egypt and brought you out of the house of slavery, and I delivered you from the hand of the Egyptians and from the hand of all who oppressed you, and drove them out before you, and gave you their land, and I said to you, 'I am the Lord your God; you shall not pay reverence to the gods of the Amorites in whose land you live.' But you have not given heed to my voice."

Normally, it is a judge that the Lord sends to his people when they cry out to him, not a prophet. The unexpected narrative element here is all the more surprising since the individual it mentions is—apart from Deborah, who is also described as "judging" Israel (4:4)—the only prophet who appears in the book of Judges. Judges 6:8–10 clearly represents a theological lesson that emphasizes the guilty behavior of the Israelites. Scholars have long surmised that these verses are an interpolation, but until recently all the available manuscripts included this passage. The situation changed when 4QJudges[a] was deciphered, for in this scroll the text passes directly from v. 7 to v. 11! To be more precise, a line of this scroll contains the words "the Israelites cried to the Lord" (cf. v. 7a), then there is a lacuna, and the next preserved words, on the next line, belong to v. 11. There was clearly no place on the scroll for the story of the prophet. The missing part most likely started with "the Lord sent a prophet"; that is to say, it was the paragraph quoted above.

Could the absence of vv. 8–10 from 4QJudges[a] be due to an accidental omission? This seems unlikely, as no repetition (*homoioarcton* or *homoioteleuton*) could have prompted an instance of haplography. Could it be an intentional omission? This is unlikely: the theology of this passage is in line with that of the rest of the historical books, so there is nothing special here that might have bothered a copyist and led him to remove it.

8:1–11 in Light of the Septuagint," *Textus* 28 (2019): 45–66. Nevertheless, the stress on the unity of Israel and on the role of the Levites is characteristic of Chronicles.

> It seems therefore that this passage is an addition, one that was clearly inspired by similar descriptions of theological judgment that one finds elsewhere in the historical books (e.g., 2 Kgs 17). In the end, 4QJudges[a] reflects an older compositional stage of Judges, one prior to the addition of the passage on the prophet,[11] which is an intrusion into the cyclical pattern that is characteristic of the book of Judges.
>
> This does not mean that the presence of this passage (in most manuscripts) does not contribute to the narrative. Gregory Wong notes a similar disruption of the cyclical pattern in 10:11–14, where it is God himself who intervenes. As Wong points out, the cyclical pattern in Judges progressively deteriorates because the people's behavior worsens. God shows an "increasing reluctance to respond to their cries," which "suggests that their cries were becoming increasingly perfunctory and manipulative."[12] So, it makes sense in ch. 6 that a prophet criticizes the people before God appoints a savior (Gideon).

2.6 EXPLORE THE IMPACT OF THE VARIANTS

When we study the text's reception in chapter 13, we will see examples in which variants have impacted the way in which one or more ancient interpreters interpreted the text. For now, I will give a taste of the most fascinating kind of situation that occurs in this regard—namely, when two variant readings give rise to two different lines of interpretation.

> **EXAMPLE 2.6 ▸ Ezekiel 28:11–19**
>
> Ezekiel 28:11–19 is a famous oracle about the king of Tyre. My aim here is not to analyze in detail the variants in this passage or explain their origins.[13]

---

11. Eugene Ulrich, "Deuteronomistically Inspired Scribal Insertions into the Developing Biblical Texts: 4QJudg[a] and 4QJer[a]," in *Houses Full of All Good Things: Essays in Memory of Timo Veijola*, ed. Juha Pakkala and Martti Nissinen (Helsinki: Finnish Exegetical Society, 2008), 489–506.

12. Gregory T. K. Wong, *Compositional Strategy of the Book of Judges: An Inductive, Rhetorical Study*, VTSup 111 (Leiden: Brill, 2006), 183–85.

13. I have published my views on this subject in Matthieu Richelle, "Le portrait changeant du roi de Tyr (Ézéchiel 28) dans les traditions textuelles anciennes," in *Phéniciens d'Orient et d'Occident: Mélanges Josette Elayi*, ed. André Lemaire, CIPOA 2 (Paris: Maisonneuve, 2014), 113–25. For a more detailed study, see Hector Patmore, *Adam, Satan, and the King of Tyre: The Interpretation of Ezekiel*

Instead, I want to take note of the most important differences and indicate how two diverging lines of interpretations have stemmed from them. Table 2.9 serves to compare the MT and the LXX of vv. 14–16. The most significant differences are presented in italics.[14]

Table 2.9: Ezekiel 28:14–16 in the MT and in the LXX

Masoretic Text (NRSVue)	Septuagint (NETS)
You were a cherub [אַתְּ־כְּרוּב]; I placed you on the holy mountain of God; you walked among the stones of fire.	I placed you *with the cheroub* [μετὰ τοῦ χερουβ] in a holy, divine mountain; you were born in the midst of fiery stones.
In the abundance of your trade you were filled with violence, and you sinned; so *I cast you as a profane thing* from the mountain of God, and *I drove you out, O guardian cherub*, from among the stones of fire.	You were born blameless in your days from the day you were created until acts of iniquity were found in you.
You were blameless in your ways from the day that you were created, until iniquity was found in you.	From the abundance of your commerce you filled your storehouses with lawlessness, and you sinned and *were wounded* [ἐτραυματίσθης] from God's mountain, and *the cheroub drove you* [ἤγαγέν σε τὸ χερουβ] from the midst of the fiery stones.

The most striking difference appears in v. 14: the king of Tyre *is* a cherub according to the MT, whereas he is *accompanied by* a cherub according to the LXX. The divergence ultimately comes from the fact that the Hebrew word את can be vocalized אֶת ("with") or אַתְּ ("you," an archaic form of אַתָּה). Then, in v. 16, we read in the MT that, because of the king-cherub's sins, God expels him from the holy mountain; by contrast, in the LXX, it is the cherub who drives out the king.

When we add to this the fact that just before this passage, in v. 13, the original location of the king of Tyre is described as "Eden, the garden of God," we can see that the situation is reminiscent of Gen 2–3. In that story, a

---

28:11–19 in Late Antiquity, JCI 20 (Leiden: Brill, 2012); see also Lydia Lee, "The Tyrian King in MT and LXX Ezekiel 28:12b–15," *Religions* 12 (2021): Article 91 (online).

14. The MT of v. 14 in fact begins "You were an anointed guardian cherub" (אַתְּ־כְּרוּב מִמְשַׁח הַסּוֹכֵךְ), but the NRSVue regards מִמְשַׁח הַסּוֹכֵךְ as an addition and therefore does not translate these two words.

> man is placed in the garden of Eden and is then expelled and prevented by a cherub from going back into the garden. The scenario is not exactly the same as in Ezek 28, since Gen 3 does not say that the cherub expelled the man, but the parallels are sufficiently striking to suggest to a reader that one might compare the texts—and this is precisely what a number of ancient interpreters did. A rabbinic interpretation, based on the (oral) vocalization אֶת ("with") in v. 14 of the proto-MT, understood the king to be "with" a cherub in the holy place of God, and inferred from this that the king in question was Adam. By contrast, Tertullian, a church father who read the LXX, understood the king to be figuratively represented as a cherub. Since he conflated cherubs with angels, he concluded that Ezek 28 is about the "fall of Satan," whom he regarded as a rebellious angel whom God expelled from his presence.[15]

Exercises for Chapter 2

The following exercises are of increasing difficulty, beginning with cases for which you will only need to understand the BHS or BHQ apparatus, proceeding to cases that demand more reflection, and finally moving to cases for which you need to compare the textual witnesses on your own.

Exercise A

Read Gen 6:6 and the critical apparatus of BHQ. "Translate" this apparatus in two sentences: one that describes the variant, the other that explains it. Do you agree with this explanation?

Exercise B

Read the last entry in the BHQ apparatus on Gen 30:19, that is, the part of this apparatus that concerns the lemma יִשָּׂשכָר. In one sentence, "translate" the comparison between the witnesses. Do the same with the characterization, then explain it. Do you agree with this characterization?

Exercise C

"Translate" the BHS apparatus on 1 Kgs 22:28 and explain the textual scenario it refers to, in a couple of sentences. Do you agree with this hypothesis?

---

15. Patmore, *Adam, Satan, and the King of Tyre*, 16–79.

Exercise D

"Translate" the BHQ apparatus on Gen 35:4 in a few sentences (there are two lemmas). Explain the characterizations. Do you agree with them?

Exercise E

"Translate" the BHQ apparatus on Hag 2:13 in a few sentences (there are two lemmas). Explain the characterizations. Do you agree with them?

Exercise F

"Translate" and explain the BHQ apparatus on the lemma הַכַּפְתּוֹר in Amos 9:1. You will probably need to use Muraoka's *Two-Way Index to the Septuagint* and/or Hatch and Redpath's concordance of the LXX. Do you agree with BHQ?

Exercise G

"Translate" the BHQ apparatus on Gen 2:2. The characterization in the apparatus suggests that the reading attested by Smr, G, and S is secondary. But read the textual commentary on this variant in the same volume; you will see that there is a debate. What explanation do you find more likely? What clinches the argument for you?

Exercise H

Make a synoptic table comparing English translations of the MT and the LXX of Jer 25:8–14. It is much better if you do the translations yourself; if you lack the time, however, you can use a standard translation (e.g., NRSVue) for the MT and the NETS translation for the LXX. Use italics, bold characters, and blank lines to make the qualitative and quantitative differences apparent. Do you find that some of the variants are interconnected? How do you explain them?

CHAPTER 3

COMPOSITIONAL CRITICISM: ANALYSIS

OVERVIEW

In simple terms, compositional criticism aims to reconstruct the development of a text from its earliest form to its "final" form. It explores both the intermediary stages that were part of this process and the stage whereby the text reached its current form. It is possible to present the task of compositional criticism in two main steps: analysis and synthesis. Analysis mainly consists of detecting traces of redactional intervention (this task of detection is called *Literarkritik* in German).[1] Synthesis aims to reconstruct the stages of the formation of a passage (or a book) and, if possible, to date them and situate them in the history of Israelite or Judean traditions.[2] The present chapter is devoted to analysis; the next will address synthesis.

Compositional analysis rests on two assumptions:

(1) The composition of a biblical text generally involved several stages, may have included a reliance on *sources*, and may have entailed the text undergoing large-scale revisions (each of which is called a *redaction*). The work of a redactor can involve integrating and reworking textual material, adding or subtracting material, or reorganizing the text (for instance, changing the sequence of passages).

---

1. The expression "literary criticism" would be the formal equivalent, but in the English-speaking world this often refers to more recent methods (e.g., narrative criticism) that are primarily interested in the final form of the text.

2. My twofold presentation of the method (analysis and synthesis) follows Christophe Nihan, "L'analyse rédactionnelle," in *Manuel d'exégèse de l'Ancien Testament*, ed. Michaela Bauks and Christophe Nihan, MdB 61 (Geneva: Labor et Fides, 2008), 137–89, esp. 139.

(2) It is possible to reconstitute, at least partially, the history of this process, by engaging in analysis based on certain criteria.

Some students find it difficult to accept both (1) and (2), whether on principle or because they are skeptical about the degree of probability of the working hypotheses involved or the results obtained. To begin with, (1) proves counterintuitive to many people because we live in a time characterized by the paradigm of *authored literature*. This means that nearly all books that are produced in our day are what we might say "signed" by (i.e., accompanied by the name of) at least one author; and in the case of a book that contains contributions from multiple authors, the different contributors are mentioned.

Not so in the ancient Near East. Most literary compositions written there before the Hellenistic period (that is, before the end of the fourth century BCE) were anonymous. When there is a "signature" (called a *colophon*), it is that of the scribe who *copied* the text and not that of its author. That books were anonymous is consistent with the fact that they were sometimes updated and rewritten by scribes over centuries; they were collective works, a bit like the *wiki*s of today. For example, there is material evidence of this fact for the *Gilgamesh Epic*, a famous legend about a Mesopotamian hero: tablets from the third millennium to the first millennium attest to its growth, as new chapters were progressively added. Prophetic oracles are often exceptions to the trend of anonymous authorship, however, because the identity of the recipient of a divine revelation was deemed important in the ancient Near East; it is interesting to note that, in keeping with this, most of the prophetic books in the Hebrew Bible bear the name of a prophet. But this does not mean that it was the prophet in question who wrote down his own oracles, nor that the book was not updated. In fact, in the case of the Bible, various manuscripts attest to important changes that were made in a number of the prophetic books, changes that sometimes amounted to a reworking of the text that resulted in a new literary edition. The paramount example of this is in fact an entire prophetic book, Jeremiah, for which (as we have seen in the preceding chapter) there are attested two distinct editions, which differ from each other both quantitatively and qualitatively.

Two biblical books, Proverbs[3] and Psalms, themselves state that they are the product of a plurality of contributors. Psalms is an interesting case because the manuscripts show that at the end of the first millennium BCE, scribes tended to add superscriptions that attributed a growing number of the psalms to David.[4] At the time of the Dead Sea Scrolls, he was somehow regarded as *the* author of the Psalter, even though some of its chapters name other authors. In the same way, it became important for

---

3. Proverbs cites as "contributors" Solomon (Prov 1:1; 10:1), Agur (Prov 30:1), and Lemuel (Prov 31:1), and observes that a group of its maxims were "transmitted" or "transcribed" at the time of Hezekiah (Prov 25:1).

4. Although the meaning of the preposition often translated as "of" in the phrase "of David" is debated, it is likely that it came to be read as an indication of authorship.

many Jews to attribute the whole of the Pentateuch to Moses, even though the five books it contains are anonymous (even Deuteronomy, which presents itself as mainly a series of speeches by Moses). This tendency to ascribe books to precise authors may well be due to the influence of Hellenistic culture, and we are still living in the same paradigm. The point is that students of the Hebrew Bible should know that in most cases, traditional ideas about authorship are just that: traditional, not biblical.

Admittedly, the fact that books are often multilayered does not mean that we are able to disentangle all the layers and reconstruct the history of their formation with precision. The earliest manuscripts we have date from the third century BCE, while most of the books they contain were written long before that: we do not have copies of their earlier, successive "drafts." Moreover, the hypotheses put forward by scholars regarding how to disentangle the layers of a given text and reconstruct the history of their formation often diverge sharply. As a result, many people, even some scholars, doubt point (2) above. The reply to this criticism is twofold. First, the task is *at least partially* possible with a satisfactory degree of likelihood, especially when it comes to describing the broad strokes of the development of a book. This is why most scholars, although they delight in disagreeing among themselves, nevertheless have reached a consensus on some classic cases, such as the idea that Isa 40–66 is made up of additions from the sixth century or later. There is even a striking case where the discovery of a Dead Sea scroll has verified an earlier scholarly hypothesis: Judg 6:8–10, a passage long regarded as an interpolation, is absent from 4QJudges[a] (see chapter 2).

Second, the endeavor is worth the effort, and even *necessary*, if we wish to place the biblical texts in their historical contexts. The limits of compositional criticism are also, to a large extent, the limits of historical knowledge about the literature and the religious ideas of ancient Israel. To put it differently, whether you realize it or not, what you believe about the history of ideas in ancient Israel (e.g., when monotheism was introduced, or when the cult was centralized in Jerusalem) depends on certain hypotheses or others about the compositional history of the biblical books.

In the end, even skeptics should be aware of the methods that are used in diachronic studies, if only in order to understand the scholarly literature, including exegetical commentaries, that makes use of them. So, even if it is not to your taste, this chapter (and chapter 4) will tell you "how the sausage is made." It is also worth noting that scholars who attempt to "excavate" the text by identifying, for instance, words, phrases, or sentences that were added to the text at some point are not claiming that such additions are "inauthentic" or less valuable than the earlier text. It is simply a fact that most texts in the Hebrew Bible are the result of a gradual process of growth to which many scribes contributed. Reconstructing this history is not looking for a "purer" state of a text, but trying to understand the logic behind these successive contributions.

Be that as it may, engaging in compositional criticism may range from identifying a gloss in a verse, to elaborating complicated scenarios about the formation of a book, to reconstructing a large literary composition whose component parts stretch over several books. In the framework of the present introduction, I will focus on the most typical situation a student will encounter—that is, when you are studying a pericope and want to understand its compositional history. This entails first of all detecting scribal interventions in the pericope: changes that were made in the course of its compositional history. The most frequent such changes involve the addition of new phrases or sentences.

> **Lost in Terminology?**
>
> ---
>
> There are many ways to talk about the method examined in this chapter; do not be confused by this. For a long time, scholars made much of a distinction between "source criticism," which aimed to detect and reconstitute the sources that supposedly lay behind the current text, and "redaction criticism," which looked more at the manner in which the intermediate redactional stages were created from preexisting materials (either sources or earlier redactional stages). "Literary criticism" (*Literarkritik* in German) often designated the detection and "surgical removal" of interpolations from a given text, based on hints that the phrases or sentences were intrusive.
>
> Current exegetical practice combines all these complementary approaches, recognizing that they are difficult to disentangle. It is possible to use the term "compositional *analysis*" to speak of studying each successive scribe's work, and to use the term "compositional *history*" to refer to reconstructing the steps that led from the first written elements to the definitive text. In practice, however, this kind of terminology (which is merely a question of convention) varies by author and publication. Exegetes often interchangeably speak of "redactor," "scribe," or "editor" to designate the person who contributed to the text at some point. "Redactor" may more appropriately designate a person working on a large scale at an intermediate stage, while it could make sense to refer to a person making changes that resulted in a new literary edition of a work as an "editor." But deciding what is a "large-scale" redactional work is subjective. And distinguishing between an intermediate stage and an edition is quite difficult when we are talking about hypothetical stages. Also, some exegetes use "editor" when they want to describe the work of a person who makes edits, without claiming that it was a (large-scale) redaction. Finally, a "scribe" was a person whose job was to write down texts in a proper fashion (not just scribbling a few words), and it is generally assumed that this is precisely what redactors did when they wrote and reworked texts. As you can see, there is a lot of flexibility and overlap in the terminology exegetes use.

3.1 HOW TO DETECT SCRIBAL ACTIVITY

The first thing to do is to *take stock of changes that are materially attested in textual witnesses*, whether Hebrew manuscripts or ancient versions; this is part of the job you have already done when working on textual criticism. As we saw in chapter 2, some divergences between textual witnesses are of a redactional nature: scrolls and translations sometimes show that words, expressions, or entire passages have been added, removed, or transposed. Because these changes are materially attested, they are not hypothetical, and they must be taken into account.[5] For instance, if you are studying Judg 6, you already know—thanks to examining this text through the lens of textual criticism—that an older stage of this chapter, compared to the MT, did not include vv. 8–10 (see Example 2.5b).

The next step is to *detect traces of redactional intervention* that are not materially attested but can be reasonably identified, based on various criteria developed by scholars. Here is a list of the criteria that are often used to determine that a segment of text (a word, phrase, sentence, or section) is an addition:

- *Criterion 1:* It introduces a **redundancy** (repetition or duplication): this may be a hint that the text is based on different sources.
- *Criterion 2:* It **interrupts the flow of the text** by unexpectedly switching to another subject, another speaker, or other addressee(s), or it breaks up the text's literary structure.
- *Criterion 3:* It is only **loosely connected** to its immediate literary context.
- *Criterion 4:* It stands out from what surrounds it due to a **formal or linguistic difference** (such as a difference in literary genre, style, or vocabulary—including possibly using a different personal name for a character already mentioned by another name), or it belongs to a different linguistic stage (e.g., it contains features of Late Biblical Hebrew, whereas the rest of the text is in Classical Biblical Hebrew; see the sidebar "Linguistic Dating" below).
- *Criterion 5:* It stands out from what surrounds it on the level of content because it seems to introduce a **tension** or a **contradiction** within the text.
- *Criterion 6:* It introduces or presupposes **a later piece of information, a later idea, or a later tradition** compared to the time of the text where it appears.[6]

---

5. This has not always been the case in past scholarship: many monographs have been written on the sole basis of the MT.

6. When an exegete considers that a passage refers to an event anterior to the time of its writing although it is introduced as a prediction, he or she designates it by the Latin expression *vaticinium ex eventu* ("prophecy after the event").

* ***Criterion 7:*** It is framed by a **resumptive repetition** (*Wiederaufnahme* in German). After inserting a new element ("X") in a text, scribes sometimes took up the last sentence preceding X and repeated it after X, thus creating a frame around the new element. This serves to resume the main line of argumentation or the main storyline after the interruption, by reminding the reader what was mentioned right before it. The equivalent in a speech would be, when finishing an extended anecdote, to resume your main comment with, "As I was saying . . ." Given that one speaker or writer can diverge from his or her main storyline, however, it is often debatable whether, when we encounter resumptive repetition in the biblical text, we are dealing with a case in which a redactor deliberately marked an interpolation this way or a case in which it is simply the same writer who temporarily switched subject matter and is now signaling that he is going back to the main storyline or argument.

This last remark points to a general difficulty: the criteria mentioned above are not always decisive, since using them often involves speculation. For instance, some apparent disruptions in a narrative are simply due to differences between ancient and modern literary conventions, tastes, and expectations, not to a plurality of redactors. In the ancient Near East, the presence of repetition in a text was not necessarily seen as a problem—indeed, some writers and audiences appear to have enjoyed this as a literary technique.[7] As a result, in many cases, the criteria mentioned above merely point, with a greater or lesser degree of likelihood, to elements in the text that are *possible* additions, and this is why scholars often diverge in their conclusions. Therefore, it is much better if *several criteria are combined*: this enhances the probability that we are indeed dealing with a secondary element in the text. For this reason, rather than illustrating each of the preceding criteria one by one, most of the following examples will illustrate several of them together.

Linguistic Dating

Like all spoken languages, Hebrew developed over time. Linguists distinguish several periods in the history of Hebrew as it is attested in the Bible (see Table 3.1).

---

7. See Gary A. Rendsburg, *How the Bible Is Written* (Peabody, MA: Hendrickson, 2019), 34–71.

Table 3.1: Different Periods in the History of Biblical Hebrew

Period	Approximate Time	Examples
Archaic Biblical Hebrew (ABH)	late second millenium or early royal period	poems in Gen 49, Exod 15, Judg 5, Deut 32
Classical Biblical Hebrew (CBH)	most of the royal period and the early sixth century	most narratives in the Pentateuch and in the Deuteronomistic History (Joshua, Judges, Samuel, Kings)
Transitional Biblical Hebrew (TBH)	around the middle of the sixth century	Isa 40–66, Lamentations, Ezekiel
Late Biblical Hebrew (LBH)	Persian and Hellenistic periods	Chronicles, Ezra-Nehemiah, Esther, the Hebrew parts of Daniel

The differences between the successive periods of the Hebrew language listed here concern morphology, vocabulary, and syntax. Obviously, this model is merely a schematic description that simplifies a much more complex development and gradual changes. It cannot be used to mechanically date a text.

Recent years have seen three challenges to this model. First, the biblical scholars Ian Young and Robert Rezetko have put forward alternative explanations for the linguistic variations observed in Biblical Hebrew, such as dialectal differences and the use of different levels of language. While their insights have generated an interesting debate and led linguists to take more seriously such aspects of the discussion, this alternative approach remains a minority view that is not accepted by many linguists.

Second, some scholars accept that the difference between CBH and LBH is chronological, but they also argue that it was possible to imitate CBH for centuries after it had ceased to constitute the spoken language. This is contested by linguists, however, who do not find any convincing example of flawless imitation in ancient Hebrew literature: that is, the writers could not help introducing features that betray their own time.

Third, scholars specializing in the Pentateuch, at least in Continental European exegesis, date many of the narratives in Genesis through Deuteronomy to the Persian period, based on their contents. This produces a tension with the linguistic model above, according to which the Pentateuch contains little LBH, thus making the dating of whole swaths of the Pentateuch to the Persian period unlikely. As a solution, some suggest that the transition from CBH to LBH did not occur in the sixth century but rather in the fifth century, or at least that it was more gradual than has been suggested by many linguists.

For more details on the model above, see the following articles in *EHLL* = Geoffrey Khan, ed., *Encyclopedia of Hebrew Language and Linguistics*, 4 vols. (Leiden: Brill, 2013):

- Aaron Hornkohl, "Biblical Hebrew: Periodization" (1:315–25).
- Alice Mandell, "Biblical Hebrew, Archaic" (1:325–29).
- Avi Hurvitz, "Biblical Hebrew, Late" (1:329–38).

In practice, when studying a pericope, two questions can be raised:

(1) How do we recognize that a word or an expression is a LBH innovation? Avi Hurvitz has published an annotated list of LBH words:

- Avi Hurvitz, *A Concise Lexicon of Late Biblical Hebrew: Linguistic Innovations in the Writings of the Second Temple Period*, VTSup 160 (Leiden: Brill, 2014).

Hurvitz's methodology for establishing that a feature belongs to LBH is based on three criteria (the following quotations are from pp. 9–10 of the book just cited):

- *"Late Biblical Distribution"*: "The Biblical distribution of an LBH feature must be limited exclusively, or predominantly, to acknowledged late compositions (Esther, Daniel, Ezra, Nehemiah, Chronicles)."
- *"Linguistic Contrast with Classical Equivalents"*: the feature must have an equivalent in CBH that it came to replace (otherwise one could argue that its absence from CBH texts is due to accidental distribution).
- *"Extra-Biblical Corroboration"*: "The linguistic element under examination must be commonly attested in extra-Biblical sources contemporary with or following LBH (the DSS, Ben-Sira, RH [= Rabbinic Hebrew], IA [= Imperial Aramaic], etc.)."

(2) How do we establish that a text is late?

- Here Hurvitz uses the criterion of *"accumulation"*: "A text suspected of being of post-Classical provenance can be so classified only if it contains an abundance of late linguistic features." Indeed, "early authors could at times employ rare or foreign words whose intensified usage became typical only in the Second Temple period."

3.2 EXAMPLES

The following examples are designed to illustrate the use, often in combination, of the criteria mentioned above related to detecting scribal activity. For each example, the relevant criteria will be explicitly indicated.

EXAMPLE 3.2a ▸ Genesis 1 and 2

Criteria: 1 and 5

Both Gen 1 and Gen 2 contain an account of the creation of humans and animals. While both of these chapters also include much unique material, the overlap is undeniable and creates some redundancy. Moreover, the sequence is not the same: the animals are created before the humans in Gen 1, but it is the other way around in Gen 2. Furthermore, the terminology differs: for instance, the name of God is Elohim in Gen 1 but Yhwh in Gen 2, and the Hebrew word אָדָם designates the humans collectively in Gen 1 but a specific male character ("Adam") in Gen 2.

Two criteria (redundancy and narrative tension) converge to show that these two chapters come from two distinct hands, possibly two sources. That said, readers have always managed—by neglecting the divergences or spontaneously harmonizing them—to read these two chapters in sequence without difficulty. Thus, the creation of Adam and Eve in Gen 2 looks like a flashback that zooms in on what happened when God created humans. The texts speak of the same God, who bears several names. Some translations attempt to harmonize the chronology by speaking of the animals that "God had formed" in Gen 2:7, but this is not grammatically warranted. In fact, the formal contradiction at the level of chronology is a problem only if one reads these accounts literally, which is an idea that would probably not have crossed the minds of their authors. At any rate, the juxtaposition of the two accounts proved fruitful for the formation of Genesis.

EXAMPLE 3.2b ▸ Judean Updates in Hosea

Criterion: 2

The book of Hosea contains oracles directed at the northern kingdom of Israel, and yet it sometimes also mentions Judah. There is no *a priori* reason why a prophet talking to Israel could not, in order to make a point, occasionally mention a neighboring country, especially one where the same God was worshiped. But in at least some of these cases, the sentence mentioning Judah is directed *toward* the Judeans. In such cases, most scholars think that the verses are most probably editorial glosses designed to "update" the book and make the oracles relevant for its new audience, the Judeans. Indeed, although the core of the book comes from Israel, it was handed down to us by the Judeans, who preserved and edited it. Because Hosea's oracles and threats were vindicated by the fall of Samaria in the late eighth century BCE, they were subsequently taken seriously by some Judeans, who believed they could serve as a warning for the worshipers of the same God in Judah. Their concern was the same as that of many preachers today: to explain how the text was relevant for their contemporaries.

For instance, Hos 4 contains a series of criticisms of the people of Israel and its priests, but several statements at the end of the chapter (marked in italics below) are clearly parenthetical remarks concerning Judah:

> *Though you prostitute yourself, O Israel, do not let Judah*
> *become guilty.*
> *Do not enter into Gilgal, or go up to Beth-aven,*
> *and do not swear, "As the Lord lives."*
> Like a stubborn heifer, Israel is stubborn;
> can the Lord now feed them like a lamb in a broad pasture?
> Ephraim is joined to idols—*let him alone.*
>
> (Hos 4:15–17)

The objective behind these additions is to say, "Do not make the same mistakes that Israel did!," by saying in particular, "Do not go to Israel's cultic centers at Gilgal and Beth-aven." (Beth-aven, which means "house of iniquity," is a pun on Bethel, "house of God.")

Another telling case of Judean updating is found in 12:2 [3]:

> The Lord has an indictment against *Judah*
> and will punish Jacob according to his ways
> and repay him according to his deeds.

Here both the literary context (which exclusively concerns Israel) and the poetic parallelism with "Jacob" in the next line indicate that Judah is most probably a secondary correction for "Israel."

EXAMPLE 3.2c ▸ Job 32–37

Criteria: 2 and 3

Most of the book of Job consists of a debate between Job and his friends Eliphaz, Bildad, and Zophar. However, in ch. 32, another man suddenly intervenes:

> So these three men ceased to answer Job, because he was righteous in his own eyes. Then Elihu son of Barachel the Buzite, of the family of Ram, became angry. He was angry at Job because he justified himself rather than God; he was angry also at Job's three friends because they had found no answer, though they had declared Job to be in the wrong. Now Elihu had waited to speak to Job, because they were older than he. (32:2–4)
>
> After this introduction, Elihu speaks for a long time—until the end of ch. 37, in fact! Three reasons lead many scholars to think that chs. 32–37 are an interpolation. First, Elihu's intervention is entirely unexpected, since he is never introduced before ch. 32, contrary to Eliphaz, Bildad, and Zophar, who are mentioned in the narrative prologue (Job 2:11). While the debate unfolding in chs. 4–31 looks like an intimate discussion between friends, we now learn that another person, not presented as a friend of Job's, was listening, which seems odd. Moreover, 32:4 ("Now Elihu had waited to speak to Job . . .") sounds like a justification for Elihu's unexpected appearance, which suggests that the redactor who inserted the passage was aware of the difficulty created by Elihu's presence.
>
> Second, right after Elihu's speeches, God reacts to *Job's* discourses, not Elihu's, as if the latter had not occurred or as if God were ignoring them. Third, Elihu is not mentioned in the epilogue, whereas Job's friends are (42:7–10). If God reacts to what these men said in their speeches to Job, why would he ignore Elihu's long and interesting speeches?
>
> To sum up, in this case it is both the interruption created by the presence of chs. 32–37 and the absence of the expected literary connections between it and the surrounding context that indicate that these chapters are an interpolation.
>
> That said, it has also been noted that Elihu's speeches serves as a bridge between the debate of Job and his friends (chs. 3–31) and God's intervention (chs. 38–40). Elihu already turns the attention of Job to the mysteries of God's creation (36:22–37:24), and this anticipates an important theme in God's own speeches.[8] Could this somehow counterbalance the strong impression that Elihu's speeches are an interpolation and hint at the fact that they come from the same author who wrote chs. 3–31 and 38–40? Some scholars think this is the case, though many find it unlikely. In the opinion of the latter group, a redactor may well have written these speeches in light of the context into which he wanted to insert them, precisely to serve as a bridge between Job's and God's speeches. At any rate, we can appreciate how Elihu's speeches were written in a more artful manner than exegetes once thought.

---

8. Choon-Leong Seow, *Job 1–21: Interpretation and Commentary*, Illuminations (Grand Rapids: Eerdmans, 2013), 31–37, esp. 37.

> **EXAMPLE 3.2d** ▸ **Isaiah 19:16–25**

Criteria: 4 and 6

Isaiah 19 begins with an oracle about Egypt (vv. 1–15) that predicts a series of afflictions, which are presented as a judgment of the Lord. The passage is written in a poetic style, as is typical for an oracle in Isaiah. Then, starting in v. 16 (and going through v. 25), the text suddenly switches to prose. In addition, this prose section contains five instances of the introductory formula "in that day" (vv. 16, 18, 19, 23, and 24), which serves as a backbone to this part of the chapter but which did not appear at all in vv. 1–15. Moreover, the text soon shifts to a series of astoundingly positive predictions (vv. 18–25). Five cities in Egypt will speak "the language of Canaan" (i.e., Hebrew) and swear allegiance to the Lord (v. 18), and the Egyptians will worship him (v. 21). The text ends with an extraordinary sentence: "Blessed be Egypt my people, and Assyria the work of my hands, and Israel my heritage." Furthermore, according to some scholars, vv. 19–21 allude to Jewish communities and worship in Egypt, which they regard as postexilic realities.[9] For all these reasons, many (though not all) commentators regard vv. 16–25 as an addition.

It could be countered that it would be gratuitous to assume that a prophet could not complete his negative oracle (concerning the present or the near future) with a positive one (concerning a remote future). This would impose unrealistic limitations on what a person in ancient Judah could have thought or imagined. That is correct. While exegetes in the past were often prone to ascribe only judgment oracles to preexilic prophets and to regard all the positive promises contained in the prophetic books as postexilic additions, scholars now regard this approach as simplistic. In the present case, however, the use of prose for oracular discourse is altogether unusual in Isaiah, and this creates a surprising contrast with the first part of the chapter.

But the most interesting issue concerns the universalistic perspective in vv. 16–25. This is not attested in the oracles that scholars unanimously ascribe to Isaiah himself, and the same holds true for all the other preexilic prophets. By contrast, universalistic ideas are a mark of the second half of Isaiah (chs. 40–66), which most exegetes date to the sixth century and later. The few universalistic texts found in the first half of the book, notably the one in 2:1–5, are thus often regarded as interpolations made in the sixth century or later. But is this not the result of circular reasoning? Why would

---

9. The sole attested Jewish temples in Egypt were located in Elephantine and Leontopolis; we have evidence of the existence of the former in the late fifth century BCE, while the latter was built in the second century BCE. The text does not necessarily allude to the Leontopolis temple (that would be quite late for a text that is present in Greek Isaiah, which was translated in the second century BCE, and in several Dead Sea scrolls), but we do not know of similar temples that existed prior to the Persian period.

2:1–5 not, on the contrary, show that Isaiah himself, in the eighth century, entertained universalistic ideas? While this is theoretically possible, this too rests on a hypothesis, since it is not possible to prove that Isaiah himself wrote this passage. The clinching argument, for most scholars, is the fact that the universalistic perspective is very well attested in the sixth century, whereas its possible earlier attestations are rare and exceptional. Moreover, these exceptions stand out from their immediate literary contexts; if Isaiah really did have universalistic ideas, then one would expect many of his other oracles to be colored by them. Given that the book was updated over centuries, it is not far-fetched to hypothesize that these exceptions are additions.

By way of a tentative conclusion, there are good reasons to think that vv. 16–25 are an addition, although it must be acknowledged that these reasons do not amount to absolute proof.[10] This is a typical situation in redactional analysis.

Now, even among the majority of scholars who think that the end of the chapter is secondary, there is hesitation about vv. 16–17. Since these two verses contain *negative* predictions about Egypt, some regard them as an integral part of the first part of the chapter. If so, the redactor responsible for the addition of vv. 18–25 imitated the introductory formula "in that day" found in v. 16a. On the other hand, the fact that vv. 16–17 are in prose makes it likely that they constitute the beginning of the interpolation. Moreover, since these verses state that the Egyptians will be frightened of the Lord and of the Judeans, which already represents a shift in their attitude, they serve as a bridge from the first to the second half of the chapter. Writing such a bridge makes more sense if at least part of vv. 18–25 is already present or is added at the same time as vv. 16–17. In fact, a number of exegetes surmise that vv. 16–25 are actually made up of successive additions, each new redactor adding to the work of his predecessors by imitating them in introducing his own contribution with the same formula, "in that day."[11] If so, these subparts could date from various times. Nevertheless, this hypothesis does not necessarily entail ascribing a very late date to the last ones: interestingly, because the Assyrian empire, named here, vanished at the end of the seventh century BCE, while later ancient Near Eastern powers (such as Babylonia and Persia) are not mentioned here, J. J. M. Roberts argues that vv. 23–25 would not have made much sense after the seventh century BCE.[12] Unless,

---

10. For instance, J. J. M. Roberts does not rule out the possibility that most of these verses come from Isaiah himself. The exception, however, is v. 18, which Roberts finds difficult to ascribe to this prophet (see J. J. M. Roberts, *First Isaiah: A Commentary*, Hermeneia [Minneapolis: Fortress, 2015], 262–64).

11. See Joseph Blenkinsopp, *Isaiah 1–39: A New Translation with Introduction and Commentary*, AB 19 (New York: Doubleday, 2000), 317.

12. Roberts, *First Isaiah*, 264.

of course, Assyria serves here as a cypher for an "eastern empire"—which is not impossible, though this is far from clear.

EXAMPLE 3.2e ▸ Isaiah 17:7–8

Criteria: 2 and 6

Isaiah 17 contains an oracle about Damascus (the capital of Aram) that, in reality, concerns the downfall of both Aram and Israel, the Northern Kingdom (vv. 1–6 and 9–10). Around 732 BCE, the Assyrians took Damascus, put an end to the kingdom of Aram, and annexed the northern regions of Israel. A decade later, they took Samaria and annexed what remained of the Northern Kingdom. This seems to be the background of this oracle.

However, vv. 7–8 apparently have nothing to do with this historical context: "On that day people will look to their Maker, with their eyes on the Holy One of Israel; they will not have regard for the altars, the work of their hands, and they will not look to what their own fingers have made, either the sacred poles or the altars of incense."

These verses have an eschatological sound and a universalistic perspective to them; they envision a time when humans in general will turn to the Lord. As a result, most exegetes regard vv. 7–8 as an interpolation, perhaps made by a redactor who had in mind the tradition of "the Day of the LORD," an important theme in some prophetic books. In the context of an oracle that concerned both a foreign nation and Israel, a redactor may have felt the need to add a note of hope to the effect that all humans will, "on that day," repent and turn to the Lord. The fact that these verses are secondary does not mean that their contribution to the theological contents of this passage is irrelevant—quite the contrary.

Interestingly, it seems that vv. 7–8 were themselves later subjected to minor editing. The expression "and the sacred poles or the altars of incense" is not part of the symmetrical structure of v. 8:[13]

    A they will not gaze at

        B *the altars*, the work of their hands,

        B′ and at what their own fingers have made

    A′ they will not look,

    ? *and the sacred poles or the altars of incense.*

---

13. This is my own translation; the NRSVue modifies the sequence of the text.

In fact, this expression is appended to the sentence like an afterthought. Furthermore, it introduces the theme of sacred poles, which is never mentioned elsewhere in Isaiah (Isa 27:9 is the exception that proves the rule, since Isa 24–27 is regarded by virtually all scholars as an addition). The same scribe probably inserted "the altars" too, since this word betrays the same concern; lists of illicit cultic paraphernalia often include both altars and sacred poles (e.g., Deut 12:3). Also, the parallelism between B and B′ would be neater without "the altars." This redactor wanted to make explicit what, according to his own interpretation, remained implicit in v. 8.

EXAMPLE 3.2f ▸ Genesis 24

Criteria: 4 and 6

Two lines of evidence indicate that Gen 24 is most probably an addition made to the Abraham cycle in the Persian period.[14] First, it contains a number of features of Late Biblical Hebrew, for instance "let me sip" (הַגְמִיאִינִי) in v. 17. It uses the expression "God of heaven" (אֱלֹהֵי הַשָּׁמַיִם) (vv. 3, 7), which is typical of—and as far as we know, an innovation from—the Persian period. In the Hebrew Bible, this expression is elsewhere found only in texts dating from the Persian period or later (Jonah 1:9; Ezra 1:2; Neh 1:4–5; 2:4, 20; 2 Chr 36:23). It is a calque of the Aramaic phrase אֱלָהּ שְׁמַיָּא, which is typically found in texts from the Persian and Hellenistic periods, both in the Bible (Dan 2:18–19, 37, 44) and in epigraphic sources (the Elephantine papyri).

Second, this chapter presupposes a prohibition against marrying a foreign woman, which plays a crucial role in a book from the Persian period (Ezra-Nehemiah). This last argument would probably not be decisive on its own, since one could imagine that the same issue was a concern in certain circles before its Persian-period attestations. But this argument reinforces the two previous ones by showing that Gen 24 is very much at home in the Persian period. The author of Gen 24 wanted to make it clear that Abraham, the great ancestor, already cared about avoiding mixed marriages.

---

14. See Konrad Schmid, "How to Identify a Persian Period Text in the Pentateuch," in *On Dating Biblical Texts to the Persian Period: Discerning Criteria and Establishing Epochs*, ed. Richard J. Bautch and Mark Lackowski (Tübingen: Mohr Siebeck, 2019), 115.

EXAMPLE 3.2g ▸ Numbers 22:22–35

Criteria: 5 and 7

Numbers 22:22–35 is one of the most surprising narratives in the Hebrew Bible, since one of its main characters is a speaking donkey. A combination of factors indicate that this passage is an interpolation. First, the story introduces a tension with its immediate context. Just before this narrative, in v. 20, God permits Balaam to go with the Moabite officials, and the next day, Balaam does so (v. 21). But v. 22 says that "God's anger was kindled because he [viz., Balaam] was going, and the angel of the LORD took his stand in the road as his adversary." This does not seem consistent with the divine permission given the previous night.

Second, the narrative is framed by a *Wiederaufnahme*: that is, v. 35 echoes vv. 20–21:

vv. 20–21

That night God came to Balaam and said to him, "If the men have come to summon you, get up and go with them, but do only what I tell you to do." So Balaam got up in the morning, saddled his donkey, and went with the officials of Moab.

v. 35

The angel of the LORD said to Balaam, "Go with the men; but speak only what I tell you to speak." So Balaam went on with the officials of Balak.

Why did a scribe insert the narrative of vv. 22–35? The irony it presents is that Balaam, the renowned seer who claims to be "the man whose eye is clear, . . . who sees the visions of the Almighty, who falls, but with eyes uncovered" (Num 24:3–4) is not able to see an angel, whereas his donkey is! In the claim just quoted, Balaam may allude to ecstatic trances during which he falls but receives a divine revelation; the verb "uncover" (גלה) often means "to reveal" in Hebrew. But this is the same Hebrew verb that is used in the story of the donkey when the angel "opened [lit., uncovered] the eyes of Balaam" so that he could finally see the angel (22:31). It is plausible that the story of the donkey was added as a counterpoint to the main narrative about Balaam in Num 22–24, which sheds a positive light on this character. Indeed, another tradition, attested in several texts, notably elsewhere in Numbers (31:16), had a clearly negative view of him (see also Josh 13:22 and, later, 2 Pet 2:15; Jude 11; Rev 2:14). The redactor who inserted the donkey story chose to preserve for us both perspectives about Balaam, which renders the text more interesting.

> **EXAMPLE 3.2h** ▸ Exodus 3:1–4:18 and 6:2–7:7

Criterion: 1

In Exod 6:2, the Lord introduces himself to Moses, as if they had not already met earlier (in Exod 3). Then he announces that he will deliver his people from bondage in Egypt and bring them into the country promised to the patriarchs (vv. 5–7). He orders Moses to speak to Pharaoh, and Moses does so (vv. 10–13), albeit saying that he has difficulty speaking, which leads the Lord to make Aaron Moses' spokesperson (6:28–7:7). All of this has already been told, in the same sequence, in chs. 3:1–4:18, and yet it is reported in ch. 6 as if it were fresh news. At the same time, there are interesting differences. Notably, in ch. 6 (v. 30) Moses is afraid to speak in front of Pharaoh, whereas in ch. 4 (vv. 1, 10) he is afraid to speak in front of the people.

Therefore, there are good reasons to consider Exod 3:1–4:18 and Exod 6:2–7:7 as parallel accounts from different sources or redactions. This does not exclude the possibility that either of them is itself multilayered, as the next example will show.

> **EXAMPLE 3.2i** ▸ Exodus 6:14–25

Criteria: 2, 4, and 7

Exodus 6 contains a genealogy of Moses and Aaron (vv. 14–25). It clearly stands out in the middle of the narrative, not only due to its literary genre and style but also because it interrupts the flow of the text. In addition, it is framed by a *Wiederaufnahme* composed of vv. 12–13, on the one hand, and vv. 26–30, on the other.[15] In sum, vv. 14–25 (and vv. 26–30, written to create the resumptive repetition) are an addition to Exod 6.

vv. 12–13

  A *Moses' difficulty speaking*

    But Moses spoke to the LORD, "The Israelites have not listened to me; why should Pharaoh listen to me, poor speaker that I am?"

---

15. Also, the latter passage does not simply echo vv. 12–13: it parallels its main elements *in reverse order* (see below), in keeping with Seidel's law (see the sidebar "Inverted Quotations, or Seidel's Law" in chapter 12). Here, this literary device reinforces the link between the two parts of the *Wiederaufnahme*.

B   *The Lord's command to urge Pharaoh to free the Israelites*

> Thus the LORD spoke to Moses and Aaron, and gave them orders regarding the Israelites and Pharaoh king of Egypt, charging them to free the Israelites from the land of Egypt.

[vv. 14–25 = **genealogy of Moses and Aaron**]

vv. 26–30

B′   *The Lord's command to urge Pharaoh to free the Israelites*

> It was this same Aaron and Moses to whom the LORD said, "Bring the Israelites out of the land of Egypt, company by company." It was they who spoke to Pharaoh king of Egypt to bring the Israelites out of Egypt, the same Moses and Aaron. On the day when the LORD spoke to Moses in the land of Egypt, the LORD said to Moses, "I am the LORD; tell Pharaoh king of Egypt all that I am speaking to you."

A′   *Moses' difficulty speaking*

> But Moses said to the LORD, "Since I am a poor speaker, why should Pharaoh listen to me?"

EXAMPLE 3.2j ▸ **2 Kings 17:34–40**

Criteria: 5 and 7

Second Kings 17 serves as an epilogue to the history of the Northern Kingdom. After an account of the kingdom's demise (vv. 1–6) and a theological analysis (vv. 7–23), the text mentions the forced settlement of foreign peoples in the former territory of Israel (v. 24), characterizing their religious activity as a syncretistic mix of their own traditions and Yahwistic practices (vv. 25–34a). This section concludes with the statement "So *they worshiped the* LORD but also served their own gods, after the manner of the nations from among whom they had been carried away. To this day they continue to practice their former customs" (vv. 33–34a).

Then, surprisingly, we read: "*They do **not** worship the* LORD" (v. 34b). In fact, the section spanning vv. 34–41 seems to introduce another perspective on the inhabitants of the northern territories. This section regards them as "sons of Jacob" who are bound by the law of Moses, recalls the command of the Lord to obey this law, and concludes that "they would not listen" (v. 40a).

The next, final sentences of the chapter, however, take up the other, preceding view, according to which the inhabitants are syncretistic "nations." The way in which these sentences do this is by using expressions from

vv. 33–34a (or synonyms of them), as marked here in italics: "but *they continued to practice their former custom*. So *these nations worshiped the* LORD, *but also served their carved images*; to this day their children and their children's children *continue to do as their ancestors did*" (vv. 40b–41).

How do we disentangle this complicated situation? The key is the repetitive resumption I just mentioned: it is clearly a *Wiederaufnahme* that fittingly frames the paragraph putting forward the "alternative view" (vv. 34b–40a). This indicates that vv. 34b–40a is an addition that provides another perspective on the subject.

EXAMPLE 3.2k ▸ 2 Kings 18:13–19:37

Criteria: 1 and 5

The invasion of Judah by the Assyrian king Sennacherib in 701 BCE—as well as the concomitant siege of Jerusalem—was one of the most important events in the history of the country. The second book of Kings devotes a good deal of space to this subject. First, 18:13–16 comprises a sober report according to which Hezekiah apologized to Sennacherib and paid him tribute. But then a long narrative begins that spans 18:17–19:9a: Assyrian envoys try to scare the Judeans, Hezekiah reacts, the prophet Isaiah gives an oracle, and then the Assyrians hear news about an imminent attack by a Kushite, which seems to suggest that they will leave to address this issue. Yet the narrative continues (19:9b–37), and we read again about speeches by Assyrian envoys designed to intimidate the Judeans, Hezekiah's reaction, and oracles by Isaiah; finally, an "angel of the LORD" decimates the Assyrian army, so Sennacherib leaves. In sum, we read in 18:17–19:37 two successive accounts that have the same structure, although their endings differ:

    a Intimidating speeches by Assyrian envoys (18:17–35)

       b Hezekiah's reaction (18:36–19:4)

          c Isaiah's oracle (19:5–7)

             d Motive for the departure of the Assyrian king (19:8–9a)

    a′ Intimidating speeches by Assyrian envoys (19:9b–13)

       b′ Hezekiah's reaction (19:14–19)

          c′ Isaiah's oracles (19:20–34)

             d′ Motive for the departure of the Assyrian king (19:35–37)

> But it is not just that the narratives are similar. Amazingly, the characters behave in the second narrative as if they had not gone through the same steps in the first. For instance, Hezekiah is completely surprised, as if he had not already heard about the Assyrian threats. In addition, the two narratives provide two different reasons for the Assyrian army leaving without taking Jerusalem. Exegetes have long recognized that we are dealing here with *two alternative versions of the same story*. In fact, 18:13–16 already formed a brief version, since it provided a reason why Sennacherib left: Hezekiah paid him tribute. In the end, then, one can distinguish three successive parts: A (18:14–16), B1 (18:13; 18:17–19:9a; 19:37) and B2 (19:9b–36).[16] The final redactor of this section of Kings has chosen to preserve for us three different accounts of the same events.[17]

Exercises for Chapter 3

Exercise A

Read 1 Kgs 6:7–15 in the NRSVue (or any other modern translation that is essentially based on the MT). Then read the NETS translation to compare, with respect to the passage's key features, the LXX equivalent of the same passage. An important textual difference should immediately appear. How do you explain it? What bearing does it have on the compositional history of the passage?

---

16. The exact limits of B1 and B2 are debated. I ascribe 18:13 to B1 because in the parallel text in Isa 37–38, the equivalent of this verse immediately precedes the equivalent of 2 Kgs 18:17–19:9a. Also, I consider 2 Kgs 19:37 to really be the end of B1, though it also serves as the end of the combined narratives. Note that other models than that of the three successive accounts have been proposed, but I find this one to be more compelling; see, recently, e.g., Dan'el Kahn, *Sennacherib's Campaign Against Judah: A Source Analysis of Isaiah 36–37*, SOTSMS (Cambridge: Cambridge University Press, 2020).

17. Interestingly, this means that this final redactor did not make a mistake by preserving these diverging versions; doing so was a deliberate move. Likewise, in other examples that were presented in this chapter, we have encountered situations where a redactor inserted a passage in a book as a counterpoint to a previous redaction; and yet, the later redactor chose to preserve what his or her predecessor had written, rather than deleting it. The preservation of diverging traditions or views is a very significant feature of the Hebrew Bible, which foreshadows the love for debate that is found in later Judaism. On this subject, see Benjamin D. Sommer, *Revelation and Authority: Sinai in Jewish Scripture and Tradition* (New Haven: Yale University Press, 2015), 216–18.

Exercise B

Genesis 36 contains a list of rulers from Edom. Find an indication in this passage that helps to determine that it was not written before a certain date (see v. 31).

Exercise C

The books of Kings normally follow this compositional rule: the information concerning a king is provided within a framework delimited by standard formulae. Thus, a typical section concerning a reign

- is introduced by chronological indications about when the person became king and the duration of his reign, as well as by a theological evaluation (see, e.g., 2 Kgs 15:1–3), and

- concludes with formulae about further sources concerning his reign, and about his death, burial, and successor (e.g., 2 Kgs 15:6–7).

A number of verses that appear to lie outside these boundaries are considered additions by exegetes. Read 2 Kings 15 and find two such verses.

Exercise D

Read Hos 1:7, identifying possible glosses and determining their function. Then identify a possible gloss in Hos 5:5, and infer what would be the earliest possible date for it.

Exercise E

Read the narrative about Elijah on Mount Horeb in 1 Kgs 19:8–18. This passage contains a lengthy repetition: find it. Some commentators regard this repetition as a *Wiederaufnahme* marking an interpolation,[18] while others are skeptical and note that this hypothesis "impoverishes the basic story greatly."[19] What is your opinion? Do you think there is an addition or that the repetition was there from the start, as a literary device?

Exercise F

Although today the patriarchs are among the most-well-known figures from the Hebrew Bible, they are rarely mentioned in the historical books from Judges to Kings. Many scholars believe that the earliest texts about them were written relatively late in the monarchic period (in the seventh century BCE). They also tend to think that the oral traditions about the patriarchs, despite being older, were originally restricted to certain regions and only spread to the whole country at a late date.

Against this background, depending on your own understanding of this issue, what do you make of the rare and isolated mentions of Abraham, Isaac, and Jacob in the books of Kings (1 Kgs 18:36; 2 Kgs 13:23)? Would you regard these as additions?

---

18. E.g., Ernst Würthwein, *Die Bücher der Könige: 1. Kön. 17 – 2. Kön. 25*, ATD 11.2 (Göttingen: Vandenhoeck & Ruprecht, 1984), 160–61.

19. Mordechai Cogan, *1 Kings: A New Translation and Commentary*, AB 10 (New York: Doubleday, 2001), 456n1.

CHAPTER 4

COMPOSITIONAL CRITICISM: SYNTHESIS

OVERVIEW

In the preceding chapter, we saw how it is possible to detect scribal activity. If you have detected *several* scribal interventions—additions, for instance—scattered throughout a text, the next step is to determine whether these are interconnected and form a redactional layer. At any rate, it is important to situate the scribal activity you have detected within the history of the formation of the biblical book in which the text is found. Two general scenarios are possible here: Perhaps you will be able to recognize features that are characteristic of a known composition or redaction. If so, then the setting and date of the latter will *ipso facto* apply to the scribal activity you have detected. If correlating this activity with a known composition or redaction is not possible, however, you can use a number of criteria to try to date the activity. Since scribal activity typically involved the addition of a (portion of) text, the general, underlying question is thus, "How do we date a portion of text?" What is at stake is not ascribing this text a *precise* date, but understanding the purpose of the scribal activity in question and the role it played in the compositional history of the book under consideration.

In sum, we need to explore the following four issues:

❶ HOW TO DETERMINE IF SEVERAL SCRIBAL INTERVENTIONS BELONG TO THE SAME COMPOSITIONAL LAYER

❷ HOW CERTAIN SCRIBAL ACTIVITY CAN BE CORRELATED WITH KNOWN COMPOSITIONS OR REDACTIONS

❸ HOW TO DATE A TEXT

❹ HOW TO DESCRIBE THE COMPOSITIONAL HISTORY OF THE PASSAGE WE ARE STUDYING

4.1 HOW TO DETERMINE IF SEVERAL SCRIBAL INTERVENTIONS BELONG TO THE SAME COMPOSITIONAL LAYER

If you have detected several scribal interventions, a number of criteria may make it likely that they originated with the same redactor or editor:

Ⓐ They may have some **common formal features**: distinctive vocabulary (including proper names), phraseology, or Late Biblical Hebrew features.

Ⓑ They may reflect the **same ideas** or serve the **same purpose**.

Ⓒ They may belong to the **same subplot** that was not part of the earliest form of the text.

Ⓓ They may be **plusses** found in a single textual witness.

As always, if only one such criterion is met, that may prove insufficient to show that the scribal interventions in question are related. And even if more than one of these criteria are met, it may be that a series of similar additions in the text are due to *successive* scribal interventions that were made over a long period by scribes whose method was to imitate their predecessors. Nevertheless, a combination of these criteria being met increases the likelihood that we are indeed dealing with one compositional layer. The examples below will illustrate both the usefulness and the limits of this line of inquiry.

> **EXAMPLE 4.1a ▸ Judean Updates in Hosea**
>
> In Example 3.2b, we saw that some glosses and changes in Hosea were designed to make the oracles relevant to a Judean context. The exact list of these "updates" is debated, however. In his commentary, Andrew Macintosh lists the following verses as places where he detects interventions by Judean redactors: 1:7; 3:5; 4:5, 15; 5:5; 6:11a, 11b; 9:4; 10:11; 11:10; 12:1 [2], 3 [4].[1] Because these interventions betray the same overall concern (applying the oracles to a Judean context), we could at first be tempted to hypothesize that they are all elements of the same compositional layer. But it is also conceivable that they were made in several stages. On closer inspection, it becomes apparent that not all of them presuppose exactly the same background; for instance, some allude to the Babylonian exile while others could be criticisms made earlier, during the royal period. Macintosh therefore suggests that "they were made

---

1. Andrew A. Macintosh, *A Critical and Exegetical Commentary on Hosea*, ICC (Edinburgh: T&T Clark, 1997), lxxi–lxxii.

piecemeal over the course of two centuries," though he tentatively dates the majority of them to the seventh century BCE.

EXAMPLE 4.1b ▸ **Isaiah 19:16–25 and Other Positive Statements about the Nations**

In Example 3.2d, we saw that the end of the oracle against Egypt in Isa 19 may be an addition or a series of additions (vv. 16–25). The most distinctive feature of these verses is that they mark a sudden turn to positive statements about Egypt. However, it should be observed that in general the oracles against the nations in Isaiah (chs. 13–23) do not only contain judgment: quite often their criticisms are followed by promises of restoration for these peoples, so much so that one could call these chapters "oracles *about* the nations." For example, such positive statements can be found in 14:32; 16:1–5; 18:7; 19:16–25; and 23:15–18 (and perhaps also 14:1–2). This raises the question whether these statements could constitute a compositional layer.

This is conceivable, but it is not certain that all of these statements were made at the same time. In the latest study on the subject, Jongkyung Lee notes that the positive stance and inclusive attitude toward the nations in 14:1–2, 32; 16:1–5; and 18:7 are comparable to what we find in Isa 40–55, and he asserts that these passages constitute a compositional layer added by Deutero-Isaiah (i.e., the main redactor of Isa 40–55) or his circle. On the other hand, he argues that 19:16–25 and 23:15–18 do not belong to this layer: since the former presupposes the existence of a temple to Yhwh in Egypt and the latter alludes to the seventy years of exile, he regards them as postexilic additions.[2]

4.2 HOW CERTAIN SCRIBAL ACTIVITY CAN BE CORRELATED WITH A KNOWN COMPOSITION OR COMPOSITIONAL LAYER

How can you determine if a scribal change can be attributed to a known composition, redaction, or compositional layer? The answer is simple: you need first to **become familiar with the most important compositions and redactions found in the Hebrew**

---

2. Jongkyung Lee, *A Redactional Study of Isaiah 13–23*, OTRM (Oxford: Oxford University Press, 2018), 179–82. Lee also adds 14:1–2 to the same compositional layer as 14:32, 16:1–5, and 18:7.

Bible and with their **characteristic features**. Then you will be able to **recognize** the latter when you meet them in a particular text. This is not the place to describe the existing theories; that is done in most introductory courses and handbooks on the Hebrew Bible, as well as in exegetical commentaries. In this chapter, sidebars will serve as reminders of what is necessary to know in some select cases (the Pentateuch, and P in particular; the Deuteronomistic History), and this will serve as background for this chapter's examples.

> **EXAMPLE 4.2a** ▸ **Genesis 1 and 2**
>
> In Example 3.2a, we saw that Gen 1:1–2:3 and Gen 2:4–3:24 are two distinct creation accounts. As it happens, Gen 1 is the starting point of P (for this siglum, see the sidebar "Current Models for the Formation of the Pentateuch" below). Many scholars believe that, in similar fashion, Gen 2 (in fact, Gen 2–3) belongs to a continuous story, named J (for "the Yahwist" [German *der Jahwist*]) in the Documentary Hypothesis. Others doubt this and prefer to regard Gen 2–3 as one of many non-P fragments, or complements to P.

Current Models for the Formation of the Pentateuch

Two main models currently exist to explain the formation of the Pentateuch:

The Documentary Hypothesis. Developed in the nineteenth century and synthesized by Julius Wellhausen, this theory posits that four documents (i.e., standalone works) were merged: J (the Yahwist), E (the Elohist), P (the Priestly document), and D (the Deuteronomic document). The division of these sources was based on a variety of criteria; some of them, especially those based on style and vocabulary, came to be regarded by many scholars as weak. In addition, in the version of the theory put forward by Wellhausen, the four documents corresponded to specific periods in the history of Israel and reflected the development of religious views. These ideas also came to be severely criticized. That said, many scholars, especially in North America, still hold to the Documentary Hypothesis, albeit avoiding the preceding excesses.

A number of scholars, often called **Neo-Documentarians** (e.g., Baruch Schwartz, Joel Baden, and Jeffrey Stackert), have recently refined this hypothesis and introduced some differences, notably:

- The criteria used to disentangle and recognize the documents mostly concern literary inconsistencies (which are used to separate documents) and narrative continuity (which is used to link passages); more

- questionable elements, such as differences in style, are used only minimally and in combination with more solid arguments.
- The approach is purely literary; it sets aside arguments related to historical criticism and questions of dating and of the historical setting of the documents.
- The four documents are, in practice, treated as independent sources that a single compiler, whose goal was that they would all be preserved, merged with much care and minimal intervention.

For an excellent introduction, see:

- Joel S. Baden, *The Composition of the Pentateuch: Renewing the Documentary Hypothesis*, AYBRL (New Haven: Yale University Press, 2012).

For a detailed description of the characteristic features of this approach, and a thoughtful criticism, see:

- Konrad Schmid, "The Neo-Documentarian Manifesto: A Critical Reading," *JBL* 140 (2021): 461–79.

The Traditio-Historical Model. In the eyes of its critics, the most important weaknesses of the Documentary Hypothesis—whether in its old form or in the Neo-Documentarian version—concern the viability of J and E and the underlying model of the formation of the Pentateuch. First, E is considered to be so fragmentarily attested that its very existence is regarded as implausible. As for J, its existence presupposes that the stories in Genesis about the patriarchs are linked to the story of the exodus. But most scholars today admit that these were originally two separate traditions corresponding to two models of the origins of Israel, one endogenous (according to which the ancestors—i.e., the patriarchs—already lived in the land), the other exogenous (according to which the ancestors came from another country, Egypt). While the Documentary Hypothesis states that J combined these two traditions into a separate written document, some of its critics deny this; they argue that P was the only separate document to bridge Genesis and Exodus.

More generally, a number of scholars, following Rolf Rendtorff, believe that—rather than constituting continuous strands that stretch from (more or less) the beginning of the Pentateuch to its end and thus cover most periods of the same overall story—the writings that lay behind the Pentateuch developed around more limited traditions concerning different periods (the Primeval History, the patriarchal period, the exodus, etc.). Even P is often regarded as originally stretching from Gen 1 to Exod 40 or Lev 16 only. This traditio-historical model (as it is known) sees the growth of the Pentateuch as having mainly involved a process whereby one or two strands (P, at any rate) was or were supplemented by successive additions, rather than the Pentateuch's formation being the result of the merging of documents.

Yet this approach encompasses a great variety of theories, with no consensus in view. The most divisive issue is whether a non-P writing (perhaps anterior to P) existed that joined some patriarchal traditions and an exodus story (which would be a sort of J). One's view on this depends on how one analyzes a limited series of passages that bridge Genesis and Exodus, including Gen 15:13–15, Exod 1:1–6, Exod 3, and Exod 6.

Excellent introductions to the diachronic study of the Pentateuch are:

- Jean-Louis Ska, *Introduction to Reading the Pentateuch*, trans. Pascale Dominique (Winona Lake, IN: Eisenbrauns, 2006).
- Joel S. Baden and Jeffrey Stackert, eds., *The Oxford Handbook of the Pentateuch* (New York: Oxford University Press, 2021); see the chapters in section II ("The Formation of the Pentateuch").

In addition to J, E, P, and D, there is another letter that you need to know: H. This stands for "the Holiness Code," a name scholars have given to Lev 17–26. This section of Leviticus contains a number of distinctive features with regard to both its terminology (even compared to Lev 1–16) and its ideas. H is very much concerned with holiness, which it "democratizes": compared to the situation in Exodus and the first part of Leviticus, holiness, according to H, is no longer the exclusive characteristic of the sanctuary and the priests but must also extend to the whole land and the whole people of Israel. Moreover, in H's view, impurity can now be contracted through ethical misbehavior. These ideas are part of an innovative and fascinating theological project. H presupposes chs. 1–16 and is a development of their theology and laws. Following the seminal work of Israel Knohl, many scholars admit that a Holiness School added passages in a number of places in the Pentateuch:

- Israel Knohl, *The Sanctuary of Silence: The Priestly Torah and the Holiness School* (Minneapolis: Fortress, 1995).

EXAMPLE 4.2b ▸ Exodus 3:1–4:18 and 6:2–7:7

In Example 3.2h, we saw that Exodus contains two parallel accounts of Moses' commission: 3:1–4:18 and 6:2–7:7. The latter story contains a new statement: here the Lord indicates that the patriarchs did not know him by the name Yhwh; instead, they called him "God Almighty" (Exod 6:2). This represents a striking difference with certain texts in Genesis (e.g., 4:26) but is consistent with P texts, in which the patriarchs use the term "God Almighty" rather than "Yhwh." In fact, this notion of the use of different divine names in different historical periods is a major hallmark of P. As a result, most scholars ascribe Exod 6:2–7:7 to P. We also saw in Example 3.2i that the genealogy of Moses and Aaron in Exod 6:14–25 is likely an interpolation. Therefore, this genealogy is either a post-P addition or simply an internal development of P.

What about 3:1–4:18? The Documentary Hypothesis sees in this passage a mixture of J and E.[3] Joel Baden, a leading Neo-Documentarian, assigns most of it to E because it contains features that are characteristic of the core E texts and features that are at variance with J. For instance, the mountain where the Lord appears to Moses is called "Horeb, the moutain of God" (3:1), which is typical of E; Moses' uncle is called Jethro, not Reuel, as in the previous passage (2:18), which belongs to J; the Lord's name is revealed in 3:13–16, whereas in J it is known from the beginning of human history (4:26).[4]

Scholars who do not believe in the existence of J or E regard 3:1–4:18 as a "non-P" text.[5] But "non-P" is not a unified source or document. The same kinds of differences between 3:1–4:18 and the surrounding passages that were noted just above, together with the fact that this section of text interrupts the flow of the non-P texts (in Exod 2 and 4:19–20) concerning Moses in Midian, indicate that 3:1–4:18 was a non-P text interpolated within another non-P strand.

The numerous features that 3:1–4:18 and 6:2–7:7 have in common suggest to many scholars that one of these accounts constitutes a rewriting of the other. However, exegetes disagree about the direction of "literary dependence" (that is, they debate which text was rewritten in light of which).[6] There are two possibilities:

- 6:2–7:7 depends on 3:1–4:18. If this is correct, P was not necessarily the first to create a bridge between the ancestral stories and the exodus, since there was already a non-P strand (3:1–4:18) that did this. That is, in this scenario there existed a pre-Priestly composition that stretched from the patriarchal narratives to the exodus story.

- 3:1–4:18 is a reinterpretation of Exod 6:2–7:7. In this case, 3:1–4:18 is post-Priestly; it is a non-P text written in light of a P text.

---

3. Samuel Rolles Driver, *An Introduction to the Literature of the Old Testament*, 2nd ed. (New York: Scribner's Sons, 1914), 23.

4. Joel S. Baden, *The Composition of the Pentateuch: Renewing the Documentary Hypothesis*, AYBRL (New Haven: Yale University Press, 2012), 120–21.

5. See David M. Carr, *The Formation of the Hebrew Bible* (New York: Oxford University Press, 2011), 118–24.

6. See the thoughtful discussion in Carr, *Formation of the Hebrew Bible*, 140–44. We will explore the notion of "literary dependence" in chapter 12.

| EXAMPLE 4.2c | ▸ | Exodus 12:15–20 |

Before the Hebrews leave Egypt, the Lord prescribes various actions for them to do (Exod 12:1–28). Some of these, like slaughtering a lamb (12:1–13, 21–23), are designed to be done immediately: that is, they concern what the people are to do the night before they leave Egypt. Some verses add that this will be the basis for future, annual commemorations (12:24–28). By contrast, the prescriptions about the Feast of Unleavened Bread (12:15–20) concern later commemorations only. This festival will echo the fact that the Hebrews will have left Egypt in a hurry, taking "their dough before it was leavened" (v. 34). But the Hebrews are not to eat unleavened bread for seven days before crossing the Sea of Reeds.

Because the prescription in 12:15–20 presupposes a reality that has not yet taken place (when Moses is supposed to have given this prescription, the Hebrews had not yet left Egypt in a hurry), it is clear that this prescription was not really said at the time when the narrative situates it.[7] Rather, it seems to be a prescription from elsewhere that was placed here because of its connection to v. 34. As a matter of fact, another law concerning the Feast of Unleavened Bread is found in Lev 23:5–8. A close comparison of the two texts shows that most of the material in Lev 23:5–8 also appears in Exod 12:15–20, *including some terminology that is proper to Lev 17–26*, that is, to H.[8] Therefore, scholars have concluded that Exod 12:15–20 was composed in light of Lev 23:5–8, rather than the other way around. Exodus 12:15–20 is a version of the same law but has been adapted to its present context in the Passover narrative (cf. Exod 12:17) and has been updated.[9] As Christophe Nihan writes, "the function of this supplement is clear: in conformity with Lev 23:5–8, it connects P's legislation on Passover in Ex 12:1–3 with the celebration of Unleavened Bread and thus harmonizes it with H's calendar."[10]

Depending on the scholarly theory that one adopts regarding the passages in the Pentateuch that were influenced by H, it may or may not be possible to suggest a more precise date for them. There are at least two important positions:

---

7. There is a famous rabbinic saying: "there is no before nor after in the Torah," meaning that the narratives in the Pentateuch are not (always) arranged chronologically.

8. See Christophe Nihan, *From Priestly Torah to Pentateuch: A Study in the Composition of the Book of Leviticus*, FAT 2.25 (Tübingen: Mohr Siebeck, 2007), 564. Among other examples, see "holy assembly" in v. 16a, although this is obscured in the NRSVue, which translates it as "solemn assembly."

9. Nihan, *From Priestly Torah to Pentateuch*, 564–65. There is a debate about whether v. 14 belongs with vv. 1–13 or with vv. 15–20 (thus Nihan). Some exegetes prefer to think that only vv. 14b–17 are an addition influenced by H (Graham I. Davies, *A Critical and Exegetical Commentary on Exodus 1–18*, vol. 2, *Commentary on Exodus 11–18*, ICC [London: T&T Clark, 2020], 29–30, 58).

10. Nihan, *From Priestly Torah to Pentateuch*, 565. In addition, he observes (565) that "the inclusion of Ex 12:24–20 was also the opportunity to complete and even revise the law of Lev 23:5–8."

- H is preexilic, and the work of the Holiness School spread over centuries, during which time scribes inserted H-like additions here and there in the Pentateuch (Knohl). In this case, Exod 12:15–20 would be later than H.

- The same Holiness School, in the Persian period, was responsible for both H and the H-like additions found in the Pentateuch. Thus, Nihan writes that "the *same* scribes who composed the so-called 'Holiness Code' as the conclusion of the Sinaitic legislation gradually extended their redactional activity to other portions of the Torah," the objective being to harmonize them with H.[11] In this case, Exod 12:15–20 would date to roughly the same time ascribed to H (the late fifth century, according to Nihan).

Juxtaposition, Conflation, and Supplementation

According to the Documentary Hypothesis, the growth of the Pentateuch involved two main processes: **juxtaposition** and **conflation**. That is, in some cases a compiler deemed it preferable to have two stories on the same subject appear consecutively (e.g., the two creation accounts in Gen 1 and Gen 2–3). But in other cases, his or her sources were so closely parallel that the compiler preferred to *interweave* their elements and thus create a new, combined narrative. The standard example is the flood story, which contains so many doublets that most scholars identify two originally separate strands, one belonging to P (6:9–22; 7:6, 11, 13–16a, 17*, 18–21, 24; 8:1–2a, 3b–5, 13a, 14–19; 9:1–17), the other not (6:5–6, 7aα*; 7:1–2, 3b–5, 10, 7*, 16b, 12, 22, 23*; 8:2b–3a, 6–12, 13b, 20–22), plus some additions.[12]

While recognizing juxtaposition and conflation in some cases, proponents of the competing theory—that is, the traditio-historical approach—tend to privilege the model of **supplementation**. In other words, they tend to conclude that fragments were added, not necessarily all at the same time, to one or two main textual strands.

Both models have advantages and disadvantages. The strength of the supplementation model is that supplementation is a well-documented scribal practice, whereas interweaving is rarely attested in extant manuscripts (though this may be because they are too late to attest to the earliest stages of the text's compositional history). A limitation of the supplementation model is that it is

---

11. Nihan, *From Priestly Torah to Pentateuch*, 563 (emphasis original).
12. Cf. David M. Carr, *The Formation of Genesis 1–11: Biblical and Other Precursors* (New York: Oxford University Press, 2020), 141–52, esp. 144.

often difficult to determine what motives lie behind isolated interpolations that interrupt the flow of the text and obscure the story. In support of conflation, it makes sense that *entire* stories about the same topics from different traditions existed in ancient Israel and that the desire of scribes to preserve them trumped the concern for literary clarity. In practice, both models are useful: conflation by interweaving has to be considered when compositional analysis leads us to identify two series of sentences that constitute complete or quasi-complete narratives, while supplementation is more probable when what we encounter consists only of isolated additions, or of additions that would not, together, come close to constituting a continuous narrative.

4.3 HOW TO DATE A TEXT

In addition to our ability to ascribe some redactional activity to a dated composition or layer, there are various means of dating a text, even if the text in question consists only of a small addition. Let's now turn to the data that can help in this task. I will first give an overview of this topic, and will then discuss each point further and illustrate it with examples.

First of all, it is important to note that you can rarely determine a precise date for a text. Quite often, the best you can do is determine temporal limits. Scholars generally use the following Latin phrases to designate these:

- *terminus a quo*, that is, the earliest possible date for the composition of a text.
- *terminus ad quem*, that is, the latest possible date for the compositon of a text.

Two types of data can help us determine a *terminus a quo* or a *terminus ad quem* for a text. The first type is data based on features that are present in the text itself (a, b, and c below); the second type is data based on dating relative to other elements (d, e, and f below):

- **A** The earliest manuscript attestations of the text (possibly in the **Dead Sea Scrolls**), or its earliest translation (in the **Septuagint**), provide a *terminus ad quem*.

- **B** The **linguistic profile** of the text may point to a broad period of the history of the Hebrew language, suggesting that the text was composed during this period.

- **C** The text was likely **written for an audience living in a specific period**, and its contents may shed light on this.

Ⓓ The text refers or alludes to **datable events or realities**.

Ⓔ There is **literary dependence** between the text being studied and other, **dated texts** (from the Hebrew Bible or elsewhere).

Ⓕ The text shows either awareness or lack thereof about a tradition or an idea.

A. Attestation in the Dead Sea Scrolls or the Septuagint

The Dead Sea Scrolls provide a *terminus ad quem* (latest possible date) for the texts that are preserved among them. Most scholars date these manuscripts between the third century BCE and the first or second century CE; depending on the text you are studying, you need to check the dates usually ascribed to the manuscripts that preserve it.

The situation is similar with the Septuagint: if a biblical book was translated, say, in the second century BCE, this provides a *terminus ad quem* for its composition. As with the production of the Dead Sea Scrolls, the translation process for the Septuagint continued over several centuries (from the third century BCE to the first century CE), and you need to check the current hypothesis concerning the date of the book you are studying. There is a difference between the Septuagint and the Dead Sea Scrolls, however: the extant manuscripts of the LXX are generally from much later than the time when their contents were translated. As a result, it is possible that changes were made in the interim. This is not a problem if you are trying to date a book, but it is if you are trying to date a particular passage: its presence in the standard editions of the LXX does not constitute absolute proof that it was already present in the book in question at the time the book was translated.

EXAMPLE 4.3a   ▸   Genesis 14:18–20

The brief episode about Melchizedek found in Gen 14:18–20 interrupts the flow of the surrounding narrative: the king of Sodom approaches Abram in v. 17, but it is only in v. 21 that he speaks to him. In the meantime, Melchizedek arrives out of the blue. As a result, vv. 18–20 look like an interpolation. Because Melchizedek combines the royal and priestly offices, a phenomenon that some suggest is only attested in Israel during the Hasmonean period (second to first centuries BCE), many scholars date vv. 18–20 to that time.

However, vv. 18–20 are present in the Septuagint. (Genesis 14 is not preserved in the Dead Sea Scrolls, by contrast, so they do not contribute anything to answering the question of when to date these verses.) The Pentateuch was translated into Greek in the third century BCE. Therefore, it is difficult to argue that vv. 18–20 were added in the Hasmonean period. The only way to maintain this hypothesis would be to argue that the following steps occurred:

> - Verses 18–20 were originally absent from the Greek translation made in the third century (because they were absent from the Hebrew text at that time).
>
> - They were added in Hebrew manuscripts (that were ancestors of the MT) in the second or first century BCE.
>
> - They were subsequently incorporated into the Greek manuscripts in order to harmonize them with the MT.[13]
>
> This is theoretically possible, but is somewhat speculative; in addition, these verses are present in all the textual witnesses, which would be surprising if they were a late textual addition.
>
> Moreover, the notion that kings in Israel and in Judah did not have priestly functions before the Hasmonean period is debatable. This would contrast, for example, with the situation in Ugarit and in Phoenicia. Moreover, some biblical passages point to kings and princes having priestly functions: David, Solomon, and Jeroboam I offer sacrifices (2 Sam 6:18; 24:25; 1 Kgs 3:4, 15; 12:32–33); David wears an ephod and leads a procession of the ark (2 Sam 6:14); his sons are priests (2 Sam 8:18); and Solomon plays a priestly role during the dedication of the temple in Jerusalem, leading the procession of the ark, pronouncing a public prayer, and blessing the people (1 Kgs 8). Even if all these elements were deemed fictional, they would suggest that the combination of royal and priestly offices was a concept present in the mind of the redactors who wrote these texts long before the Hasmonean period.
>
> In the end, it is likely that vv. 18–20 are an interpolation in Gen 14, but not necessarily one that dates to the Hasmonean period.

B. Linguistic Profile

We saw in chapter 3 (see the sidebar "Linguistic Dating") that linguistic features can have a bearing on questions of chronology. Thus:

- If a *long* passage is written entirely in Classical Biblical Hebrew, this enhances the likelihood that it was written in the sixth century at the latest.

- If a passage contains an *accumulation* of Late Biblical Hebrew features, this enhances the likelihood that it comes from the postexilic period.

---

13. This interesting suggestion is made by Thomas Römer and Israel Finkelstein, "Comments on the Historical Background of the Abraham Narratives: Between 'Realia' and 'Exegetica,'" *HeBAI* 3 (2014): 22–23.

- If a passage contains a mixture of CBH and LBH features, it may be that the verses containing the LBH features are late additions, or that the text was written in Transitional Biblical Hebrew (therefore, in the sixth century).

These considerations have allowed us to see why, for example, many scholars date Gen 24 to the Persian period (see Example 3.2f). As we have seen, however, linguistic dating is a very approximative method that often is not sufficient in itself but must be corroborated by other elements in the text.

> **EXAMPLE 4.3b** ▸ **2 Kings 17:24–34**
>
> In Example 3.2j, we saw that 2 Kgs 17:34b–40a can be regarded as an addition that was inserted in the chapter after vv. 24–34a, 41 were written. It is possible to go further, however, thanks to linguistics: vv. 24–34a contain a number of Late Biblical Hebrew features, which contrasts with the beginning of the chapter and, in fact, with most of Kings.[14] In combination with other arguments, this suggests that vv. 24–34a were added to the text at a time when it consisted only of vv. 1–23.
>
> In sum, 2 Kgs 17:1–23 was supplemented, probably during the Persian period, in two successive stages that reflect two different ways of polemicizing against the inhabitants of Samaria. First, a scribe added vv. 24–34a, 41 in order to argue that these people were actually foreigners and syncretists. Then, later, another scribe inserted vv. 34b–40a, looking at the situation from another angle; perhaps, as Magnar Kartveit argues, this section contains "a criticism of the same population from the point of view that they professed themselves Israelites—if so, then their practices are against the covenant that would bind them to the Torah. But in fact, they did not worship Yahweh, v. 34b, because they violated the covenant."[15]

C. Texts Written for an Audience Living in a Specific Period

Various situations are possible here:

- The story addresses a problem that was especially relevant in a particular historical context.
- The setting of the story is so firmly anchored in a specific historical context that the narrative seems to have been written in and/or for people living in that context.

---

14. See Magnar Kartveit, "The Date of II Reg 17,24–41," *ZAW* 126 (2014): 31–44, with further arguments.
15. Kartveit, "Date of II Reg 17,24–41," 43.

- The story mirrors a historical situation and is designed to provide a model attitude or an antimodel.

In the last situation, exegetes make use of a "mirror reading" of the text: that is, they see it as a reflection of (akin to an allegory on) a particular historical situation, not a description of that situation itself. A modern example of this is the novel *The Plague*, which Albert Camus began writing in 1941 (and which was published in 1947). This book—which narrates the arrival of rats in Oran, Algeria, and the plague that ensues—can be read as an allegory of the European resistance against Nazism, a point that many readers understood and that Camus himself acknowledged.[16]

This approach is widely used in compositional criticism, especially by scholars who regard most of the Pentateuch as consisting of fictional retrojections of first-millennium realities. The underlying idea is that retrojections often take the form of "allegorical" narratives. However, it is of the essence of an "allegory" to be readable without reference to the realities that it figuratively represents. That is, the texts do not give away their own allegorical nature, which is implicit. As a result, these exegetical inquiries are inevitably subjective. Moreover, history repeats itself, so it is quite rare to see an issue be a concern in only one specific period. Therefore, using this kind of reading to pin down the time when a text could have been written is interesting but conjectural.

In sum, arguments attempting to show that a text was written for an audience living in a specific period are often debatable. For this reason, it is best to use this criterion for dating a text in combination with other criteria.

> **EXAMPLE 4.3c** ▸ **Genesis 11:28, 31; 15:7**
>
> Most readers of the Hebrew Bible know that Abraham's birthplace is Ur, in Mesopotamia. However, this information is proper to P and is mentioned in only a few verses in the Pentateuch (Gen 11:28, 31; 15:7).[17] And yet, this tiny detail has an important consequence: Abraham, the great ancestor, has already gone through the same journey as the exiles who, beginning in 539 BCE, came back from Babylonia to Judah. Hence, some scholars have hypothesized that a Priestly writer introduced the aforementioned references to Ur into Genesis in order to create this precedent, either making Abraham a model for the people coming back from exile or highlighting the value of their experience. This is one reason that has led many (though not all) scholars to date P to the sixth century BCE.

---

16. In a letter to Roland Barthes dated January 11, 1955.
17. A number of scholars regard 15:7 as post-P.

> **EXAMPLE 4.3d** ▸ **Genesis 37–50**

In the last several years, various aspects of the Joseph story (Gen 37–50) have inspired (at least) two models for dating it.[18] To begin with, this story is about a Hebrew immigrant who settles in Egypt and, after overcoming certain difficulties with the help of the Lord, becomes very successful. It is plausible that members of the Jewish people living in Egypt found in Joseph a model of successful integration and life in Egyptian society. Thomas Römer, among others, has argued that this concerns not only the reception of this story, but its very composition as well: in his view, it is a Diaspora novel, written in the Persian period and probably in Egypt.[19]

Erhard Blum and Kristin Weingart, on the other hand, are not convinced; they mention the Sinuhe Story, a very popular Egyptian story from the second millenium BCE, as a counterexample: "The Sinuhe Story is set abroad, its protagonist travels to a foreign country, rises to a position of power at a foreign court and raises a family there. Nevertheless, no one would search for an Egyptian Diaspora in the Levant in order to account for its existence."[20] Therefore, Blum and Weingart explore another scenario: namely, that the story is mostly about the relationships between the tribes, represented by the eponymous ancestors. Thus, the story highlights Joseph's primacy over his brothers (Gen 42:8; 50:18) in order to promote the leadership of the tribe of Joseph in Israel. In addition, the story highlights a close relationship between Benjamin and Joseph, one that is recognized by Judah; this, they suggest, is a narrative transposition of a political program of hegemony over the territories of Benjamin and Judah on the part of Israel (the Northern Kingdom, represented by Joseph). Based on these considerations (and others), Blum and Weingart situate the core of the Joseph story in the Northern Kingdom, during the eighth century BCE.

The debate continues (and it also involves other considerations, such as the linguistic profile of the Joseph cycle).[21] But this brief summary suffices to illustrate how complex narratives such as the Joseph story may contain

---

18. The older, conservative view is still defended by some scholars: e.g., Kenneth A. Kitchen, *On the Reliability of the Old Testament* (Grand Rapids: Eerdmans, 2003), 313–72.

19. Thomas Römer, "The Joseph Story in the Book of Genesis: Pre-P or Post-P?" in *The Post-Priestly Pentateuch: New Perspectives on Its Redactional Development and Theological Profiles*, ed. Federico Giuntoli and Konrad Schmid, FAT 101 (Tübingen: Mohr Siebeck, 2015), 185–201.

20. Erhard Blum and Kristin Weingart, "The Joseph Story: Diaspora Novella or North-Israelite Narrative?" *ZAW* 129 (2017): 516.

21. See Konrad Schmid, "Die Datierung der Josephsgeschichte: Ein Gespräch mit Erhard Blum und Kristin Weingart," in *Eigensinn und Entstehung der Hebräischen Bibel: Erhard Blum zum siebzigsten Geburtstag*, ed. Joachim J. Krause, Wolfgang Oswald, and Kristin Weingart, FAT 136 (Tübingen: Mohr Siebeck, 2020), 99–109; Thomas Römer, "How 'Persian' or 'Hellenistic' Is the Joseph Narrative?" in *The Joseph Story between Egypt and Israel*, ed. Thomas Römer, Konrad Schmid, and Axel Bühler, ArchBib 5 (Tübingen: Mohr Siebeck, 2021), 35–53.

> several plots and subplots that generate various mirror readings that are mutually incompatible.

D. Links to Datable Events or Realities

Several possibilities exist here, depending on whether the text:

- refers to, alludes to, or presupposes a past event or reality (hence providing a *terminus a quo* [earliest possible date])
- looks forward to a reality that ceased to be current at some point in history, or refers to this situation as being current (hence providing a *terminus ad quem* [latest possible date])
- is an oracle that announces an event that took place and is dated, provided that this oracle was not written *ex eventu* (i.e., after the event, in light of it)
- is an oracle that announces an event that, in the end, did not take place or did not take place in the way it was announced (hence providing a *terminus ad quem*, since nobody would have written such an announcement after the fact).

This criterion is important but, like the preceding one, it must be used with caution. For example, it is inappropriate to presuppose that a writer *could not have imagined a situation* before it took place in history.[22] So, if a text mentions a deportation, for instance, this is not sufficient grounds to argue that it was necessarily written after 586 BCE. Deportations were a recurrent reality in the ancient Near East; if you wanted to conceive of a calamity that could happen to your country during the Neo-Assyrian period, exile would have been near the top of the list. To use a modern analogy, novels about pandemics were written well before the COVID-19 pandemic started; future historians would obviously be wrong to date these books after 2019.

> **EXAMPLE 4.3e** ▸ **Nahum 3:8**
>
> The third chapter of Nahum is addressed to Nineveh and announces to this city that it will be destroyed. To shake Nineveh's confidence in its fortifications, the text alludes to a precedent, the fall of Thebes (Hebrew "No-Amon") in Egypt: "Are you better than Thebes that sat by the Nile, with water around her, her rampart a sea, water her wall?" (Nah 3:8). Since we know that the fall

---

22. For a thoughtful criticism of the use of such criteria for dating texts, see Benjamin D. Sommer, "Dating Pentateuchal Texts and the Perils of Pseudo-Historicism," in *The Pentateuch: International Perspectives on Current Research*, ed. Thomas B. Dozeman, Konrad Schmid, and Baruch J. Schwartz, FAT 78 (Tübingen: Mohr Siebeck, 2011), 85–108.

of Thebes occurred in 663 BCE, Nah 3:8 must have been written after that date. And insofar as there is little reason to suspect that this is an addition to the chapter, this relative dating also applies to Nah 3.

EXAMPLE 4.3f ▸ "Until This Day" in Judges and Kings

The books of the Deuteronomistic History sometimes note that something holds true "until this day." This suggests that the redactor regards the thing in question—which is generally a practice—as having been instituted in the remote past. This hints that the redaction is from a later time than the one referred to in the narrative; and in certain cases the text contains information that gives us at least some idea of what this later time is.

For example, the book of Judges contains a sort of appendix (Judg 17–21), which is punctuated by the recurring phrase "In those days, there was no king in Israel" (Judg 17:6; 18:1; 19:1; 21:25). This suggests that at least these four verses, and perhaps even these five chapters, were not written before the monarchic period. Moreover, 18:30 mentions "the time [when] the land went into captivity," an allusion to the deportations of the late eighth century BCE, which provides a *terminus a quo* (earliest possible date).

Similarly, in 1 Kgs 8:8, we read that in Solomon's temple "the poles [of the ark of the covenant] were so long that the ends of the poles were seen from the holy place in front of the inner sanctuary; but they could not be seen from outside; they are there to this day." Yet the end of Kings mentions the destruction of the temple and the removal of its cultic furnishings (2 Kgs 25:9–18). The fact that there is no way the ark and its poles were still there when the book was completed indicates that 1 Kgs 8:8 was probably not written by the same redactor who wrote 2 Kgs 25. This is one of several hints that a redaction of Kings took place in the preexilic period.[23]

EXAMPLE 4.3g ▸ Jeremiah 50–51

Jeremiah 50–51 announces the violent conquest of Babylon, including, notably, the plundering of the city (50:10) and the destruction of its walls (50:15). Jeremiah 51:11 specifies the identify of the attacker: the Medes. However, when Cyrus the Great, a Mede who founded the Achaemenid empire, entered Babylon in 539 BCE, he was welcomed by the inhabitants; Babylon was neither destroyed nor plundered—in fact, it was not even attacked. The lack

---

23. See further Jeffrey C. Geoghegan, "'Until this Day' and the Preexilic Redaction of the Deuteronomistic History," *JBL* 122 (2003): 201–27.

of fulfillment of what looks like a prophetic prediction may sound controversial to some readers and may lead to discussions about hermeneutics, but for the present purpose, the point is that this discrepancy is what leads many scholars to date the core of Jer 50–51 before 539 BCE.

EXAMPLE 4.3h › 2 Kings 18:13–19:37

We saw in Example 3.2k that 2 Kgs 18–19 contains three successive accounts of the Assyrian siege of Jerusalem in 701 BCE: A (18:14–16), B1 (18:13; 18:17–19:9a; 19:37), and B2 (19:9b–36). Nadav Na'aman has noted that 19:12–13 alludes to Babylonian victories from the late seventh century and that 19:17–18 alludes to the Babylonian practice of destroying the statues of the deities worshiped in conquered lands.[24] This implies that B2 was written, at the earliest, in the Neo-Babylonian period. Na'aman himself prefers a date at the end of this period or slightly later. Amitai Baruchi-Unna opts for a slightly earlier date, suggesting that B2 was written in the last days of the kingdom of Judah, when history repeated itself and Jerusalem was, or was about to be, besieged by the Babylonians, as it had been by the Assyrians in 701.[25] On either view, B2 would be a rewritten version of B1 intended to make it relevant to the new context.

E. Literary Dependence

Two situations are relevant here:

- The text depends on an earlier text whose dating we know (hence providing a *terminus a quo* [earliest possible date]).
- The text is used (referred to, alluded to, quoted, used, etc.) in another text whose dating we know, whether a text from the Hebrew Bible or from any Second Temple work (hence providing a *terminus ad quem* [latest possible date]).

The idea here is very simple: if passage B uses text A (whether it alludes or refers to it, or was written in light of it), then B is necessarily later than A. This reasoning is widespread in compositional criticism, especially because certain key texts—the dating of which is a matter of broad consensus—are used as benchmarks. It should be noted that scholars sometimes apply this principle repeatedly to multiple related texts—for example, to date text C, which depends on text B, which in turn depends

---

24. Nadav Na'aman, "New Light on Hezekiah's Second Prophetic Story (2 Kgs 19,9b–35)," *Bib* 81 (2000): 393–402.

25. Amitai Baruchi-Unna, "The Story of Hezekiah's Prayer," *JSOT* 39 (2015): 281–97.

on text A (for which a reasonable dating can be proposed). Needless to say, piling up inferences in this manner enhances the hypothetical character of the dating, and this should be borne in mind.

> **EXAMPLE 4.3i** ▸ Isaiah 17:7–8
>
> In Example 3.2e, we saw that Isa 17:7–8 is likely an interpolation and that these verses, in turn, were augmented with small additions (marked here in italics): "they will not have regard for *the altars,* the work of their hands, and at what their own fingers have made they will not look, *and the sacred poles or the altars of incense*" (author's translation).
>
> Criticism of illicit altars and sacred poles is a hallmark of the Deuteronomistic History (see Deut 12:3 and many passages in Kings). Their mention here is akin to the "fingerprints" of a redactor who was influenced by this idea, which is often dated to the seventh or sixth centuries BCE. This therefore provides a *terminus a quo* (earliest possible date) for these additions.

Models for the Formation of the Deuteronomistic History

It is obvious that Joshua, Judges, Samuel, and Kings—which narrate the story of the Hebrews from the time they entered the land of Israel to the time they were expelled from it—can be read as a continuous story. Moreover, a number of passages scattered over this collection of books promote a theological interpretation of history based on ideas such as the exclusive worship of the Lord. Several models attempt to explain how this collection was formed:

The single historian model. Martin Noth hypothesized that this collection—which, together with Deuteronomy, he called "the Deuteronomistic History" (or DH)—was the work of a single historian living during the Babylonian exile (in the sixth century BCE), who wanted to provide an explanation (etiology) of the fall of Israel and Judah.

The blocks model. According to Frank Moore Cross, a first version of the DH was written by a certain **Dtr1** during the reign of Josiah (in the late seventh century); it highlighted the positive theme of the dynastic promise made to David (2 Sam 7) and ended with a celebration of Josiah's reform (2 Kgs 23:25). Then, after the catastrophe, this composition was updated, during the exile, by **Dtr2**. Some scholars hypothesize the existence of earlier redactions, notably one made during the reign of Hezekiah (ca. 700 BCE), the mention of whose reform (2 Kgs 18) some consider to be the original climax of the work.

The layers model. Some German scholars have proposed a model of **successive layers** that originated during the exile: DtrG (or DtrH), the original narrative; DtrP, made up of additions about prophets; and DtrN, a layer introducing passages about the law (N stands for *nomos*, the Greek word for "law").

Combinations of aspects of the blocks and layers models also exist: for instance, some add to Dtr1 and Dtr2 a stage during the Persian period when most of the prophetic stories were added. On the other hand, many doubt the existence of the DH altogether, or restrict it to a nucleus based on Kings or Samuel–Kings.

A common criticism raised against the theory of a robustly unified DH is that the books that are supposed to constitute it are in fact very different from one another. Still, there are connections between all of these books. The following two models are designed to take into account these insights:

The gradual connection of originally autonomous books model. According to this hypothesis, the books constituting the DH first grew autonomously from each other, and were all subjected to some Dtr editing, before they were gradually connected by means of redactional links.

The two poles model. This hypothesis integrates recent developments in Continental European scholarship on the Pentateuch, notably the notion that a narrative encompassing the life of Moses, the exodus, and the conquest developed independently of the stories about the patriarchs (in particular, the stories in Genesis and in Exodus were connected relatively late). According to this model, a Dtr composition can be identified in Exodus to 2 Kings. This Dtr composition results from the connection between the narrative mentioned above, which constitutes the first pole, and stories that were precursors to Samuel and Kings, which is the second pole. These two poles grew over time and were finally connected by a Dtr redactor who intervened throughout Exodus to 2 Kings.

To go further, see the following important discussions:

- Reinhard G. Kratz, *The Composition of the Narrative Books of the Old Testament*, trans. John Bowden (New York: T&T Clark, 2005; original German edition, 2000), 153–215.

- Jan Christian Gertz, Angelika Berlejung, Konrad Schmid, and Markus Witte, *T&T Clark Handbook of the Old Testament: An Introduction to the Literature, Religion and History of the Old Testament* (New York: T&T Clark, 2012; original German [3rd] edition, 2008), 237–71, 351–82, esp. 260–66, 351–56.

- Thomas Römer, "The So-Called Deuteronomistic History and Its Theories of Composition," in Brad E. Kelle and Brent A. Strawn, eds., *The Oxford Handbook of the Historical Books of the Hebrew Bible* (New York: Oxford University Press, 2020), 303–22.

In practice, scholars have detected "deuteronomistic" interventions in virtually every part of the Hebrew Bible, based on Dtr ideas and style. The standard description of these ideas and style is:

- Moshe Weinfeld, *Deuteronomy and the Deuteronomistic School* (Oxford: Clarendon, 1972).

However, an indiscriminate use of this approach has led to a sort of "pan-deuteronomism" that sees Dtr interventions everywhere based on phraseology that is not always proper to the Dtr redactors. In addition, it seems that after the great Dtr period (in the seventh and sixth centuries BCE), scribes imitated the Dtr style for centuries. Hence, there is a need to distinguish carefully between scribal interventions that can safely be correlated with a Dtr redaction and later imitations.

EXAMPLE 4.3j ▸ **Exodus 34:11–26**

Exodus 34:11–26 contains a series of prescriptions the Israelites are to follow. This text is, in fact, a reworking of Exod 23 that is adapted to a new context. The laws here are focused on worship, which fits the literary context, inasmuch as they appear right after the Golden Calf episode, where the problem of illicit worship is emphasized (Exod 32–33). Moreover, Exod 34 adds a new prescription compared to Exod 23: the Israelites are forbidden to make "molten gods" (אֱלֹהֵי מַסֵּכָה). This harks back to the golden calf episode (32:4, 8). Exodus 34 was a fitting place to include revised laws: Verse 1 speaks of God's intention to replace the tablets that originally contained the Ten Commandments and that Moses broke, but the chapter originally did not spell out the contents of the text that would be written on these new tablets. The addition fills this gap; it shows that the new tablets given by God contain the same commandments as before—the same, but slightly updated. At least, this is a possible reading of this passage.

A close inspection reveals that Exod 32 has reworked Exod 23 in light of the concerns of, and using the terminology of, both Priestly texts (notably H) and D. For instance:[26]

- Exodus 34:11 includes the typical Deuteronomic expression "Observe what I command you today" (cf. Deut 4:40, 6:6; etc.).
- Exodus 34:25 reproduces 23:18 word for word, except for the verb meaning "to slaughter" (שחט), which has been substituted

---

26. Shimon Bar-On (Gesundheit), "The Three Festival Calendars in Exodus XXIII 14–19 and XXXIV 18–26," *VT* 48 (1998): 161–95.

> for "to sacrifice" (זבח) in order to fit the Priestly terminology of animal sacrifice.²⁷
>
> ♦ Exodus 34 treats the Sabbath together with the annual festivals, listing it between the Festival of Unleavened Bread (vv. 18–20) and the Festival of Weeks (v. 22a). This is a feature unique to Priestly texts; more precisely, it appears in H (cf. Lev 23; see also Num 28–29).²⁸
>
> ♦ Like Exod 23:14–17, Exod 34 prescribes three festival pilgrimages, but it contains a subtle addition that takes into account the centralization of the cult, which is a hallmark of D. As long as there were local temples in all the regions of the country, the Israelites could go to a festival and be back home on the same day. Once the cult was centralized in Jerusalem, however, they had to leave their homes for a number of days, without protection from intruders.²⁹ Hence the reassuring promise: "*no one shall covet your land when you go up to appear before the* LORD *your God three times in the year*" (Exod 34:24).
>
> Because it depends both on Priestly texts and on D, Exod 34:11–26 is a post-Priestly text (see the sidebar "P as a Benchmark"). More than that, this passage represents a harmonization between the Covenant Code, Priestly writings (including H), and the Deuteronomic Code. Because it presupposes knowledge of most of the strands of the Pentateuch, it represents the work of scribes who knew the Pentateuch at an advanced stage of its formation, compared different laws on the same subjects, noticed the differences among them, and created a compromise between them. The same concern for the harmonization of laws is apparent in some Dead Sea scrolls (e.g., the Temple Scroll).

---

27. The root זבח is common in non-Priestly texts but very rare in P and H, where its use is restricted to the זֶבַח שְׁלָמִים, "offering of well-being" (or "peace offering").

28. Interestingly, the prohibition against making "molten gods" (Exod 34:17) appears elsewhere only in H (Lev 19:4). Since one could theoretically argue that Exod 34:17 was inspired by Exod 32:4, 8 and that Lev 19:4 was, in turn, inspired by Exod 34:17, the presence of the phrase "molten gods" in Exod 34:17 cannot be used to establish that Exod 34 depends on H. Once this fact has been accepted on the basis of other arguments, however, it seems reasonable to conclude that Exod 34:17 comes from Lev 19:4.

29. Strictly speaking, this is a programmatic idea of D; the historicity of the centralization reforms in Judah is debated. See Examples 8.1c and 8.2c for Hezekiah's reform and Exercise C in chapter 8 for Josiah's reform.

> **P as a Benchmark**
>
> One of the most important benchmarks in contemporary exegesis is P. Its dating is debated: adherents of the Documentary Hypothesis sometimes ascribe it a preexilic (e.g., eighth-century) date, but more frequently they date it to the exilic period (sixth-century); contemporary Continental European exegesis, by contrast, tends to date P to the early Persian period (fifth century).[30] Overall, the sixth- or fifth-century horizon represents a wide consensus and thus a benchmark for dating post-Priestly texts (that is, texts that are later than P): many scholars date such texts to the Persian period at the earliest.
>
> However, it is not always easy to decide whether a text that exhibits Priestly features (i.e., ideas and/or terminology proper to P) was composed in light of P, and thus later than it, or simply belongs to P. If the text lies outside the boundaries you ascribe to P (e.g., Gen 1–Lev 16, according to one theory), then chances are that it is post-Priestly. Within these boundaries, the following criterion alleviates the difficulty and is often used by Continental European exegetes: If a text exhibits a *mixture* of Priestly and non-Priestly features (for instance, D's ideas or terminology), then it is post-Priestly. Indeed, it is only once P was extant and available that P's ideas and terminology could be taken up and combined with features from non-P texts. Needless to say, such a criterion must be used with caution, especially when the arguments are based on terminology, since expressions unique to a document are a rare thing.[31]

F. The Text Shows Awareness (or Lack Thereof) about a Tradition or Idea

Two situations are relevant here, depending on whether the tradition or idea

- became relevant only from a certain point onward (hence providing a *terminus a quo* [earliest possible date])
- ceased to be relevant at some point (hence providing a *terminus ad quem* [latest possible date])

This criterion needs to be used with a good deal of caution. In particular, the fact that a text does not presuppose the knowledge of a tradition or an idea represents an argument from silence. This silence may be due to the fact that the writer lived in a time when this tradition or idea did not yet exist, but it may also be that the writer has

---

30. It should be noted that these comments concern the core of P, since most agree that it was amplified in (at least) a second stage.

31. For a critical discussion of this criterion, see Carr, *Formation of the Hebrew Bible*, 132–37.

deliberately ignored it. For instance, the Chronicler intentionally typically avoids referring to the exodus, not because he is ignorant of this tradition but because he wants to write a history of Judah that encourages his contemporaries on other grounds.[32]

For a superb description of the theological ideas contained in the Hebrew Bible, including an overview of their development through time and in connection with major compositions and redactions, see:

- Konrad Schmid, *A Historical Theology of the Hebrew Bible*, trans. Peter Altmann (Grand Rapids: Eerdmans, 2019; original German edition, 2018).

EXAMPLE 4.3k ▸ Amos 5:25; Jeremiah 7:22

In Amos 5:25, we read: "Did you bring to me sacrifices and offerings the forty years in the wilderness, O house of Israel?" Likewise in Jer 7:22: "For in the day that I brought your ancestors out of the land of Egypt, I did not speak to them or command them concerning burnt offerings and sacrifices."

It seems that the redactors responsible for these verses did not know about the Priestly traditions of the Pentateuch (especially the prescriptions found in Leviticus). They knew stories about the sojourn in the desert, but it seems that the traditions they had inherited concerning that time did not mention any sacrificial rituals. In particular, the assertion in Jer 7:22 echoes the situation presented in Deuteronomy (5:25), according to which the Lord gave the Ten Commandments *but no other law* on Mount Sinai.[33]

This may provide an argument in favor of dating these verses earlier than the composition of P, which is often dated to the sixth century BCE. In the case of Jeremiah, this makes it likely that the verse comes from the prophet himself; and in the case of Amos, this lends credibility to the same idea.

---

32. Sara Japhet, *The Ideology of the Book of Chronicles and Its Place in Biblical Thought* (Winona Lake, IN: Eisenbrauns, 2009), 296–301. She writes that in the Chronicler's view, "the bond between the people and the land, like the bond between the people and its god, is described as something continuous and abiding. This bond cannot be associated with a particular moment in history, for it has existed since the beginning of time" (301).

33. Other explanations of Jer 7:22 do exist, of course. For example, Jack R. Lundbom, *Jeremiah 1–20: A New Translation with Introduction and Commentary*, AB 21A (New York: Doubleday, 1999), 481–82, suggests that this verse contains a purely rhetorical assertion. And according to Jacob Milgrom, Jer 7:22 concerns only voluntary sacrifices made by individuals, not the temple cult ("Concerning Jeremiah's Repudiation of Sacrifice," *ZAW* 89 [1977]: 173–75). I find these interpretations unconvincing, however.

EXAMPLE 4.31 ▸ 2 Kings 5:1–19

Second Kings 5:1–19 narrates the story of an Aramean general, Naaman, who comes to Israel to be healed of a skin disease by Elisha. Once this has been done, he declares: "Now I know that there is no God in all the earth except in Israel" (v. 15). Commentators generally regard this as a monotheistic "confession" that is comparable to statements found in Isa 40–55 and Deut 4 (both of which are generally dated to the sixth century). Without necessarily excluding the possibility of roots in the preexilic period, most scholars consider that monotheism really gained traction in the exilic period. As a result, they date 2 Kgs 5 to the sixth century or later.

The situation is a bit more complicated, however. Strictly speaking, Naaman's confession firmly ties the existence of a deity to the *land* of Israel, so much so that he wants to bring some soil from there to Damascus (v. 17). As Thomas Römer remarks, this confession is less strictly "universalistic" than what one finds in Isa 40–55 and Deut 4.[34] Still, even the kind of monotheism contained in Naaman's confession does not seem to sit comfortably with preexilic ideas.

Indeed, Römer finds further arguments in favor of a postexilic dating. The story in 2 Kgs 5 is likely told not only for its own sake, but because it explores the general issue of Yahwistic worship outside of Israel. As a matter of fact, Naaman's intention of offering sacrifices to the Lord in a foreign country (vv. 17–18) is at odds with the imperative of cult centralization in Jerusalem, which is an important tenet of the Deuteronomistic History and of Kings in particular. And yet the redactor does not regard this as an absolute problem. Does the fact that 2 Kgs 5 ignores this prohibition mean that it is *pre*-Deuteronomistic? Not necessarily, because not everybody agreed with Deuteronomistic ideas, even after the sixth century. As a matter of fact, this explains the presence in the very Deuteronomistic book of Kings of stories about Elijah and Elisha, stories in which altars are built and sacrifices are made outside of Jerusalem (see 1 Kgs 18; 2 Kgs 5). These narratives were interpolated into Kings at a late date by redactors who did not mind the tension this created.

In the end, based on a mirror reading, Römer argues that 2 Kgs 5 is a postexilic text that acknowledges the existence of Yahwistic worship in Aramean territory (and provides an etiology for it) while still defending the idea that for worship of the Lord to be adequate, it should take place in Israel. The debate continues, and one may also wonder whether a redactor in the Persian period would really have created from scratch a whole

---

34. Thomas Römer, "The Strange Conversion of Naaman, Chief of the Aramaean Army," in *Research on Israel and Aram: Autonomy, Independence and Related Issues*, ed. Angelika Berlejung and Aren M. Maeir, ORA 34 (Tübingen: Mohr Siebeck, 2019), 116–18.

story involving the kings of Israel and Aram, centuries after the end of the corresponding kingdoms. It is therefore possible that the present narrative is based on an earlier kernel. Be that as it may, this example illustrates the complexity of the use of ideas (such as monotheism) and ideologies (such as Deuteronomistic thought) for dating texts.

4.4 SYNTHESIS

After completing the preceding steps, you have a basis for reconstructing the compositional history of the passage you are studying. This entails:

- drawing up a list of the successive stages
- proposing dates for each of them
- explaining the purpose of each stage, and perhaps even a setting for it.

In practice, it is wise to acknowledge the hypothetical character of your proposals. This applies to the following example, which summarizes my own analysis of a passage.

EXAMPLE 4.4 ▸ 2 Kings 3

This example illustrates the kind of complexity that can be found in many publications on compositional criticism, so you may want to have a cup of coffee before reading it and have a translation of the Bible open so you can follow the passage as you work through the example.

Second Kings 3 contains a discussion about a conflict between Israel and Moab (vv. 1–6, 24–27), and this serves as a framework that surrounds a prophetic story (vv. 7–23). As most scholars who work on the Elijah-Elisha stories acknowledge, this prophetic account is certainly an interpolation. One indication of this is that this account is in tension with its literary context. For example, the mention of a king in Edom is at odds with other statements in the book (1 Kgs 22:47 [48]; 2 Kgs 8:20). Even though some interpreters try to harmonize the text by assuming that the king was merely a governor (cf. 1 Kgs 22:47 [48]), it is unlikely that the same redactor would have written all these passages. In addition, the geographical indications in the prophetic story seem at variance with the general movement of the armies described in the framework.[35]

---

35. Erasmus Gaß, "Topographical Considerations and Redaction Criticism in 2 Kings 3," *JBL* 128 (2009): 65–84.

Once the prophetic account is removed, the oldest text goes directly from v. 6 ("So King Jehoram marched out of Samaria at that time and mustered all Israel") to its natural sequel in v. 24aβ ("the Israelites rose up and attacked the Moabites"). This kernel (vv. 4–6, 24aβ–27*)[36] described a conflict only between Moab and Israel (not between Moab, on the one hand, and Israel, Judah, and Edom, on the other).

The prophetic account contains many similarities to 1 Kgs 22:1–38, including verbal repetitions (compare, notably, 1 Kgs 22:4, 7–8 and 2 Kgs 3:7, 11). One of the most striking features of the story told in 1 Kgs 22 is that it pictures many prophets being deceived and announcing victory to Ahab, whereas in fact he ends up dying in the battle. It seems likely that the story in 2 Kgs 3 imitates 1 Kgs 22 in order to make Elisha also appear to deliberately deceive the king. Indeed, in v. 18 Elisha predicts a complete victory (this is the normal sense of "handing over" an army), whereas in reality the Israelite army will end up retreating before taking the enemy capital (v. 27). That this literary strategy of imitation is operating the other way around seems less likely, so 2 Kgs 3 appears to depend on 1 Kgs 22.

It seems possible to detect two further additions. The LXX (in the Antiochian Text) preserves a repetition in vv. 24 and 25aα: both end with "they struck Moab"; the Greek expressions render the same underlying Hebrew:

24b καὶ εἰσῆλθον εἰσπορευόμενοι καὶ τύπτοντες τὸν Μωαβ (< וַיַּכּוּ אֶת־מוֹאָב)

25aα καὶ τὰς πόλεις καθεῖλον καὶ πᾶσαν μερίδα ἀγαθὴν ἔρριψεν ἀνὴρ τὸν λίθον αὐτοῦ καὶ ἐνέπλησαν αὐτὴν καὶ πᾶσαν πηγὴν ὕδατος ἐνέφραξαν καὶ πᾶν ξύλον ἀγαθὸν κατέβαλον καὶ ἐξέσεισαν τὸν Μωαβ (< וַיַּכּוּ אֶת־מוֹאָב)

24b And they entered **and they struck Moab**

25aα and the cities they overturned, and on every good piece of land everyone threw his stone, and they filled it, and every spring of water they stopped up, and every good tree they felled, **and they struck Moab**.

(author's translation)

The second occurrence of "and they struck Moab" may have been removed from the MT to avoid a redundancy. This repetition is a *Wiederaufnahme* framing the insertion of v. 25aα, which reads, in the MT: "The cities they overturned, and on every good piece of land everyone threw a stone until it was covered; every spring of water they stopped up, and every good tree they

---

36. Here I follow Steven L. McKenzie, *1 Kings 16–2 Kings 16*, IECOT (Stuttgart: Kohlhammer, 2019), 267. The asterisk indicates that I am referring to the earliest form of the verses in question. Indeed, a bit later in this example, I will explain that some additions were made to them later on.

felled." This addition disturbed the syntax of the text, hence the enigmatic end of v. 25 (lit., "until there remained only its stone in Kir-hareseth . . .").³⁷

The gloss in v. 25aα is obviously related to v. 19: "You shall conquer every fortified city and every choice city; every good tree you shall fell, all springs of water you shall stop up, and every good piece of land you shall ruin with stones." Both were added by the same scribe, who, I suggest, was bothered by the tension between Elisha's prediction of total victory in v. 18 and the retreat in v. 27. By adding another announcement (in v. 19) and its point-by-point realization (in v. 25aα), this scribe softened the problem: Elisha had, in fact, made an accurate prediction. The scribe may even have intended v. 19 to serve to make explicit what Elisha meant in v. 18, although this was an unlikely reinterpretation.

To sum up:

(1) The earliest narrative (vv. 4–6, 24aβ–27*) may come from a source used by a Dtr redactor in the seventh century; it described a conflict between Moab and Israel only.

(2) An Elisha story (vv. 7–18, 20–24aα) was *added* in the Persian period, like the other Elijah-Elisha narratives; it was written in light of 1 Kgs 22 and therefore *composed* later, so it may be a late addition. It makes the text more relevant to a Judean audience by involving Jehoshaphat, and it has Elisha intervene in a deceptive way.

(3) A later scribe, at an indeterminate date (the LXX translation in the second century BCE provides a *terminus ad quem* [latest possible date]), added v. 19 and v. 25aα in order to dissipate the tension between Elisha's prediction and the epilogue of the narrative.

---

37. Julio Trebolle Barrera, *Centena in libros Samuelis et Regum: Variantes textuales y composición literaria en los libros de Samuel y Reyes*, TECC (Madrid: Instituto de Filología, 1989), 163–65.

Exercises for Chapter 4

Exercise A

Consider the Elijah-Elisha cycles. What, in your opinion, is their original intended audience? (Because this set of texts may have been augmented throughout time, this question is really about the earliest core of these cycles, but you do not need to delve into the details of what precisely this core comprised.) Does thinking about these stories' original intended audience help you situate them in a historical context and date them?

Exercise B

Do a compositional analysis of Exod 24:1–11, then propose your synthesis of its compositional history. In doing this, try to correlate at least one part of the text, or stage of its compositional history, with a known composition or redaction of the Pentateuch. Use exegetical commentaries to help you.

Exercise C

Choose one example from this chapter whose conclusions you find unconvincing or debatable, and write a paragraph to explain your objections to the hypothesis (or hypotheses) that was (or were) presented.

Exercise D

This exercise, which will take some time, requires reading and critically reflecting on a chapter from each of the two scholarly monographs listed below. The idea is to compare two different compositional analyses of the same pericope; please make sure that you have read the sidebar "Juxtaposition, Conflation, and Supplementation" before going further. The first chapter, using the framework of the Documentary Hypothesis, understands Num 16 as having resulted from the interweaving of two continuous narratives. The second chapter, using the framework of the traditio-historical approach to the Pentateuch, understands Num 16 as having resulted from a block and a few supplements.

- Joel S. Baden, *The Composition of the Pentateuch: Renewing the Documentary Hypothesis*, AYBRL (New Haven: Yale University Press, 2012), 149–68.

- David Frankel, *The Murmuring Stories of the Priestly School: A Retrieval of Ancient Sacerdotal Lore*, VTSup 89 (Leiden: Brill, 2002), 63–117.

Do you find one of these two analyses more convincing than the other? Why?

PART TWO

THE VARIOUS FACETS OF THE TEXT

CHAPTER 5

LITERARY GENRE

OVERVIEW

The Hebrew Bible is not, strictly speaking, a book, but a collection of books that are often very different from one another. Even within a particular book, there can be several types of text; for example, the prologue and the epilogue of the book of Job are narratives, whereas the heart of the work is made up of speeches given by different individuals. Likewise, the book of Ezra contains narratives but also lists (in chs. 2, 8, and 10) and letters (in chs. 4–7). In order to describe this kind of variety, we speak of distinct *literary genres*.

In order to better appreciate the form and content of the passage you are studying, it is of prime importance to take into account the literary genre of the passage. This is so for several reasons. First, certain literary genres are associated with *implicit conventions*. This concerns, in the first place, the *literary form* adopted for the writing of the text. Thus, a letter generally follows a typical form: announcement of the sender and the recipient, a standard greeting, the heart of the letter, and the formula for signing off. Identifying the literary genre of a passage can thus help you determine its layout, by comparing the passage to other texts of the same genre. On the other hand, a deviation with regard to the standard literary form can turn out to be significant. Another type of convention concerns the *degree of literality* of the text. Certain genres frequently employ metaphors and other figurative elements that are not meant to be taken literally. A third convention concerns the degree of *historicity* or of *fiction* that the author wants to give to his or her text. Typically, a parable should not be read like a normal narrative: the person who tells it can introduce fictional people or events without having to say so in an introduction.

In sum, appreciation of a text's literary genre allows you to avoid misinterpretations, since it helps you *adjust your expectations* to the nature of the text. Moreover, the identification of genre can help us better understand a text's original *function*, and sometimes its audience or readership; it can also help us understand the sociological and cultural setting in which the text was composed and used (which scholars refer to as the text's *Sitz im Leben*, or "life setting").

Once a passage's literary genre has been identified, the passage can be compared with other texts of the same genre. Just as you can study the occurrences of a *word* and its different usages in the Hebrew Bible, you can also compare different instances of the same literary genre.

Lastly, thanks to comparison with ancient Near Eastern texts of the same literary genre, or at least of a similar genre, it is sometimes possible to highlight aspects of the biblical text that we would otherwise miss: for example, literary conventions that appear more clearly outside of the Bible and that explain a certain detail in a passage. Conversely, when a biblical text diverges from the literary conventions employed in other texts of the same genre, this may indicate a strategy on the part of the biblical author to differentiate his message from the practices or worldview of the neighboring peoples.

In sum, we can proceed as follows:

1. IDENTIFY THE LITERARY GENRE OF THE TEXT.
2. COMPARE THE TEXT WITH OTHER TEXTS OF THE SAME GENRE THAT APPEAR IN THE HEBREW BIBLE.
3. TAKE NOTE OF THE LITERARY CONVENTIONS LINKED TO THE LITERARY GENRE IN QUESTION.
4. DETERMINE THE FUNCTION OF THE TEXT AND, IF POSSIBLE, ITS *SITZ IM LEBEN*.
5. COMPARE THE TEXT WITH EXTRABIBLICAL TEXTS WHOSE GENRE IS SIMILAR.

Before reviewing each of these steps, let me note a resource that is useful in several ways. The commentaries in the series FOTL (Forms of the Old Testament Literature) provide, for each pericope, a detailed structure and an examination of its literary genre, its context (dating, *Sitz im Leben*), and the intention that lay behind the text.

5.1 IDENTIFY THE LITERARY GENRE OF THE TEXT

Table 5.1 provides a list, with examples, of the main literary genres represented in the Hebrew Bible. It also includes a column that presents examples of possible parallels in ancient Near Eastern literature, which you may find helpful for contextualizing these biblical genres and to which you can refer back when you read the discussion later in this chapter on the comparative method.

It must be emphasized that there is no perfect or "official" list of the different literary genres attested in the Bible. This is due to at least four factors. First, the texts themselves only rarely provide explicit indications on this subject, and even when they do, making use of them is not necessarily easy. For example, the superscriptions of the psalms often contain words such as "psalm" (מִזְמוֹר) or "song" (שִׁיר), but these do not necessarily correspond to the categories that modern exegetes refer to when they use these terms; moreover, some such words that are found in the psalms are difficult to translate and seem to describe types of musical settings that are no longer known. Quite often, the genres biblicists refer to are scholarly constructs that are useful because of their heuristic function or because they can serve in exegetical discussions to distinguish different aspects of the text.

Second, and as a result of the first point, subjectivity plays a part in how one classifies texts, such that from one scholar to another there can be slight differences in terminology, especially when exegetes propose more-or-less detailed subgenres. Third, overlaps can occur: thus, the "call narrative" of a prophet could be considered to belong to either the category of "prophetic texts" or the category of "narratives." Fourth and finally, certain texts (especially in the Psalter) cannot easily be classified because they combine the characteristics of several genres.

It is important therefore to avoid regarding the identification of literary genre as a matter of scientific classification: while seeking to be as precise as possible, we must respect the freedom that the authors used and the flexibility of literary works, rather than forcing the texts into rigid categories. The most important task is not to label a passage, but to better understand its features.

Table 5.1: The Main Literary Genres in the Hebrew Bible

Genre	Subdivisions, Examples	Examples of Ancient Near Eastern Parallels
Narrative	Creation narrative (Gen 1; 2–3)	Egyptian cosmogonies (*Pyramid Texts, Sarcophagus Texts, Stone of Shabaka*) Mesopotamian myths of creation (*Genesis of Eridu, Enuma Elish, Atrahasis*)
	Flood narrative (Gen 6–9)	Mesopotamian flood narratives (*Atrahasis, Gilgamesh*, etc.)
	"Biographical" narrative or saga (Gen 12–50)	Egyptian biographical narratives (*The Story of Sinuhe, The Story of Wenamun*)
	Autobiography (Nehemiah)	Egyptian autobiography (Inscription of Udjahorresne)
	Conquest narrative (Josh 2–12)	Egyptian, Hittite, Mesopotamian conquest narratives
	Historiography (Judges; 1 and 2 Samuel; 1 and 2 Kings; 1 and 2 Chronicles)	Royal annals and chronicles from Assyria and Babylonia; royal inscriptions (Moabite Stone, a.k.a. Mesha Stele)
	Novel (Ruth, Esther)	*The Story of Sinuhe*
	Parable (Judg 9:8–15; 2 Sam 12:1–4)	Sumerian fables

Genre	Subdivisions, Examples	Examples of Ancient Near Eastern Parallels
Lists and genealogies	List (2 Sam 23:24–39)	Lists of people on Mesopotamian, Egyptian, and Syrian tablets; lists on ostraca in Paleo-Hebrew
	Genealogies of Gen 1–11 (Gen 5; 10)	Mesopotamian royal lists (esp. the *Sumerian King List*)
	Other genealogies (1 Chr 1–9)	Genealogy of the dynasty of Hammurabi; Egyptian sacerdotal genealogies
Legislative texts	Covenant narratives (Deuteronomy)	Vassal treaties (Hittite, Neo-Assyrian, etc.)
	Law codes (Exod 20–23; etc.)	Law collections (*Hammurabi's Code*, etc.)
	Ritual prescriptions (Lev 1–16)	Ritual texts (Emar, Ugarit, Hittites, etc.) Punic Marseille and Carthage Tarriffs
Lyric texts	Psalms • Wisdom or didactic psalms (Pss 1; 9–10; 25; 34; 37; 111; 112; 119) • Hymns (Pss 8; 19; 29; 33; 67; 100; 103; 104; 145) • Psalms of thanksgiving: individual (1 Sam 2:1–10; Pss 18; 32; 34; 40) or collective (Exod 15:1–21, Judg 5, Pss 66; 67; 124; 129) • Requests: individual (Pss 3; 5; 13; 22; 25) or collective (Pss 44; 79; 80; 83) • "Human" royal psalms (Pss 2; 20; 21; 45; 89; 110; 132) • Psalms about Yhwh's kingship (Pss 47; 93–99) • Songs of Zion (Pss 46; 48; 76; 87)	Egyptian, Akkadian, and Hittite hymns and prayers (*Great Hymn to the Aten*, *Hittite Plague Prayers*)
	Lamentations (Lam 1–5; Isa 14; Ezek 28)	Lamentations in Sumerian on the ruin of a city (Ur, etc.) Lamentations in Akkadian (of the type *balag* and *eršemmu*)
	Love poems (Song of Songs)	Egyptian and Mesopotamian love poems Arabic wedding songs from Syria (*waṣf*)
Prophetic texts	Salvation or restoration oracles (Ezek 36)	Prophecies of Mari (Syria) Neo-Assyrian prophecies
	Judgment oracles, including: • trial (Mic 6) • oracle about a nation (Isa 13–23; Jer 46–51)	
	Symbolic acts (Ezek 4–5)	
	Vision reports (Ezek 1–3; 8–11; 40–48; Zech 1–9)	Balaam's vision (Deir 'Alla inscription)
	"Quasi-prophecy" (Dan 11)	Akkadian "quasi-prophecies"
Letters	Letters (Ezra 4:8–24; 5:6–17)	Letters from El-Amarna, Egypt, Ugarit, Elephantine; Persian decree (*Letter to Gadatas*)

Genre	Subdivisions, Examples	Examples of Ancient Near Eastern Parallels
Wisdom texts	Proverbs (Prov 10–31; Eccl 7:1–8; 10:1–4)	Sumerian proverbs Egyptian proverbs (*Instruction of Amenemope*) Proverbs of Ahiqar (Aramaic)
	Instruction speeches (Prov 1–9)	Egyptian instruction texts (*Instruction of Amenenope, Instruction of Ptah-Hotep*, etc.)
	Reflective texts (Ecclesiastes)	Akkadian wisdom autobiographies
	"The righteous sufferer" (Job)	Mesopotamian "righteous sufferer"
	"Allegory" (Eccl 12:1–7)	*Instruction of Ptah-Hotep*

5.2 COMPARE THE TEXT WITH BIBLICAL TEXTS OF THE SAME LITERARY GENRE

Once you have identified the literary genre of the text you are studying, a whole range of comparable texts opens up to you. The steps to follow are:

Ⓐ Find passages in the Hebrew Bible that have the same literary genre.

Ⓑ Look for similarities between these passages and yours.

Ⓒ Look for differences between these passages and yours.

The differences are often the most interesting, since they point to aspects that are specific to the passage you are studying, and thus possibly to the intention that lay behind it.

Comparing a passage with others of the same genre often resembles the study of "type-scenes," which is usually undertaken as part of narrative criticism (see chapter 11). Indeed, there is a flexibility in the terminology employed in exegetical publications: some speak of identifying a literary genre, while others speak of a "type-scene."

EXAMPLE 5.2 ▸ 1 Kings 19

Micha Roi has studied what he calls the literary genre "departure on a journey";[1] this is relevant to texts such as Hagar's flight to the desert (Gen 16); Jacob's flight to Haran, which involves his famous stop at Bethel (Gen 27:41–28:22); Moses' flight to Midian, which ends with the episode of the burning bush (Exod 2:11–4:17); and Elijah's flight from Jezebel, which takes

---

1. Micha Roi, "1 Kings 19: A 'Departure on a Journey Story,'" *JSOT* 37 (2012): 25–44.

him to Mount Horeb (1 Kgs 19). The "normal" structure in these texts involves the following:

(1) a departure in the form of a flight from danger

(2) a meeting with God or a messenger of God that is not anticipated by the person and that takes place in a deserted location where he or she is alone; God reveals himself in a theophany

(3) a message of reassurance from God as well as promises of support and of blessing or prosperity to come, often linked to the person's descendants

(4) a return home.

These elements can be found in all the narratives mentioned above, with the exception of 1 Kgs 19, which is anomalous with respect to points (3) and (4). This passage is undoubtedly an example of the "departure on a journey" genre, inasmuch as Elijah flees and God reveals himself to Elijah in a theophany in a deserted place. But it is the divergences from the usual structure that constitute the most interesting aspects of this story. First, instead of receiving an assurance that he will be protected and accompanied by the divine presence for the rest of his life, Elijah receives an order entrusting him with a final mission: to anoint several people, notably the one who will replace him (vv. 15–18). There is no question here of a blessing on Elijah's descendants (of whom, indeed, nothing is known); instead, the focus is on the commissioning of Elisha, who is the son of someone else (Shaphath). And if there is an announcement about people whom God will look after, it is not about Elijah but about the seven thousand faithful ones whose knees "have not bowed to Baal" (v. 18). Second, there is no question of Elijah returning home once he has been reassured; he is asked to set out again and go to Damascus (v. 15).

What is the effect of these narrative elements that are specific to 1 Kgs 19? Certainly, God grants Elijah a theophany. However, by showing him that God is not in the violent natural phenomena that take place in front of the entrance to the cave in which he is hiding, and by letting him understand that in reality the divine presence is linked to "a sound of sheer silence" (v. 12), this revelation seems to teach a lesson to the man of God. It is all the more significant since Elijah had presided shortly beforehand over a spectacular victory over the enemy prophets, which culminated in their massacre (1 Kgs 18). In giving this spiritual lesson to Elijah and in announcing his replacement to him instead of reassuring him and promising him a blessed and prosperous new start, God is suggesting that all is not functioning well in his ministry. This will be confirmed by our further study of this text in the chapter on intertextuality (Example 12.1f below).

5.3 TAKE NOTE OF THE LITERARY GENRE'S CONVENTIONS

Next, it is important to draw conclusions from the fact that the text belongs to a certain literary genre, by taking into account the genre's conventions. I will mention three examples here: the presence of figurative language, the conditionality of prophetic announcements, and the "illocutionary stance" that an author takes regarding his own composition.

A. Figurative Language

As in any work of literature, the biblical texts contain standard rhetorical devices (or figures): comparison, metaphor, metonymy, synecdoche, etc. One of the most damaging mistakes that can occur in exegesis is when the reader takes literally elements of the text that were not meant to be read in this way. All texts can include figurative elements, of course, but their presence is especially prevalent in *lyric poems* and *prophetic oracles*, which are generally written in a poetic style.

> **EXAMPLE 5.3a** ▸ **Psalm 18 and Exodus 15**
>
> As an example, let us consider a group of texts we can call "thanksgiving songs," and more precisely those that constitute the poetic, or "lyrical," version of a narrative in which God intervened on behalf of an individual or a group. The case of Ps 18 (// 2 Sam 22)—a hymn in which an individual (David) sings about how God has delivered him—is telling. In vv. 2–16 [3–17], the psalmist employs striking images to evoke the way in which God intervened on David's behalf: an earthquake (v. 7 [8]), smoke coming out of God's nostrils (v. 8 [9]), etc. It is clear that the author does not take these images literally; rather, as a poet, his goal is simply to provide a lyrical version of the events. In this kind of text, using hyperbolic images is not only normal but is expected.
>
> Likewise, the narrative version of the crossing of the Sea of Reeds (Exod 14) is followed by a song (Exod 15:1–21) that offers a lyrical version of the events: it speaks not only of the Sea of Reeds in v. 4, but also of the "depths" in v. 5; in the place where the narrative said that God "drove the sea back" (14:21), the song pictures this as having occurred by the "blast of [God's] nostrils" (15:8). Another striking example of this method is found in Judg 4–5: a narrative version of events (ch. 4) is followed by a lyrical version in song (ch. 5).

> **EXAMPLE 5.3b ▸ Metaphors in the Prophetic Books**
>
> Prophetic texts contain many *metaphors*. We will learn in detail in chapter 10 how to study this kind of rhetorical device, so I will merely mention a few examples here:
>
> - The invasion of locusts in Joel 1–2: this serves as a metaphor for an army's attack on the people of Israel.
>
> - The conjugal metaphor in Hosea: the relationship between God and his people is likened to the one between a husband and his (adulterous) wife (Hos 1–2). This book also contains many metaphors that feature plants (e.g., 10:1 describes Israel as a vine) and animals (e.g., 4:16 describes Israel as a "stubborn heifer").
>
> - The metaphor of Zion as a mother appears in Isa 40–55 (in particular, in 49:14–26 and 55:1–10), Lamentations, and Ps 87. Specifically, Jerusalem/Zion is presented as a mother who has lost some of her children in the exile and to whom God gives new children, in abundance, when the exiles return (Isa 55 and Ps 87).

B. The Conditionality of Prophetic Announcements

An intuitive, traditional reading of the prophetic oracles might see them as comprising a large number of predictions that inevitably had to be fulfilled. But in Mesopotamia, the announcements made by prophets or seers were often contingent or conditional; they were not absolute decrees, but rather indications of what would happen if nothing intervened to change the situation. In the same way, many of the oracles in the Hebrew Bible contain an implicit conditionality and are above all calls to the people to modify their behavior so that the disasters being announced will *not* happen.[2] This does not mean that all the prophetic announcements are necessarily conditional, but it is an often-neglected point that should be kept in mind.

> **EXAMPLE 5.3c ▸ Jonah and Micah 3**
>
> When Jonah announces, "Forty days more, and Nineveh shall be overthrown!" (Jonah 3:4), he does so precisely in order that this should *not* happen. And indeed, the town is spared because the people repent (Jonah 3:10).

---

2. Lena-Sofia Tiemeyer, "Prophecy as a Way of Cancelling Prophecy—the Strategic Uses of Foreknowledge," *ZAW* 117 (2005): 329–50.

> Similarly, in Jer 26:16–19, the "elders of the land" conclude that God abstained from applying the threat of Mic 3:12—according to which Zion would be "plowed as a field" and Jerusalem would become "a heap of ruins"—because at the time Micah made this pronouncement, Hezekiah sought to appease the Lord.

C. Illocutionary Stance

Identifying the literary genre of a text can enable you not only to find out about the relevant literary conventions but also to grasp the specific purpose and nature of the text. To put it differently, the text's literary genre is a reflection of the author's project and of what he or she implicitly purports to offer the reader through the text. For instance, an author telling a story may implicitly adopt a variety of stances regarding the historicity of the events he mentions. These stances can include the following:

- "These are historical events, and I am telling you exactly how things happened."
- "This story is based upon facts, but it has been elaborated by the addition of fictional or reconstructed details."
- "Something like this must have happened."
- "This is pure fiction."

We can speak here of "illocutionary stance," in order to describe (1) the stance an author takes with regard to what he wants to achieve and (2) what he implicitly claims to be doing in his text. To confuse one stance for another is a major interpretive mistake. Biblical texts generally do not make their authors' stances explicit, and it is often by identifying a text's literary genre that an exegete can try to determine its stance.

EXAMPLE 5.3d ▸ Esther

> Does the author of the book of Esther purport to report only historical events, or only fiction, or a mixture of the two? Scholars have long noted that no extrabiblical confirmation of the events mentioned in the book exists; in particular, there is no trace that a persecution of Jews or a civil war linked to them took place in the Persian empire. Moreover, a number of aspects of the story this book tells seem unlikely from a historical point of view. For example, the principal wife of Ahasuerus (Xerxes I) was named Amestris, not Vashti or Esther; nothing allows us to assume that she bore two different names. In addition, the comical or ridiculous behavior of the characters in this book, and the nonsensicality of issuing an edict announcing a massacre eleven months in advance (Esth 3:12–13), suggest that the story is a fiction.

> In his commentary on Esther, Jean-Daniel Macchi argues that the book is a *persica*, that is, a fiction composed during the Hellenistic period about events situated in the Persian period. In this literary genre, which is well attested in Hellenistic literature, the Persian characters are depicted according to representations of them that were current in Hellenistic times. Like other works of the *persica* genre, the book of Esther projects into the Persian period concerns and topoi from Hellenistic times—notably the persecution of Jews within an empire, which reflects the situation that obtained in the early second century under Antiochus IV.[3]
>
> To some readers, asserting that Esther is a fiction is counterintuitive; some even think that asserting this is disrespectful toward the Scriptures. Yet if the author of this book wanted to compose a fiction, reading the book literally, as history, is not in line with the author's intention. As a matter of fact, the earliest reception of this book that we know about indicates that it was read as a fiction: that is, the scribes who added the supplements to the book that are canonical in Catholicism and in Orthodoxy did not hesitate to insert into the book stories that are universally recognized as fictional. Would they have done so if they had regarded the original story as purely historical?
>
> While some readers may be bothered by the idea that Esther could well be a fictional account, it is important to realize that this is because the results of scholarly investigation do not necessarily match our reading habits. Many people intuitively read stories in the Bible as history, as a sort of default position, but this is a modern expectation. Fiction is not a lower kind of literature; it is actually more powerful than history when it comes to conveying a message (which is why fictional shows on Netflix do more to shape the ideas of people today than documentaries do, for example). What would be a problem would be to "sell" a fictional account as if it were history, but that is not what the book of Esther does, since it does not claim to be historical.

5.4 DETERMINE THE TEXT'S FUNCTION AND *SITZ IM LEBEN*

The next step is to ask yourself what purpose the passage you are studying serves, and to ask what sociocultural context it could belong to. For a discussion that places each genre in its supposed *Sitz im Leben*, see:

- Rolf Rendtorff, *The Old Testament: An Introduction* (London: SCM Press, 1985), 77–128.

---

3. Jean-Daniel Macchi, *Esther*, IECOT (Stuttgart: Kohlhammer, 2018).

Numerous examples of this kind of analysis can also be found in the commentaries of the FOTL collection, which was mentioned at the beginning of this chapter. However, it is important to recognize that, generally speaking, the life settings (*Sitze im Leben*) that scholars suggest are simply hypotheses or reconstructions. Nevertheless, searching for them is stimulating and inspires us as readers to ask more questions about who the intended recipients of the text might have been.

> **EXAMPLE 5.4a ▸ Genesis 19:3–38; Kings**
>
> Certain texts have an etiological function: that is, they explain the origin of a present reality, such as a place name, the meaning of a religious festival, or the like. For example, the story about the incest of the mothers of Ammon and Moab (Gen 19:3–38) serves to show that these peoples and the people of Israel are cousins; at the same time, this story casts a bad light on these peoples. Similarly, the books of Kings (in their final redaction) provide a theological explanation for the demise of the Northern and Southern Kingdoms (describing these events as orchestrated by God as punishment for the religious unfaithfulness of Israel and Judah).

> **EXAMPLE 5.4b ▸ The Oracles against the Nations**
>
> The "oracles against the nations" (Amos 1; Isa 13–21; Jer 46–51; etc.) probably do not figure among the favorite passages of modern readers of the Bible. What are these texts for? They are addressed to nations or kings, but it is clear that this is simply a literary convention: they were not read by the rulers of Egypt or Babylon (among others), but instead were aimed at the people of Israel and Judah.
>
> In fact, the function of these texts seems to be threefold. First, they emphasize in a very practical way the sovereignty of Yhwh over all the nations, providing a "universalistic" perspective that contrasts with the common ancient Near Eastern idea that a god ruled over only one particular country. The fact that the prophets of the God of Israel can pronounce judgment against kings of all the countries that were known at the time illustrates the scope of his dominion. Second, and even more importantly, this shows that the people of all nations are accountable to God: they must answer for their actions (cf. Amos 1–2, where Judah is criticized for having disobeyed the law and Israel is criticized for transgressions of specific commandments, whereas the Arameans, Philistines, etc., are condemned for infringing the most basic of ethical standards). Third, these oracles comfort the people of Israel and Judah by affirming that the nations who are humiliating them will one day be punished by God.

> **EXAMPLE 5.4c ▸ Chronicles**
>
> Why was the book of Chronicles written? After all, a very large part of its contents are already available in other parts of the Bible—for example, the genealogies of Genesis and the narratives in Samuel–Kings. Indeed, Genesis through Kings constitutes a continuous history (which scholars sometimes call "the Primary History") ranging from creation to the end of the kingdom of Judah. Nonetheless, an author (or several) decided to write another narrative covering almost the same history, from Adam to the edict of Cyrus, which authorized the reconstruction of the temple. Since the historical project we find in Chronicles is parallel to the Primary History (both are histories of the same people), what is its purpose? And who are its target readers?
>
> The answer can be found in clues given by the text itself. First of all, in Chronicles, the story very quickly focuses in on Judah, leaving the northern kingdom of Israel aside. It is the dynasty of David that captures this narrator's attention, with King David and King Solomon being presented as "types," or models, of what a good ruler should be. Even when Chronicles mentions David's fault in ordering a census, it uses this event to explain how the place of the temple was chosen (1 Chr 21–22). Indeed, Chronicles accords great importance to this divine sanctuary. After all, the culmination of this long history is the announcement of the reconstruction of the temple (2 Chr 36:22–23). In addition, the text devotes a good deal of space to those who serve in this building (1 Chr 15–16; 23–26), especially the Levites. This specific perspective has led many exegetes to conclude that the milieu that produced Chronicles was that of the Levites in the Persian period.
>
> Second, while the books of Kings (the culmination of the Primary History) provide an etiology of the fall of the Hebrew kingdoms, Chronicles rereads the history of the entire world and specifically that of the chosen people from another, and this time positive, angle: that of a return to religious life centered on the temple in a new period ushered in by its reconstruction. Moreover, many passages in Chronicles have a "homiletic" quality that points to the pedagogical function this book was intended to have for the restored community. According to Chronicles, history furnishes examples, models, countermodels, and "types." Chronicles' insistence on "divine retribution" for the deeds of various people throughout history (1 Chr 28:8–9; 2 Chr 12:5; etc.) also has an instructive dimension. Its positive view of the reigns of David and Solomon does not amount to nostalgia for a "golden age," but reflects hope of a future renewal for Judah. In short, the function of this book is above all to draw lessons from the past in order to help the community living in the province Yehud during the late Persian period (or the early Hellenistic period) to live better in the future.

5.5 COMPARE WITH EXTRABIBLICAL TEXTS WHOSE GENRE IS SIMILAR

The extant literature from the ancient Near East considerably expands our ability to better situate a biblical passage among the range of texts that existed in antiquity. The **comparative method** has indeed proved to be a fruitful approach since the nineteenth century, when ancient Near Eastern texts began to be discovered and deciphered in significant numbers. This method can yield a variety of results:

- Reading comparable ancient Near Eastern texts may reveal some literary conventions that are less evident in biblical literature; this may shed light on an aspect of a particular biblical text that previously was neglected or surprising.

- The ability to compare biblical and extrabiblical sources that deal with the same historical period, or the same events, is a valuable tool for historians. This may help determine whether it is certain, likely, or unlikely that an event mentioned in the Bible actually occurred, and it can also provide background information or help situate an event within a larger sequence of events.[4]

- In some cases, it turns out that the redactors of a biblical text were familiar with an ancient Near Eastern text and used it when writing their own composition. This provides crucial information for the relative dating of the biblical text in question; moreover, it allows the exegete to see which elements from the extrabiblical text the biblical redactors incorporated into their composition and which they left out, as well as how else they may have deviated from their source. All of this is helpful for understanding the logic of the text.

- Most of the time, however, a biblical text that contains influences from the ancient Near East was not inspired by a particular extrabiblical text but rather was informed more generally by an ancient Near Eastern literary tradition, or at least by a cultural/religious tradition that is reflected in various ancient Near Eastern texts. By learning about the cultural "air" the redactors or their audiences breathed—that is, the ideas and motifs that were part of their cultural horizon—exegetes find themselves in a much better position to spot allusions and reactions that are implicit in the biblical texts.

---

4. These are facets of the comparative method that we will explore in chapter 8. The approach there will be broader than in the present chapter, since, as we will discuss, historical information can be drawn from texts with a wide range of literary genres, not only those with the same genre as the biblical text under study.

A methodological caveat must be noted at this point. Struck by the similarities between ancient Near Eastern documents and certain biblical texts, some scholars in the past tended to iron out the differences or to unduly project onto the biblical texts features present in the extrabiblical texts. The discovery of Babylonian texts, for instance, led to the phenomenon of "Pan-Babylonianism" in the nineteenth century, whereby some scholars tended to see Babylonian influences everywhere in the Hebrew Bible. But writers are always free, and experience shows that the biblical redactors did not hesitate to deviate from the patterns found in extrabiblical sources, sometimes for polemical purposes. This needs to be kept in mind.

Outlining the basic steps in the comparative method is not difficult:

- **Ⓐ Find relevant, comparable texts** for the biblical passage you are studying. Note that these need not always belong to exactly the same literary genre, but they should belong to a genre that bears a sufficient degree of resemblance to the genre of the biblical text in question to make the comparison reasonable.

- **Ⓑ Note the similarities** and **reflect** on how they might elucidate the biblical text. Was it composed in light of a particular text or in light of a broader tradition? Do some aspects of the text appear in a new light?

- **Ⓒ Note the differences** and **reflect** on how they might illuminate the specific characteristics of the biblical text and its underlying intentions.

The quantity of extant ancient Near Eastern literature is so vast that it resembles a maze. Where can you find a reliable translation of a particular Mesopotamian text? Has anyone already made a systematic comparison of, say, prophecy in the Bible and the ancient Near East? Table 5.2 below—which lists ancient Near Eastern parallels for each biblical literary genre—is meant to help you begin answering questions like these. Once you have identified the type of text you are looking for, you can consult one of the anthologies, text editions, or comparative studies listed in this table.

A. Consult an Anthology

The main reference books in English that present translations of ancient Near Eastern texts are:

- *ANET* = James B. Pritchard, ed., *Ancient Near Eastern Texts Relating to the Old Testament*, 3rd ed. (Princeton: Princeton University Press, 1969). A text can be quoted by its page in *ANET*. Note that *ANET* contains an index of biblical references. A two-volume pocket edition also exists: James B. Pritchard, ed., *The Ancient Near East* (Princeton: Princeton University Press, 1958–75). In addition, a more recent abridgment of *ANET*—which also incorporates parts of Pritchard's companion volume *The Ancient Near East in Pictures Relating to the Old Testament*, 2nd ed. (Princeton: Princeton University

Press, 1969)—has been published under the title *The Ancient Near East: An Anthology of Text and Pictures* (Princeton: Princeton University Press, 2011).

- *COS* = William W. Hallo and K. Lawson Younger, eds., *The Context of Scripture*, 4 vols. (Leiden: Brill, 1997–2017). A collection of English translations with philological notes; biblical parallels are indicated in columns. One disadvantage is that there is no index of biblical references. Scholarly books and articles typically refer to a text from *COS* by its "*COS* number" (for example, *COS* 2.123 means text number 123 in volume 2).

Table 5.2 provides references to *COS* for a number of ancient Near Eastern texts that provide parallels to biblical genres.

In addition, each volume of the following series contains an anthology of texts (in English translation) belonging to a literary genre as it is attested in a particular geographically defined, linguistic, or epigraphic corpus (e.g., "Hittite Prayers" or "Law Collections from Mesopotamia and Asia Minor"):

- *WAW* = the series Society of Biblical Literature, Writings from the Ancient World (Atlanta: SBL Press). Presents translations with notes.

The following one-volume anthologies of English translations are also very helpful:

- Michael D. Coogan, *A Reader of Ancient Near Eastern Texts: Sources for the Study of the Old Testament* (New York: Oxford University Press, 2013).

- Bill T. Arnold and Brian E. Beyer, *Readings from the Ancient Near East: Primary Sources for Old Testament Study* (Grand Rapids: Baker Academic, 2002).

B. Consult an Edition

When your goal is to do in-depth verification of or research on details in a particular ancient Near Eastern text, it can be desirable to consult a scholarly edition of the work that contains the text in its original language and also, if possible, a translation. For instance, you may want to read in its entirety a work for which only excerpts are provided in anthologies like *COS*, or you may wish to check a particular Akkadian or Ugaritic phrase in a text. Each chapter of the following excellent guide is devoted to a distinct literary genre and introduces the most relevant ancient Near Eastern documents, along with helpful bibliography:

- Kenton L. Sparks, *Ancient Texts for the Study of the Hebrew Bible: A Guide to the Background Literature* (Grand Rapids: Baker Academic, 2017).

In addition to its references to *COS*, Table 5.2 provides examples of useful text editions.

Table 5.2: Ancient Near Eastern Parallels and Where to Read Them

Ancient Near Eastern Parallels	Where to Read Them
Egyptian and Mesopotamian creation accounts (cf. Gen 1–3) Mesopotamian flood accounts (cf. Gen 6–9)	• *The Eridu Genesis* (*COS* 1.158), *Atrahasis* (*COS* 1.130), Egyptian cosmologies (*COS* 1.1–20). • James P. Allen, *The Ancient Egyptian Pyramid Texts*, WAW 38 (Atlanta: SBL Press, 2015). • Philippe Talon, *The Standard Babylonian Creation Myth Enūma Eliš*, SAATC 4 (Helsinki: Neo-Assyrian Text Corpus Project, 2005). • Stephanie Dalley, *Myths from Mesopotamia: Creation, the Flood, Gilgamesh, and Others* (Oxford: Oxford University Press, 1989).
King lists (cf. genealogies in Gen 4; 5; 11)	• *COS* 1.134–138. • Jean-Jacques Glassner, *Mesopotamian Chronicles*, WAW 19 (Atlanta: SBL Press, 2004).
"Biographical" narratives (cf. Gen 12–50)	• *The Story of Sinuhe* (*COS* 1.38), *The Story of Wenamun* (*COS* 1.41). • Elizabeth Frood, *Biographical Texts from Ramessid Egypt*, WAW 26 (Atlanta: SBL Press, 2007).
Conquest narratives (cf. Joshua)	• Annals of Thutmosis III (*COS* 2.2A), Annals of the tenth year of Mursili II (*COS* 2.16). • K. Lawson Younger, *Ancient Conquest Accounts: A Study in Ancient Near Eastern and Biblical History Writing*, JSOTSup 98 (Sheffield: JSOT Press, 1990).
Parables	• Sumerian fables (*COS* 1.178). • Wilfred G. Lambert, *Babylonian Wisdom Literature* (Oxford: Clarendon, 1960), 150–212.
Vassal treaties (cf. Exodus, Deuteronomy)	• Simo Parpola and Kazuko Watanabe, *Neo-Assyrian Treaties and Loyalty Oaths*, SAAS 2 (Helsinki: Helsinki University Press, 1988). • Kenneth A. Kitchen and Paul J. N. Lawrence, *Treaty, Law and Covenant in the Ancient Near East*, vol. 1: *The Texts*; vol. 2: *Text, Notes and Chromograms*; vol. 3: *Overall Historical Survey* (Wiesbaden: Harrassowitz, 2012).
Law collections (cf. Exodus-Leviticus-Numbers-Deuteronomy)	• Martha T. Roth, *Law Collections from Mesopotamia and Asia Minor*, 2nd ed., WAW 6 (Atlanta: SBL Press, 1997).

Ancient Near Eastern Parallels	Where to Read Them
Ritual texts (cf. Leviticus)	• Rituals of Emar (*COS* 1.122–127) and of Ugarit (*COS* 1.94–97, 100), Punic tariff (*COS* 1.98). • Dennis Pardee, *Ritual and Cult at Ugarit*, WAW 10 (Atlanta: SBL Press, 2002).
Egyptian, Akkadian, and Hittite hymns and prayers (cf. Psalms)	• *COS* 1.114–117. • John L. Foster, *Hymns, Prayers, and Songs: An Anthology of Ancient Egyptian Lyric Poetry*, WAW 8 (Atlanta: SBL Press, 1995). • Alan Lenzi, *Reading Akkadian Prayers and Hymns: An Introduction*, ANEM 3 (Atlanta: SBL Press, 2011). • Itamar Singer, *Hittite Prayers*, WAW 11 (Atlanta: SBL Press, 2002).
Lamentations on the ruin of a town (cf. Lamentations)	• *Lamentation on the Ruin of Sumer and Ur* (*COS* 1.166). • Mark E. Cohen, *The Canonical Lamentations of Ancient Mesopotamia* (Potomac, MD: Capital Decisions, 1988). • Piotr Michalowski, *The Lamentation over the Destruction of Sumer and Ur*, MC 1 (Winona Lake, IN: Eisenbrauns, 1989).
Love poems (cf. Song of Songs)	• Egyptian love poems (*COS* 1.49–52). • Yitzhak Sefati, *Love Songs in Sumerian Literature: Critical Edition of the Dumuzi-Inanna Songs* (Ramat-Gan: Bar-Ilan University Press, 1998). • Michael V. Fox, *The Song of Songs and Ancient Egyptian Love Songs* (Madison: University of Wisconsin Press, 1985).
Prophecies	• *COS* 1.42–45; 2.24, 27. • Martti Nissinen, *Prophets and Prophecy in the Ancient Near East*, 2nd ed., WAW 12 (Atlanta: SBL Press, 2019).
"Akkadian prophecies" (cf. Dan 11)	• *The Dynastic Prophecy* (*COS* 1.150). • Tremper Longman III, *Fictional Akkadian Autobiography: A Generic and Comparative Study* (Winona Lake, IN: Eisenbrauns, 1991). • Matthew Neujahr, *Predicting the Past in the Ancient Near East: Mantic Historiography in Ancient Mesopotamia, Judah, and the Mediterranean World*, BJS 354 (Providence, RI: Brown Judaic Studies, 2012), 13–73.

Ancient Near Eastern Parallels	Where to Read Them
Visions	• Balaam's vision: Deir 'Alla inscription (*COS* 2.27). • Jacob Hoftijzer and Gerrit van der Kooij, *Aramaic Texts from Deir 'Alla* (Leiden: Brill, 1976).
Letters (cf. Ezra-Nehemiah)	• Letters in Ugaritic (*COS* 3.45A–PP), Paleo-Hebrew (*COS* 3.41–44), and Aramaic (*COS* 3.46–54). • Edward F. Wente, *Letters from Ancient Egypt*, WAW 1 (Atlanta: SBL Press, 1990). • Harry A. Hoffner Jr, *Letters from the Hittite Kingdom*, WAW 15 (Atlanta: SBL Press, 2009). • Dennis Pardee, *Handbook of Ancient Hebrew Letters: A Study Edition*, SBLSBS 15 (Atlanta: Scholars Press, 1982). • James M. Lindenberger, *Ancient Aramaic and Hebrew Letters*, 2nd ed., WAW 4 (Atlanta: Scholars Press, 2003). • Bezalel Porten, *The Elephantine Papyri in English: Three Millennia of Cross-Cultural Continuity and Change*, 2nd ed. (Atlanta: SBL Press, 2011).
Sumerian, Egyptian, and Aramaic proverbs (cf. Proverbs)	• Sumerian proverbs (*COS* 1.174–175), *Instruction of Amenemope* (*COS* 1.47). • Wilfred G. Lambert, *Babylonian Wisdom Literature* (Oxford: Clarendon, 1960), 222–82. • Michael Weigl, *Die aramäischen Achikar-Sprüche aus Elephantine und die alttestestamentliche Weisheitsliteratur*, BZAW 399 (Berlin: de Gruyter, 2010).
Reflections of wise men (cf. Ecclesiastes)	• *Instruction of Ptah-Hotep* (cf. Eccl 12:1–8). • *The Song of the Tomb of King Intef* (*COS* 1.30). • *The complaints of Khakheperre-sonb* (*COS* 1.44). • Akkadian wisdom autobiographies (*COS* 1.151–154); Tremper Longman III, *Fictional Akkadian Autobiography: A Generic and Comparative Study* (Winona Lake, IN: Eisenbrauns, 1991).
"The righteous sufferer" of Mesopotamia (cf. Job)	• *COS* 1.151–154. • Amar Annus and Alan Lenzi, *Ludlul bēl nēmeqi: The Standard Babylonian Poem of the Righteous Sufferer*, SAACT 7 (Helsinki: Neo-Assyrian Text Corpus Project, 2010). • Wilfred G. Lambert, *Babylonian Wisdom Literature* (Oxford: Clarendon, 1960), 21–91. • Takayoshi Oshima, *Babylonian Poems of Pious Sufferers*, ORA 14 (Tübingen: Mohr Siebeck, 2014).

In addition to printed editions of ancient Near Eastern literature, a number of websites provide editions and translations:

- *ETCSL = The Electronic Text Corpus of Sumerian Literature. Contains a variety of Sumerian texts (original and English translation).

- *Archibab = Archives babyloniennes. Covers the twentieth through seventeenth centuries BCE. Brings together many texts (in the original, and sometimes in French translation) that originate, notably, from the royal palace of Mari and that concern "current affairs" (administrative documents, letters, etc.).

- *SAAo = State Archives of Assyria Online. This is the online equivalent of the series SAA (State Archives of Assyria), offering scholarly editions of Assyrian texts.

- *Knowledge and Power in the Neo-Assyrian Empire. This site is devoted to Assyria in the seventh century. It includes not only texts (letters, oracles, etc.) but also much historical information.

- *RINAP = The Royal Inscriptions of the Neo-Assyrian Period. Aims to publish all the royal texts dating from the reigns of Tiglath-Pileser III, Shalmaneser V, Sargon II, Sennacherib, and Esarhaddon—that is, from the period 744–669 BCE.

- *CTIJ = Cuneiform Texts mentioning Israelites, Judeans, and Related Population Groups. Aims to bring together all the texts from the period 744–300 BCE (from Tiglath-Pileser III to Alexander the Great) that mention Israel, Judah, or neighboring peoples.

- *eTACT = Electronic Translations of Akkadian Cuneiform Texts. Brings together English translations of classic Akkadian works (*Enuma Elish*, etc.).

C. Consult a Comparative Study

For an even more in-depth study, you may want to turn to articles and monographs that provide a detailed comparison between biblical and ancient Near Eastern texts that belong to a particular literary genre. Table 5.3 offers *examples* of comparative studies for most genres. To find recent publications, notably scholarly articles, you can search for keywords in a library catalogue or a search engine such as Google Scholar.

As a model for the application of the comparative method to most literary genres, I recommend the following book (which provides translations and thoughtful reflections):

- Christopher B. Hays, *Hidden Riches: A Sourcebook for the Comparative Study of the Hebrew Bible and Ancient Near East* (Louisville: Westminster John Knox, 2014).

Table 5.3: Examples of Comparative Studies for Most Genres

Genres	Examples of Comparative Studies
Egyptian and Mesopotamian creation accounts (cf. Gen 1–3) Mesopotamian flood accounts (cf. Gen 6–9)	• Richard J. Clifford, *Creation Accounts in the Ancient Near East and in the Bible*, CBQMS 26 (Washington, DC: Catholic Biblical Association, 1994). • Michaela Bauks, *Die Welt am Anfang: Zum Verhältnis von Vorwelt und Weltentstehung in Gen 1 und in der altorientalischen Literatur*, WMANT 74 (Neukirchen-Vluyn: Neukirchener Verlag, 1997). • Helge S. Kvangig, *Primeval History: Babylonian, Biblical, and Enochic; An Intertextual Reading*, JSJSup 149 (Leiden: Brill, 2011).
King lists (cf. genealogies in Gen 4; 5; 11)	• Richard S. Hess, "The Genealogies of Genesis 1–11 and Comparative Literature," *Bib* 70 (1989): 241–54, reprinted in *I Studied Inscriptions from before the Flood: Ancient Near Eastern, Literary, and Linguistic Approaches to Genesis 1–11*, ed. Richard Hess and David T. Tsumura (Winona Lake, IN: Eisenbrauns, 1994), 58–72.
Conquest narratives (cf. Joshua)	• James K. Hoffmeier, "The Structure of Joshua 1–11 and the Annals of Thutmose III," in *Faith, Tradition, and History*, ed. Alan R. Millard, James K. Hoffmeier, and David W. Baker (Winona Lake, IN: Eisenbrauns, 1994), 165–79. • John Van Seters, "Joshua's Campaign and Near Eastern Historiography," *SJOT* 2 (1990): 1–12.
Vassal treaties (cf. Exodus, Deuteronomy)	• Kenneth A. Kitchen and Paul J. N. Lawrence, *Treaty, Law and Covenant in the Ancient Near East*, vol. 3: *Overall Historical Survey* (Wiesbaden: Harrassowitz, 2012). • William S. Morrow, "Treaties/Loyalty Oaths and Biblical Law," in *The Oxford Handbook of Biblical Law*, ed. Pamela Barmash (New York: Oxford University Press, 2019), 319–32.
Collections of "laws" (cf. Exodus-Leviticus-Numbers-Deuteronomy)	• Richard Westbrook, *Studies in Biblical and Cuneiform Law*, CahRB 26 (Paris: Gabalda, 1988). • Pamela Barmash, ed., *The Oxford Handbook of Biblical Law* (New York: Oxford University Press, 2019) [specifically Part IV].

Genres	Examples of Comparative Studies
Ritual texts (cf. Leviticus)	• Dennis Pardee, *Ritual and Cult at Ugarit* (Leiden: Brill, 2002), 233–41. • David W. Baker, "Leviticus 1–7 and the Punic Tariffs: A Form-Critical Comparison," *ZAW* 99 (1987): 188–97. • Yitzhaq Feder, *Blood Expiation in Hittite and Biblical Ritual: Origins, Context, and Meaning*, WAWSup 2 (Atlanta: SBL Press, 2011). • Samuel L. Balentine, ed., *The Oxford Handbook of Ritual and Worship in the Hebrew Bible* (New York: Oxford University Press, 2020).
Egyptian, Akkadian, and Hittite hymns and prayers (cf. Psalms)	• Alan Lenzi, ed., *Reading Akkadian Prayers and Hymns: An Introduction*, ANEM 3 (Atlanta: SBL Press, 2011).
Lamentations on the ruin of a town (cf. Lamentations)	• Paul W. Ferris Jr., *The Genre of Communal Lament in the Bible and the Ancient Near East*, SBLDS 127 (Atlanta: Scholars Press, 1992).
Love poems (cf. Song of Songs)	• Michael V. Fox, *The Song of Songs and Ancient Egyptian Love Songs* (Madison: University of Wisconsin Press, 1985).
Prophecies	• Jonathan Stökl, *Prophecy in the Ancient Near East: A Philological and Sociological Comparison*, CHANE 56 (Leiden: Brill, 2012). • Martti Nissinen, *Ancient Prophecy: Near Eastern, Biblical, and Greek Perspectives* (Oxford: Oxford University Press, 2017).
"Akkadian prophecies" (cf. Dan 11)	• Matthew Neujahr, *Predicting the Past in the Ancient Near East: Mantic Historiography in Ancient Mesopotamia, Judah, and the Mediterranean World* (Providence, RI: Brown Judaic Studies, 2012).
Balaam's vision (cf. biblical visions reports)	• Jacob Hoftijzer and Gerrit van der Kooij, eds., *The Balaam Text from Deir 'Alla Re-Evaluated* (Leiden: Brill, 1991). • George H. van Kooten and Jacques van Ruiten, ed., *The Prestige of the Pagan Prophet Balaam in Judaism, Early Christianity and Islam*, TBN 11 (Leiden: Brill, 2008).
Letters (cf. Ezra-Nehemiah)	• Dirk Schwiderski, *Handbuch des nordwestsemitischen Briefformulars: Ein Beitrag zur Echtheitsfrage der aramäischen Briefe des Esrabuches*, BZAW 295 (Berlin: de Gruyter, 2000).

Genres	Examples of Comparative Studies
Sumerian, Egyptian, and Aramaic proverbs (cf. Proverbs)	• Glendon E. Bryce, *A Legacy of Wisdom: The Egyptian Contribution to the Wisdom of Israel* (Lewisburg, PA: Bucknell University Press, 1979). • Diethard Römheld, *Wege der Weisheit: Die Lehren Amenemopes und Proverbien 22.17–24.22*, BZAW 184 (Berlin: de Gruyter, 1989). • John Day, "Foreign Semitic Influence on the Wisdom of Israel and Its Appropriation in the Book of Proverbs," in *Wisdom in Ancient Israel: Essays in Honour of J. A. Emerton*, ed. John Day, Robert P. Gordon, and Hugh G. M. Williamson (Cambridge: Cambridge University Press, 1998), 55–70. • Michael V. Fox, "From Amenemope to Proverbs: Editorial Art in Proverbs 22,17–23,11," *ZAW* 126 (2014): 76–91.
"The righteous sufferer" of Mesopotamia (cf. Job)	• R. G. Albertson, "Job and Ancient Near Eastern Wisdom Literature," in *Scripture in Context*, vol. 2, *More Essays on the Comparative Method*, ed. William W. Hallo, James C. Moyer, and Leo G. Perdue (Winona Lake, IN: Eisenbrauns, 1983), 213–30.

Let us now turn to some examples.

EXAMPLE 5.5a ▸ **Exodus 22:2–3 [1–2]**

While studying the law against burglary found in Exod 22:2–3 [1–2], you may wonder if there is an equivalent in the laws of the ancient Near East. Table 5.2 indicates that such legislation does exist outside the Bible, notably in the famous "Code of Hammurabi." Of the four volumes of *COS*, the second ("Monumental Inscriptions") proves to be the most helpful here (since the Code of Hammurabi is engraved on a large basalt stela): the table of contents indicates that there is a section in the volume called "'Functional' Inscriptions" that contains laws, notably "The Laws of Hammurabi." The easiest approach is to examine the central column, which lists biblical parallels: indeed, Exod 22:2–3 [1–2] is noted as being linked to the law found in §21 of the Code of Hammurabi, which stipulates that if a man breaks into a house, he must be killed and hanged in front of the place where he broke in.

Comparing this law with Exod 22:2–3 [1–2] is interesting, since—beyond the obvious similarity between the laws—this reveals two differences. On the one hand, Exodus provides for a case in which the burglar is caught red-handed and is killed. In such a scenario, the one who caused his death will be considered guilty if the break-in happened during the day but innocent if it took place at night; the notion of mitigating circumstances is implicitly present and concerns the owner of the house. On the other hand, if the burglar is seized, he will not be killed but must provide compensation (or, if he cannot, he must sell himself as a slave).

EXAMPLE 5.5b ▸ Job

If you are studying the book of Job, you may wish to compare it to similar texts from the ancient Near East. Table 5.2 indicates the existence of a corresponding literary genre in Mesopotamia: that of the "righteous sufferer." To find out more, you can consult *COS*, for example. Of the four volumes of this work, volume 1 (on "Canonical Compositions") is most relevant. The table of contents lists a section called "Akkadian Canonical Compositions"; this has a subcategory called "Individual Focus," which in turn contains another subcategory called "Just Sufferer Compositions," which comprises four texts. The introductions to these texts are relatively short, but the one for *COS* 1.153 specifies that the text it presents—called *Ludlul bēl nēmeqi* (after its opening words)—has often been compared to Job. Similarly, the introduction for *COS* 1.154 ("The Babylonian Theodicy") indicates that this is another text that, from a formal point of view, forms a close parallel to the book of Job.

There are interesting similarities and differences between Job and these two works. The "Babylonian Theodicy" is made up of speeches that are exchanged between a "righteous sufferer" and his friend, and moreover, these speeches are written in poetic form, as are the speeches in Job. However, this Mesopotamian work merely states the problem of the righteous man suffering, but it does not provide any solution or explanation.

Ludlul bēl nēmeqi is more relevant in terms of its substance. The fates of Job and of his Mesopotamian counterpart, Shubshi-meshre-shakkan, are similar, and their complaints resemble each other in many ways; in addition, the circumstances of both men are ameliorated in the end. An important difference, however, is that whereas the book of Job contains a narrative frame that explains the hidden reasons why Job suffers, *Ludlul bēl nēmeqi* does not. Moreover, only in Job do we find dialogues between the sufferer and his friends. Furthermore, in *Ludlul bēl nēmeqi* the god Marduk never speaks, whereas in Job the Lord delivers extended speeches and intervenes on Job's behalf. The most important question is whether either text provides any justification for circumstances that are prompted by the deity. The answer is not straightforward: in *Ludlul bēl nēmeqi*, no reason is provided as to why Marduk caused Shubshi-meshre-shakkan's predicament, and the reason provided in the prologue to Job is linked to a wager that the Lord makes with

> Satan. Christopher Hays writes: "If either Marduk or Yhwh is vindicated, it is not by some intellectual breakthrough, but by the practical restoration that each offers in the end."[5]

EXAMPLE 5.5c ▸ Genesis 5 and 11

The genealogies in Gen 5 and 11 contain striking similarities with some Mesopotamian king lists. The latter are not genealogies; instead, they compile the names of kings who supposedly reigned successively in important cities and specify the length of their reigns. The most classic example is the "Sumerian King List" (henceforth SKL); an extract, taken from Michael Coogan's anthology of ancient Near Eastern texts, reads as follows:

> When kingship had come down from heaven, kingship was at Eridu. Alulim was king; he reigned 28,800 years; Alalgar reigned 36,000 years; two kings reigned 64,800 years. Eridu was abandoned; its kingship was taken to Bad-tibira.
>
> At Bad-tibira, Enmen-lu-ana reigned 43,200 years; Enmen-gal-ana reigned 28,800 years; the divine Dumuzi, the shepherd, reigned 36,000 years; three kings reigned 108,000 years. I abandon Bad-tibira; its kingship was taken to Larak.
>
> . . .
>
> Five cities; eight kings ruled 385,200 years.
>
> The Flood swept over. After the Flood had swept over, when kingship had come down from heaven, kingship was at Kish.
>
> At Kish, Gishur was king; he reigned 1,200 years; Kullassina-bel reigned 900 years . . . Etana the shepherd, the one who went up to heaven, who put all countries in order, was king; he reigned 1,500 years.[6]

A close comparison between this text and Gen 5 and 11 reveals both similarities and differences. Some of them you will be able to spot when comparing the texts on your own. However, this is a case where consulting comparative studies may help. Richard Hess's article, mentioned in Table 5.3, surveys the research on the subject up to 1989, so it is a good starting point.

---

5. For a more detailed discussion, see Christopher B. Hays, *Hidden Riches: A Sourcebook for the Comparative Study of the Hebrew Bible and Ancient Near East* (Louisville: Westminster John Knox, 2014), 331–36 (with quotation on 336).

6. Michael D. Coogan, *A Reader of Ancient Near Eastern Texts: Sources for the Study of the Old Testament* (New York: Oxford University Press, 2013), 65–66.

Then, if you look for keywords such as "genealogies," "Genesis 5," "Genesis 11," and "Sumerian King List" in a library catalogue or in an online search engine, you will easily find more publications on the subject.[7]

Here is a list of similarities:

- The formulaic style, with indications of durations (whether of someone's life or a king's reign). In SKL, before the flood, the total length of the reigns of kings of the same town is often added up; after the flood, it is omitted. In the same way, Gen 5 indicates the total number of years lived by an antediluvian patriarch before and after he begat his son (for example, 5:23 states that "all the days of Enoch were three hundred sixty-five years"); after the flood, this is no longer the case.

- The presence, within this repetitive pattern, of narrative parentheses. For example, SKL states that Etana "ascended to heaven" and "put all the land in order"; compare the statement in Gen 5:24 that "Enoch walked with God, and he was not, for God took him."

- The caesura between two periods created by the flood (cf. Gen 6–9).

- The astronomically high numbers for the lengths of someone's life or a king's reign, with a net decrease in both cases after the flood.

- The number of stages of royal succession before the flood in SKL tends to be ten (although in some tablets it is eight), like the number of generations in the genealogy of Gen 5.

- The numbers in SKL are often multiples of 3,600 before the flood and multiples of 60 afterward. In Genesis, the numbers before the flood are often multiples of 5, sometimes with the addition of 7 or of 14 (i.e., 7 + 7).

At the same time, significant differences emerge:

- Genesis is not talking about kings, but about ordinary people without titles, and the link between adjacent individuals in

---

7. For instance: Dwight W. Young, "A Mathematical Approach to Certain Dynastic Spans in the Sumerian King List," *JNES* 47 (1988): 123–29; Young, "On the Applications of Numbers from Babylonian Mathematics to Biblical Life Spans and Epochs," *ZAW* 100 (1988): 332–61; Young, "The Influence of Babylonian Algebra on Longevity among the Antediluvians," *ZAW* 102 (1990): 321–25; Casper J. Labuschagne, "The Life Spans of the Patriarchs," in *New Avenues in the Study of the Old Testament*, ed. Adam S. van der Woude, OTS 25 (Leiden: Brill, 1989), 121–27; Donald V. Etz, "The Numbers of Genesis V 3–31: A Suggested Conversion and Its Implications," *VT* 43 (1993): 171–89.

the list is not one of dynastic succession but of the line of descent. In addition, unlike SKL, Genesis provides the total number of years in two stages (dividing them at the point at which a father begets a son).

- Similarly, the starting point in Genesis is not the "descent" of royalty from heaven to earth, but (taking into account the larger context of the Genesis narrative) the creation of human beings.
- SKL constantly jumps from one city to another, whereas the biblical text evokes a linear succession.

All in all, there are enough formal resemblances to justify the hypothesis that the author of Genesis drew inspiration from some version of SKL.[8] The similarities may explain some puzzling features of Gen 5 and 11. For example, the brief parentheses about certain individuals in the list are not necessarily later additions, since this seems to be a normal feature of the literary genre in question (or, at least, such parentheses were likely to have been present in the document the author of Genesis used as a model for his text). Moreover, while I noted above a feature common to Etana in SKL and Enoch in Gen 5, some compare the latter with Enmen-dur-ana (also called Enmenduranki), the seventh king mentioned in SKL, because there are traditions according to which he ascends to heaven and meets the sun god Shamash. As David Carr notes: "This theory then might explain why Enoch is placed in a similar seventh position in Genesis 5, lives a lifespan whose 365 years mirror the days in a solar year (//Shamash), and enjoys a heavenly audience with YHWH akin to that which Enmenduranki is described as having with Shamash."[9]

Another interesting point of comparison is the fact that in SKL the numbers are often multiples of 3,600 (= 60 x 60) and of 60, and in Gen 5 they are multiples of 5. In SKL, this is obviously a play on numbers, 60 being the basis of the sexagesimal system that was used in Mesopotamia. While the situation is less clear in Gen 5, the use of such formulaic numbers in SKL suggests that the numbers in Gen 5 are also a literary construction that follows a pattern. Many publications are devoted to elucidating what this pattern might be.[10]

Nevertheless, the differences between SKL and the biblical text indicate that the author of Genesis did not simply wish to write an "alternative history" for the Hebrew people. Behind the change from kings to ordinary people may lie a polemical intention, one that is in line with the idea that the image of God is not the prerogative of leaders but the privilege of every person (Gen 1:27).

---

8. Carr, *Formation of Genesis 1–11*, 104–7.
9. Carr, *Formation of Genesis 1–11*, 107.
10. See footnote 7 on p. 151.

EXERCISES FOR CHAPTER 5

Exercise A

What is the literary genre of Job? Do you think it is a historical account, a fictional story, or a mixture of the two? Justify your view.

Exercise B

Read an English translation of *Enuma Elish* (a Mesopotamian creation myth), for instance in *COS* or in Michael Coogan's anthology of ancient Near Eastern Texts. Then read Gen 1. What, in your view, are the most striking similarities? What are the most striking differences? What light do these similarities and differences shed on the biblical text?

Exercise C

Read an English translation of Tablet XI of the *Gilgamesh Epic* (which contains the story of the flood). Draw up a list of similarities between this text and Gen 6–9. How do you explain the fact that there are so many resemblances? What are the most striking differences? What light do these similarities and differences shed on the biblical text?

Exercise D

Find the *Great Hymn to the Aten* in an anthology and compare it to Ps 104. What, in your view, are the most striking similarities, and how do you explain them? What are the most striking differences? What light do these similarities and differences shed on the biblical text?

Exercise E

A surprising feature of some complaint psalms is the sudden shift from complaint to praise that one encounters in them. Read, for instance, Ps 22. Some scholars suggest logical explanations for the shift just mentioned (e.g., a sudden change of mood, a reply from the Lord given by a priest or a prophet), while others believe this shift is due to a juxtaposition of texts from different sources or to redactional activity. Could prayers from the ancient Near East shed some light on this issue? To find out, read Alan Lenzi, ed., *Reading Akkadian Prayers and Hymns: An Introduction*, ANEM 3 (Atlanta: SBL Press, 2011), 279–81 (an open-access version is available on the SBL Press website). Then summarize Lenzi's conclusions.

CHAPTER 6

LITERARY CONTEXT

OVERVIEW

It is a well-known and fundamental rule that a text must be read in its context. The advantage of taking into account the literary context is that this enables us (1) to obtain useful (background) information and (2) to avoid incorrectly interpreting the text's nature and subject matter. More precisely:

- We must often peruse the text just before the passage we are studying in order to obtain information on the characters who appear in our text, as well as (for a narrative text) information on the circumstances in which our episode takes place or (for a prophetic oracle) information on the message that is being delivered.
- The context sometimes indicates the genre of the passage we are studying (e.g., speech, vision) or the passage's function.
- The passage can be part of a literary progression or larger whole that forms a coherent subunit within the biblical book in which it is found.

Taking into account the context sometimes merely amounts to reading a little before and a little after the passage in order to find out some useful information. But, as we will see, it is possible to go much further and discover subtler contextual features, ones that have even more important implications for the exegesis of the text in question. In other words, this stage of exegesis can be completed in five minutes . . . or two hours.

How to proceed? You can search in two directions:

❶ IDENTIFY, **IN THE TEXTS SURROUNDING THE PASSAGE IN QUESTION**, USEFUL CONTEXTUAL INFORMATION (CIRCUMSTANCES, CHARACTERS, FUNCTION OF THE PASSAGE, ETC.).

❷ LOCATE THE PASSAGE **WITHIN A POSSIBLE PROGRESSION OR LARGER LITERARY WHOLE**.

6.1 HOW TO IDENTIFY USEFUL INFORMATION IN THE CONTEXT

This is the easiest step. However, it sometimes demands more discernment than might be imagined.

EXAMPLE 6.1a ▸ Genesis 12:10–20

The narrative found in Gen 12:10–20 could simply be read as the account of a particular event that took place in the lives of Abram and his wife Sarai, one that concerns their relationship and that raises questions about the morality of the patriarch's behavior: When he and Sarai go to Egypt in this passage, he claims that she is his sister, so that he will not be killed by the Egyptians who otherwise would want to take her away from him. This has terrible consequences for Sarai, since Pharaoh does take her into his palace—presumably not just to have coffee with her, but to add her to his "harem." But limiting one's interpretation to these aspects of the story would entail missing the principal concern of the text itself, which can be discerned only if we take into account the broader context. Indeed, the previous pericope (12:1–9) recounts a promise that God makes to Abram, a central element of which is God's declaration that Abram will have descendants so numerous that they will constitute a "great nation" (v. 2). But at this stage, Abram does not have a single child. Consequently, when he "loses" his wife in 12:10–20, a crucial actor in the fulfillment of the promise seems to disappear! In other words, the issue in this passage, in its present literary context, is not so much the drama the couple experiences or the moral aspects of the attitudes and actions of Abram or Pharoah, but the future of God's promise—and even of the origins of the Hebrew people—which is (temporarily) put in jeopardy.

EXAMPLE 6.1b ▸ Genesis 23

Further on in the Abra(ha)m cycle, a whole chapter is dedicated to negotiations that this patriarch enters with the Hittites in order to buy some land (Gen 23). What is the purpose of this passage? On the surface, it might seem to be merely the boring account of a somewhat "technical" episode in the life of the patriarch. But again, if the promise (12:1–9) that introduces the whole Abraham cycle is taken into account, it becomes clear that ch. 23 has a much deeper meaning: it is about the *first piece of the promised land* that comes into Abraham's possession; in other words, this story describes the beginning of the fulfillment of an important element of the promise (12:7).

EXAMPLE 6.1c ▸ Ezekiel 40–48

Ezekiel 40–48 contains a lengthy description of a temple. It would not make sense for a reader to randomly open his or her Bible to Ezek 41:1–4 and think that they were reading here a description of the Holy Place (vv. 1–2) and of the Holy of Holies (vv. 3–4) belonging to *the historical temple that was located in Jerusalem* (whether Solomon's temple or the later second temple). Ezekiel 40:1–4, which introduces chs. 40–48, clearly indicates that these chapters constitute a *vision*. This is a very simple case in which the context gives us information about the literary genre of the passage being studied.

EXAMPLE 6.1d ▸ Psalms 1 and 2

It is very common to read the psalms one by one, in isolation from one another. But the Psalter opens with two psalms that form a "gateway" to the rest of the book by introducing key themes that will recur throughout it.[1]

Psalm 1, which contrasts divergent ways of life and standard characters ("the righteous," "the wicked," "mockers") in the style of the book of Proverbs, resembles a *wisdom* text. This sets the tone for the entire Psalter, and there are several implications to this. First, this prologue transforms Psalms from the status of a "simple" song book that is meant generally for public worship to a book that is meant to be useful for personal edification and instruction. Second, Ps 1 indicates, at the very beginning of the Psalter, that the spiritual situation of the reader of the various texts in the Psalter matters. This psalm describes the personal piety of the individual who meditates day and night on the law of the Lord (vv. 1–2), before mentioning the community of the righteous (v. 5). Implicitly, it suggests that the only people who can truly "enter" this collection of psalms are those who are pious and righteous. This contrast between the righteous and the wicked in Ps 1 calls to mind the one between "Lady Wisdom" and "Lady Folly" found in Prov 8, which serves to prepare for the antithetical character of many of the statements found in the rest of the book of Proverbs. In fact, a "wisdom flavor" is regularly present in the Psalter. Here are some examples to illustrate the point:

---

1. In antiquity, Pss 1 and 2 were in fact considered by some readers to be one single psalm. In Acts 13:33, Paul quotes Ps 2:7, evoking what "is written in the second psalm," but some manuscripts have "in the first psalm" here.

> O LORD, who may abide in your tent? Who may dwell on your holy hill? Those who walk blamelessly and do what is right and speak the truth from their heart; who do not slander with their tongue . . .
>
> (Ps 15:1–3)
>
> Keep your tongue from evil and your lips from speaking deceit.
>
> (Ps 34:13 [14])
>
> Better is a little that the righteous person has than the abundance of many wicked. For the arms of the wicked shall be broken, but the LORD upholds the righteous.
>
> (Ps 37:16–17)[2]
>
> Psalm 2 describes a man whom the Lord has enthroned on his "holy hill," who has received an anointing, and who benefits from particular divine protection. It draws attention to the person of the king, who keeps appearing throughout the Psalter. Moreover, this text lends itself easily to a messianic interpretation, at least in the strictest sense of the word (since "messiah" means "anointed one").
>
> This double opening to the book of Psalms provides a lens for reading the whole collection. From the point of view of compositional criticism, it remains important to look into the origins of any particular psalm; but when studying the final form of the text, we can take into account the desire on the part of the final editors of the Psalter that the collection as a whole be read with the double perspective of wisdom and "messianism."

6.2 HOW TO LOCATE THE PASSAGE WITHIN A POSSIBLE LITERARY PROGRESSION

Paying careful attention to echoes and developments in an unfolding narrative may help you identify an artful literary progression.

> **EXAMPLE 6.2a ▸ Passages about Women in Judges**
>
> Women play a significant role in many passages in the book of Judges. When you are studying one of these texts, it would be a shame to ignore the fact that this is a major theme of the book. The place of women in society and the

---

2. Without this reference, one might think this was a passage from Proverbs!

treatment that they experience at the hands of men constitute an important *leitmotif* in the book, and the successive episodes bring to light a clear deterioration in this respect (see Table 6.1). The accounts progress from describing women who have a place in society (thus, Deborah is a judge and a prophet) to women who are treated increasingly worse and are increasingly anonymous. This negative development is a sort of parallel to the deterioration that can be observed in the religious behavior of the Israelites and the judges themselves, suggesting perhaps that the way in which women are treated acts as a barometer for the spiritual health of the country.[3] At the same time, the intelligence that women exhibit—from Achsah to Deborah to Manoah's wife to Delilah—seems constant. Consequently, if you are studying a specific text in the book of Judges and a woman plays a role in the story, it is worth situating it within this general literary arc.

Table 6.1: Passages about Women in Judges

Passage	Woman/Women	Events
Judg 1:12–15	Achsah	Woman who is given in marriage by her father but who also obtains springs of water from him
Judg 4–5	Deborah	Woman who is a prophetess and judge (Deborah)
	Jael	Woman who kills the enemy leader (Jael)
Judg 9:50–57	Woman of Thebez	(Anonymous) woman who kills Abimelech
Judg 11	Daughter of Jephthah	(Anonymous) daughter who is sacrificed by her father
Judg 12:9	Daughters of Ibzan	(Anonymous) daughters who are given in marriage and women who are brought from outside the clan
Judg 13	Wife of Manoah	(Anonymous) wife who is more insightful than her husband
Judg 17	Delilah	Woman who manages to manipulate her husband

---

3. Alternatively, some of the redactors of Judges may have wanted to suggest that the absence of a monarchy leads to chaos; indeed, politics and religion were entangled in ancient Israel. We will come back to the issue of women in Judges in chapter 14 (Feminist and Gender Studies), in Example 14.2c.

| Judg 19 | Levite's concubine | (Anonymous) woman who is raped, beaten up, and cut into pieces |
| Judg 21 | Women of Jabesh-gilead | (Anonymous) women who are abducted to be taken as wives |

Sometimes, the links between the passage you are studying and its literary context are numerous, and the shared elements create a network of connections. When a large number of similarities are present, this brings the differences between your passage and its context into greater relief (as illustrated in the two next examples). In such cases, overlooking the network means missing an important literary strategy that is likely to affect the message of the text.

EXAMPLE 6.2b ▸ Genesis 4:1–16

If you are studying the story of Cain and Abel (Gen 4:1–16), it would be a shame not to take the time to look back at the previous section, not only because it provides the general background (humans are now living outside Eden) but also—and most importantly—because the redactor of Gen 4 deliberately used terms that recall Gen 3 when he wrote his own account, something that is apparent only through close observation.

In Gen 3, Adam and Eve disobey God, who encounters them and pronounces a series of punishments against them. In the following chapter, Cain murders his brother; God speaks to him and again pronounces a punishment. A comparative examination (see Table 6.2) shows a series of echoes of ch. 3 in ch. 4, right down to the very expressions that have been employed.

Table 6.2: Comparison of Genesis 3 and Genesis 4

Genesis 3	Genesis 4
"But the LORD God called to the man and said to him, 'Where are you?'" (v. 9)	"Then the LORD said to Cain, 'Where is your brother Abel?'" (v. 9)
"What is this that you have done?" (v. 13)	"What have you done?" (v. 10)
"Your desire shall be for your husband, and he shall rule over you" (v. 16)	"Its [sin's] desire is for you, but you must master it" (v. 7)

"Cursed is the ground because of you" (v. 17)	"And now you are cursed from the ground, which has opened its mouth to receive your brother's blood from your hand" (v. 11)
"In toil you shall eat of it [the ground]" (v. 17)	"When you till the ground, it will no longer yield to you its strength" (v. 12)
"until you return to the ground, for out of it you were taken; you are dust, and to dust you shall return" (v. 19)	"You will be a fugitive and a wanderer on the earth" (v. 12)
God's kindness: tunics (v. 21)	God's kindness: mark (v. 15)
God banishes the man to the east of the garden of Eden (v. 24)	Cain goes out from before God and lives in the land of Nod, to the east of Eden (v. 16)

Through this subtle network of connections, the narrator encourages us to compare Gen 3 and 4, and this leads us to note important differences. Thus, when God asked Adam where he was, he replied by admitting that he had hidden himself and by explaining why he had done so, showing that he was conscious that he was the source of the problem ("I was afraid, because I was naked," 3:10). By contrast, when the Lord asks Cain where his brother is, the murderer—who is the last person to have seen the lifeless body of his victim—lies ("I do not know," 4:9). Even worse, by adding to his answer the question "Am I my brother's keeper?," he throws the problem back on the Lord.

What's more, while Adam remains silent when he listens to the punishments pronounced by God, Cain dares to respond and even to comment on the condemnation that he must undergo: "my punishment is greater than I can bear" (4:13). Far from showing the least sign of regret or repentance, he fears for his life; in other words, he is afraid of suffering the fate that he inflicted on his own brother. Strikingly, Cain frames this risk as a consequence of what God has planned: "Today you have driven me away from the soil, . . . and anyone who meets me may kill me" (4:14). He thus continues to deflect the blame from himself by arguing about what the Lord has said. In parallel, the punishments increase in intensity: it was the ground, not Adam, that was cursed in Gen 3; in ch. 4, however, it is Cain himself who becomes cursed (4:11). And whereas Adam is banished to the east of the garden of Eden, Cain wanders to the east of *the entire region of Eden*—in other words, further still.

Taken on its own, the narrative about Cain and Abel could be read as the story of a fratricide only. But when its context is taken into account, we see it as the continuation of the transgression of Gen 3—and indeed, as an aggravation of it, both in the transgression itself and in the ensuing consequences.

EXAMPLE 6.2c ▸ Exodus 15:22–17:7

Exodus 17:1–7, in which Moses strikes a rock with his staff, is the third of a group of consecutive accounts in which the Hebrew people go through the same kind of trial and exhibit the same kind of reaction. Immediately after leaving Egypt, they get stuck in several similar situations (Exod 15:22–27; 16:1–36; 17:1–7). Many similarities can be observed among these three accounts (see Table 6.3 below): each time, after a journey, the people go through a trial linked to their provisions (food or drink) and complain about their leaders, in particular disputing Moses' authority; each time, God intervenes miraculously (the first and the third times through a staff). Such a series of resemblances among three consecutive pericopes is hardly fortuitous. In fact, while these passages seem at first glance very repetitive, interesting differences appear (again, see the table).

First, we can note a *steady increase in the complaints*. A question that seems justified in the first episode ("What shall we drink?," 15:24) gives way in the second to an expression of nostalgia for Egypt and a surprising imputation of evil motives to Moses and Aaron ("for you have brought us out into this wilderness to kill this whole assembly with hunger," 16:3). In the third episode, the people issue a command to Moses and Aaron ("Give us water," 17:2), impugn their motives again, and doubt the presence of God. In addition, in this last episode, three verbs (not just one) are used to describe the dispute.

Second, we can observe an *evolution in who is targeted by the complaint*: in the first account, Moses alone is targeted; in the second account, Moses and Aaron are; and in the third account, even God himself is the target of the complaint. More importantly, in the first two passages, it is God who puts the people to the test through rules they are to respect; by contrast, in the final episode, there are no rules or test for the people: in an astounding reversal, the text states that this time *it is the people who put God to the test*.

In short, these three episodes are tightly linked to one another, and taken together, they describe a negative development on the part of the people during the difficulties they experience: at the end of a series of similar trials that exposes their insubordination, the situation ends up being turned into a trial of God himself. Another element, this time having to do with the wider context of the Pentateuch, could also be taken into account in analyzing these texts: the comparable episode of Num 20:1–13. But that is another story.

Table 6.3: Exodus 15, 16, and 17

	Marah (Exod 15:22–27)	Desert of Sin (Exod 16)	Massah and Meribah (Exod 17:1–7)
Journey	From the Sea of Reeds to the wilderness of Shur (v. 22)	From Elim to the wilderness of Sin (v. 1)	From the wilderness of Sin to Rephidim (v. 1)
Problem	No water, water is bitter (vv. 22–23)	Hunger (v. 3)	No water (v. 1)
Verbs	Murmur (v. 24)	Murmur (v. 2)	• Find fault (vv. 2, 7) • Murmur (v. 3) • Put to the test (v. 7)
Complaints	"What shall we drink?" (v. 24)	"If only we had died . . . in the land of Egypt, . . . for you have brought us out into this wilderness to kill this whole assembly" (v. 3)	• "Give us water to drink" (v. 2) • "Why did you bring us out of Egypt, to kill us . . . with thirst?" (v. 3) • "Is the Lord among us or not?" (v. 7)
Against	Moses (v. 24)	• Moses and Aaron (v. 2) • God: "Your complaining is not against us but against the Lord" (v. 8)	• Moses (find fault, murmur) • God (put to the test): "Why do you test the Lord?" (v. 2)
Solution	Staff thrown into water (v. 25)	Manna and quail (vv. 4–5, 11–18)	Rock struck with staff (v. 6)
Rules	"the Lord made for them a statute and an ordinance" (v. 25)	Rules about manna (vv. 4–5)	
Test	God tests the people (v. 25)	God tests the people (v. 4)	The people test God (v. 7)

> **EXAMPLE 6.2d ▸ Psalms 111 and 112**

The Psalter is not simply a compendium of songs appended one after the other without any logic. It contains subcollections, recurrent formulae that unite series of psalms, and so on. Let us consider a simple case: it would be a shame to look at Ps 112 without a glance at the psalm that comes before it. When these two psalms are compared, a whole series of connections appears (see Table 6.4).[4]

Table 6.4: Psalms 111 and 112

Psalm 111	Psalm 112
Starts with "Praise the LORD"	Starts with "Praise the LORD"
Ends with "The fear of the LORD is the beginning of wisdom"	Opens with "Happy are those who fear the LORD"
Subject: description of the works of the Lord	Subject: description of the works of the man who fears the Lord
"the LORD is gracious and merciful" (v. 4)	"They rise in the darkness as a light for the upright; they are gracious, merciful, and righteous" (v. 4)
"his righteousness endures forever" (v. 3)	"their righteousness endures forever" (v. 3)
"He provides food" (v. 5)	"they have given to the poor" (v. 9)
"He has gained renown by his wonderful deeds" (v. 4)	"the righteous . . . will be remembered forever" (v. 6)

What is the meaning of these parallels? For its part, Ps 111 describes the righteous acts of God and enjoins the reader to fear him. Psalm 112 reminds the reader that those who fear God are "happy," and it describes the actions of such people in terms that evoke the ones used about God in the preceding psalm. Like God, the righteous are "gracious" and "merciful," "their righteousness endures forever," they give to those in need, and they "will be remembered." Thus, the diptych that these two texts form suggests that *those who fear God act in a manner that reflects the manner in which God himself acts*. We would miss this message if we read Ps 112 on its own, without taking into account the previous psalm.

---

4. These two psalms are also linked by the fact that each is an acrostic (see p. 210).

Literary Context, Synchronic and Diachronic Approaches

The approach followed in this chapter is mostly *synchronic*: that is, we have been analyzing the text in its final state, regardless of the history of its composition. Reading the text continuously leads us to discover echoes, parallels, developments, differences, and other literary features that exegetes (more or less implicitly) consider to be due to a deliberate act of arrangement that they attribute to a writer, a redactor, or a narrator. Indeed, it is often the case that an artful composition seems to reveal a unified literary project that originated in a single mind. But it may also be that the current sequence of the text is the product of a long compositional development. *Diachronic* studies are devoted to understanding how a text developed over time.

To take a simple illustration, two adjacent pericopes may have their origins in the work of two different redactors, even though their juxtaposition has given rise to the kind of literary connections just mentioned. This could be the result of deliberate composition, whereby the redactor who wrote the newer pericope did so in light of the older one or whereby a redactor combined two earlier sources. Moreover, once two passages have been placed next to each other, they may also have been further modeled on each other by means of small, later additions that created more links between them. It is often difficult to say what happened. For instance, we have seen that Gen 4 echoes Gen 3 (Example 6.2b). It may simply be that Gen 4 was modeled on Gen 3. But it is also conceivable that, *after* Gen 4 was written in light of Gen 3 and placed immediately following it, some expressions from Gen 4 were inserted back into Gen 3, thus bringing both chapters even more into conformity with each other.[5] This is sometimes called the "boomerang phenomenon."[6] The same question can be raised for Pss 111 and 112 (Example 6.2d), which may have been edited to echo each other. Likewise, we have seen that there are many parallels between Exod 15:22–27, 16:1–36, and 17:1–7 (Example 6.2c); however, many scholars think that these stories resulted from a long and complicated compositional history. In other cases, the situation may be, at least in part, "accidental": a scribe may have interpolated a passage into a narrative without anticipating all the consequences, on a literary level, of the combination he thus created.

To sum up, ascribing the literary features we observe in the final state of the text to the strategy of a single writer or redactor is not necessarily a reflection

---

5. See, more generally, the nuanced discussion about the similarities between Gen 2–3 and Gen 4 in Carr, *Formation of Genesis 1–11*, 66–73.

6. Yair Zakovitch, "The Book of the Covenant Interprets the Book of the Covenant: The 'Boomerang Phenomenon,'" in *Texts, Temples, and Traditions: A Tribute to Menahem Haran*, ed. Michael V. Fox et al. (Winona Lake, IN: Eisenbrauns, 1996), 59*–64* [Hebrew]. The Hebrew expression often translated by "boomerang phenomenon" in English-language publications is תופעת הבומראנג.

of what actually happened. In practice, exegetes who work in a synchronic perspective generally proceed *as if* these features stemmed from the intentions of a single redactor; for narrative texts, they speak of a "narrator" to designate the "voice" that speaks in the book. But it is important to remember that these are scholarly conventions; they are helpful conventions, to be sure, but they must not be confused with the historical claim that a single person wrote the whole text and planned all its features. What can be said with certainty is that the final redactor or editor left us a text that contains these literary features, whether this person was aware of all of them or not.

This does not mean that the kinds of features that are germane to a text's literary context are relevant only for synchronic studies. On the contrary: because such features may stem from strategies used by redactors to (for instance) artfully insert a passage into a preexisting work, it is very important for scholars working in a diachronic perspective to identify such features. It would not make sense to discuss the compositional history of Gen 2–4, for example, without taking into account the presence of echoes between Gen 3 and Gen 4.

To put it simply, diachronic studies are interested in the possible redactional reasons that lie behind the presence of certain literary features, while synchronic studies are interested in the literary consequences of the presence of these features. Where these two approaches may diverge is when they yield competing explanations about the origins of these features. Some scholars will regard the links between certain passages as hints that the text is a unified composition originating with a single writer, whereas others will explain them as techniques used by successive redactors to expand the text. Deciding what is the best explanation in any given case is a matter of judgment.

Exercises for Chapter 6

Exercise A

Read Gen 22 and consider it on its own. How would you describe the main problem that this narrative evokes? Now take into account the literary context of the whole Abraham cycle (Gen 12–25), especially Gen 12. In light of this context, what is at stake in ch. 22?

Exercise B

In 2 Kgs 4:42–44, Elisha multiplies a modest amount of food so that it will feed a hundred people. Is this brief episode the sequel of the preceding narrative (vv. 38–41) or is it a standalone story? Are vv. 42–44 presented as occurring in a time of famine? In other words, what changes when we read this brief episode in connection with the one that precedes it rather than as an independent story?

Exercise C

Compare 1 Sam 24 and 26, and highlight the similarities and differences between them. What changes when you read ch. 26 *after* reading ch. 24? For instance, does David's attitude evolve between these chapters? Does it matter that ch. 25 is "sandwiched" between these two similar chapters?

Exercise D

Forget everything you know about Job and read Job 3 as if for the first time. (If you actually have never read the entire book, do not read chs. 1–2 first.) From your reading of ch. 3, what is your understanding of the man Job and of his situation? Now read Job 1–2. How do these chapters affect your understanding of Job 3?

Exercise E

This is a follow-up exercise to the previous one. The book of Job comprises a long core made up of poetic speeches (Job 3–41), and this core is embedded in a narrative framework that includes a prologue (Job 1–2), which sets the stage, and an epilogue, which provides a happy ending (Job 42). Some exegetes believe that the book once existed without this narrative framework. Others think that the core of the book does not make sense without this framework because the latter provides the context for the debate that takes place between Job and his friends. What is your opinion?

Exercise F

What difference does it make to read Ps 106 while taking into account Ps 105?

CHAPTER 7

HISTORICAL GEOGRAPHY

OVERVIEW

The study of geography is essential for understanding the literature of ancient Israel and Judah, since these two small countries were each composed of very different regions and marked by a rather varied terrain. Indeed, the very logic of some biblical passages is difficult to grasp without understanding their geographical references. Specialists distinguish between two areas of study, which are interrelated. On the one hand, physical geography is concerned with natural features like the topography of a country, the presence of a river in a region, etc. On the other hand, human geography focuses on the interaction between human beings and the places where they live. One example of a topic that is of interest to scholars is the place names (*toponyms*) of populated sites, especially those that are mentioned in the Bible. Indeed, study of these place names helps situate them on a map and associate them with archaeological sites (if possible), and all this may shed light on what the Hebrew Bible says about human activities that took place in these locations.

Here are some elements that matter in terms of geography, irrespective of whether the situation described in the text is historical or fictional:

- *Situating places on a map* can enable you to better understand the logic behind where the characters in a story are located (for instance, this can help clarify the tactics employed in a battle).

- *Assessing the distance between two places* allows you to understand the distance a person travels from one to the other or to better assess the dynamics of a situation (e.g., the proximity of danger).

- When you come across a *series of places*, situating them on a map can help you realize, for example, that it is not a random accumulation of names that is being described but rather an *itinerary*.

- Beyond purely topographical questions, the mention of a place can be a way of *implicitly evoking the whole of the history associated with it*, or at least some *connotations the name bears*. Sources that help us find out about the history of a place include not only the relevant biblical and ancient Near Eastern texts but also the results of archaeological surveys and excavations.

This last point serves as a reminder that geography and history are inextricably linked.

How to proceed? The following steps can be followed:

❶ NOTE THE RELEVANT PLACES IN THE TEXT AND **SITUATE THEM ON A MAP**.

❷ WHEN DEALING WITH MORE THAN ONE PLACE, **ASSESS THE DISTANCE** BETWEEN THEM OR THEIR **RELATIVE POSITIONS**.

❸ IN THE CASE OF AN **ITINERARY**, IDENTIFY AND INTERPRET IT AS SUCH.

❹ FIND OUT ABOUT THE **HISTORY OF A PLACE** THROUGH ARCHAEOLOGY.

❺ DETECT ALLUSIONS TO THE POSSIBLE **OVERTONES** A PLACE NAME MIGHT HAVE.

7.1 SITUATE PLACES ON A MAP

In the case of a *narrative text*, the first task is to simply look for the places that are named in order to find out where the episode takes place. In an *account of a journey* or in a *prophetic or poetic text*, it may be that a whole series of places are named. Situating a place within a region can provide helpful information about its climate, how the site could be accessed, whether it was far from another, central location, etc. In addition to the towns and cities that are mentioned in the text, regions (e.g., Gilead) are of great importance because the topography of Israel is quite varied.

Atlases

The most helpful resources here are atlases; here are some examples:

- Anson F. Rainey and R. Steven Notley, *The Sacred Bridge: Carta's Atlas of the Biblical World*, 2nd ed. (Jerusalem: Carta, 2015). A magnificent and very rich atlas, with maps for numerous biblical episodes. An excellent resource.

- Adrian Curtis, *Oxford Bible Atlas* (Oxford: Oxford University Press, 2007).
- Meir Ben-Dov, *Carta's Illustrated History of Jerusalem*, 2nd ed. (Jerusalem: Carta, 2006). Contains numerous drawings and maps.
- Siegfried Mittmann and Götz Schmitt, eds., *Tübinger Bibelatlas* (Stuttgart: Deutsche Bibelgesellschaft, 2001). Includes very large, very detailed bilingual German/English map sheets.

Because you often do not know in advance exactly where to look on a map to situate a place, when you first pick up an atlas it can be useful to consult the index, which will point out the section of the map to look at. Once you find the location on a map, you may also wish to enter the location in Google Earth or Google Maps, which can provide you with an even more precise view of the region in which the place is located; this is especially helpful if you wish to study the place's topography (by viewing it in relief, looking for nearby waterways, etc.). If you want to learn more about the history of a place, you can consult an encyclopedia.

EXAMPLE 7.1 ▸ Tyre in Ezekiel 26–28

The book of Ezekiel contains a series of oracles about Tyre (Ezek 26–28). A quick look at an atlas will show you that this city was situated to the north of Israel, on the maritime coast (in what is now Lebanon and what in antiquity was a Phoenician territory). This already explains the numerous references to the sea in Ezek 26–28. But you may be struck by some verses that state that God will "bring up the deep" over Tyre so that the "great waters" will cover it (26:19) or that Tyre was "in the midst of the sea" (27:32) or "in the heart of the seas" (28:2), which implies that it was an island.

If you check a more detailed atlas or consult Google Earth or Google Maps and zoom in on Tyre, you will notice that today this city is located on a peninsula. If you are curious enough to consult an encyclopedia entry on Tyre, you will learn that, by contrast, at the time of Ezekiel Tyre was in fact an island. It became a peninsula only in the late fourth century BCE, when Alexander the Great had a dam built in order to besiege it (although the decisive battle was largely a naval one). Before that, the city was impregnable. Hence the references, in the verses noted above, to Tyre being situated in the middle of the sea.

For Further Reading on Historical Geography

Identifications of places mentioned in the Bible with locations known from extrabiblical sources from the Near East are often uncertain. If such an identification proves crucial for your study, it may be necessary to go beyond the mere use of an atlas and to critically examine the reasons behind the standard identification. This will be all the more pertinent when scholars have suggested several hypotheses. The encyclopedia EBR (= Hans-Josef Klauck et al., eds., *Encyclopedia of the Bible and Its Reception* [Berlin: de Gruyter, 2009–]) has an entry for every geographical name contained in the Bible, and the entries often mention, even if very briefly, the most probable identifications. To find out more, you can consult the following classic works on historical geography (especially by using their indexes):

- Félix-Marie Abel, *Géographie de la Palestine*, 2 vols., Ebib (Paris: Gabalda, 1967).

- Michael Avi-Yonah, *The Holy Land from the Persian to the Arab Conquests, 536 B.C. to A.D. 640: A Historical Geography*, rev. ed. (Grand Rapids: Baker, 1977).

- Yohanan Aharoni, *The Land of the Bible: A Historical Geography* (Philadelphia: Westminster, 1979).

- Othmar Keel, *Orte und Landschaften der Bibel: Ein Handbuch und Studien-Reiseführer zum Heiligen Land*, 2 vols. (Göttingen: Vandenhoeck & Ruprecht, 1982–84).

- Zecharia Kallai, *Historical Geography of the Bible* (Jerusalem: Magnes, 1986).

To these should be added the following books, the first of which was already mentioned above:

- Anson F. Rainey and R. Steven Notley, *The Sacred Bridge: Carta's Atlas of the Biblical World*, 2nd ed. (Jerusalem: Carta, 2015).

- Paul H. Wright, *Holman Illustrated Guide to Biblical Geography: Reading the Land* (Nashville: Holman Reference, 2020).

In some cases, there are technical works dedicated to a particular biblical book or section of a book: e.g.,

- Jan Svensson, *Towns and Toponyms in the Old Testament: With Special Emphasis on Joshua 14–21* (Stockholm: Almqvist & Wiksell, 1994).

- Erasmus Gaß, *Ortsnamen des Richterbuchs in historischer und redaktioneller Perspektive*, ADPV 3 (Wiesbaden: Harrassowitz, 2005). On the book of Judges.

Note that in discussions of historical geography, Eusebius's *Onomasticon*, which is a valuable ancient source, is often referred to. To consult it, see:

- G. S. P. Freeman-Grenville, Rupert L. Chapman III, and Joan E. Taylor, *The Onomasticon by Eusebius of Caesarea: Palestine in the Fourth Century A.D.* (Jerusalem: Carta, 2003).

- R. Steven Notley and Ze'ev Safrai, *Eusebius, Onomasticon: A Triglott Edition with Notes and Commentary*, JCP 9 (Leiden: Brill, 2004).

For a study of toponyms contained in the *Onomasticon* that are relevant for the Hebrew Bible, see:

- Yoel Elitzur, *Ancient Place Names in the Holy Land: Preservation and History* (Jerusalem: Magnes, 2004).

The following book—although not pertinent for toponymy—provides descriptions of the different regions of the land of the Bible:

- Denis Baly, *Geography of the Bible: A Study in Historical Geography* (New York: Harper & Brothers, 1957).

Finally, the website *Ortsangaben der Bibel (odb), funded by the Deutsche Forschungsgemeinschaft (DFG) and edited by Jan Christian Gertz and Erasmus Gaß, is an extremely helpful database that provides information on hundreds of toponyms mentioned in the Hebrew Bible.

7.2 ASSESS THE DISTANCE BETWEEN PLACES

To measure the distance between two places, you can use a map whose scale is indicated or the tool on Google Earth or Google Maps that calculates the distance between two points. In addition, you can sometimes find this information in a note in a study Bible or in a commentary. In the case of battle accounts, visualizing the topography of the places, the relative positioning of the armies, and the armies' movements can help you understand the tactics employed by one of the sides. The atlas by Rainey and Notley mentioned above (*The Sacred Bridge: Carta's Atlas of the Biblical World*) includes numerous precise maps illustrating all sorts of biblical events with indications of places and journeys.

> **EXAMPLE 7.2** ▸ **2 Chronicles 20:2**
>
> In 2 Chr 20:2, Jehoshaphat finds out that an immense army is coming to attack him and that it is currently located at En-gedi. The importance of this information can only be appreciated if the reader knows that this place is very close to Jerusalem—barely twenty-five miles away, as the crow flies. This information indicates that the episode describes a situation that, from a human perspective, is hopeless. The king and the people are completely dependent on God, and indeed, the rest of the text will underline this reality, since the Judeans are called to not fight but rather to take up their positions on the battlefield in order to "see the victory of the LORD on [their] behalf" (v. 17).

7.3 IDENTIFY AN ITINERARY AND INTERPRET IT AS SUCH

Once you have identified a series of place names as an itinerary, it can be helpful to plot the itinerary on a map. Depending on your objective, you can use Google Maps to place "pins" on the relevant towns or cities and/or to place an arrow that indicates the direction of movement.

> **EXAMPLE 7.3** ▸ **Isaiah 15**
>
> Isaiah 15 lists a number of places that are found in modern-day Jordan (Ar, Kir, Dibon, Medeba, etc.) in a way that seems impressionistic to many readers, since these toponyms are obscure to them. Yet in reality, this oracle against Moab depicts the journey of inhabitants who are fleeing this country because of an invasion coming from the east. Not all the sites can be identified definitively, but on the whole, the movement from the north to the south of Moab seems certain. The next part of the text, in ch. 16, seems to criticize the pride of the Moabites and presents the catastrophe as a punishment from the Lord: the idea seems to be that this people will not be able to escape his judgment.
>
> In other words, the mention of all these place names is an integral part of the content of this passage: it is an oracle of judgment pronounced not in vague terms, but in terms that are striking in their specificity (the historical reality in question could be the Assyrian invasion of Moab that took place in 715 BCE).

7.4   EXPLORE A PLACE'S HISTORY

If you are studying a passage that mentions a place name that seems significant, you may want to learn more about its history. You can do so first by looking at other texts—both texts in the Hebrew Bible and ancient Near Eastern sources—that mention this place. If archaeological excavations have been undertaken at the site in question, the findings can shed new light on the history of its settlement, the presence in it of public buildings (notably palaces and temples), dramatic events (such as destructions) that took place there and that have left traces, and so on. One difficulty, though, is that the identification of a place name mentioned in the Bible with a specific archaeological site is sometimes uncertain.

EXAMPLE 7.4 ▸ Tel Dan

> The Hebrew Bible often mentions Dan as the northern extremity of the country, most notably in the expression "from Dan to Beer-sheba" (e.g., Judg 20:1; 1 Sam 3:20). The books of Kings also regard Dan as an important cult site that was established as such by Jeroboam I (1 Kgs 12:29–30).
>
> Archaeological excavations at the site of Tel el-Qadi have shed important light on this site.[1] First of all, the discovery of a Hellenistic dedicatory inscription reading "to the god who is at Dan, Zoilos made a vow" has proven that Dan was the name of Tel el-Qadi in antiquity. The site's very close proximity to Mount Hermon makes it understandable that it represented, during certain periods, the northernmost city belonging to Israel.
>
> Second, excavations have established that Tel Dan was an important fortified city during the Iron Age. Moreover, it contained a religious complex that included a large sacrificial altar, a platform that probably served as a support for another building, and a series of rooms where priests performed rituals—as indicated by the presence of another modestly sized altar, iron shovels (probably used to handle ashes when incense was burned), and a scepter. In sum, archaeology fleshes out what we know of Dan during the royal period. What continues to be debated is whether the temple was first built by Jeroboam I (in the tenth century BCE) or by Jeroboam II (in the eighth century BCE).[2]

---

1. Avraham Biran, *Biblical Dan* (Jerusalem: Israel Exploration Society, 1994), 159–233; Andrew R. Davis, *Tel Dan in Its Northern Cultic Context*, ABS 10 (Atlanta: SBL Press, 2013).
2. Eran Arie, "Reconsidering the Iron Age II Strata at Tel Dan: Archaeological and Historical Implications," *TA* 35 (2008): 6–64.

Where to Find Out about an Archaeological Site

The first resources that should come to mind here are the following encyclopedias, which contain articles summarizing the results of excavations on many sites:

- *NEAEHL* = Ephraim Stern et al., eds., *The New Encyclopedia of Archaeological Excavations in the Holy Land*, 4 vols. (New York: Simon & Schuster, 1993); vol. 5 (update), 2008. A reference encyclopedia, with lengthy technical articles often written by the excavators themselves.

- *OEANE* = Eric M. Meyers, ed., *The Oxford Encyclopedia of Archaeology in the Near East*, 5 vols. (New York: Oxford University Press, 1997). Less technical than *NEAEHL*.

For Transjordanian sites (ancient Ammon, Moab, and Edom, as well as some Israelite settlements), see:

- Russell B. Adams, ed., *Jordan: An Archaeological Reader* (London: Equinox, 2008).

When conducting in-depth research, you can consult the official excavation report of a site, which is often a multivolume publication containing many technical chapters. Check the table of contents; the last chapter often consists of a historical synthesis that summarizes the most relevant findings. That said, archaeologists often publish preliminary reports as articles in specialized journals. These journals are also the ideal place to search for discussions on specific findings (notably inscriptions) and issues (such as the historical interpretation of a specific aspect of the site). Here is a selected list of peer-reviewed journals germane to this subject:

- *BASOR* = *Bulletin of ASOR*, the flagship journal of ASOR, one of the most important learned societies of archaeologists.
- *IEJ* = *Israel Exploration Journal*, published by the Israel Exploration Society.
- *Levant*, the journal of the British School of Archaeology.
- *TA* = *Tel Aviv*, the journal of the Archaeological Institute of the University of Tel Aviv.
- *JJAR* = *Jerusalem Journal of Archaeology*, published by the Institute of Archaeology at the Hebrew University of Jerusalem.
- *ZDPV* = *Zeitschrift des deutschen Palästina-Vereins*, the journal of a network of German archaeological institutes.

The following two journals are less technical:

- *NEA = Near Eastern Archaeology*. Published by ASOR (like *BASOR*); more accessible, though still a bit technical. Contains many fine articles and is magnificently illustrated.
- *BAR = Biblical Archaeology Review*. A semi-popular journal. Archaeologists often publish an article for laypeople in *BAR* alongside a technical article in a specialized journal. Also magnificently illustrated.

Obviously, printed books on the subject of archaeology cannot remain up-to-date for long, since any new season of excavations can change the picture. The best way to check this is to consult the official website of the excavations or an associated blog, when these exist. You can also type keywords like "[site name]" and "excavations" into a search engine. Many other websites discuss new discoveries, but reliable information is difficult to find. Here again, the database *Ortsangaben der Bibel (odb) proves very helpful.

7.5 DETECT ALLUSIONS TO THE POSSIBLE OVERTONES OF A PLACE NAME

For French people, the name "Waterloo" is a synonym of defeat, because it was the location of the last battle of Napoleon, which he lost. It is common to speak of "un véritable Waterloo" to designate a bitter failure. Not so for the British people, who were the enemies of Napoleon and named a train station in London "Waterloo." This illustration is a reminder that a place name may have overtones stemming from historical events that took place there, and the mere evocation of the name can convey these overtones, without the need to make the allusions explicit. This situation sometimes occurs in the Hebrew Bible. Therefore, even when a place name is not strongly associated with a particular event, it is still worth looking into its history to see what overtones the place name may have when it is mentioned in the text you are studying.

> **EXAMPLE 7.5a** ▸ **Micah 1:10–15**
>
> Micah 1:10–15 laments the fate of no fewer than twelve places. Most of these places are not well known and are difficult to locate on a map.³ Since the Hebrew text contain puns on the place names—for example, "in Beth-leaphrah [בְּבֵית לְעַפְרָה] roll yourselves in the dust [עָפָר, *'aphar*]" (v. 10)—

---

3. Matthew J. Suriano, "A Place in the Dust: Text, Topography and a Toponymic Note on Micah 1:10–12a*," *VT* 60 (2010): 433–46; Rainey and Notley, *Sacred Bridge*, 242–43.

some of the toponyms may well have been chosen by the writer in order to create such soundplay. However, it should also be noted that Micah came from one of the cities he mentions (Moresheth; cf. 1:1, 14) and that there is more to this passage than a haphazard series of toponyms. The sites that can be definitively identified on a map (including Gath, best known as a Philistine city) are located in a region that belonged to Judah during Hezekiah's reign and Micah's lifetime, and this region was conquered by the Assyrian king Sennacherib in 701 BCE. What Micah is doing in this passage, therefore, is lamenting a precise series of events that occurred in his very own region—namely, the destruction of particular places in it by the Assyrian army in 701 BCE.

EXAMPLE 7.5b ▸ Micah 5:2 [1]

In Mic 5, the prophet announces the arrival of someone who will come from Bethlehem to rule Israel and "feed his flock in the strength of the LORD" (v. 4 [3]). Verse 2 [1] addresses this town, saying, "you ... who are one of the little clans of Judah"—indeed, Bethlehem was a small town without great importance. But this place nevertheless had historical significance, since it was the hometown of King David (1 Sam 16). By announcing that a future king would come from this small town, Mic 5 subtly evokes an important theme, that of a return to a monarchy similar to King David's. This explains why the text then adds that his "origin is from of old, from ancient days." If, as readers, we do not pay attention to the historical weight carried by the name Bethlehem, we will not notice this important allusion.[4]

EXAMPLE 7.5c ▸ Amos 6:14

When most readers come across Amos's announcement to the Israelites that God will send a nation to oppress them "from Lebo-Hamath to the Wadi Arabah" (Amos 6:14), they find this phrase meaningless. But here Amos is alluding to the maximal borders of the Northern Kingdom, which were either established or reestablished by King Jeroboam II during the prophet's lifetime (2 Kgs 14:25). One way to discover this would be to look up the other occurrences of "Lebo-Hamath" in the Bible, which include 2 Kgs 14:25, where this historical information is mentioned. Further research indicates that Lebo-Hamath was situated at the entrance of the kingdom of Hamath

---

4. It can also be noted in passing that the theme of "the return of David" appears—this time explicitly—in another prophetic book (Ezek 34:23–24; 37:24).

> (the name literally means, "entrance of Hamath")—in the Beqa' region, to the north of Israel—and that the Wadi Arabah was situated to the south.
>
> Thus, Amos is saying that God will strike Israel "from top to bottom"—that is, from the northernmost border to the southernmost border of the country.

Exercises for Chapter 7

Exercise A

Isaiah 10:27–34 mentions a number of places. Where are they located, and how does this knowledge help us understand the meaning of this passage?

Exercise B

Isaiah 9:1 [8:23] mentions the lands of Zebulun and Naphtali, then the "way of the sea" and "Galilee of the nations." Can you situate these places on a map, and can you explain why they are mentioned here?

Exercise C

In Hos 11:8, God asks:

> How can I give you up, Ephraim?
> How can I hand you over, O Israel?
> How can I make you like Admah?
> How can I treat you like Zeboiim?

What do we know about Admah and Zeboiim, and why are they mentioned here?

Exercise D

In Hos 4:15, Judah is told not to go to Gilgal or Beth-Aven. Where are these places, and why shouldn't the Judeans go there?

Exercise E

How do you interpret the significance of "the valley of Jehoshaphat" mentioned in Joel 3:2, 12 [4:2, 12]?

CHAPTER 8

HISTORY

OVERVIEW

The most obvious advantages of situating a text in its historical context are related to our own ignorance. This context is often *implicit* in the text: originally, there was no point in reminding the readers or hearers of it, since they knew it quite well. For us, however, effort is required in order to rediscover the historical context. This is all the more pressing since the texts of the Hebrew Bible are deeply "incarnated" in the context of Israel, Judah, and the surrounding peoples; that is to say, most of the biblical books deliver their messages in specific settings, even when these messages are of universal value. For instance, the prophets often *allude* to historical events. If we read their texts without any knowledge of this historical background, we may perhaps grasp the thrust of their argument, but we risk missing part of their message or its rhetorical force.

There is no absolute rule that governs historical analysis. Paul Veyne, a leading historian specializing in the Roman Empire, provocatively gave the second chapter of his book *Writing History: Essay on Epistemology* the title "History Does Not Exist." In his view, "the historical method that is dinned into us does not exist."[1] Nevertheless, he distinguishes three steps we can use:

- **Reading documents:** Philological analysis allows historians to determine which events the documents claim to report.
- **Critically analyzing the documents:** This is the object of historical criticism, which, according to Veyne, consists of answering the following question: "I believe that this document teaches me this; may I trust it to do that?"

---

1. Paul Veyne, *Writing History: Essay on Epistemology*, trans. Mina Moore-Rinvolucri (Middletown, CT: Wesleyan University Press, 1984), 12. The quotations below from Veyne's book are also found on this page.

- **Historical synthesis**, which consists of "retrodiction"—that is, putting the events learned from the documents into an orderly sequence based on causal links. Because our knowledge is fragmentary, this task entails a significant degree of extrapolation and making analogies from similar situations. According to Veyne, "other than the techniques of handling and checking documents, there is no more a method of history than one of ethnography or of the art of traveling."

It remains to be seen what ethnographers and travelers would think of this assertion, but for our purposes, the distinction between the three stages above remains helpful. Nevertheless, Veyne's perspective is that of a historian who gathers all the relevant documents in order to fulfill one main objective: to relate what happened (i.e., the history of events).[2] By contrast, when we approach a biblical passage in order to exegete it, our perspective is oriented *toward the text*. That is, our primary aim is to study the passage from a historical point of view, not to reconstruct the entire history of the period of ancient Israel that the passage evokes, which would be a much more ambitious project. For this reason, our starting point is one precise "document" (the biblical passage), and studying it from a historical perspective is based on comparing it with other historical sources. As a result, below I will adapt Veyne's method and tailor it to the needs of the student of the Hebrew Bible. Finding the historical sources and extracting relevant information from them is the most time-consuming task here. You may also be interested in the light that extrabiblical sources can shed on, say, practices that are mentioned in your passage.

A number of factors make studying the Hebrew Bible from a historical perspective complicated (and exciting). First, even historiographical texts in the Bible are far from being modern handbooks of history (which also have their own limits, of course). For example, the books of Kings do not seek to be exhaustive or to give an objective description of the events they relate; the authors of these books are transparent about the fact that they report only a selection of events and that they interpret these in light of their theological convictions.

Second, a temporal gap (whether short or long) may have elapsed between the *period of reference* (the one in which the action takes place or to which the text refers) and the *period(s) of composition* of the text. Therefore, historians wonder whether the redactors of a particular narrative may have, consciously or not, retrojected realities from their own time into the narrative, thus introducing anachronisms into the text.[3] For instance, a redactor from, say, the fifth century may have modeled his narrative

---

2. Of course, few historians today would claim that it is possible to reconstruct the past "exactly as it happened" based on "pure facts," since our access to past events is always mediated through sources that report them from particular perspectives.

3. To illustrate by means of an analogy, some modern translations of the Bible do the same when they mention "coins" in texts such as 1 Sam 13:21, since coins did not exist in the early first millennium and were not, in fact, introduced in the region before the fourth century. Prior to this time, people used various sorts of ingots that they weighed in order to determine their value.

about a story situated in the seventh century on realities from his own time. If so, the text provides information about *representations or realities* from the time of redaction.

Third, and related to the two preceding points, the relationship between biblical texts and history is more flexible than what modern readers intuitively expect. The biblical writers had at their disposal—and indeed, they used—a large array of literary genres, some of which involve pure fiction and others of which involve a mix of fact and fiction.

The following steps can be followed when studying a passage historically:

❶ BASED ON A CAREFUL **READING** AND **ANALYSIS** OF THE TEXT, DETERMINE EXACTLY WHAT YOUR **RESEARCH QUESTION** IS.

❷ OBTAIN RELEVANT HISTORICAL INFORMATION FROM **EXTRABIBLICAL SOURCES** (INCLUDING ARCHAEOLOGY).

❸ **COMPARE** THE BIBLICAL AND EXTRABIBLICAL SOURCES.

❹ **SYNTHESIZE** THE INFORMATION FROM THE PRECEDING STEPS, RECONSTRUCTING THE SEQUENCE OF EVENTS, AND IF POSSIBLE, THE CAUSAL LINKS BETWEEN THEM.

8.1 DETERMINE EXACTLY WHAT YOUR RESEARCH QUESTION IS

Suppose you are interested in a precise event mentioned in the Bible (for instance, the exodus) and you want to find out what we know about it. In a case like this, you need to find the passages that deal with this event. Most of the time, however, you probably just want to exegete a given passage but you do not know in advance what historical questions it raises. Here is a series of steps you can follow in such cases:

Ⓐ Draw up a list of (potentially) historical aspects of the text and choose the ones you want to investigate. That is, identify the aspects of the text that may be worth investigating. These might include an event (e.g., a battle), a person (e.g., King David), a practice (e.g., making a sacrifice), a place (e.g., Jerusalem), and so forth.

Ⓑ Check the literary genre of the text to see whether it really claims to report historical events. There is no point in looking for historical information about a fictional event or character! Thus, you may want to determine if the literary genre of your passage makes it likely that the text contains mainly historical facts, mainly fiction, or a mixture of both. It is possible, for example, that the text is based upon a historical kernel that has been elaborated with reconstructed or fictional features. It is also possible that it retrojects into the past realities from the time when it was written, which leads us to the next step.

(C) Check the compositional history of the text to determine, if possible, what period it is really about. It may well be that a diachronic study of the text leads you to conclude that, while it seems to report events from, say, the time of Moses, it was actually written in the seventh century BCE and reflects realities from that time. This question may concern the entire passage or each of its successive redactions, if it is multilayered; for instance, it may be that the event you are interested in is only mentioned in a verse that is secondary and reflects a later period. Note that "early" here does not necessarily mean "genuine," and "late" does not necessarily mean "fictional." The earliest literary core of a text is not necessarily a "pure" historical account; conversely, the information contained in a late addition could theoretically come from an ancient source that was used by the interpolator.

At this juncture, it is important to remember that historical considerations may already have played a role in the compositional analysis of the passage. For instance, a reference made in the text to a historical event may have prompted you to infer a relative dating for the text. You should be attentive to this in order to avoid the risk of circularity in your argumentation.

(D) In light of the preceding steps, decide what you are interested in:

- Do you want to **assess the historicity** of an event (or person or practice)? This may entail determining whether an event occurred or not, or whether it occurred at the time mentioned in the text or at another time; whether the existence of a person is corroborated by extrabiblical sources; or whether a practice is attested at the time when it was in use according to the chronology of the text.

- Do you want to **learn more about the historical background** of an event—for instance, about the relationships between Israel or Judah and a foreign country at a time when they entered into battle?

- Do you want to **obtain historical information that may shed light** on an aspect of the life of the ancient Israelites—for example, a practice—regardless of whether it was actually participated in by the particular person (or people) and in the precise circumstances the text you are studying says it was? For instance, ancient Near Eastern texts or archaeology can provide details that the Bible does not.

| EXAMPLE 8.1a ▸ 2 Chronicles 33 |

Second Kings criticizes Manasseh, who reigned over Judah in the seventh century BCE, for his religious behavior (2 Kgs 21), notably his building of high places, altars, and a statue of Asherah. Indeed, this book blames him for having gone so far that his actions led the Lord to reject Jerusalem and put an end to the kingdom of Judah, despite Josiah's reform (2 Kgs 23:26–27).

The second book of Chronicles takes up some of the criticisms found in 2 Kgs 21 (see 2 Chr 33:1–10), but it also adds new episodes that have no parallel in Kings (2 Chr 33:11–19). According to the Chronicler, Manasseh was taken prisoner to Babylon and repented by turning to the Lord, who brought him back to Jerusalem. Manasseh then destroyed the altars and the statue he had made, and he rebuilt the altar of the Lord. In fact, 2 Chr 33:15–17 ascribes to him a reform that Kings ascribes to Josiah. In a word, Chronicles rehabilitates Manasseh.

What about the historicity of these events that only occur in Chronicles? In terms of literary genre, scholars generally regard Chronicles as a mix of history and fiction, that is, as a sort of historical theology. Chronicles rewrites Samuel and Kings by removing some episodes and adding others; the new ones may originate partly in genuine historical sources used by the Chronicler, but most scholars suspect that they also emanate partially from his own creativity. The stories contained in Chronicles are clearly designed to create a program of restoration for the inhabitants of Yehud in the Persian and Hellenistic periods; the Chronicler finds positive examples from the past and offers them as illustrations of the attitudes he encourages (see Example 5.4c).

In the case of Manasseh, it is not difficult to see that the personal experience that 2 Chr 33:11–13 describes him as having is a sort of brief summary of the Babylonian exile: he is deported to Babylon, he repents, the Lord brings him back, and he brings renewal to the worship of the Lord in Jerusalem. Manasseh's story recapitulates the story of the deported Judeans. More than that, in this passage, the Chronicler tells his readers how the experience of the exile can be interpreted theologically. In fact, the story of Manasseh serves as an illustration of the general statement found in 2 Chr 7:14: "if my people who are called by my name humble themselves, pray, seek my face, and turn from their wicked ways, then I will hear from heaven and will forgive their sin and heal their land." These considerations do not prove beyond doubt that the events in question did not happen, but they lend credibility to the view that the Chronicler created them to serve his theological program.

EXAMPLE 8.1b ▸ Leviticus 18

Let's imagine that your professor has assigned you an exegesis paper on Lev 18. Congratulations ... and good luck. At first glance, this passage appears to contain prescriptions the Lord gave to Moses in the Sinai desert (cf. v. 1). If taken *prima facie*, this gives us information about the time of Moses; notably, the text mentions certain customs of the Canaanites—both sexual practices (vv. 6–20, 22–23) and child sacrifice (v. 21)—that the Lord forbids the Hebrews to imitate. Intriguingly, we also learn from vv. 24–30 that the land itself can become impure, not just the temple. In addition, it turns out that the ethical behavior of the Hebrews (not just the physical contaminations mentioned in Lev 1–16) can make them (and their land) impure. Accordingly, the text seems to indicate that purity and impurity had to do with morality from the start, that is, from the time of Moses.

From the point of view of biblical criticism, however, things are not that simple. To start with, most scholars regard Leviticus as having been written in the monarchic period at the earliest, and more probably during the exile or the early Persian period (though the priestly regulations it contains were probably in use before they were put into writing). Nevertheless, in keeping with a long-standing tradition according to which such regulations were merely a development of the Torah given to Moses,[4] the compilers of the laws of Leviticus chose to formally present them as having been received by Moses in the Sinai desert. Moreover, ch. 18 belongs to the Holiness Code (Lev 17–26), i.e., "H," for which scholars have proposed dates varying from the eighth century to the fifth century, with a tendency today to prefer the end of this spectrum.

The consequences of all of this for your paper are important, at least if you accept these results of biblical criticism. For example, the mention of certain practices in Lev 18 is not evidence about the life of the Canaanites in the second millennium BCE, and the theological ideas this passage contains cannot be regarded as information about the time of Moses. Instead, strictly speaking, this chapter provides us with information about the period when H was written, let us say the sixth century, if that is the dating you adopt. Of course, there is little doubt that the sexual practices in question already existed in the second millennium. But this is less evident as far as child sacrifice is concerned. If anything, we learn from this chapter that this was probably a reality in, say, the sixth century in Judah. Indeed, there is no point in forbidding things that people never do. And the most striking consequence of the observations above concerns the idea of moral impurity, which seems to be a new development proper to H. Indeed, although the Holiness Code may record ideas that are older than the text, it essentially has a programmatic character.

---

4. On this subject, see Hindy Najman, *Seconding Sinai: The Development of Mosaic Discourse in Second Temple Judaism*, JSJSup 77 (Leiden: Brill, 2003).

> **EXAMPLE 8.1c** ▸ **Hezekiah's Reform in 2 Kings 18:4, 22**
>
> Second Kings 18 attributes to King Hezekiah a religious reform in which he centralizes the cult. The most pressing question is whether this actually happened. A further interesting question is: if the reform did indeed happen, how did it take place in practice? For instance, did it entail destroying temples? Before looking for possible reflections of this reform in the archaeological record, it is important to check the biblical evidence. Hezekiah's reform is mentioned in only two verses: 2 Kgs 18:4 and 22 (and the parallel to the latter verse in Isa 36:7). From the viewpoint of literary genre, v. 4 occurs in a regnal account and it has all the appearance of information that could have come from a royal annal. The case of v. 22 is more complicated, as it appears in a speech given by an Assyrian official that is embedded in a "historical narrative"; that is, it could be a fictional reconstruction. In addition, both verses are sometimes regarded as glosses, for the following reasons:
>
> - Verse 4 seems to interrupt the flow of the text because its syntax differs from that of the surrounding verses: it begins with the personal pronoun "he" and could be translated as: "It is he who removed [הוּא הֵסִיר] the high places, broke down the pillars, and cut down the sacred pole." Moreover, some scholars suspect that the preceding list of cultic material is drawn from the account of Josiah's reform (2 Kgs 23:14) and suggest on this basis that an editor who wanted to ascribe to the pious King Hezekiah the same reform as Josiah may have inserted v. 4 in imitation of 2 Kgs 23:14.
>
> - Verse 22 is the only verse in the Assyrian official's speech in vv. 20–25 that is addressed not to Hezekiah (who is absent) but to his officials (who are present and whose job is to report the speech to the king).
>
> These arguments are debatable, however:
>
> - There is a good reason why v. 4 begins with "he": this deliberately creates a contrast with a long series of negative statements concerning Hezekiah's predecessors, according to which "he [the king in question] did not remove the high places," which serves as a *leitmotif* in the book (1 Kgs 15:14; 2 Kgs 12:3 [4]; 14:4; 15:4, 35; 16:4). Against this background, 2 Kgs 18:4 sounds like a climax: at last, the reformer has come![5] In addition, it is not certain that this verse was inspired by 23:14.

---

5. See Benjamin D. Thomas, *Hezekiah and the Compositional History of the Book of Kings*, FAT 2.63 (Tübingen: Mohr Siebeck, 2014), 320–22.

> It is also possible that 18:4 originally mentioned the high places only, since, as we have just seen, they were really the main concern, as the aforementioned *leitmotif* makes clear. Perhaps the "pillars" and the "sacred pole" were added to make the sentence resemble 23:14, but there is good reason to think that the "high places" were topically relevant in 18:4.
>
> ◆ It is perfectly conceivable that the Assyrian official momentarily turns toward his actual audience (which consists of Hezekiah's officials), inserting a parenthetical remark into his speech that is directed at them.
>
> While this merely scratches the surface of a complicated debate, it turns out that the historicity of Hezekiah's reform is based on a couple of verses that are debated, albeit not with sufficient evidence to prove that both are glosses. It is worth keeping in mind the existence of this debate as we continue our investigation on this reform below.

8.2 OBTAIN RELEVANT HISTORICAL INFORMATION FROM EXTRABIBLICAL SOURCES

This is the part of your study that will most depend on the work of historians. You may be led to consult both *primary sources* (e.g., ancient historiographical works by authors such as Flavius Josephus; texts from the ancient Near East, such as Mesopotamian annals or royal inscriptions; the results of archaeological excavations) and *secondary literature* (handbooks on the history of Israel, commentaries, encyclopedias, etc.). From a practical point of view, there is no need to reinvent the wheel, so you may want to look at the secondary literature first and then go back and check the primary sources, depending on the depth of your study. In fact, you can go in several directions when looking for information:

Ⓐ Consult a publication that comments on the historical background of the *passage* you are studying. This is a sort of shortcut that can give you a brief overview of what we know about the historical aspects of the passage. Note that not all exegetical commentaries give much information of this kind, and also, be mindful of the date of publication of the works you consult, since both new archaeological discoveries and new historical arguments may have been made since. The following commentary deals specifically with the geographical, historical, and cultural aspects of the Hebrew Bible, and its endnotes provide further bibliographical references:

- ZIBBC = John Walton, ed., *Zondervan Illustrated Bible Backgrounds Commentary*, 5 vols. (Grand Rapids: Zondervan, 2009).

B Obtain information about a *person, event, practice*, or *place* that is referred to in the text. If your research concerns such a specific topic, then your first thought should be to consult a good dictionary or an encyclopedia. Although it is now dated, the *Anchor Bible Dictionary* remains an excellent resource. The *Encyclopedia of the Bible and Its Reception* is also of high quality and is more recent (actually, its publication is still in progress). If you are interested in the daily life of Israelites, see the sidebar below titled "Where to Find Out about Daily Life in Ancient Israel." If you are specifically interested in a place, it may also be worth checking whether the site has been excavated and, if it has, what the relevant archaeological results may be for your study. For this, see the sidebar in chapter 7 titled "Where to Find Out about an Archaeological Site." In addition, iconographic sources may provide useful information, notably about religious representations; see the sidebar below titled "Where to Find Out about Iconography."

C Obtain information about the *period* in which the events are purported to have taken place, and information about (if known) the period in which the passage was written. For useful resources, see the sidebars below titled "Where to Find Out about the History of Israel and Judah" and "Where to Find Out about the History of Other Ancient Near Eastern Countries."

Again, what secondary literature cannot always provide, or at least not for long, is up-to-date information, since new discoveries are constantly made during excavations and new interpretations of old findings are published every year. Depending on the depth of your inquiry, you may want to consult websites, journals, and other recent publications to make sure that you are not missing anything significant. Several sidebars below indicate useful references in this regard.

Where to Find Out about Daily Life in Ancient Israel

The following books are very informative:

- Philip J. King and Lawrence E. Stager, *Life in Biblical Israel*, LAI (Louisville: Westminster John Knox, 2001).
- Oded Borowski, *Daily Life in Biblical Times* (Atlanta: SBL Press, 2003).
- William G. Dever, *The Lives of Ordinary People in Ancient Israel: Where Archaeology and the Bible Intersect* (Grand Rapids: Eerdmans, 2012).

- Edwin M. Yamauchi and Marvin R. Wilson, eds., *Dictionary of Daily Life in Biblical and Post-Biblical Antiquity*, 4 vols. (Peabody, MA: Hendrickson, 2014–16).

See also:

- Avraham Faust, *The Archaeology of Israelite Society in Iron Age II* (Winona Lake, IN: Eisenbrauns, 2012).
- Victor H. Matthews, *The Cultural World of the Bible: An Illustrated Guide to Manners and Customs*, 4th ed. (Grand Rapids: Baker Academic, 2015).

The following are useful for researching specific topics:

Religion

- Ziony Zevit, *The Religions of Ancient Israel: A Synthesis of Parallactic Approaches* (London: Continuum, 2001).

Food

- Nathan MacDonald, *What Did the Ancient Israelites Eat? Diet in Biblical Times* (Grand Rapids: Eerdmans, 2008).
- Cynthia Shafer-Elliott, *Food in Ancient Judah: Domestic Cooking in the Time of the Hebrew Bible* (London: Equinox, 2013).
- Janling Fu, Cynthia Shafer-Elliott, and Carol Meyers, eds., *The T&T Clark Handbook of Food in the Hebrew Bible and Ancient Israel* (London: T&T Clark, 2021).

Agriculture

- Oded Borowski, *Agriculture in Iron Age Israel* (Winona Lake, IN: Eisenbrauns, 1987).

Music

- Joachim Braun, *Music in Ancient Israel/Palestine: Archaeological, Written, and Comparative Sources*, trans. Douglas W. Stott (Grand Rapids: Eerdmans, 2002; original German edition, 1999).

EXAMPLE 8.2a ▸ Judges

The exact function of the "judges" (שֹׁפְטִים) described in the book of Judges can elude modern readers, since it often seems very far removed from what is meant by the term "judge" today. The nature of these characters' "judging" activity is not clearly defined, except that some of them are described as "saviors" or "liberators." The rest of the Hebrew Bible does not give any indication either. Can data from the rest of the ancient Near East shed light on this question? A good reflex here is to consult a dictionary or encyclopedia: for instance, the *Anchor Bible Dictionary* or the more recent *Encyclopedia of the Bible and Its Reception*. These sources reveal an interesting parallel. In texts from the Syrian city of Mari (eighteenth century BCE), a *šāpiṭum* (again the same root) was appointed by the king for special tasks, such as assisting in the administration of a territory, leading a military campaign, arbitrating disputes linked to domestic affairs, or serving as the governor of a province.

This parallel suggests that the roles we find the biblical "judges" playing, as well as their regionally focused jurisdiction, should not surprise us. Even if they may sometimes have engaged in judicial arbitration, this was at most only one of the facets of a wider function their office entailed. Thus, it may be best to translate the term in the book of Judges as "governor," to avoid misapplying the typical meaning of the Hebrew (and English) verb "to judge" to them.

Where to Find Out about the History of Israel and Judah

Take your pick! Here is a choice of books, listed according to their publication date, that attempt to reconstruct the history of the Hebrew people, whether in its totality or by concentrating on one period:

- J. Alberto Soggin, *An Introduction to the History of Israel and Judah*, trans. John Bowden, 3rd ed. (London: SCM Press, 1999; original Italian edition, 1998).

- Israel Finkelstein and Neil Asher Silberman, *The Bible Unearthed: Archaeology's New Vision of Ancient Israel and the Origins of Its Sacred Texts* (New York: Touchstone, 2002). A best seller cowritten by a top archaeologist and a journalist, this is a popular book with the associated limits of the genre, but it is helpful for a first approach.

- Iain Provan, V. Philips Long, and Tremper Longman III, *A Biblical History of Israel* (Louisville: Westminster John Knox, 2003). A conservative approach.

- J. Maxwell Miller and John H. Hayes, *A History of Ancient Israel and Judah*, 2nd ed. (Louisville: Westminster John Knox, 2006). Contains detailed discussions.

- Lester L. Grabbe, *Ancient Israel: What Do We Know and How Do We Know It?* (London: T&T Clark, 2007). Covers the second millennium through the sixth century BCE; very helpful in that it presents the epigraphic sources and archaeological data and debates, then compares them to the biblical data.

- Mario Liverani, *Israel's History and the History of Israel*, trans. Chiara Peri and Philip R. Davies (London: Equinox, 2009; original Italian edition, 2003). A unique feature of this book is that it contains two parts, one about "normal history" and the other about "invented history" that is contained in the Hebrew Bible.

- Bill T. Arnold and Richard S. Hess, eds., *Ancient Israel's History: An Introduction to Issues and Sources* (Grand Rapids: Baker Academic, 2014). A volume of collected essays, with a chapter on each period.

- Reinhard G. Kratz, *Historical and Biblical Israel: The History, Tradition, and Archives of Israel and Judah*, trans. Paul Michael Kurtz (New York: Oxford University Press, 2015; original German edition, 2013). Contains effective overviews of the history of Israel and Judah and of the relevant written sources—both the traditions that found their way into the Hebrew Bible and the extrabiblical "archives" (including epigraphic texts).

- Philippe Guillaume and Ernst-Axel Knauf, *A History of Biblical Israel: The Fate of the Tribes and Kingdoms from Merenptah to Bar Kochba*, WANEM (Sheffield: Equinox, 2016).

- William G. Dever, *Beyond the Texts: An Archaeological Portrait of Ancient Israel and Judah* (Atlanta: SBL Press, 2017). Written mostly from the point of view of archaeology, which is regarded as the primary source of data.

- Bernd U. Schipper, *A Concise History of Ancient Israel: From the Beginnings through the Hellenistic Era*, CSHB 11 (University Park, PA: Eisenbrauns, 2019; original German edition, 2018). As the title indicates, this book is concise; it provides very helpful summaries of the relevant sources and historical debates.

- Lester L. Grabbe, *A History of the Jews and Judaism in the Second Temple Period*, 4 vols., LSTS (London: T&T Clark, 2004–21). As the title indicates, this book concerns only the Second Temple period; very detailed and helpful.

The book *The Sacred Bridge*, already mentioned several times, also offers an enormous amount of historical information. In addition, the twelve volumes of the German series Biblische Enzyklopädie (Stuttgart: Kohlhammer) cover the entire history of Israel and Judah; this work is currently being translated into English by SBL Press as the series Biblical Encyclopedia (half of the volumes have appeared to date).

| EXAMPLE 8.2b   ▸   Multiple Places of Worship |

Deuteronomy 12 forbids animal sacrifice outside of the Jerusalem temple (understanding this as the referent of the phrase "the place that the LORD your God will choose" [Deut 12:5, etc.], which we also find in other books, especially in 1 Kgs 8).[6] In spite of this, various passages in the Hebrew Bible accuse the Israelites and the Judeans of worshiping in many places, indeed "on every high hill and under every green tree" (1 Kgs 14:23; 2 Kgs 16:4; 17:10; Isa 57:5; Jer 2:20; 3:6; Ezek 6:13). In this vein, Jeremiah goes so far as to say: "For your gods have become as many as your towns, O Judah, and as many as the streets of Jerusalem are the altars to shame you have set up, altars to make offerings to Baal" (Jer 11:13).

Have archaeological excavations uncovered places of worship in Judah? They have. But how can you find out? In practical terms, you could consult the entry "temple" in a good encyclopedia or another reference book. In this case, however, the answer to your question could be affected by archaeological findings—such as the discovery of a temple—that have occurred after the printed resource in question was published. For this reason, my advice would be to supplement your initial inquiry in a reference book by searching keywords (such as "temple," "Judah" or "Israel," "archaeology," etc.) in a good library catalog, a bibliographical database, or a search engine. If you use a standard search engine, such as Google, your search will return popular websites, while a search in Google Scholar will focus on academic publications. Because archaeological discoveries are often made public first on news websites, you may hear about a recent, exciting find that is not dealt with in scholarly publications yet. In such cases, caution is in order, since the correct interpretation of a new find generally requires time and scholarly discussion, whereas the news industry tends to favor sensationalist announcements.

After some digging around in printed and online publications, you will arrive at a (provisional) list of temples or altars that have been found at archaeological sites. For example:

- *Tel Arad:* In the eighth century BCE, this fortress included a temple, which housed a huge sacrifice altar in stone and a cella ("holy of holies") containing incense altars and standing stones (*maṣṣēvôt*).[7]
- *Tel Beersheba:* Several stones belonging to a dismantled sacrificial altar, with "horns" (elevated corners), were found in

---

6. In the Samaritan Pentateuch, the expression is "the place that the LORD your God has chosen," and the Samaritan tradition interprets this as a reference to the temple on Mount Gerizim (the books of Kings are not part of the Samaritan canon).

7. Ze'ev Herzog, "The Fortress Mound at Tel Arad: An Interim Report," *TA* 29 (2002): 63.

secondary use in the wall of a storehouse here.⁸ This altar was apparently in use in the eighth century BCE. Interestingly, no temple has been found on this site, although its Iron Age II levels have been thoroughly excavated, which raises the possibility that this altar was used in an open-air place of worship.

- *Tel Lachish:* According to the archaeologists who recently renewed the excavations at the gate of this city, one of the rooms in this gate contained a double sacrificial horned altar during the eighth century BCE.⁹ This interpretation of the stones has recently been challenged, however.¹⁰ According to another archaeologist, another room in the same gate also had a cultic function.¹¹

- *Tel Moza:* A temple with the same architectural outline as Solomon's temple, albeit a bit smaller, has been found only seven kilometers (about 4.3 miles) from Jerusalem. The building contains two main rooms (the equivalent of the holy place and the holy of holies), side rooms, two columns at its front, and a sacrificial altar; figurines were found close to this altar. This temple was built in the late tenth or early ninth century BCE, over an earlier temple tentatively dated to the tenth century.¹²

In light of these data, the answer to our initial question ("Have archaeological excavations uncovered places of worship in Judah?") should be nuanced. Yes, there were a number of worship sites in Judah, but not many temples have been found.¹³ It may well be that a number of places, especially in the countryside, served as open-air places of worship, and this may correspond to the expression "on every high hill and under every green tree." Archaeology has difficulty detecting such sites, however, probably because

---

8. Ze'ev Herzog, "Perspectives on Southern Israel's Cult Centralization: Arad and Beer-Sheba," in *One God – One Cult – One Nation: Archaeological and Biblical Perspectives*, ed. Reinhard G. Kratz and Hermann Spieckermann, BZAW 405 (Berlin: de Gruyter, 2010), 169–99.

9. Saar Ganor and Igor Kreimerman, "An Eighth-Century B.C.E. Gate Shrine at Tel Lachish," *BASOR* 381 (2019): 211–36.

10. David Ussishkin, "Was a 'Gate Shrine' Built at the Level III Inner City Gate of Lachish? A Response to Ganor and Kreimerman," *BASOR* 385 (2021): 153–70.

11. Elad Liraz, "A Second Cult Room at the Lachish Gate?" *NEA* 81 (2018): 269–75.

12. Shua Kisilevitz and Oded Lipschits, "Tel Moẓa: An Economic and Cultic Center from the Iron Age II (First Temple Period)," in *The Mega Project at Motza (Moẓa): The Neolithic and Later Occupations up to the 20th Century*, ed. Hamoudi Khalaily, Amit Re'em, Jacob Vardi, and Ianir Milevski (Jerusalem: Israel Antiquities Authority, 2020), 303–5.

13. On this subject, see Avraham Faust, "Israelite Temples: Where Was Israelite Cult [*sic*] Not Practiced, and Why," *Religions* 10 (2019): Article 106 (online).

they did not leave many remains. On the other hand, the existence in Tel Moza of a temple that is very similar to, and that is contemporary with, Solomon's temple, raises tantalizing questions. Notably, it seems inconceivable that the existence of such a temple, so close to Jerusalem, was not sanctioned by the king.

In addition, it seems clear that the prohibitions found in Deut 12 were not applied until at least the eighth century BCE. In fact, most scholars think that they constitute an innovation from the seventh century.

EXAMPLE 8.2c ▸ Hezekiah's Reform

Let us resume our inquiry about Hezekiah's reform, which (as we saw in Example 8.1c above) is mentioned in 2 Kgs 18:4, 22. Is there archaeological evidence for this reform? In light of the preceding example, we can reformulate this question as follows: are there hints that the shrines at Tel Arad, Tel Beersheba, Tel Lachish, and Tel Moza were closed? Here is what we find in the publications on these sites:[14]

- *Tel Arad:* At the end of the eighth century BCE, the temple was deliberately buried under a layer of several meters of dirt. Some scholars regard this as confirmation that Hezekiah dismantled the shrine. Others interpret this as a method of safeguarding the temple right before the Assyrians attacked the city, or even after this invasion, until the city could be rebuilt. However, new, secular buildings were built over it in the next archaeological stratum.

- *Tel Beersheba:* At the end of the eighth century BCE, the altar was dismantled and reused to build a wall.

- *Tel Lachish:* According to the excavators, at the end of the eighth century BCE the horns of the altar were chopped away and a toilet seat was put in the cult room to desecrate it. However, we have seen that this interpretation is debated.

- *Tel Moza:* Cultic objects were buried, then the temple itself was buried, under a layer of earth; Kisilevitz and Lipschits interpret these actions as having been "performed as part of a

---

14. See the references already given in the preceding example. For discussions (published before the recent discoveries at Tel Lachish and Tel Moza), see, e.g., Lisbeth S. Fried, "The High Places (*bāmôt*) and the Reforms of Hezekiah and Josiah: An Archaeological Investigation," *JAOS* 122 (2002): 437–65; Diana Edelman, "Hezekiah's Alleged Centralization," *JSOT* 32 (2008): 395–434; Herzog, "Perspectives on Southern Israel's Cult Centralization: Arad and Beer-Sheba."

a religious ritual during which cultic paraphernalia were decommissioned to make room for new artifacts—an act of reverence rather than signifying a break in religious traditions." However, they specify that the figurines close to the altar were intentionally broken, which (in my view) favors the idea of a reform.[15]

Here again, the conclusion needs to be nuanced and provisional. There are striking hints that all the cult places were intentionally closed, but in three cases, some scholars interpret the evidence otherwise. It seems fair to say that the evidence favors the view that a reform did occur, but the debate continues. Note that an interesting situation would obtain if we concluded that the cult was interrupted in some shrines but not in others. This might indicate that Hezekiah led only a partial reform, perhaps due to local resistance in some places.

Where to Find Out about the History of Other Ancient Near Eastern Countries

For recent overviews, see:

- Bill T. Arnold and Brent A. Strawn, eds., *The World around the Old Testament: The People and Places of the Ancient Near East* (Grand Rapids: Baker Academic, 2016). Contains chapters on the Amorites, Assyria, Babylonia, Ugarit, Egypt, the Hittites and the Hurrians, the Arameans, the Phoenicians, Transjordanian peoples, the Philistines, Persia, the Arabians, and Greece.

- Brian R. Doak, *Ancient Israel's Neighbors*, EBS (Oxford: Oxford University Press, 2020). A student-friendly introduction with chapters on the Canaanites, the Arameans, the Ammonites, the Moabites, the Edomites, the Philistines, and the Phoenicians.

The Ancient Near East

- Amélie Kuhrt, *The Ancient Near East c. 3000–330 BCE*, 2 vols., RHAW (London: Routledge, 1995). Covers the history of Mesopotamia, Egypt, the Hittites, and the Levant.

---

15. Kisilevitz and Lipschits, "Tel Moẓa: An Economic and Cultic Center from the Iron Age II (First Temple Period)," 303.

Aramaeans

- Edward Lipiński, *The Aramaeans: Their Ancient History, Culture, Religion*, OLA 100 (Leuven: Peeters, 2000).
- K. Lawson Younger, *A Political History of the Arameans: From the Origins to the End of Their Polities*, ABS 13 (Atlanta: SBL Press, 2016).

Transjordan (Ammon, Moab, Edom)

- Craig W. Tyson, *The Ammonites: Elites, Empires, and Sociopolitical Change (1000–500 BCE)* (London: Bloomsbury, 2014).
- Erasmus Gaß, *Die Moabiter: Geschichte und Kultur eines ostjordanischen Volkes im 1. Jahrtausend v. Chr.*, ADPV 38 (Wiesbaden: Harrassowitz, 2009).
- Bradley L. Crowell, *Edom at the Edge of Empire: A Social and Political History*, ABS 29 (Atlanta: SBL Press, 2021).
- Edward Lipiński, *On the Skirts of Canaan in the Iron Age: Historical and Topographical Researches*, OLA 153 (Leuven: Peeters, 2006).

Phoenicians

- Josette Elayi, *The History of Phoenicia* (Atlanta: Lockwood Press, 2015).
- Hélène Sader, *The History and Archaeology of Phoenicia*, ABS 25 (Atlanta: SBL Press, 2018).
- Mark Woolmer, *A Short History of the Phoenicians*, rev. ed. (London: Bloomsbury Academic, 2022).

Ugarit

- Wilfred G. E. Watson and Nicholas Wyatt, eds., *Handbook of Ugaritic Studies* (Leiden: Brill, 1999). Still an excellent introduction to many aspects of ancient Ugarit.

Mesopotamia (including Persia)

- Marc Van De Mieroop, *A History of the Ancient Near East, ca. 3000–332 BC*, 3rd ed., BHAW (Malden, MA: Wiley-Blackwell, 2016).

Egypt

- Ian Shaw, ed., *The Oxford History of Ancient Egypt* (New York: Oxford University Press, 2000).
- Marc Van De Mieroop, *A History of Ancient Egypt*, 2nd ed., BHAW (Hoboken, NJ: Wiley-Blackwell, 2021).

Persia

- Pierre Briant, *From Cyrus to Alexander: A History of the Persian Empire*, trans. Peter T. Daniels (Winona Lake, IN: Eisenbrauns, 2002).

- Maria Brosius, *A History of Ancient Persia: The Achaemenid Empire*, BHAW (Hoboken, NJ: Wiley-Blackwell, 2021).

Hittites

- Trevor Bryce, *The Kingdom of the Hittites*, 2nd ed. (Oxford: Clarendon, 2005).

- Billie Jean Collins, *The Hittites and Their World*, ABS 7 (Atlanta: SBL Press, 2007).

EXAMPLE 8.2d ▸ Tyre in Ezekiel 26:7–12

Tyre is mentioned a number of times in Ezek 26–29. At the time of the prophet, this city was an impregnable fortress located on an island (see Example 7.1). Yet in 586, Ezekiel foretells that the Babylonian king Nebuchadnezzar will conquer it by force, destroying its walls (26:1, 7–12). Is there extrabiblical confirmation of this event?

The answer is yes and no. We can find out about this in several ways: for instance, by consulting a good commentary on Ezekiel that briefly summarizes what we know (e.g., Moshe Greenberg's commentary in the Anchor Bible series), or by consulting a history of Phoenicia (see the book by Josette Elayi that is mentioned under the heading "Phoenicians" in the sidebar "Where to Find Out about the History of Other Ancient Near Eastern Countries"). From such sources we can learn that, on the basis of Phoenician records that had been preserved in the writings of Hellenistic authors, Flavius Josephus mentions the siege and says that it lasted thirteen years (*Against Apion* 1:121). Chronological calculations indicate that Tyre capitulated in ca. 573 or 572 BCE. On the other hand, we also learn that there is no indication in Josephus or any other extrabiblical sources that Tyre was taken by force (which is the kind of detail these sources usually record). Modern historians therefore think that the city surrendered after negotiations, and in fact, this is what we see in another passage in Ezekiel. About two years after the city capitulated (that is, about sixteen years after the prediction Ezekiel made in 586; compare 26:1 and 29:17), the prophet acknowledged the relative failure of Nebuchadnezzar's army, noting that it did not get any spoils (29:18)—which is a veiled way of saying that it did not take the city by force. Therefore, Tyre did surrender to Nebuchadnezzar, but not in the way described in Ezek 26:7–12.

Where to Find Out about Iconography

Iconography deals with the study of figurative representations (of deities, for example). Ancient Near Eastern sources that provide iconographic data include painted frescoes, graffiti, sculptures, bas-reliefs, decorated stelae, seals, etc. In order to obtain information in this area that might inform our exegesis, we can search in at least two ways.

By Biblical Book or Passage

- ANEP = James B. Pritchard, *The Ancient Near East in Pictures Relating to the Old Testament*, 2nd ed. (Princeton: Princeton University Press, 1969). An anthology of pictures: search via the index of biblical references.
- ZIBBC = John Walton, ed., *Zondervan Illustrated Bible Backgrounds Commentary*, 5 vols. (Grand Rapids: Zondervan, 2009).

Here are examples of monographs that analyze specific biblical books in light of ancient Near Eastern iconography:

- Othmar Keel, *The Symbolism of the Biblical World: Ancient Near Eastern Iconography and the Book of Psalms*, trans. T. J. Hallett (Winona Lake, IN: Eisenbrauns, 1997).
- Othmar Keel, *The Song of Songs: A Continental Commentary* (Minneapolis: Fortress, 1994).
- Izaak J. de Hulster, *Iconographic Exegesis and Third Isaiah*, FAT 2.36 (Tübingen: Mohr Siebeck, 2009).

The following book provides examples of "iconographic exegesis" from all sections of the Hebrew Bible:

- Izaak J. de Hulster, Brent A. Strawn, and Ryan P. Bonfiglio, eds., *Iconographic Exegesis of the Hebrew Bible/Old Testament: An Introduction to Its Method and Practice* (Göttingen: Vandenhoeck & Ruprecht, 2015).

By Figure or Motif

Another way of proceeding is to identify a figure (e.g., a goddess) or a motif in the text that may have inspired figural representations and to then look in the secondary literature for an article or book dedicated to the subject. Here are a couple examples:

- Othmar Keel and Christoph Uehlinger, *Gods, Goddesses, and Images of God in Ancient Israel*, trans. Thomas H. Trapp (Minneapolis: Fortress, 1998).

- Martin Klingbeil, *Yahweh Fighting from Heaven: God as Warrior and as God of Heaven in the Hebrew Psalter and Ancient Near Eastern Iconography*, OBO 169 (Göttingen: Vandenhoeck & Ruprecht, 1999).

EXAMPLE 8.2e › **Cherubim**

Cherubim appear in many contexts in the Hebrew Bible:

- Cherubim guard access to the garden of Eden (Gen 3:24).

- In the tabernacle and the temple, cherubim are represented on curtains, walls, and doors (Exod 26:1, 31; 36:8, 35; 1 Kgs 6:23–35; 7:29, 36).

- Sculpted cherubim spread their wings above the ark of the covenant in the holy of holies (Exod 37:7–9; 1 Kgs 8:6).

- The Lord is said to be "enthroned on the cherubim" (1 Sam 4:4; 2 Sam 6:2; cf. also Ps 80:1 [2]; etc.).

- In the vision of Ezek 10, cherubim are associated with wheels located under a platform that supports God's throne.

- The Lord traverses the heavens riding on a cherub (Ps 18:10 [11]).

What is the nature of the cherubim? Similar winged beings appear in other ancient Near Eastern sources, notably in iconographic sources. For example, creatures of this kind appear in the form of sculptures at the entrances of temples and palaces, or carved on walls; sometimes, they flank a throne. Scholars have devoted much study to these beings, and it turns out that they were perceived as having two main functions: to guard the entrances of sanctuaries and palaces and to serve as "throne-bearers."[16] The common denominator shared by these two roles is that cherubim marked and protected the frontier between the "profane" world of humans and the "sacred" or divine realm of the gods (note that kings were, in some way,

---

16. For important studies, see Othmar Keel and Christoph Uehlinger, *Gods, Goddesses, and Images of God in Ancient Israel*, trans. Thomas H. Trapp (Minneapolis: Fortress, 1998), 168–69; Dale Launderville, "Ezekiel's Cherub: A Promising Symbol or a Dangerous Idol?" *CBQ* 65 (2004): 165–83; Alice Wood, *Of Wings and Wheels: A Synthetic Study of the Biblical Cherubim*, BZAW 385 (Berlin: de Gruyter, 2008).

regarded as associated with this higher sphere, which is also reflected in the fact that they are sometimes called "sons of God"). This sheds light on the various roles of cherubim in the Hebrew Bible:

- They guard the entrance of the garden of Eden, which can be regarded as a proto-temple—that is, a place where (before the fall) humans could meet God.

- They mark the frontier between the exterior and the interior of the temple, and, within the temple, the frontier between the holy place and the holy of holies.

- They support or flank the throne of the king and the Lord's throne. This is seen most notably in the vision in Ezek 10: what the prophet beholds there is the Lord's chariot, with wheels below and a throne above a platform supported by the cherubim.

8.3 COMPARE THE BIBLICAL AND EXTRABIBLICAL SOURCES

Most reasoning about the history of events involves comparing biblical texts and other sources. By the end of the preceding step, you should have found the relevant extrabiblical sources. Before moving on to comparing these with the biblical text, however, it is necessary to subject these extrabiblical sources—whether they are texts, archaeological findings, or otherwise—to the same kind of critical analysis you have applied to the biblical texts. You can do this using the following steps:

Ⓐ Critically assess the extrabiblical sources, considering their dating, interpretation, and possible ideological underpinnings. If, for instance, you are dealing with a royal inscription from Mesopotamia, you should remember that these are, by definition, propaganda; although they often contain important data, they are biased. If you are dealing with archaeological findings, it is worth checking whether their dating and interpretation are a matter of consensus or debate among archaeologists.

Ⓑ Compare the sources. The easiest situation occurs when independent sources *converge*, since this enhances the credibility of their shared claims. When the sources *diverge*, it is worth assessing their relative credibility, but this must be done carefully, in a manner that avoids simplistic approaches. Let us briefly consider the following situations:

- *A biblical text and an epigraphic text diverge:* The latter has the advantage that it is more or less contemporary with the events it describes; biblical texts, by contrast, were often written later and were subjected to successive redactions. That said, it should be kept in mind that inscriptions that have historiographical bearing are generally the product of royal ideology and propaganda, so it would be naïve to accept everything they say uncritically. In addition, it should be remembered that relatively late biblical books may be based on early sources.

- *A biblical text and archaeological data diverge:* The latter have the advantage of being "objective" and contemporary with the period under study, whereas biblical texts were written from a particular perspective and often much later than the events they describe. Nevertheless, archaeological data also need to be interpreted and dated—and unfortunately, archaeologists often differ among themselves with regard to both of these matters.

- *Two biblical texts diverge:* Here it is important not only to determine the relative chronology of the texts (though the earlier text is not necessarily the more accurate one), but also, and more crucially, to find out what the underlying theological projects of their authors are.

C Determine the answer to your initial research question:

- If you want to learn more about the background of an event or about a practice, you should—on the basis of the preceding steps—be able to compare it with extrabiblical data that are truly comparable (in terms of dating, interpretation, and so on).

- If you want to assess the historicity of an event, it is important to remember that the answer to your question may take several forms. If the event is attested in an extrabiblical source, you may be able to reach a definitive conclusion about its historicity. If not, you may nevertheless be able to assess the *degree of plausibility* that such an event occurred, depending on how well it fits the historical context or whether similar events took place during the same period.

Finally, while most historians studying ancient Israel and Judah are interested in the history of events, another fascinating perspective is provided by cultural memory (see the sidebar "Communicative Memory and Cultural Memory" below).

EXAMPLE 8.3 ▸ The Murder of Joram and Ahaziah (2 Kings 9:14–28)

According to 2 Kgs 9:14–28, Jehu killed both Joram, king of Israel, and Ahaziah, king of Judah. Do we have corroboration of these events in extrabiblical sources? As it happens, the Tel Dan inscription, a fragmentary Aramaic victory stela from the late ninth century BCE, seems to corroborate some aspects of this story while challenging another one. Although the name of the king who speaks in the text is not preserved, the dating suggests that it was Hazael, who is mentioned in 2 Kgs 8 and 10. In the stela, he makes the following claim: "[I killed Jo]ram son of [Ahab], king of Israel, and [Ahaz]iah son of [Jehoram, king] of the house of David" (in other words, of the kingdom of Judah). Although the names of the two victims are broken, the end of each name is preserved, and if we look in the Bible for two kings of Israel and Judah whose names ended in this way and were contemporaries, there is only one possible match: Joram and Ahaziah, precisely the kings that 2 Kgs 9 claims were killed almost simultaneously. Therefore, the inscription seems to corroborate this part of the story. Where the accounts diverge is about the identity of the killer: according to the Bible, it is Jehu, but according to the stela, it is an Aramaean king (most probably Hazael). This raises an interesting question from a methodological viewpoint: which source should we believe? Some scholars prefer to give priority to the epigraphic text because it was written soon after the events described, whereas the main redactions of the books of Kings were completed centuries later. At first, this sounds like a logical approach. On second thought, however, it is important to remember that royal inscriptions cannot be trusted without reservation. The artifact in question is a victory stela, that is, a propagandistic document by nature. There is no shortage of ancient rulers who declare that they were victorious in battles that they actually lost or who claim to have accomplished things that were in fact done by others. Moreover, despite the fact that the main redactions of Kings date from the seventh and sixth centuries BCE, they are partly based on sources that are much older. In the case of Jehu's reign, such sources can hardly postdate the end of the Northern Kingdom (ca. 720).

What is more, it is likely that the original account used in 2 Kgs 9 comes from the time of Jehu himself, because this is when some people were still interested in reacting to his coup. This story could have been told to vindicate his actions. It could also have been designed to criticize Jehu's violence. Either way, it is plausible that 2 Kgs 9 is based on an account that is more or less contemporary with the Tel Dan stela. Even though this account was probably subjected to a good deal of editing when it was incorporated into Kings, it is unlikely that the identity of the person responsible for the double regicide was changed.

Yet another possibility, which would harmonize both documents, is that Jehu acted on Hazael's behalf. After all, these two individuals came to the throne at approximately the same time, and both were illegitimate outsiders (that is, they did not belong to the reigning dynasties). It is possible that they had a secret agreement to perpetrate the murders and that Jehu, the one who was in Israel, was the one who actually performed the job. Hazael may have been, or may have perceived himself as, the suzerain, in which case he could have claimed responsibility for something that his vassal did.

8.4 SYNTHESIS: RECONSTRUCT THE SEQUENCE OF EVENTS

This is the task whose results are the most uncertain, since the historical sources at our disposal are fragmentary and do not necessarily discuss the same events as each other.

> **EXAMPLE 8.4** ▸ **The Assyrian Siege of Jerusalem (2 Kings 18:13–19:37)**
>
> The two main historical sources about the Assyrian siege of Jerusalem in 701 BCE are the biblical narratives in 2 Kgs 18–19 (as well as their parallels in Isa 36–39, along with a sort of summary in 2 Chr 32) and Assyrian annals. The main historical question is why the Assyrians, after conquering all the rest of Judah, did not take Jerusalem but instead retreated from it.
>
> Let's begin by assessing the biblical texts. As we saw in chapter 3, 2 Kgs 18:14–19:36 combines three sources: A (18:14–16), B1 (18:13; 18:17–19.9a; 19:37), and B2 (19:9b–36). These sources provide different explanations for Sennacherib's retreat:
>
> - According to A, Hezekiah paid tribute to the Assyrian king.
> - According to B1, Sennacherib heard news about an attack by Tirhakah the Kushite.
> - According to B2, an angel of the Lord killed the Assyrian soldiers.
>
> Most scholars consider A to be a sober report that may come from, or summarize, an annalistic source. The situation is more complicated with B1 and B2, however. A number of scholars have attempted to harmonize them—arguing, for example, that they narrate two successive Assyrian attacks—but this does not do justice to the internal logic of either account, each of which seems clearly to provide an alternative explanation for the same event.
>
> According to one theory, A reports events that took place *after* those narrated in B1. On this view, after a period of siege in which Assyrian officials tried to intimidate the Judeans with speeches such as those found in B1, Hezekiah paid tribute and the Assyrian army left. This does not correspond to the internal logic of B1, however, since there the prophet Isaiah predicts that Sennacherib will leave due to a rumor he will hear (19:7), and this is in fact what happens at the end of B1 (19:9a). Nevertheless, B1 could still

contain a historical kernel that could be combined with A. Another theory builds on a mention of the Kushite king Tirhakah at the end of B1 (19:9) to argue that this king played a part in Sennacherib's retreat from Jerusalem.

Let's now turn to the Akkadian sources—which are mainly royal annals—and compare them to the biblical texts.[17] Royal annals are by nature biased due to their royal ideology, but nevertheless are relatively sober in their descriptions of events; indeed, historians generally consider them to contain much historical information. In this particular instance, the relevant annals report Sennacherib's invasion of Judah and the destruction of dozens of cities there. Sennacherib says that he "shut him [i.e., Hezekiah] up like a bird in a cage within Jerusalem," but he does not claim to have taken this capital city. Carved panels from his palace (now in the British Museum) abundantly illustrate the siege of Lachish, not of Jerusalem. This absence of a claim that Jerusalem was taken is in itself significant: Sennacherib did not distort history on this point to aggrandize his successes. What the Assyrian sources state is that Hezekiah submitted and paid tribute. This corroborates the main event mentioned in A of the biblical account.

Although the last decade of Sennacherib's reign is not documented in the royal annals, what we know of the Assyrian empire during this time makes it very unlikely that its army came back to attack Jerusalem a second time, which further undermines the hypothesis that B1 and B2 narrate two distinct attacks. In addition, 19:12–13 seems to allude to victories made by the Babylonians in the late seventh century BCE, which confirms that B2 is not a direct historical source for 701 BCE (see Example 4.3h). By contrast, B1 accurately mentions several titles (e.g., the "Rabshakeh") that Assyrian officials bore in the late eighth century BCE, and the speeches presented in this text fit quite well what we know of Assyrian methods of intimidation, thus giving B1 a ring of authenticity.

In the end, it seems safe to say that Hezekiah submitted to Sennacherib and paid him tribute. The precise circumstances and chronology of these events still elude us (did they take place while Sennacherib was at Lachish, as 18:14–16 seems to suggest, or later?). Whether Tirhakah played a role—and if so, precisely what kind—is still debated. It is plausible that during the siege some officials tried to intimidate the inhabitants of Jerusalem, although we have no means of saying whether this happened in the way that is narrated in B1. As for B2, it does not seem to provide direct information on the events that unfolded in 701 BCE, but it does yield important information on the *cultural memory* associated with these events in the kingdom of Judah a century later.

---

17. Josette Elayi, *Sennacherib, King of Assyria*, ABS 24 (Atlanta: SBL Press, 2018), 69–88.

Communicative Memory and Cultural Memory

Since the publication of Jan Assmann's seminal study *Cultural Memory and Early Civilization*,[18] historians speak of ancient literature as potentially preserving two kinds of memories:

- *Communicative memory*, which "comprises memories related to the recent past. These are what the individual shares with his contemporaries."

- *Cultural memory*, which focuses on what Assmann calls "figures of memory," that is, events or narratives that are situated in a remote past. "What counts for cultural memory is not factual but remembered history. One might even say that cultural memory transforms factual into remembered history, thus turning it into myth." Here, myth does not mean "fiction" but "foundational history that is narrated in order to illuminate the present from the standpoint of its origins."[19]

A related distinction is the following:

- When scholars study the *history of events*, they are interested in assessing the historicity of events mentioned in texts and do so by raising questions such as: Did they happen? Did they happen as they are narrated? Did they happen when the texts say they occurred? and so forth.

- When scholars study the *history of cultural memory* (also called *mnemohistory*), they put aside the issue of the historicity of events and instead focus on the following: the manner in which they have been told and retold, how these stories have been transformed through time, how they have shaped the self-understanding of a people, how they have helped a people maintain its identity in times of trial, how such stories have met resistance in some circles and prompted counternarratives, and so on.

Assmann himself analyzed the examples of Exodus and Deuteronomy in the aforementioned book, and since then, mnemohistory has been used to understand various texts (both narratives and oracles) in the Hebrew Bible. Here are a few examples:

- Ronald Hendel, *Remembering Abraham: Culture, Memory, and History in the Hebrew Bible* (New York: Oxford University Press, 2005).

---

18. Jan Assmann, *Cultural Memory and Early Civilization: Writing, Remembrance, and Political Imagination* (New York: Cambridge University Press, 2012; original German edition, 2007).
19. Assmann, *Cultural Memory and Early Civilization*, 36–38.

> - Ronald Hendel, "The Exodus as Cultural Memory: Egyptian Bondage and the Song of the Sea," in *Israel's Exodus in Transdisciplinary Perspective: Text, Archaeology, and Geoscience*, ed. Thomas E. Levy, Thomas Schneider, and William H. C. Propp (Cham: Springer, 2015), 65–77. Provides references to previous articles on the subject by the same author.
> - Hugh G. M. Williamson, "History and Memory in the Prophets," in *The Oxford Handbook of the Prophets*, ed. Carolyn J. Sharp (New York: Oxford University Press, 2016), 133–48.

Exercises for Chapter 8

Exercise A

In 1 Kgs 18:28, we read that when the prophets of Baal called on their god at Mount Carmel, "they cried aloud and, as was their custom, they cut themselves with swords and lances until the blood gushed out over them." Do any ancient Near Eastern sources attest to such a custom?

Exercise B

In Gen 16, because Sarai does not have any children, she suggests to Abram that he should have children with her slave Hagar and that she (Sarai) will then take these children as her own. Abram complies, and this subsequently leads to a conflict between the two women. Hagar "looked with contempt on her mistress" (v. 4), presumably because of a sense of superiority. Sarai complains to Abram, and he then tells her to do what she wants with her slave. The text then reports that "Sarai dealt harshly with [Hagar], and she ran away from her" (v. 6).

This episode raises various question for the modern reader, particularly because the narrator does not provide any explicit assessment of the behavior of the characters. Was using a slave to get children for oneself a common practice in the ancient Near East? Or is it a unique idea of Sarai's here?

Exercise C

According to 2 Kgs 22–23, King Josiah led a reform of cult centralization in Judah. Investigate the historicity of this event. In addition to learning what archaeology can say about this, do not forget to look into historical-critical analyses that scholars have offered on these chapters.

Exercise D

Many biblical texts discuss the Babylonian exile, which took place in the sixth century BCE. Find out what epigraphic and archaeological sources can tell us about the historicity of the deportations. In particular, are deportations mentioned in these sources? Did the population of Judah decrease in the sixth century BCE?

Exercise E

Compare the text of the Moabite Stone (a.k.a. Mesha Stele) and 2 Kgs 3. Note the ways in which the accounts agree and disagree. How do you explain the disagreements?

CHAPTER 9

LITERARY STRUCTURE

OVERVIEW

Biblical writers often took pains to give their texts a well-crafted structure. As a result, many books and passages exhibit a relatively clear "outline" that can be laid out like the table of contents in a modern book. As we will see, a number of literary devices serve as "structural markers" that can help us in this task. In addition, writers sometimes arranged their texts by repeating a pattern. And often, they made use of more sophisticated structures based on correspondences between parts of the text.

Discerning the structure of a biblical passage can have several advantages:

- At the very least, there is an aesthetic satisfaction that comes from perceiving that a text is a harmonious literary construction.

- In antiquity, symmetrical structures undoubtedly helped people memorize texts more easily. Likewise today, describing the structure of a text helps us better understand its contours and form and remember its contents.

- Identifying structure in the text helps us delineate the exact limits of a pericope, since the whole of it is therefore "of a piece."

- Fairly often, *structure reflects the logic of the text*; that is, a passage's form may fit closely with its content and can even guide our interpretation. For instance, parallels within a literary structure often enable the author to highlight similarities or create meaningful contrasts.

- The relevance of a passage or verse within its larger context is sometimes unclear, especially when the passage or verse in question appears to disrupt the chronology of events or when its position does not seem to be the result of any logical arrangement. Sometimes, however, such an apparently poorly placed segment of text in fact serves as a parallel to another segment of text (e.g., passage or verse) in a larger literary structure.

- On a larger scale, situating a whole passage within a larger structure allows us to better grasp the passage's literary context.

Detailed publications about the structure of biblical texts include:

- Roland Meynet, *Rhetorical Analysis: An Introduction to Biblical Rhetoric*, LHBOTS (Sheffield: Sheffield Academic, 1998). A detailed introduction.

- Jerome T. Walsh, *Style and Structure in Biblical Hebrew Narrative* (Collegeville, MN: Liturgical Press, 2001). A good introduction focusing on narratives.

Studying the literary structure of a text can sometimes feel like unwinding a ball of yarn by pulling on one of the strands: that is, we look for clues that might be suggestive of the text's structure and that might show us in which direction we should continue our research. Here are some helpful steps you can follow:

❶ LOOK FOR INCLUSIOS.

❷ NOTE STRUCTURAL MARKERS.

❸ DISTINGUISH AMONG SECTIONS IN THE TEXT BASED ON FORMAL DIFFERENCES BETWEEN THEM OR DIFFERENCES IN CONTENT.

❹ IDENTIFY A REPEATED PATTERN.

❺ LOOK FOR STANDARD SYMMETRICAL STRUCTURES IN THE TEXT.

9.1 LOOK FOR INCLUSIOS

Inclusio (the Latin word for "inclusion") is a technique as simple as it is frequent. It consists of finishing a text by echoing the text's beginning, often by repeating a formula or a few words found there. The main advantage of detecting an inclusio is that it indicates the *limits* of a passage, which is useful for cases in which determining these limits may otherwise be difficult.

> **EXAMPLE 9.1a** ▸ **Psalms 1 and 2**
>
> We saw earlier (Example 6.1d) that Pss 1 and 2 serve as an introduction to the whole Psalter and that certain readers in antiquity considered them to be a single text. This does not mean that they were written by the same author or at the same time, but it does reflect the fact that the final editors wanted to make them a unit in the final edition of the Psalter. Indeed, this is

confirmed by an inclusio that brackets the two texts: Ps 1 starts with "Happy are those who . . ." and Ps 2 ends with "Happy are all who . . ." The implicit message seems to be: "Happy is the reader who takes into account these two dimensions—wisdom/morality and kingship/messianism—during his or her reading of the book."

EXAMPLE 9.1b ▸ **Psalm 8 and Psalm 103**

Psalm 8 begins and ends with the same statement: "O Lord, our Sovereign, how majestic is your name in all the earth!" Similarly, Ps 103 begins and ends with "Bless the Lord, O my soul."

9.2 NOTE STRUCTURAL MARKERS

"Structural markers" here refers to expressions or phrases that indicate boundaries or transitions. For example:

- *Introductory and concluding formulae.* In prophetic books, expressions such as "oracle of the Lord" (נְאֻם־יְהוָה; often rendered "thus says the Lord") and "in that day" (בַּיּוֹם הַהוּא) often play this role (though these expressions sometimes also appear in the middle of a speech).

- *Apostrophes*, such as "listen!" (שִׁמְעוּ) or a vocative, can also serve to introduce sections.

- *Transition markers and logical linking words*—for example, "because" (כִּי) or "therefore" (לָכֵן).

Two notes of caution are in order. First, the kind of structural markers just cited sometimes plays a merely *local* structural role; in other words, they are sometimes only relevant on the scale of one or several verses but are not relevant for the structure of the whole text. For example, as noted above, the formula "thus says the Lord" often appears in the middle of an oracle, without a particular structural function. Likewise, the expression "in that day" sometimes serves to introduce a new oracle, but at other times it serves to take up the speaker's line of argument again by adding new information. Second, logical linking words prove relatively rare in Hebrew texts. A single letter in the original (the conjunctive *waw*) is often used to say "and," "but," or "yet," so translators usually need to rely on context to determine the logical relationship between two statements. Moreover, the word "but" can indicate either a turning point in a story or a simple opposition within a sentence.

EXAMPLE 9.2a ▸ Habakkuk

The expression "Woe to him who . . ." (author's translation) is found five times at the heart of the book of Habakkuk (2:6b, 9, 12, 15, 19). Each time, this formula introduces a new aspect of condemnation against those who are generally accused of being "treacherous." Thus, this formula structures the section 2:6b–20 into five parts, as follows:

> A1   Woe to the plunderers (2:6b–8)
> A2   Woe to the dishonest (2:9–11)
> A3   Woe to the violent (2:12–14)
> A4   Woe to those who mistreat others (2:15–17)
> A5   Woe to the idolatrous (2:18–20)

EXAMPLE 9.2b ▸ Micah 3

Micah 3 contains three introductory formulae marking the beginning of three oracles:

"And I said: Listen, you heads of Jacob and rulers of the house of Israel!" (3:1).

"Thus says the Lord concerning the prophets" (3:5).

"Hear this, you rulers of the house of Jacob and chiefs of the house of Israel" (3:9).

Note that the first and third formulae are very similar. In addition, the first and third oracles are both on the same subject, that is, the attitude of the leaders of the people. Consequently, the chapter follows an ABA′ structure, where A = 3:1–4, B = 3:5–8, and A′ = 3:9–12. Moreover, a closer comparison between A and A′ shows that their inner progressions are similar (see Table 9.1).[1] Both mention, successively, an inversion of values (hatred of good or justice), a bloody oppression, and an illusory confidence that the Lord will support the rulers in spite of all this.

---

1. Matthieu Richelle, "Un triptyque au coeur du livre de Michée (Mi 4–5)," *VT* 62 (2012): 234–35.

Table 9.1: First and Third Oracles in Micah 3

Theme	First Oracle (Mic 3:1–4)	Third Oracle (Mic 3:9–12)
(1) Inversion of values	"you who hate the good and love the evil" (3:2)	"you . . . who abhor justice and pervert all equity" (3:9)
(2) Oppression of the people, likened to a crime	"who eat the flesh of my people, flay their skin off them, break their bones in pieces" (3:3)	"who build Zion with blood and Jerusalem with wrong" (3:10)
(3) Illusory confidence in the Lord's support	"Then they will cry to the Lord, but he will not answer them" (3:4)	"yet they lean upon the Lord. . . . Therefore because of you Zion shall be plowed as a field" (3:11–12)

Acronym Poems

A special way of marking the different parts of a text—one found in a handful of poetic texts in the Hebrew Bible—is where (in general) the first letter of the first word of each verse or poetic line follows the order of the Hebrew alphabet. Here is a fictitious example in English:

Alleluia!
Bless the Lord;
Call on the Creator God;
Do good and obey the God of our redemption.
etc.

Sometimes, it is only the first letter of each stanza that is marked with this kind of acrostic pattern. An extreme case of the acrostic form is Ps 119, which is composed of twenty-two stanzas (the number of letters in the Hebrew alphabet), each of which comprises eight poetic lines starting with a successive letter of the alphabet.

Those who read Hebrew can easily observe the presence of this feature in the original of the poems in question. Here is a list: Pss 9–10; 25; 34; 37; 111; 112; 119; 145; Prov 31:10–31; and Lam 1; 2; 3; 4. Nahum 1:2–11 is often added to this list, but it needs to be "corrected" in several places in order for it to be a true acrostic, so there is some doubt about whether it was written with this intention.

9.3 DISTINGUISH DIFFERENT SECTIONS IN THE TEXT

In addition to the help provided by possible structural markers, identifying discrete sections in a text and delimiting them is generally achievable thanks to the inner coherence of each of these sections and their differences from one another. For instance, it may be that a narrative is clearly composed of successive scenes, each of which has its own coherence in terms of place, time, or characters. To take another example, a speech may be composed of several parts, each of which is about a distinct theme or puts forward a distinct argument.

EXAMPLE 9.3 ▸ Song of Songs 2:8–17

Song of Songs 2:8–17 is a beautiful poem that, to the best of my understanding, does not exhibit a parallel or symmetrical structure but nevertheless is arranged in a well-crafted manner. Let's begin by noting that we are warranted in considering these verses a literary unit. Just prior to this passage, in 2:7, we find the following refrain, which marks the end of the preceding pericope: "I charge you, O daughters of Jerusalem, by the gazelles or the wild does: do not stir up or awaken love until it is ready!" That pericope is a dialogue, whereas all of vv. 8–17 (even vv. 10–14, which are a quotation of the beloved) is spoken by the woman. At the other end of the passage, in 3:1 (which immediately follows 2:17), a clearly distinct scene opens, one that takes place at nighttime. In addition, there is a structural feature that corroborates this delimitation: vv. 8–9a and 17 constitute an inclusio, with a long sentence that is repeated ("My beloved is like a gazelle or a young stag" [v. 9a] and "Be like a gazelle or a young stag" [v. 17]) and synonymous expressions ("upon the moutains" [v. 8] and "on rugged mountains" [v. 17]). All of this serves to clearly delimit this passage as a literary unit (see Table 9.2).

Table 9.2: Song of Songs 2:8–9, 17

vv. 8–9	v. 17
The voice of my beloved! Look, he comes, leaping **upon the mountains**, bounding over the hills. (v. 8) *My beloved is like* *a gazelle or a young stag.* (v. 9)	Until the day breathes and the shadows flee, turn, *my beloved, be like a gazelle or a young stag* **on rugged mountains**.

As we move on to consider the internal structure of 2:8–17, we see that it contains three discrete scenes. First, the woman says that her beloved is approaching her home (vv. 8–9). Second, the beloved invites the woman to come out (vv. 10–14). Third, the woman replies (vv. 16–17). Verse 10 represents a turning point, because vv. 10–14 constitute a relatively long speech by the beloved, which is explicitly introduced by the formula "my beloved speaks and says to me." By contrast, the verses that surround vv. 10–14 are clearly utterances by the woman. A possible exception is v. 15: we do not really know the identity of the person who says here, "Catch us the foxes, the little foxes, that ruin the vineyards—for our vineyards are in blossom." Is this the end of the man's speech or the beginning of the woman's reply? The resemblance between "vineyards are in blossom" in v. 15 and "vines are in blossom" in v. 13 lends support to the first possibility, but since the tone and substance of v. 15 differ from those of the optimistic invitation that precedes, some regard it as a cautious reaction by the woman.

In the end, we can outline the following structure:

(1) The beloved approaches the woman's house (vv. 8–9).

(2) The beloved invites the woman to come out and enjoy the spring (vv. 10–14).

Injunction about little foxes (v. 15).

(3) The woman replies (vv. 16–17).

While some exegetes have tended to read here mere fragments with little cohesion, this is not the case. Indeed, a number of repeated keywords subtly build bridges between one section and another. For example, (1) mentions the "voice" of the beloved (v. 8), while (2) mentions the "voice" of the turtledove (v. 12) and the "voice" of the woman (v. 14). In fact, there is a coherent progression from (1) to (2): the woman first hears the voice (or sound) of her beloved from afar, then she hears his words. As a result, even the formula that introduces the quotation of the man ("my beloved speaks and says to me") echoes the theme of the "voice."

Also, as we have seen, "vineyards are in blossom" in v. 15 harks back to "vines are in blossom" in v. 13, which either reinforces the internal cohesion of the man's speech (if v. 15 is spoken by the man) or builds a bridge between his speech and the woman's reply (if v. 15 is spoken by her). We have also seen that v. 17 echoes vv. 8–9. In addition, v. 17 constitutes a reply to the beloved's invitation in vv. 10–14—although, intriguingly, the woman does not explicitly say yes or no: her reply is exquisitely ambiguous. The verb rendered "turn" in the NRSVue (v. 17) can also mean "come back." Moreover, when she tells her beloved to be like a gazelle on the mountains, she actually tells him to do what he was already doing when he first appeared in v. 8, which ties the beginning and end of the passage together.

There is still another feature of the text that adds to its cohesion: The formula "*X* [my beloved, in this case] speaks and says to me" is actually unusual in poetry, and unique in Song of Songs. This kind of phraseology is, however, typical of narratives. This reinforces the continuity between vv. 8–9 and vv. 10–14, and also underscores the fact that all of vv. 8–17 constitutes one speech made by the woman.

In summary, Song 2:8–17 is a coherent and well-organized poem, and the study of its literary structure is a key to understanding it.

9.4 IDENTIFY A REPEATED PATTERN

As the following examples will show, another way to structure a text is to repeat a pattern.

EXAMPLE 9.4a ▸ Amos 1:3–2:16

The book of Amos opens with a series of eight oracles against various nations (1:3–2:16). Each of these passages follows the same pattern:

"Thus says the LORD."

"For three transgressions of [a certain nation], and for four, I will not revoke the punishment."

"Because they have . . ." (motives for the condemnation).

"I will . . . [do this]" (divine action in the form of judgment).

To describe the relationship between these oracles, it is best to speak not of a simple series (ABCDEFGH) but of a group of parallel oracles that follow the same pattern (A1 to A8):

> A1   Oracle against the Arameans of Damascus (1:3–5)
> A2   Oracle against the Philistines (1:6–8)
> A3   Oracle against the Phoenicians (1:9–10)
> A4   Oracle against the Edomites (1:11–12)
> A5   Oracle against the Ammonites (1:13–15)
> A6   Oracle against the Moabites (2:1–3)
> A7   Oracle against Judah (2:4–5)
> A8   Oracle against Israel (2:6–16)

EXAMPLE 9.4b ▸ Malachi

The case of the book of Malachi is more interesting because the point at which one oracle ends and another begins is not explicitly marked. Apart from a superscription (1:1) and an epilogue (4:4–6 [3:22–24]), this book is structured in terms of six debates, each of which follows the same pattern. Here is what this looks like:

(1) *An assertion involving God* (the fact that he loves his people [1:2], that he is Father and Master and therefore must be honored [1:6], etc.).

(2) *A quotation of a question (or more than one question) asked by the people* ("How have you loved us? Is not Esau Jacob's brother?" [1:2], "How have we despised your name?" [1:6], etc.).

(3) *The response to the question* (God will punish the Edomites [1:2–5], thus showing his attachment to Israel in preference to Edom/Esau; by despising rules about food purity, the Israelites have despised God's name [1:7–8], etc.).

Based on the recurrence of this pattern, the debates in the book of Malachi can be outlined as follows:

> A1   Debate concerning God's love and the case of Edom (1:2–5)
> A2   Debate concerning despising God's name (1:6–2:9)
> A3   Debate concerning the profaning of the covenant (2:10–16)
> A4   Debate concerning God's justice (2:17–3:5)
> A5   Debate concerning repentance (3:6–12)
> A6   Debate concerning criticism of God (3:13–4:3 [3:13–21])

9.5 RECOGNIZE A STANDARD SYMMETRICAL STRUCTURE

Israelite and Judean redactors often had recourse to a number of standard literary structures based on symmetries. Scholars refer to parallel parts of a text by using the letters A, B, C (etc.) for the initial elements and A', B', C' (etc.) for their parallels. The structure of a passage containing such symmetries can be denoted by using a "formula" that combines all these letters (e.g., ABCDA'B'C'). Parallels can be of at least three different kinds:

- **Semantic parallels**, based on verbal repetitions and synonyms (and antonyms). These are the most obvious, since they are based either on the common occurrence of a number of words or phrases in two parts of a text or on echoes between the two parts created by synonyms. These techniques can of course be combined. Here, it is best to begin by looking for repetitions and then synonyms. Needless to say, this search does not imply that any given repetition or synonym in a text necessarily points to structural parallels. But if there is an accumulation of such lexical echoes and if these echoes are distributed throughout the text in a symmetrical order, the chances of their presence pointing to a specific structure increase.

- **Thematic parallels**, based on shared topics or subject matter. These are more difficult to identify than semantic parallels.

- **Parallels based on other distinctive, shared features**—for instance, the appearance of text segments belonging to the same literary genre that are embedded in a larger literary structure (e.g., when two songs appear within a larger narrative work). This kind of parallel only appears clearly if the parallel sections are neatly distinguished from what surrounds them within the larger structure.

Once you have discovered two parallel sections in a text, you can search for others nearby. Note that when you make a proposal about the literary structure of a passage, it is of crucial importance to justify your claims by highlighting the features that "prove" that the parallels are sound: verbal repetitions, shared themes, etc.

A. Regular Parallelism

A simple method of structuring a passage involves the writer beginning the text with sections that can be denoted A, B, C, etc., then going through these same steps, as it were, by means of parallel sections that echo the previous ones and that follow the same order: A', B', C', etc. The "formula" for the entire structure can therefore be described as ABCA'B'C' (the number of parts can of course be extended).

> **EXAMPLE 9.5a** ▸ **Psalm 132**

When reading Ps 132, you may be struck by the presence of two almost identical phrases:

> Let your priests be clothed with righteousness,
> and let your faithful shout for joy. (v. 9)
>
> "Its priests I will clothe with salvation,
> and its faithful will shout for joy." (v. 16)

This is a hint that there might be a parallel structure in this psalm. By looking for repetitions or synonymous terms, we can discern that the psalm contains two sections (vv. 1–10; vv. 11–18), which are linked by a series of correspondences (see Table 9.3). Moreover, two particular parts stand out from the rest: vv. 3–5 and 11b–12, which are oaths (these are set in italics in Table 9.3). The psalm thus exhibits a "regular parallelism" that can be described as ABCDEA′B′C′D′E′. This structure accentuates the parallel between the oaths made by David and by God, as well as the invitation to come to God's "resting place" (i.e., Jerusalem; v. 8) and God's choosing of this city (vv. 13–14).

Table 9.3: Structure of Psalm 132

A David swore to the Lord (vv. 1–2)	**A′ The Lord swore to David (vv. 11a)**
O Lord, remember in **David's** favor all the hardships he endured; **how he swore to the Lord** and vowed to the Mighty One of Jacob,	The **Lord swore** to David a sure **oath** from which he will not turn back:
B Quotation of the oath (vv. 3–5)	**B′ Quotation of the oath (vv. 11b–12)**
"I will not enter my house or get into my bed; I will not give sleep to my eyes or slumber to my eyelids, until I find a place for the Lord, a dwelling place for the Mighty One of Jacob."	*"One of the sons of your body I will set on your throne. If your sons keep my covenant and my decrees that I shall teach them, their sons also, forevermore, shall sit on your throne."*
C The resting place of the Lord (vv. 6–8)	**C′ The resting place of the Lord (vv. 13–15)**
We heard of it in Ephrathah; we found it in the fields of Jaar. "Let us go to his **dwelling place**; let us worship at his footstool." Rise up, O Lord, and go to your **resting place**, you and the ark of your might.	For the Lord has chosen Zion; he has desired it for **his habitation**: "This is my **resting place** forever; here I will reside, for I have desired it. I will abundantly bless its provisions; I will satisfy its poor with bread.

D The priests and the saints (v. 9) Let your **priests be clothed** with righteousness, and let your **faithful shout for joy**.	**D' The priests and the saints (v. 16)** Its **priests I will clothe** with salvation, and **its faithful will shout for joy**.
E David, the anointed (v. 10) For your servant **David**'s sake do not turn away the face of **your anointed one**.	**E' David, the anointed (vv. 17–18)** There I will cause a horn to sprout up for **David**; I have prepared a lamp for **my anointed one**. His enemies I will clothe with disgrace, but on him, his crown will gleam."

B. Inverse Parallelism (Concentric Structure, Chiasmus)

Another structure that is very common in the Hebrew Bible is similar to the previous one, except that parts A, B, C, etc. are repeated in the opposite order. Hence, the "formula" for this structure can be described as ABCC'B'A' (again, any number of elements is theoretically possible). This kind of structure is called inverse parallelism or, more often, "chiasmus." This configuration of elements also introduces the possibility of including a central element that is not repeated (which can be called a "pivot"), whence the "formula" ABCDC'B'A'. This specific kind of chiasmus is known as a "concentric structure" (meaning it has a center), though scholars sometimes refer to this particular variation on the pattern simply with the general term "chiasmus." Finally, it should be noted that chiasmus necessarily involves an inclusio (created by A and A'). Therefore, it is worth glancing at the beginning and end of a text to see if there is an inclusio: if there is, sometimes these are sections A and A' of a chiasmus.

EXAMPLE 9.5b ▸ Leviticus 6:8–13 [1–6]

The prescription about the whole burnt offering (Lev 6:8–13 [1–6]) exhibits a concentric structure.[2] The passage is reproduced in its entirety below, with the parallel elements between A and A', B and B', and so forth set in italics:

(Introduction:) The LORD spoke to Moses, saying, "Command Aaron and his sons: This is the rule of the burnt offering.

    A The *burnt offering* itself *shall remain* on the hearth *upon the altar*

        B all night *until the morning*,

---

2. See Didier Luciani, *Sainteté et pardon: Structure littéraire du Lévitique*, 2 vols., BETL 185A–B (Leuven: Peeters, 2005) 1:33–34, 2:363.

     C while *the fire on the altar shall be kept burning.*

       D *The priest shall put on his linen vestments after putting on his linen undergarments* next to his body, and he shall take up *the ashes* to which the fire has reduced the burnt offering on the altar and place them beside the altar.

       D′ *Then he shall take off his vestments and put on other garments* and carry *the ashes* out to a clean place outside the camp.

     C′ *The fire on the altar shall be kept burning*; it shall not go out.

   B′ *Every morning* the priest shall add wood to it, lay out the burnt offering on it, and turn into smoke the fat pieces of the offerings of well-being.

A′ A perpetual *fire shall be kept burning on the altar*; it shall not go out.

Interestingly, D and D′ have the same internal microstructure: they first speak about the garments of the priest and then what he needs to do with the ashes.

EXAMPLE 9.5c ▸ **Daniel 2–7**

The stories found in chs. 2 to 7 of the book of Daniel (the section of this book written in Aramaic, from 2:4b to the end of ch. 7) can easily be paired up with each other, as follows:

- In ch. 2, King Nebuchadnezzar has a dream whose interpretation reveals that it concerns four kingdoms to come as well as a fifth that is eternal. In ch. 7, Daniel has a vision of four beasts, which represent kingdoms, then another vision in which eternal dominion is given to a heavenly being.

- In both chs. 3 and 6, the faith of a group of Jews (ch. 3) or an individual Jew (ch. 6) in exile is tested, and they are miraculously saved (from the fiery furnace [ch. 3], from the lions' den [ch. 6]).

- In chs. 4 and 5, two Babylonian kings (Nebuchadnezzar and Belshazzar, respectively) receive a cryptic vision or message (vision of a great tree [ch. 4], writing on the wall [ch. 5]) that announces that the king will fall because of his pride. In both cases, it is Daniel who provides the interpretation.

Putting all this together, we discover that the Aramaic portions of Daniel have a chiastic structure:

> A   Dream about four kingdoms (ch. 2)
>> B   The faith of a group of Jews is tested, and they are delivered from a fiery furnace (ch. 3)
>>> C   King Nebuchadnezzar has a vision of his downfall (ch. 4)
>>> C'   King Belshazzar receives a message about his downfall (ch. 5)
>> B'   The faith of a Jew is tested, and he is delivered from a lions' den (6)
> A'   Vision about four kingdoms (ch. 7)

EXAMPLE 9.5d ▸ Psalm 1

We have already had several occasions to consider Ps 1. Now it can be observed that this brief poem has an elegant chiastic structure:

> A   Contrast between the righteous and the wicked (vv. 1–2)
>> B   Plant comparison: the righteous person is like a tree that bears fruit (v. 3)
>> B'   Plant comparison: the wicked are like chaff (v. 4)
> A'   Contrast between the way of the righteous and the way of the wicked (vv. 5–6)

Parts A and A' imitate each other with multiple echoes. As for content, each plays on the contrast between two categories of people: the man who meditates on the law versus "the wicked," "sinners," and "scoffers" (A); the "righteous" versus "the wicked" and "sinners" (A'). As for form, the parallels fall into four categories:

- The "path" or the "way" (vv. 1, 6): In part A, the man who avoids "the path that sinners tread" is said to be blessed; in part A', this contrast is reinforced by the explicit opposition between "the way of the righteous" and "the way of the wicked."

- Movement or position: "follow" (v. 1), "take" (v. 1), "sit" (v. 1), and "stand" (v. 5).

- The idea of "company": Part A describes the man who "does not sit in the seat of scoffers" (v. 1); part A' describes the opposite reality—that sinners "will not stand" in "the assembly of the righteous" (v. 5). In this life, the person who avoids the company of the wicked is right to do so; on the day of judgment, the wicked will regret not being able to stand in the assembly of the righteous.

- Vocabulary with judicial connotations: law (v. 2) and judgment (v. 5).

Moving on to parts B and B′, the parallel here is fairly clear: both parts make use of contrasting plant comparisons (a tree that bears fruit versus chaff that is blown away by the wind).

Chiasmo-Mania and Chiasmo-Phobia

In the quest to understand the literary structure of a text, two extremes must be avoided. On the one hand, some exegetes see chiasmus everywhere. While it is clear that this classic structure was widely used by biblical authors, this is obviously not a reason for forcing any given text into this mold. Many erroneous, even fanciful, proposals about chiasmus can be found in the secondary literature (commentaries, articles, etc.), so it is always important to verify for yourself a scholar's proposal that a text is structured in this way. Here are three tips that can help you exercise discernment in this area:

- Do not be fooled by titles a scholar has deliberately given to parts of the text that make them seem to be parallels. Check whether these titles actually reflect the contents of the text.

- Make sure that the parts making up the chiasmus (A, B, C, etc.) correspond to actual sections within the text, and that they do not overlap.

- Verify that the parallels are based on significant elements in the text and not on trivial words such as prepositions.

One author has undertaken an experiment in order to illustrate this last point: he took twenty verses here and there in the book of Isaiah and put them together, thus forming an artificial "Isaiah chapter 67." Then, he demonstrated that by choosing certain words, a chiasmus could be reconstructed. In fact, he often deliberately chose insignificant words in order to create parallels. This experiment is found in:

- Mike Butterworth, *Structure and the Book of Zechariah*, JSOTSup 130 (Sheffield: JSOT Press, 1992), 53–57.

On the other hand, the excesses mentioned above have led some scholars to be wary of looking for chiasmus. To do so is to throw out the baby with the bathwater, however. Deliberately neglecting a structure that is actually present in a text is as unjustified as inventing one that does not exist.

EXAMPLE 9.5e ▸ **Psalms 26–32**

Psalms 26–32 form a subcollection that exhibits a chiastic form. Table 9.4 lists both the broad symmetries and sentences in the psalms that echo each other. It is as if the reader is invited to read Ps 32 opposite Ps 26, Ps 31 as the twin of Ps 27, Ps 30 as a sort of response to Ps 28, and Ps 29 as a sort of apex dedicated to the glory of God.

Table 9.4: Psalms 26–32

A = Ps 26: Affirmation of innocence	A′ = Ps 32: Affirmation of sin and forgiveness
"Vindicate me, O Lord, for I have walked in my integrity" (v. 1)	"Then I acknowledged my sin to you" (v. 5)
B = Ps 27: Confidence in the Lord's protection	B′= Ps 31: Confidence in the Lord's deliverance
Conclusion: "be strong, and let your heart take courage; wait for the Lord!" (v. 14)	Conclusion: "Be strong, and let your heart take courage, all you who wait for the Lord!" (v. 24)
C = Ps 28: Call for help	C′ = Ps 30: Thanksgiving
because: "if you are silent to me, I shall be like those who go down to the Pit." (v. 1)	because: "you . . . restored me to life from among those gone down to the Pit" (v. 4)
D = Ps 29: Glorify the Lord	

EXAMPLE 9.5f ▸ **Proverbs 1:22–33**

The last in this series of examples is a case where the presence of logical linking words can help us discern a structure. In the speech by Lady Wisdom in Prov 1:22–33, the recurrence of the words "simple" and "fools" can be seen at the beginning and the end (vv. 22 and 32). Could this be an inclusio? As a matter of fact, v. 32 is not the final verse in this passage; instead, the passage concludes in v. 33, which contains a promise from Lady Wisdom: "those who listen to me will be secure and will live at ease without dread of disaster." Interestingly, the same phenomenon occurs after v. 22, which likewise is followed by a promise: "Give heed to my reproof; I will pour out my thoughts to you; I will make my words known to you." Thus, vv. 22–23 and 32–33 both have the form "criticism of the simple + promise" and therefore echo each other, forming a robust inclusio around Lady Wisdom's speech.

Next, we can see if there are other parallels in vv. 24–31. A quick glance shows that vv. 24–28 describe a case of cause and effect, as marked in v. 24a by a term meaning "because": "Because [יַעַן] I have called and you refused, … I also will laugh at your calamity." A similar statement is found in vv. 29–31, which is introduced, in v. 29, by another term meaning "because": "Because [תַּחַת כִּי] they hated knowledge … , (therefore) they shall eat the fruit of their way."[3] Thus, vv. 24–28 and vv. 29–31 form parallel sections, and vv. 22–33 have a chiastic structure, as follows:[4]

    A "How long, O **simple ones**, will you love being simple?
         How long will scoffers delight in their scoffing
         and **fools** hate knowledge?
         Give heed to my reproof;
         I will pour out my thoughts to you;
         I will make my words known to you.

        B *Because* [יַעַן] I have called and you refused,
           have stretched out my hand and no one heeded,
           and (because) you have ignored all my counsel
           and would have none of my reproof,
           I also will laugh at your calamity;
           I will mock when panic strikes you …

        B′ *Because* [תַּחַת כִּי] they hated knowledge
           and did not choose the fear of the Lord,
           would have none of my counsel
           and despised all my reproof,
           (therefore) they shall eat the fruit of their way
           and be sated with their own devices.

    A′ For waywardness kills the **simple**,
         and the complacency of **fools** destroys them;
         but those who listen to me will be secure
         and will live at ease without dread of disaster."

---

3. I have added the parentheses around "therefore" and "because" both here and below in order to indicate that these words are implicit, not explicit, in Hebrew.

4. I regard v. 28 as an elaboration on vv. 26–27, not the beginning of a new subparagraph. For a different view on this passage, see Bernd U. Schipper, *Proverbs 1–15: A Commentary*, Hermeneia (Minneapolis: Fortress, 2019), 87–88.

Exercises for Chapter 9

Exercise A

In the book of Genesis, search all the occurrences of the expression "these are the generations of" (אֵלֶּה תוֹלְדוֹת). Are these introductory or concluding formulae? Can they provide a literary structure for the book?

Exercise B

Second Samuel 21–24 has a chiastic structure: prove this.

Exercise C

Many exegetes think that the flood story (Gen 6:9–9:29) exhibits a chiastic structure. Form your own view and justify it.

Exercise D

What is the literary structure of Ps 57?

Exercise E

What is the literary structure of the book of Jonah?

CHAPTER 10

POETRY

OVERVIEW

A significant part of the Hebrew Bible is written in poetry. This is the case not only for the so-called "poetic books" (such as Psalms and Song of Songs), but also for most of the prophetic literature. Poetic texts exhibit special features that are worth considering together.

Because these features are, in a sense, merely stylistic, some readers may wonder if there is really more to them than literary aesthetics (though I would suggest that this is interesting in itself!). There is. Perhaps more than in prose texts, in poetry *the form often conveys the meaning.* After all, why compose a long, elaborate discourse in subtle poetry to say that Nineveh will be destroyed (Nah 3)? Could not the same message be spelled out in a few words, such as "The God of Israel says that Nineveh will be destroyed"? Why spend so much energy to describe at length the sufferings and hopes of believers (Psalms, Lamentations)? Could not the same ideas be expressed in a few sentences? Why write a poem to say to a man or to a woman than you love him or her? The same thing could be said in a few words . . . but, of course, it would not really be the same! Expressing feelings in poetry can convey in itself a powerful message. As we will see below, no literal paraphrase can capture the full cognitive richness and meaning of a metaphor. Poetry has a cognitive and emotional power that prose does not.

Above all, a poet aims to produce an effect on his or her reader or audience, and this often involves more than just making a brief and dry statement. This is especially true when the poet is also a prophet: in this case, he wants to convince his audience of his point, to make them realize they are at fault, to make them change their behavior, to reassure them, to make them lift their heads and consider better times that lie ahead in the future, and so on. Style and poetry do not dilute ideas and arguments—they *enhance* their impact on the speaker's audience and readers.

To study a poetic text, it seems appropriate to look first at stylistic features, to then reflect on figures of speech and other poetic devices, and finally to reflect on the rhetorical function of the poem. In practical terms, we will learn in this chapter how to:

❶ ANALYZE THE **MICROSTRUCTURE** OF THE POEM (LAY OUT THE TEXT IN COLA, BICOLA, TRICOLA, AND SO ON).

❷ ANALYZE THE **MACROSTRUCTURE** OF THE POEM.

❸ STUDY THE POEM'S **FIGURES OF SPEECH** AND OTHER POETIC DEVICES.

❹ DETERMINE THE **RHETORICAL FUNCTION** OF THE POEM: WHAT DOES THE POET/PROPHET WANT TO ACHIEVE?

Approaches to Biblical Poetry

Biblical poetry has many facets, and this chapter can only introduce you to some of them. Here are some helpful books for going further:

- Luis Alonso Schökel, *A Manual of Hebrew Poetics*, SubBi 11 (Rome: Pontifical Biblical Institute, 2000).

- J. P. Fokkelman, *Reading Biblical Poetry: An Introductory Guide*, trans. Ineke Smit (Louisville: Westminster John Knox, 2001).

- Robert Alter, *The Art of Biblical Poetry*, 2nd ed. (New York: Basic Books, 2011).

- F. W. Dobbs-Allsopp, *On Biblical Poetry* (New York: Oxford University Press, 2015).

An intriguing topic is the relationship between poetry and oral performance (it is a striking fact that much biblical poetry takes the form of speeches). On this subject and for a new approach, see:

- Jacqueline Vayntrub, *Beyond Orality: Biblical Poetry on Its Own Terms* (New York: Routledge, 2019).

10.1 ANALYZE THE MICROSTRUCTURE

A poem is composed of units and subunits:

- The basic unit is the poetic line, also called a "colon" (plural "cola"). It is sometimes possible to distinguish two halves in a colon, each of which is called a "hemistich."

- When a number of consecutive cola are interconnected, they constitute a strophe, which can be described—depending on the number of cola they comprise (two, three, four, etc.)—as a bicolon, tricolon (or triplet), quadricolon (or quatrain), and so forth. Sometimes, a colon remains isolated (i.e., it is not part of a strophe), in which case it is called a monocolon.

For instance, Ps 117:1 is a bicolon since it comprises two successive poetic lines that are clearly interrelated:

> Praise the LORD, all you nations!
> Extol him, all you peoples!

And Ps 93:4 is a tricolon:

> More majestic than the thunders of mighty waters,
> more majestic than the waves of the sea,
> majestic on high is the LORD!

Segmenting a poetic text into cola and strophes, and laying out the text on the page accordingly—e.g., by starting a new line every time there is a new colon and a new paragraph every time there is a new strophe—constitute the basic tasks of *stichography*. Of course, this is already done in a number of publications (see the sidebar "Where to Find the Biblical Text Already Laid Out in Cola" below). That said, scholars often disagree among themselves about the stichography of a given passage. Moreover, it is always better to first examine a poem yourself and only then to consult (with a critical eye) the proposals that have been made by exegetes.

Where to Find the Biblical Text Already Laid Out in Cola

Here are three places to look:

Bible translations. Not all printed translations lay out poetic texts by starting a new line every time there is a new colon. And some do this but not everywhere. Study editions tend to lay out poetic texts as poetry more than "simple" editions of the Bible do. The NJPS, whether in the form of a study edition or not, is very helpful since it always tries to reflect the poetic outline of the text; moreover, bilingual (Hebrew-English) editions of the NJPS exist that allow you to easily check the choices made by the editors.

Editions of the MT. Masoretic manuscripts (e.g., the Aleppo Codex or the Leningrad Codex) often segment the cola of poetic texts by leaving blank spaces between them rather than by starting a new line, although they do not

> do so for all poetic texts. BHS and BHQ attempt to reflect the divisions of the Leningrad Codex wherever possible. In addition, the Masoretic accentuation divides every verse into constituent parts, and you may want to consider the most important of these accents (e.g., *atnach*) when determining how to divide a given verse into poetic lines. When doing so, keep in mind that the Masoretic accentuation in Psalms, Job, and Proverbs differs from that of rest of the Hebrew Bible.
>
> **Exegetical commentaries** may also be helpful. However, not all commentators are interested in poetic structures. Below, another sidebar ("Where to Find Detailed Analysis of Poetic Texts") will list commentaries and monographs that not only segment the text into cola but also provide exhaustive analysis of certain poetic books (or parts of books).

How can you segment the text into cola? In traditional English poetry, the ends of cola are typically marked by rhyme—that is, similar-sounding final (or near-final) syllables. While this sometimes occurs in Hebrew, it remains relatively rare. Hebrew poets often preferred to create "rhymes," as it were, on the level of meaning rather than on the level of sound. In other words, after writing a phrase or clause, they often wrote another one that echoes the contents of the first. In this case, since the phrases or clauses reflect each other in some sense, they can be said to exhibit "parallelism." For instance, the two cola of Ps 117:1 are easy to distinguish because they say basically the same thing. In such a case, we speak of "synonymous parallelism."

Thus, the point where a verse can be broken into two cola is often precisely the point where the text "starts again" with a new phrase or clause that echoes the preceding one. However, parallels can also exist between cola that are not consecutive, as in Ps 118:17–18, where the fourth line (A′) echoes the first (A) by revisiting the topic of not dying, while the third (B′) echoes the second (B) by again mentioning God and his actions:

> A **I shall not die**, but I shall live
>> B and recount the deeds of *the* LORD.
>> B′ *The* LORD has punished me severely,
> A′ but **he did not give me over to death**.

In addition to considering *where* parallel statements occur, it should be noted that there are various *ways* to create parallels: by mentioning a contrary situation, by adding complementary information, by reusing certain words or by using synonyms, and so forth. As a result, it is important to be attentive to echoes in a text, even when they occur at a distance. The point is that parallelism represents the most basic feature of Hebrew poetry, and knowing the usual patterns can help you identify them in a particular text—which, in turn, will enable you to delineate the cola. The most typical kinds of parallelism that occur in a bicolon are as follows:

Synonymous Parallelism [similitude]

> To get wisdom is to love oneself;
> > to keep understanding is to prosper. (Prov 19:8)

Antithetic Parallelism [opposition, contrast]

> A wise child makes a glad father,
> > but a foolish child is a mother's grief. (Prov 10:1)

Synthetic Parallelism [extra information]

> Leave the presence of a fool,
> > for there you do not find words of knowledge. (Prov 14:7)

Numerical Progression [n // n+1]

> Three things are never satisfied;
> > four never say, "Enough" (Prov 30:15)

Some typical patterns that may characterize a bicolon, tricolon (triplet), quadricolon (quatrain), and so forth are:

Regular Parallelism

Bicolon [AA′]

> A How great are your works, O LORD!
> A′ Your thoughts are very deep! (Ps 92:5 [6])

Quadricolon (Quatrain) [ABA′B′]

> A Trust in the LORD and do good;
> > B live in the land and enjoy security.
>
> A′ Take delight in the LORD,
> > B′ and he will give you the desires of your heart. (Ps 37:3–4)

Inverse Parallelism (Concentric Structure or Chiasmus) [ABA′, ABB′A′, etc.]

> A I shall not die, but I shall live
> > B and recount the deeds of the LORD.
> > B′ The LORD has punished me severely,
>
> A′ but he did not give me over to death. (Ps 118:17–18)

Staircase Parallelism

[anaphora at the beginning of the first lines; apostrophe that delays the appearance of the complement, then synonymous complements; possible last line(s) of equivalent meaning but longer]

The floods | have lifted up, | O Lord,
  a   *b*   *c*
the floods | have lifted up | their voice;
  a   *b*   *d*
the floods | lift up | their roaring.
  a *b*   *d'*

(Ps 93:3; anaphora of *ab*; apostrophe *c*; complements *d//d'*)

Ascribe | to the Lord, | O families of the peoples,
 a   *b*   *c*
ascribe | to the Lord | glory and strength.
 a   *b*   *d*
Ascribe | to the Lord | the glory due his name;
 a   *b*   *d'*
E bring an offering, and come into his courts.
F Worship the Lord in holy splendor

(Ps 96:7–9; anaphora of *ab*; apostrophe *c*; complements *d//d'*; two longer extra lines E and F)

It is also possible to look more closely at parallel cola and examine precisely the way in which the elements of one colon are echoed in another. In addition, parallels sometimes exist *within* a colon (that is, between two hemistiches). A number of typical situations are illustrated below. Proper study of this subject presupposes access to the word order of the Hebrew text. Readers who do not know Hebrew can find out this order by consulting an interlinear translation.

Regular or Ordinary Parallelism [ab/a'b'; abc/a'b'c']

Praise the Lord, | all you nations!
  a   *b*
Extol him, | all you peoples!
 a'   *b*   (Ps 117:1)

Inverted Parallelism [abc/c'b'a']

For great is | toward us | his steadfast love,
 a   *b*   *c*
and the faithfulness | of the Lord | endures forever.
  c'   *b'*   *a'* (Ps 117:2, author's translation)

Ellipsis (Gapping)

[disappearance of an element as one moves from one line to another (often this element is implied in the second line)]

It is good . . .
to declare | in the morning | your steadfast love
    a   *b*   *c*
and your faithfulness | by night
       c'   *b'*

(Ps 92:2 [3], author's translation; ellipsis of *a*; note the inversion *bc/c'b'*)

Compensation

[the ellipsis of an element is sometimes compensated for by the appearance of another]

The voice | of the Lord | breaks | the cedars;
   a   *b*   *c*   *d*
he breaks, | the Lord, | the cedars | of Lebanon.
  c'   *b'*   *d'*   *e*

(Ps 29:5, author's translation; the ellipsis of *a* is compensated for by the appearance of *e*; note also the partial inversion *bcd:cbd*)

Terrace Pattern (Anadiplosis)

[the beginning of a line repeats the end of the previous line]

Then shall all the trees of the forest sing for joy
   before the Lord, *for he is coming,*
   for he is coming to judge the earth.   (Ps 96:12b–13)

Internal Regular Parallelism [aba'b']

Jacob | will rejoice; | Israel | will be glad.
 a   *b*   *a'*   *b'*   (Ps 14:7)[1]

Internal Inverse Parallelism [abb'a']

For it has stumbled, | Jerusalem, | and Judah | has fallen.
     a   *b*   *b'*   *a'*

(Isa 3:8, author's translation)

---

1. Note that in the case of Ps 14:7, one could also consider "Jacob will rejoice" and "Israel will be glad" to be two distinct, parallel cola. However, the length of the surrounding cola makes this unlikely: they would be much too short. The same holds true for the next example (Isa 3:8).

For more detailed presentations of most poetic patterns and techniques, you can consult:

- Wilfred G. E. Watson, *Classical Hebrew Poetry: A Guide to Its Techniques*, JSOTSup 26 (Sheffield: JSOT Press, 1986).

- Wilfred G. E. Watson, *Traditional Techniques in Classical Hebrew Verse*, JSOTSup 170 (Sheffield: JSOT Press, 1994).

- Adele Berlin, *The Dynamics of Biblical Parallelism*, rev. ed. (Grand Rapids: Eerdmans; Dearborn, MI: Dove Booksellers, 2008).

EXAMPLE 10.1a ▸ Psalm 29

Let us go through Ps 29, trying to recognize standard patterns and to segment the text. To begin with, we encounter in vv. 1–2 a triple repetition of the same phrase ("ascribe to the Lord"). We may therefore surmise that here there are three successive cola that begin in the same way (an example of anaphora).

> Ascribe to the Lord, O heavenly beings,
> ascribe to the Lord glory and strength.
> Ascribe to the Lord the glory of his name;
> worship the Lord in holy splendor.

Interestingly, the second half of the first line is an apostrophe ("O heavenly beings"); the object of the verb "ascribe" is delayed until the second half of the next line. In addition, the three cola are immediately followed by a sentence that seems to summarize them: "worship the Lord in holy splendor." We recognize here the features of a well-known pattern: staircase parallelism (see p. 229).

The next verses (vv. 3–9) contain a long series of statements about the voice of the Lord. We need to look closely in order to untangle this ensemble. A proper approach consists of proceeding step by step, recognizing first the most obvious (and therefore warranted) examples of parallelism, and then seeing whether they can be extended upstream or downstream. Verse 4 stands out in this regard, since it contains two sentences that are almost identical and that therefore clearly constitute an instance of synonymous parallelism:

> The voice of the Lord is powerful;
> the voice of the Lord is full of majesty.

Does this parallelism extend upstream? That does not seem to be the case, for the preceding sentence is very different. Does the parallelism extend downstream? Although the next sentence, in v. 5, begins the same way

("The voice of the Lord"), its second half ("breaks the cedars") differs so much that the sentence as a whole would constitute a weak parallel. Indeed, while the second halves of the cola in v. 4 are two simple assertions of the same form ("the voice of the Lord is" + adjective), v. 3a describes an action ("breaks the cedars").

The same kind of remark applies to v. 5, which is an instance of synonymous parallelism that cannot be extended upstream or downstream:

> The voice of the Lord breaks the cedars;
> the Lord breaks the cedars of Lebanon.

In passing, note the subtle changes from the first to the second colon: the shortening of "the voice of the Lord" to "the Lord," and the expansion of "the cedars" to "the cedars of Lebanon." This is a standard case of "compensation" (cf. p. 230).

Again, the same situation obtains in v. 6, where there is ellipsis (gapping) of the verb from the first colon in the second colon:

> He makes Lebanon skip like a calf
> and Sirion like a young wild ox.

We also find a similar instance of compensation in v. 8, where "the voice of the Lord" is shortened to "the Lord" and "the wilderness" is expanded into "the wilderness of Kadesh":

> The voice of the Lord shakes the wilderness;
> the Lord shakes the wilderness of Kadesh.

Now let's go back to the verses that we have left aside. Because v. 3 is sandwiched between vv. 1–2 and v. 4, which have already been identified as self-contained units, it should be considered on its own. It contains two assertions ("the voice of the Lord is over the waters" and "the God of glory thunders"), and these are followed by a verbless clause ("the Lord, over mighty waters") that clearly echoes the first assertion. Thus, this verse is a tricolon of the form ABA′:

> A The voice of *the Lord* is *over the waters*;
> B the God of glory thunders,
> A′ *the Lord, over* mighty *waters*.

Verse 7 is sandwiched between v. 6 and v. 8, so it is a monocolon:

> The voice of the Lord flashes forth flames of fire.

Then, in v. 9a, we find two assertions that describe, by mentioning "oaks" or "the forest," the effect of the voice of the Lord (i.e., the thunder) on the trees:

> The voice of the Lord causes the oaks to whirl
> and strips the forest bare.
>
> It seems clear that v. 9b ("and in his temple all say, 'Glory!'") does not belong together with v. 9a, nor with v. 10, so v. 9b is a monocolon (and v. 9a a bicolon).
>
> Finally, v. 10 is clearly a bicolon, since it comprises two parallel assertions:
>
> > The Lord sits enthroned over the flood;
> > the Lord sits enthroned as king forever.
>
> The same holds true for v. 11, which describes two wishes about what the Lord should do for his people:
>
> > May the Lord give strength to his people!
> > May the Lord bless his people with peace!
>
> To conclude, we have identified a quadricolon (the staircase parallelism of vv. 1–2), seven bicola (vv. 4, 5, 6, 8, 9a, 10, and 11), a tricolon (v. 3), and two monocola (vv. 7 and 9b).

What about Meter?

A significant feature of much traditional English poetry is meter, which refers to the number of "feet" (syllabic units) in a line. Counting these metrical feet involves recognizing stressed and unstressed syllables. Is it possible to do the same with ancient Hebrew poetry? The difficulty is that we do not know what should be counted (words, syllables, stressed syllables, etc.?), or how they should be counted (should we count long and short vowels differently, for example?) Numerous attempts have been made based on various criteria, with results that most scholars regard as unsatisfactory. Consequently, an increasing number of scholars doubt the very existence of meter in ancient Hebrew poetry, although some commentators still try to measure the meter of cola in biblical poems. *Rhythmic parallelism* seems more apt as a description of what we see in Hebrew poetry.[2]

That said, there is a general consensus that the Hebrew poets generally constructed the cola of a given strophe so that they would have, at least very approximately, the same length. Even though we cannot really measure this length, we can perceive the difference between very short and very long lines, and it happens that huge variations in line length within a strophe are unusual. When they do occur, it is often in order to create a special effect.

---

2. See Michael Wade Martin, "Does Ancient Hebrew Poetry Have Meter?" *JBL* 140 (2021): 503–29.

> A particular situation in which a specific rhythm is used, however—one that is based on the relative length of the poetic lines—is in laments. Indeed, some texts belonging to this genre follow the so-called *qinah* pattern (*qinah* is the Hebrew word for "lament"), in which the second line of a bicolon is shorter than the first (scholars often mention a ratio of 3:2). This imbalance and shortening creates an impression of disappointment, or lack, in the second line.[3] For instance:
>
> > Her infants have gone into captivity
> > Before the enemy.   (Lam 1:5b NJPS)

EXAMPLE 10.1b ▸ Song of Songs 2:8–17

Let's examine some selected verses—vv. 8–9, 12, and 14—from Song 2:8–17 (for the overall structure of this passage, see Example 9.3). First, vv. 8–9 constitute a regular parallelism of the form ABA′B′:[4]

A The voice of **my beloved**!
  B *Look, there he is* (הִנֵּה־זֶה),
    (a) coming (בָּא)
    (a′) leaping (מְדַלֵּג) upon the mountains,
    (a″) bounding (מְקַפֵּץ) over the hills.
A′ **My beloved** is like a gazelle or a young stag.
  B′ *Look, there he is* (הִנֵּה־זֶה),
    (b) standing (עוֹמֵד) behind our wall,
    (b′) gazing (מַשְׁגִּיחַ) in at the windows,
    (b″) looking (מֵצִיץ) through the lattice.

(NRSVue, with alterations)

Note that the parallelism B//B′ is built not only on the repetition of "look, there he is," but also on the use of three consecutive participles in both sentences. In most modern translations, this is not apparent, which means that reading the Hebrew proves necessary here.

The accumulation of these participles has another effect. Although the woman is observing and describing her beloved in these verses, she is de-

---

3. For a more precise description, see W. Randall Garr, "The Qinah: A Study of Poetic Meter, Syntax, and Style," *ZAW* 95 (1983): 54–75.

4. Elie Assis, *Flashes of Fire: A Literary Analysis of the Song of Songs*, LHBOTS 503 (London: T&T Clark, 2009), 78–79.

scribing him as *peering into the house*. Therefore, the woman is both the observer and the observed. This can be compared to the fact that in the next verses (vv. 10–14) she is both speaking words of her own and quoting words that her beloved has said.

Verse 12 is a subtle construction due to the polysemy of the word זָמִיר, which can be translated either "pruning" or "singing." The former meaning creates a parallel with the first colon, which contains a floral description, and the latter creates a parallel with the third colon, which mentions the song of the turtledove. In this way, the second colon plays a "janus" role; that is, it contains a double entendre that points both backward and forward.[5]

> The **flowers** appear on the earth;
> the time of **pruning**/*singing* has come,
> and the *voice* of the turtledove is heard in our land.

Verse 14 is no less astonishing. It begins with a regular parallelism. There is an ellipsis in the second colon, since it does not contain any parallel to "O my dove" in the first colon, which does double duty for the entire sentence:

> A   O my dove, in the clefts of the rock,
> A'   in the covert of the cliff,

The verse continues with a quadricolon that lends itself to *two alternative but complementary analyses*, depending on the elements that we compare. On the one hand, it can be read as two consecutive bicola. First, the beloved asks the woman to show him two different aspects of her:

> B   *let me see* your face;
> B'   *let me hear* your voice,

Then he makes two parallel assertions about physical features of hers:

> C   for *your voice is sweet*,
> C'   and *your face is lovely*.

On the other hand, the same four cola can be read as forming a chiasmus:[6]

> D   let me see **your face** [מַרְאַיִךְ],
>   E   let me hear *your voice* [קוֹלֵךְ]
>   E'   for *your voice* [קוֹלֵךְ] is sweet,
> D'   and **your face** [מַרְאַיִךְ] is lovely.

Yet this is not the end of our surprises, for v. 14 contains a number of echoes of v. 12 (see Table 10.1).

---

5. Rendsburg, *How the Bible Is Written*, 360–62.
6. In Example 2.4d, we saw that although there is a variant in the manuscript 4Q107, the chiasmus is still present there.

Table 10.1: Song of Songs 2:12, 14

Verse 12	Verse 14
The flowers **appear** [נִרְאוּ] on the earth; the time of singing/pruning has come, and <u>the voice</u> [קוֹל] of the turtledove *is heard* [נִשְׁמַע] in our land.	**Let me see** [lit., **make appear to me**] [הַרְאִינִי] **your face,** *let me hear* [הַשְׁמִיעִינִי] <u>your voice</u> [קוֹלֵךְ], for <u>your voice</u> [קוֹלֵךְ] is sweet, and **your face** [מַרְאֵיךְ] is lovely.
(NRSVue, with alterations)	(NRSVue)

This mirroring effect has a lovely implication for the meaning of the passage. After describing the delightful natural elements that *reappear* because the spring has come, the beloved asks his love to do the same: to *appear*, that is, to go out of her house to join him and show him her (visual and aural) beauty. A literary device reinforces this logic: the description of the spring is framed by an inclusio, which consists of the repetition of the call to come: "Arise, my love, my fair one, and come away" (vv. 10 and 13b).

Thus, this passage illustrates the importance of looking at the microelements of a poetic text, both its microstructure and the echoes among small elements that are sprinkled throughout it.

10.2 ANALYZE THE MACROSTRUCTURE

Once you have segmented the text into monocola, bicola, tricola, and so on, you can look for larger units that structure the poem as a whole. Here, however, terminology varies among scholars, as does the number of possible levels of units they distinguish within a poem. For instance:

- For Wilfred Watson, a poem may comprise several stanzas, and each stanza may comprise a number of strophes; a monocolon, a bicolon, and so on, are strophes.
- According to Johannes C. de Moor and more generally the "Kampen School," a poem may comprise the following units, from largest to smallest: cantos, subcantos, canticles, strophes, and verses. These scholars often base their proposals for how the text should be segmented into strophes on the

MT's division of the text into paragraphs (*petuhot* and *setumot*), while paying attention to similar paragraph divisions in other manuscript traditions.

To identify units that are larger than strophes, there are two complementary approaches:

- gathering a number of strophes that "belong together" because they exhibit a high level of thematic unity
- identifying a literary structure (e.g., chiasmus) based on (possibly distant) parallelism between strophes or groups of strophes (A and A′, B and B′, etc.).

EXAMPLE 10.2a ▸ Psalm 29

Let's return to Ps 29. We have already divided the text into strophes (Example 10.1a). Now, we can make the interesting observation that these strophes are organized in a chiastic structure (see Table 10.2).

Table 10.2: Chiastic Structure of Psalm 29

	Strophe	**Theme**
A	Ascribe to the Lord, O heavenly beings, ascribe to the Lord glory and strength. (v. 1) Ascribe to the Lord the glory of his name; worship the Lord in holy splendor. (v. 2)	gift *to* the Lord from his people (here "ascribe" is a translation of the same Hebrew verb translated as "give" in v. 11)
B	the voice of the Lord is over the waters; the God of glory thunders, the Lord, over mighty waters. (v. 3)	the voice of the Lord over the waters
C	The voice of the Lord is powerful; the voice of the Lord is full of majesty. (v. 4)	the voice of the Lord is majestic
D	The voice of the Lord breaks the cedars; the Lord breaks the cedars of Lebanon. (v. 5)	impact of the voice of the Lord on trees

E	He makes Lebanon skip like a calf and Sirion like a young wild ox. (v. 6)	the voice of the Lord makes natural elements skip
F	The voice of the LORD flashes forth flames of fire. (v. 7)	(center of the concentric structure)
E′	The voice of the LORD shakes the wilderness; the LORD shakes the wilderness of Kadesh. (v. 8)	the voice of the Lord makes natural elements shake
D′	The voice of the LORD causes the oaks to whirl and strips the forest bare,	impact of the voice of the Lord on trees
C′	and in his temple all say, 'Glory!' (v. 9)	all the people say that the Lord is glorious
B′	The LORD sits enthroned over the flood; the LORD sits enthroned as king forever. (v. 10)	the Lord over the waters
A′	May the LORD give strength to his people! May the LORD bless his people with peace! (v. 11)	gift *from* the Lord to his people

EXAMPLE 10.2b ▸ Psalm 93

In Ps 93, it is not difficult to segment the text into a series of strophes.

Verse 1a can be read as a quadricolon with intricate inner parallelisms. The three last cola mention being clothed ("robed," "robed," "girded"); in addition, "majesty" in the second colon echoes "king" in the first and also finds an echo in "with strength" in the fourth colon:

> The LORD is **king**;
> he is *robed* in **majesty**;
> the LORD is *robed*;
> he is *girded* **with strength**.

That said, given the typical length of the cola in the following strophes, it is also possible to read v. 1a as a bicolon:

> The LORD is king; he is robed in majesty;
> the LORD is robed; he is girded with strength.

Verses 1b–2 are a quadricolon of the form ABA'B' in which A and A' share the idea that something (the world, God's throne) is "established," while B and B' describe stability:

> A He has established the world;
>
> > B it shall never be moved;
>
> A' your throne is established from of old;
>
> > B' you are from everlasting.

Verse 3 can be analyzed as a tricolon on the basis of the triple mention of "the floods" and the triple use of the verb "to lift." The apostrophe at the end of the first colon and the delay of the object of the verb until the second line show that this strophe is an example of staircase parallelism:

> The floods have lifted up, O LORD,
> the floods have lifted up their voice;
> the floods lift up their roaring.

Verse 4 is also a tricolon, as is apparent from the repetition of the adjective "majestic" and the fact that it constitutes a single sentence:

> More majestic than the thunders of mighty waters,
> more majestic than the waves of the sea,
> majestic on high is the LORD!

Finally, v. 5 is a tricolon in which the two first lines are assertions about things related to the Lord (his decrees, his house), while the third colon contains an apostrophe ("O LORD") and an adverbial complement to the second colon:

> Your decrees are very sure;
> holiness befits your house,
> O LORD, forevermore.

Now that we have identified the strophes in this psalm, we can ask whether the poem exhibits a macrostructure. The most obvious possible hint in this direction is the fact that v. 3 and v. 4 share the same theme (God's superiority over the waters). Thus, they may constitute two parallel strophes. Similarly, it is striking that vv. 1b–3 and v. 5 both highlight stability (of the world in v. 1b, of the Lord's decrees in v. 5a) and the places the Lord dwells (his throne in v. 2, his temple in v. 5; note that the Lord's throne is generally envisaged as a celestial temple). Therefore, these too may be deemed parallel strophes. In the end, it is possible to read vv. 1b–5 as a chiasmus: A = vv. 1b–2, B = v. 3, B' = v. 4, A' = v. 5. As for v. 1a, it serves as an introduction to the psalm. It states the main thesis (the Lord is king), while the rest of the poem explores two complementary manifestations of this kingship: first, the

Lord's superiority over the waters, which in biblical imagery are a symbol of threatening forces; second, the stability of the world and of the Lord's temple. The psalm's overall structure can be represented as follows:

Introduction and main statement: the Lord is king (v. 1a)

    A (vv. 1b–2)   *stability*
        B (v. 3)   *waters*
        B' (v. 4)   *waters*
    A' (v. 5)   *stability*

Where to Find Detailed Analysis of Poetic Texts

The following works provide exhaustive analyses of the poetic structure of various biblical books (or portions of books), using the principles of the "Kampen School":

- Haggai (analyzing it as poetic prose): William T. Koopmans, *Haggai*, HCOT (Leuven: Peeters, 2017), 299–365.
- Nahum: Klaas Spronk, *Nahum*, HCOT (Kampen: Pharos, 1997).
- Obadiah: Johan Renkema, *Obadiah*, HCOT (Leuven: Peeters, 2003).
- Isaiah 40–55: Marjo C. A. Korpel and Johannes C. de Moor, *The Structure of Classical Hebrew Poetry: Isaiah 40–55*, OTS 41 (Leiden: Brill, 1998).
- Psalms: Pieter van der Lugt, *Cantos and Strophes in Biblical Hebrew Poetry*, 3 vols., OTS 53, 57, 63 (Leiden: Brill, 2006–14).
- Lamentations: Johan Renkema, *Lamentations*, HCOT (Leuven: Peeters, 1998).
- Exod 15; Deut 32; Psalms; Job: J. P. Fokkelman, *Major Poems of the Hebrew Bible: At the Interface of Prosody and Structural Analysis*, 4 vols., SSN 37, 41, 43, 47 (Assen: Van Gorcum, 1998–2004).

In addition, Wilfred G. E. Watson has published an article in which he provides a classification of the verses of Canticles:

- Wilfred G. E. Watson, "Verse Patterns in the Song of Songs," *JNSL* 21 (1995): 111–22.[7]

---

7. Other analyses of the literary structure of the Psalms have been published, in French, by three scholars: Pierre Auffret, Marc Girard, and Roland Meynet.

10.3 STUDY FIGURES OF SPEECH AND OTHER POETIC DEVICES

Figures of speech are far more frequent in poetry than in prose. They include comparison, metaphor, metonymy, personification, hyperbole, and so forth. It is important not only to notice their presence, but to study their effects—that is, to determine their function. Do they convey or enhance an idea? What connotations do they carry with them? How do they affect the perception of a character, for instance?

Perhaps the most interesting and complex figure of speech is metaphor.[8] For most people, a metaphor simply assimilates one thing to another, and studying a metaphor simply consists of "decoding" a correspondence between two words. Thus, when we read "the Lord is my shepherd" (Ps 23:1), the two words that are in correspondence are immediately apparent: the Lord and a shepherd. It is not uncommon for readers to conclude that this is a nice way to express the fact that God takes care of the psalmist like a shepherd takes care of his sheep; after all, the psalmist immediately adds "I shall not want" (v. 1b). In other words, many readers tend to "retrovert" this poetic formulation into a literal assertion about God's relationship to humans. However, this does not do justice to the richness of this metaphor. As Pierre van Hecke writes:

> Everyone readily understands what the psalmist meant by saying that "The Lord is my shepherd", and yet any literal paraphrase would reduce the metaphor's meaning. If we would say that the metaphor means "God takes care of me", we would drastically limit the cognitive strength of the metaphor because we would exclude all other possible structurings we could come up with on the basis of what we know about the [sic] shepherds, e.g. that God makes sure I do not go astray on the way of life.[9]

Indeed, the psalmist does not only say "I shall not want" (v. 1b) and "he restores my soul" (v. 3a), but also "he leads me in right paths" (v. 3b).

Therefore, what is needed is an approach that considers not just one correspondence between two "discrete" realities but multiple possible correspondences between whole "domains." This is the objective of **Conceptual Metaphor Theory** (CMT), which studies metaphors as cognitive phenomena. According to CMT, the use of a metaphor involves understanding something (the target domain) *in terms of* another thing (the source domain). By doing so, one transfers *some* aspects from the source domain to the target domain: this is called "mapping."

---

8. I have chosen to take metaphor as the main illustration in this section; for a comparable analysis of metonymy, see, for instance, Travis J. Bott, "Praise and Metonymy in the Psalms," in *The Oxford Handbook of the Psalms*, ed. William P. Brown (New York: Oxford University Press, 2014), 131–46.

9. Pierre van Hecke, "Are People Walking After or Before God? On the Metaphorical Use of הלך לפני and הלך אחרי," *OLP* 30 (1999): 42.

For instance, Ps 23 uses the conceptual metaphor GOD IS SHEPHERD. The source domain is ANIMAL HUSBANDRY, and the target domain is GOD'S RELATIONSHIP WITH HUMANS. (In keeping with standard scholarly practice, small capital letters have been used here to designate the metaphor, the source domain, and the target domain.) The next questions are: what are the various aspects of ANIMAL HUSBANDRY, and which of them are mapped to GOD'S RELATIONSHIP WITH HUMANS in the framework of this metaphor? ANIMAL HUSBANDRY may involve providing food, leading the flock, protecting against wild animals, attending to the special needs of weak animals and healing those who are hurt, keeping the flock together, looking for lost animals, etc. Note that in this case, the psalmist elaborates on his metaphor and refers to several of these aspects (in vv. 1–4). In many other biblical texts, however, the writer does not elaborate, which makes it all the more necessary to explore the aspects of the source domain. For this purpose, it is worth examining what we learn about this domain in the Hebrew Bible and in ancient Near Eastern literature.

In sum, to study a metaphor, the following steps may be relevant:

Ⓐ Identify the metaphor, the source domain, and the target domain.

Ⓑ Explore the various aspects of the source domain (by studying it in the Hebrew Bible and in ancient Near Eastern literature).

Ⓒ Identify the aspects of the source domain that are mapped onto the target domain.

Ⓓ Analyze how the metaphor informs the meaning of the text.

The ABC of CMT, and More

For a brief and useful theoretical introduction to CMT, see:

- Johan de Joode, *Metaphorical Landscapes and the Theology of the Book of Job: An Analysis of Job's Spatial Metaphors*, VTSup 179 (Leiden: Brill, 2019), 12–45.

The seminal work on this subject is the following book:

- George Lakoff and Mark Johnson, *Metaphors We Live By* (Chicago: University of Chicago Press, 1980).

A refined approach is the Conceptual Blending Theory of Metaphor; for an introduction and illustration (with further bibliography), see:

- Pierre van Hecke, "Conceptual Blending: A Recent Approach to Metaphor. Illustrated with the Pastoral Metaphor in Hos 4,16," in *Metaphor in the Hebrew Bible*, ed. Pierre van Hecke, BETL 187 (Leuven: Peeters, 2005), 215–31.

> **EXAMPLE 10.3a** ▸ **Song of Songs 2:8–17**

Song of Songs 2:8–17 contains a number of figures of speech. For example, in v. 9 the woman explicitly compares her beloved to a gazelle. This image is anticipated in the preceding verse (v. 8), where she describes him "leaping upon the mountains" and "bounding over the hills." Thus, in v. 8 she is already speaking of him as of a gazelle, showing that the statements about him leaping and bounding are actually metaphorical. Interestingly, she uses the gazelle image in v. 9 in a statement of fact ("my beloved *is* like a gazelle"), while in v. 17 she uses it in an injunction ("*be* like a gazelle"). In any case, the source domain in these verses is GAZELLE and the target domain is BELOVED.

Let's explore the aspects of the source domain GAZELLE. In Song of Songs, this animal is also used as a metaphor for the woman's breasts (4:5; 7:3 [4]). In Prov 5:19, the gazelle is an image for a woman characterized by her grace and loveliness. In fact, the same Hebrew word (צְבִי) also means "beauty." Elsewhere in the Hebrew Bible, the gazelle connotes agility and rapidity (2 Sam 2:18; 1 Chr 12:8 [9]). In ancient Near Eastern iconography and texts, this animal seems associated with goddesses of love. All of these aspects (beauty, agility, rapidity, love) seem relevant for the target domain in Song 2:8, 17, although agility and rapidity seem to be at the forefront.

That said, these verses picture the gazelle leaping upon mountains, and a number of commentators believe that the mountains here serve as symbols for the woman's breasts. Indeed, in 4:6 we read a statement that is very similar to 2:17:

> Until the day breathes
> and the shadows flee,
> I will hasten to the mountain of myrrh
> and the hill of frankincense.

As one exegete has noted, "these mountains cannot be literal places, as myrrh and frankincense are not indigenous to Palestine."[10] Also, 4:6 immediately follows a mention of the woman's breasts (4:5), and it is not that difficult to imagine how the form of hills or mountains could be compared to breasts. Thus, many commentators think that in 4:6 the man is speaking about his desire to enjoy the woman's breasts, and that in 2:17 the woman is encouraging her beloved to do so. This interpretation is both plausible and difficult to prove. Indeed, it rests on a metaphor (the breasts as mountains) that is not explicit in the text. The fact that myrrh and frankincense are not indigenous to Palestine does not necessarily rule out the possibility of the author invoking them in a description of imaginary places in this land; that is, the author need not necessarily be using these images as symbols for breasts or for

---

10. Brian P. Gault, *Body as Lanscape, Love as Intoxication*, AIL 36 (Atlanta: SBL Press, 2019), 104.

> anything else. This kind of situation—where an erotic, symbolic interpretation is plausible but difficult to prove—occurs frequently in Song of Songs.[11]

EXAMPLE 10.3b ▸ Song of Songs 2:8–17

> In Song 2:14, as a sort of response to the statements we looked at in the previous example, the beloved describes his love by means of a metaphor inspired by another creature: the source domain is DOVE and the target domain is WOMAN. Again, this animal is chosen for its connotations. It enables the poet to evoke two aspects at the same time: the dove is sometimes hidden in clefts (v. 14a; cf. Jer 48:28), in the same way that the women is "hidden" in her house while the beloved invites her to come out. In addition, the dove is a beautiful bird and has a pleasant "voice" (v. 14b).

EXAMPLE 10.3c ▸ Song of Songs 2:8–17

> Besides metaphors, Song 2:8–17 also has recourse to an interesting literary device: the repeated mention of the word "voice" serves to blend two worlds—that of nature ("voice of the turtledove" in v. 12, "voice" of the dove in v. 14a) and that of the couple ("voice" of the beloved in v. 8, "voice" of the woman in v. 14b). More generally, there is a nice progression in this passage: the beloved walks in nature (vv. 8–9), describes it to his love (vv. 10–13), and encourages her to imitate nature (v. 14), and finally, she sends him back to nature (vv. 16–17).

10.4 DETERMINE THE RHETORICAL FUNCTION OF THE TEXT

Beyond its aesthetic value, poetry serves a purpose. Even when the expression of one's own feelings or emotions is the primary goal of a poetic composition, the act of writing it down and making it available to readers enables it to have an effect on them.

---

11. What complicates the matter further is that the same element can serve as an image for different things in Song of Songs: e.g., the gazelle can designate breasts in 4:5 and 7:3 [4], on the one hand, and the man in 2:8, 17, on the other. Therefore, one must often be cautious about trying to deduce from one passage what the meaning of a similar metaphor is in another.

That is, poems are not just intended for personal expression; they are a means of *communication* with others. Their effect on readers or on an audience may be cognitive (e.g., arousing compassion, regret, or fear) or may provoke the reader or audience to a certain action (e.g., a change in attitude toward God or other humans). Thus, an important task in exegeting a poetic text is to determine its rhetorical function.

To evoke categories from the field of "speech-act theory," this process entails passing from the realm of *locutionary acts* to that of *illocutionary acts*. To illustrate, when a prophet says "do not be afraid," the utterance itself is the locution, but the illocutionary act is *what the prophet intends to achieve* (in this case, to give strength to or to reassure his audience). So, when we are trying to determine what a poet or a prophet is aiming at, it is useful to think of various verbs that can describe what they are trying to do—reassure, admonish, convince, give hope, promise, forewarn, arouse compassion, etc. Here are a few examples of typical goals we encounter in the Hebrew Bible's poetic texts:

- to convince people to change their attitude—for instance, giving up the worship of gods other than the Lord (many oracles of judgment)
- to give hope and encouragement (oracles of salvation)
- to describe the intoxication and wonder of love in order to share one's experience and/or to help lovers find the words to celebrate their own experience (Song of Songs)
- to describe one's sufferings in order to arouse compassion in the audience and/or in the Lord (Lamentations)
- to obtain forgiveness from the Lord (psalms of repentance)
- to call for help in order to convince the Lord to intervene (psalms of petition)

Now, as any teacher will tell you, there is often a difference between the acts we want to perform when we talk and their actual effect on our audience. Speech-act theory refers to the latter as *perlocutionary acts*. In the relatively rare cases when the text mentions the reaction of the people who listened to a prophet or read an oracle, you may be able to determine the perlocutionary act.

> **EXAMPLE 10.4a ▸ Micah 3:2–3**
>
> In Mic 3:2–3, the prophet accuses the rulers of Israel of cannibalism:
>
> > you . . . who tear the skin off my people
> > and the flesh off their bones,
> > who eat the flesh of my people,
> > flay their skin off them,
> > break their bones in pieces,
> > and chop them up like meat in a kettle,
> > like flesh in a caldron.

It seems safe to say that this is not a literal description, but rather a figurative and hyperbolic way of saying that these leaders' actions lead to terrible suffering among the population. The parallel accusations against the same rulers in vv. 9–11 suggest that they are corrupt. Why use such a radically hyperbolic description in vv. 2–3? Its illocutionary function seems to be to provide an electroshock to the rulers by underscoring the gravity of their wrongdoing, in the hope of convincing them to change their behavior.

This chapter of Micah ends (in v. 12) with the following threat:

> Therefore because of you
> Zion shall be plowed as a field;
> Jerusalem shall become a heap of ruins,
>   and the mountain of the temple a wooded height.

Interestingly, Jer 26:17–19 quotes this verse and tells us about its perlocutionary effect, since the elders of Judah say that the prophet achieved the outcome he wanted:

> And some of the elders of the land arose and said to all the assembled people, "Micah of Moresheth, who prophesied during the days of King Hezekiah of Judah, said to all the people of Judah: 'Thus says the LORD of hosts, Zion shall be plowed as a field; Jerusalem shall become a heap of ruins and the mountain of the house a wooded height.' Did King Hezekiah of Judah and all Judah actually put him to death? Did he not fear the LORD and entreat the favor of the LORD, and did not the LORD change his mind about the disaster that he had pronounced against them? But we are about to bring great disaster on ourselves!"

EXAMPLE 10.4b ▸ Haggai

The book of Haggai represents an interesting case since the prophet's main task is to make the Judeans launch a new project and to then sustain it until completion. Moreover, this book is set in a brief period of a few months, and the dates of the oracles are even provided. It is interesting to see how the contents of each oracle seem adapted to the time when it was given (see Table 10.3). Like a coach, Haggai motivates the people, then helps them sustain hope when their initial enthusiasm might fade; and when their motivation needs to be renewed, he sketches a glorious future for them. At the same time, when the work is well advanced, he raises a concern about impurity; and yet even at this point, he immediately adds a promise.

Table 10.3: Oracles in Haggai

Date	Context	Oracles and Their Illocutionary Function
1st day of 6th month (= August 29)	The work of reconstructing the temple has been interrupted for years	*Oracle to stimulate action:* Haggai calls for the reconstruction of the temple. (1:1–11)
24th day of 6th month (= September 21)	The work resumes	*Narrative:* motivated by Haggai's speech, the people begin work on the temple. *Oracle to give courage by showing support to the people in their new task:* "I am with you." (1:12–15)
21st day of 7th month (= October 17)	Last day of the festival of Sukkot	*Oracle to keep their courage alive, a few weeks after the beginning of the work:* Haggai promises that the glory of the reconstructed temple will be greater than that of the former temple. (2:1–9)
24th day of 9th month (= December 18)	Three months into the work	*Oracle raises an issue and announces a change:* Haggai denounces impurity. At the same time, he promises abundant harvests. (2:10–19)
		Oracle of promise: Haggai gives long-term hope. (2:20–23)

Although the book of Haggai does not narrate the end of the project, it records some initial success (1:12–15) and indicates that the project lasted at the very least three months. According to the historiography found elsewhere in the Bible (Ezra 5–6), the project was completed; thus, the perlocutionary act was positive. Could this be due to Haggai's rhetorical strategy? It is interesting to note that Haggai is perhaps the prophet in the Hebrew Bible who argues the most. He encourages the people to reflect on their own situation: "consider how you have fared" (Hag 1:5, 7). He raises questions to make them take a step back and participate in his own reasoning (1:4, 9; 2:3, 12, 13, 19). Far from trying to silence potential objections, he voices them in order to counter them. Thus, he quotes a widespread opinion ("the time has not yet come to rebuild the LORD's house") and questions it (1:2–4). He anticipates a possible concern those in his audience might have (2:3). As we have seen, he speaks at critical junctures and when their motivation could fade. He gives long-term perspectives in order to encourage the people to go beyond their short-term concerns. It may well be that this leadership strategy, which respects the people as thinking persons rather than instilling fear in them through constant threats, was both appreciated and effective.

> **EXAMPLE 10.4c** ▸ **Song of Songs 2:8–17**

Song of Songs 2:8–17, which we examined in several examples above, makes use of yet another literary device: *indetermination*. This is apparent in several ways. First, note the use of polysemous words or expressions: gazelle/beauty (צְבִי); singing/pruning (זָמִיר); grazing among the lilies / feeding on the lilies (רעה); go/come back (סב); and, perhaps, speak/reply (עָנָה) and before/while the day breathes (עַד שֶׁיָּפוּחַ הַיּוֹם). Only in the case of צְבִי does the context allow the reader to decide that only one meaning is intended, because it is clear that "gazelle" fits the context perfectly whereas it would be odd to compare the man to an abstract concept ("beauty"). Even so, in both vv. 9 and 17 the word צְבִי appears in a phrase that is equivocal in another way: "a gazelle *or* a young stag." In this case, it is striking that the ambiguity is actually conveyed explicitly, through the word "or." In addition, as we saw in Example 9.3, the identity of the person who utters v. 15 is unclear.

What is the function of this literary technique? At first, the overall effect may seem to be one of blurring, which may sound like a shortcoming, but it also has an advantage: it creates room for the reader's imagination. Indeed, this phenomenon is a facet of a more general feature of this passage: the reader's involvement is *required* to resolve some questions or fill in some details. It is a well-known feature of all literary texts that they are more or less *open* and require the reader's participation. This is particularly true in poetry, and in this passage especially. Thus, the indetermination regarding the speaker (and the addressee) in v. 15 may lead to different interpretations. Also, who is referred to by the plural pronoun in the phrase "our wall" (v. 9)? The woman and the man? The woman and her parents? Even when we arrive at the final scene in this passage (vv. 16–17), where the woman answers her beloved, we are not told whether the woman has done what her beloved wanted her to do (that is, whether she has come out of her home). Moreover, as we have seen, the woman's reply in v. 17 can be read in two ways: "go back" or "come back"; some even understand both senses to be present ("go and come back"). And here too, we are not told whether the beloved complies. If you had to produce a theatrical play based on Song of Songs, you would need to make choices about who is speaking in any given instance and with what tone, what movements the characters make, and so forth. But these decisions must also be made in our minds simply as readers of the text. In fact, ancient and modern editions of the Bible often add "didascalies" that identify the speakers in Song of Songs. These are interpretations, however, and they are often debatable. But debate in interpretation, and some degree of liberty in performance, are precisely the fruits of good poetry.

EXERCISES FOR CHAPTER 10

Exercise A
Analyze the microstructure and the macrostructure of Ps 96.

Exercise B
Analyze the microstructure and the macrostructure of Lam 3.

Exercise C
Psalm 1 uses arboreal images to characterize the fate of two opposite kinds of people. Study the metaphor that is used here.

Exercise D
In Hos 1–3, the relationship between the Lord and his people is likened to a marital relationship. Study this metaphor.

Exercise E
In Isa 49:14–26, Zion is likened to a mother. Look more precisely at what is said about her, identify and study the metaphor, and draw conclusions regarding the function of this passage.

CHAPTER 11
NARRATIVE CRITICISM

OVERVIEW

The study of narratives *as narratives* has received new impetus since the 1970s. New approaches and concepts were initially developed in the area of modern literature and were then "imported" into the field of biblical studies. Narrative criticism has significantly revitalized the study of books such as Genesis and Samuel, for example. Scrutinizing a text from this angle is rewarding, and students often seem to find this approach one of the most satisfying of the exegetical methods, because it is undeniable that many stories in the Hebrew Bible are sophisticated and delightful literature.

Narrative criticism enables you to discover that there is a whole range of angles from which you can look at the narratives in the Hebrew Bible and that these narratives are richer that you have previously imagined. Often, readers tend to be struck by a single aspect of a narrative, and this risks them basing their exegesis almost entirely on intuition or on only one of the narrative's effects on the reader. By contrast, asking of the text the questions that are suggested by narrative criticism allows a systematic and ordered study that uncovers "pearls" hidden from our intuition.

Before going further, it is necessary to address some potential misunderstandings. First, narrative criticism is a synchronic approach that sets aside the text's compositional history; but this does not imply denying the possibility that redactional stages existed during the formation of the text. The latter is simply not the focus of this approach; rather, its object is the text in its "final form." Of course, there are differences between the textual witnesses, so the notion of a "final form" is somewhat abstract. In practice, scholars often think of the Masoretic Text when they think of the "final form," but it is also possible to conduct the work of narrative criticism on a version (e.g., the Septuagint), and it is also interesting to compare the narrative features of different textual witnesses. For instance, there are significant divergences in the story of Esther between the MT and the LXX. Second, and similar to the first point, narrative criticism sets aside the issue of the historicity of the events related in the narrative, even though the language used by practitioners of this method ("characters," "story," and so on) might seem to implicitly affirm that the text is a fiction.

In what follows, the reactions of the reader will often be mentioned. In this context, the term "reader" typically means, strictly speaking, "implied reader," since nothing indicates that these reactions are necessarily those that a real reader chosen at random would have. That is, the "implied reader" is a sort of "ideal reader" who is presupposed by the text; such a reader is sufficiently attentive, insightful, and knowledgeable about the context to react to all the underlying strategies in the account. In the same way, "narrator" does not signify "author"; rather, this denotes the voice that tells the story. In the Hebrew Bible, the narrator is implicitly *omniscient*: he seems to be able to relate the words or thoughts of anyone he wishes, including those of God himself. Above all, his voice is authoritative and the reader presumes that what he says is always true. The same holds for certain characters as well: namely, God, angels/messengers (the Hebrew word often translated by "angel" in English means, literally, "messenger"), and true prophets when they are saying something on behalf of God.[1]

Lastly, scholars often present their narrative analyses in a fairly technical way and using specialist terms. Two extremes must be avoided here as readers of this kind of material. On the one hand, we should appreciate the use of such terminology, since it has an important heuristic function and forces the analyst to study the text more closely. On the other hand, one must avoid using this technical vocabulary for its own sake, since in doing so one runs the risk of inventing technical formulations about realities in the text that are simple enough to be detected and discussed without a complex conceptual apparatus.

The present chapter is far from exhaustive and will focus on the most important aspects of narrative criticism (an entire book would be needed to cover this method in sufficient depth). It is a simple and practical introduction to this subject that intentionally avoids the excessive use of technical terms.[2]

---

1. However, in some narratives, a "true" prophet of Yhwh seems to lie to another character (see 1 Kgs 22:15 and 2 Kgs 3:18, 27, which are discussed in Example 4.4). In addition, in 1 Kgs 22 we read that God "has put a lying spirit in the mouth" of Ahab's prophets (v. 23). But these are exceptions.

2. In addition, I should note that I use the "classical approach" to narrative criticism. Other sophisticated approaches exist as well, including the "optional-narrator theory," on which see, e.g., Sylvie Patron, ed., *Optional-Narrator Theory: Principles, Perspectives, Proposals* (Lincoln: University of Nebraska Press, 2021).

Classic Studies

There is no shortage of interesting studies on narrative criticism of the Hebrew Bible. The following books are widely regarded as important:

- Robert Alter, *The Art of Biblical Narrative*, 2nd ed. (New York: Basic Books, 2011).
- Meir Sternberg, *The Poetics of Biblical Narrative: Ideological Literature and the Drama of Reading* (Bloomington: Indiana University Press, 1987).
- J. P. Fokkelman, *Narrative Art in Genesis: Specimens of Stylistic and Structural Analysis*, 2nd ed., BS 12 (Sheffield: JSOT Press, 1991; repr., Eugene, OR: Wipf & Stock, 2004).
- J. P. Fokkelman, *Narrative Art and Poetry in the Books of Samuel: A Full Interpretation Based on Stylistic and Structural Analyses*, 4 vols., SSN 20, 23, 27, 31 (Assen: Van Gorcum, 1981–93).
- J. P. Fokkelman, *Reading Biblical Narrative: An Introductory Guide*, trans. Ineke Smit (Louisville: Westminster John Knox, 2000).
- David M. Gunn and Danna Nolan Fewell, *Narrative in the Hebrew Bible* (New York: Oxford University Press, 1993).

Another helpful resources is:

- Danna Nolan Fewell, ed., *The Oxford Handbook of Biblical Narrative* (New York: Oxford University Press, 2016).

For a very informative and systematic introduction to narrative criticism, as applied to the Hebrew Bible, see:

- Jean-Louis Ska, *"Our Fathers Have Told Us": Introduction to the Analysis of Hebrew Narratives*, SubBi 13 (Rome: Pontifical Biblical Institute, 2000).

For a very readable introduction, see:

- Yairah Amit, *Reading Biblical Narratives: Literary Criticism and the Hebrew Bible* (Minneapolis: Fortress, 2001).

The following steps can be followed:

❶ IDENTIFY THE PLOT(S).

❷ STUDY THE CHARACTERS.

❸ IDENTIFY ANY "MISE EN ABYME"/MIRRORING THAT MAY BE PRESENT.

❹ STUDY ANY TYPE-SCENES THAT MAY BE PRESENT.

⑤ IDENTIFY DISCREPANCIES OR ANOMALIES.

⑥ STUDY THE FOCALIZATIONS.

⑦ LOOK FOR THE PRESENCE OF IRONY, DOUBLE MEANINGS, AND MISUNDERSTANDINGS.

⑧ LISTEN TO THE NARRATIVE VOICE.

11.1 IDENTIFY THE PLOT(S)

Plot lies at the heart of narrative analysis. It is what differentiates a narrative proper from a mere list of descriptions and accumulated facts that are not tied together with a storyline. A narrative requires an initial question or issue that governs the whole of what happens—something that creates a dynamic and provokes behavior and actions and that creates suspense for the reader. This does not mean that every narrative must be written as a thriller, of course; but the important thing to observe is that every narrative has a plot, even when a superficial reading does not enable one to pick up on it. Discerning the plot (and moreover, some narratives combine *several* plots) allows us as readers to identify what is at stake in the events of the narrative. We must always ask what the problem is in the particular text we're reading.

A. Identify the Type of Plot

The first step is to identify the type of plot. There are two basic types:

- *Resolution plots* involve concrete problems that need to be solved. The question is, "What will happen?" or "Will this problem be solved, and if so, how?"

- *Revelation plots* involve a character gaining knowledge.

EXAMPLE 11.1a   ▸   Judges 13

> The story found in Judg 13 will serve as a recurring example in this chapter. The very first verse of Judg 13 mentions a problem: the Israelites are oppressed. A first plot is hereby established: will they be delivered, by whom, and how?
>
> When the reader comes to this text, he or she has already learned from the prologue of the book of Judges and from the previous pericopes that the history of this period follows a cyclical pattern that comprises four stages:

(1) the people act in a way that is displeasing to God; (2) God is angry and hands Israel over to foreign peoples; (3) the people endure oppression and, often, call out to God; (4) God sends a judge to deliver them. In ch. 13, the first two stages are found in v. 1: "The Israelites again did what was evil in the sight of the LORD, and the LORD gave them into the hand of the Philistines forty years." The reader then expects stage (3), but it doesn't come. Instead, the account passes blithely on to the story of a couple: "There was a certain man . . ." (v. 2). In short, stage (3) has been skipped: God has taken the initiative and has intervened even though the people have not cried out to him. In addition, a certain equivalent of stage (4) can be detected, when a messenger announces the following to the woman who will conceive a son who will end up being named Samson: "It is he who shall begin to deliver Israel from the hand of the Philistines" (v. 5). However, the choice of words here is striking: he will merely "*begin* to deliver," whereas the judges normally provide complete liberation from oppression.

Therefore, knowledge of the usual cyclical pattern in Judges creates in the reader an expectation that increases the suspense. But, as seen above, the narrator abandons the subject straightaway and passes to another problem! He immerses the reader in the life of a couple without children. New problem, new plot. Will the couple finally have a child? The narrator immediately gives a positive answer to this question, by revealing the words of a messenger of the Lord (v. 3). This kind of character is imbued with an authority that comes from his status as an envoy of God, which renders his words trustworthy in the eyes of the reader. Consequently, the reader already knows in v. 3 that the problem will be resolved. The problem is barely announced when the suspense evaporates! Admittedly, it is not before the end of the chapter that Samson is born, but the certainty that it will happen is present right from the start.

In fact, v. 6 introduces yet another plot. Manoah's wife, not content to convey the message given to her in v. 3, makes comments about the messenger himself—about his appearance, and above all about his identity, which she did not dare ask about. Further on, the problem of the identity of the messenger reemerges, and it finally becomes the main subject, until the messenger ascends in the fire of the sacrifice, at which point Manoah understands that he is a messenger from the Lord. Before that, he thinks of him as a "man of God." In short, Judg 13 contains no fewer than three successive plots! But it must be noted that the third problem is not posed in the same terms for Manoah as for the reader. The latter already knows that the mysterious man is a messenger of the Lord, since the narrator has told the reader so in v. 3. For the reader, the question does not concern this individual's identity but is rather, "When and how will Manoah realize who he is dealing with?" This third plot is thus a *revelation plot*, whereas the first two were *resolution plots*.

B. Identify the Plot Structure

The second stage involves identifying what we often understand intuitively—that is, the *plot's structure*. This structure may include the following elements:

- the initial situation
- the complication (a problem arises)
- the transformative action
- the denouement
- the final situation

We must not expect to necessarily find each of these elements clearly present in every narrative; a narrator can very well skip some of them. This is simply a heuristic model to encourage us to analyze the text more precisely.

EXAMPLE 11.1b ▸ **2 Kings 6:8–23**

Second Kings 6:8–23 will serve as another recurring example in this chapter.[3] The "initial situation" and "final situation" are presented in vv. 8a and 23, respectively, which together form an inclusio: "the king of Aram was at war with Israel" (v. 8a) and "the Arameans no longer came raiding into the land of Israel" (v. 23). The "complication" arises when the Aramean ruler decides to lash out at Elisha, who has informed the king of Israel about the Aramean ruler's plans (vv. 8b–17). The "transformative action" is the blinding of the Aramean soldiers (v. 18), and the "denouement" takes place before the king of Israel (vv. 19–23).

EXAMPLE 11.1c ▸ **Judges 13**

The story of Manoah (Judg 13) and its three plots[4] is a fairly complicated case. These can be summarized as follows:

General plot. The "initial situation" and the "complication" are indicated in v. 1 (the Israelites behave badly and are oppressed); v. 5 announces a "transformative action": the child to come will "begin to deliver Israel." At the end of the chapter, this child is born, but that is all. To find out what happens

---

3. I have reused in this chapter some elements from my article "Une cécité ordinaire: Analyse narrative de 2 R 6.8–23," *ThEv* 10 (2011): 1–13.

4. For a detailed study of the plots in the Samson cycle, with a different presentation of the structures of the plots, see Robert H. O'Connell, *The Rhetoric of the Book of Judges* (Leiden: Brill, 1996), 203–20.

next, we must read the rest of the Samson cycle. But as 13:5 already indicates, Samson will only *begin* to deliver the people. The story of this last judge marks the final stage of a slow deterioration that can be observed throughout the book. In fact, it is only during the monarchic period that the Israelites will truly be delivered from the Philistines, thanks to Saul.

Infertility plot. Here we find the opposite situation: in this plot, the problem is resolved so easily that it is difficult to clearly distinguish the stages. The "initial situation" is the couple's lack of a child (v. 2), and the "final situation" is marked by the birth of Samson (v. 24). Analyses of what comes between these two points vary. It could be supposed that the "complication" is announced at the same time as the "initial situation" (sterility) and that the "denouement" occurs at the same time as the birth. The "transformative action" is implicit (presumably, God miraculously grants the couple the ability to procreate). The fundamental point here is that the announcement of the denouement is put off for a long moment by Manoah's questions about the rules that must be respected for the child and by his interest in the mysterious man.

Plot of the identity of the mysterious man. In a sense, the "complication" here comes into play as soon as Manoah's wife mentions the problem: the appearance of a man of God who has the likeness of a messenger of the Lord (v. 6). Manoah focuses first of all on the precepts that must be respected for the child, and he then wonders about the identity of the man and asks him his name. The "transformative action" is the supernatural manifestation of v. 20, and the denouement occurs immediately afterward: Manoah realizes that he has spoken to a messenger of the Lord.

11.2 STUDY THE CHARACTERS

A. Study the Characterization

A narrator can give the reader information about a character in two different ways:

- *Telling.* The narrator makes statements that (through the use of titles, adjectives, etc.) explicitly define the character. In this case, the narrator *tells* the reader something. This can have an immediate impact on the perception that the reader will have of the character, by making him or her favorably disposed toward the character, or, on the contrary, by instilling in his or her mind a sense of distrust about the character.

- *Showing.* The narrator *shows* the reader what the character is like by reporting the character's words and actions. In this case too, the narrator influences the reader's opinion about the character, since the narrator deliberately selects the specific words and actions to present.

> **EXAMPLE 11.2a ▸ Job 1:8**
>
> The beginning of the book of Job (the narrative prologue) presents Job as an "upright man" (1:8), thus setting up one of the essential conditions of the drama that will follow: the main problem of the story consists in the fact that such a man is afflicted with various ills that do not seem to be linked to any wrongdoing he may have done.

> **EXAMPLE 11.2b ▸ 1 Kings 17**
>
> In 1 Kgs 17:1, Elijah is simply introduced as an inhabitant of a certain place: "Elijah the Tishbite, of Tishbe in Gilead."[5] If the narrator had right from the beginning explicitly called him a prophet or a man of God, this would have immediately endowed him with great authority. But the narrator does not do this. Thus, when Elijah declares that there will be no rain in the land for several years (v. 1), at this stage the reader might perceive this as the word of a simple Israelite. It is true that here in v. 1 Elijah also mentions "the LORD ... before whom I stand," an expression that is normally used by prophets. But someone reading the story for the first time would not necessarily make this connection.
>
> On the other hand, immediately after Elijah says, "there shall be neither dew nor rain these years, *except by my word*" (v. 1), the text says that "*the word of the* LORD *came to him*" (v. 2), ordering him to flee and hide near the Wadi Cherith. This formula likewise is normally used about prophets, but it is still an indirect way of suggesting that Elijah may be one. In addition, the message from God sends Elijah away. And the mention in v. 2 of "the word of the LORD" that is then quoted in v. 3 seems to be a counterreaction to Elijah's excessive showcasing, in v. 1, of the power of his own word.
>
> From this point on, it is this divine word that is in the driver's seat, as it were. It is this word that provokes Elijah's journey to Sidon (v. 8). And when the miracle of the multiplication of the flour and oil takes place, this happens

---

5. Although certain manuscripts of the Septuagint have "Elijah the prophet" in this verse, the title "the prophet" is most likely a gloss added by a copyist who felt it awkward to introduce Elijah simply as one man among others. See Philippe Hugo, *Les deux visages d'Élie: Texte massorétique et Septante dans l'histoire la plus ancienne du texte de 1 Rois 17–18*, OBO 217 (Göttingen: Vandenhoeck & Ruprecht, 2006), 201–4.

"according to the word of the Lord that he spoke by Elijah" (v. 16). At the end of the chapter, the widow comes to the following conclusion: "I know that you are a man of God and that *the word of the Lord* in your mouth is truth" (v. 24). The next verse (18:1) indicates that it is the "word of the Lord" that announces the end of the drought, not Elijah's own word (as he had proclaimed in 17:1). In sum, the narrator takes care to show that it is *the Lord's* word that matters and that directs events, and that when Elijah's word is right, this is only because in reality it is "the word of the Lord in [his] mouth" (17:24), a conclusion that takes the entirety of ch. 17 to be reached;[6] that is, it is only in this final verse that the widow declares, "now I know that you are a *man of God*" (compare v. 18). And it is a declaration made by a character, not by the narrator. In the end, this very cautious presentation of the character raises the question of whether the narrator is distancing himself from Elijah's attitude.

Moreover, the words of the prophet are telling:

- "There shall be neither dew nor rain these years, *except by my word*" (17:1). See the comments on this above.

- Elijah prays, "let it be known this day that you are God in Israel," but also "that *I am* your servant, and that *I have done* all these things at your bidding" (18:36). He is anxious for his work to be recognized.

- "It is enough; now, O Lord, take away my life, *for I am no better than my ancestors*" (19:4). Elijah's reasoning involves him comparing himself with his predecessors.

- "I, even I only, am left a prophet of the Lord" (18:22); and yet Elijah has heard about one hundred prophets of the Lord who are hidden in two caves (18:13)! He repeats the same false statement from 18:22 when speaking to God on Mount Horeb: "I have been very zealous for the Lord, the God of hosts, for the Israelites have forsaken your covenant, thrown down your altars, and killed your prophets with the sword. I alone am left, and they are seeking my life, to take it away" (19:10). And he basically repeats this statement after having been granted a theophany (19:14). However, the subsequent declaration of the Lord that there are seven thousand who have not bowed the knee to Baal (19:18) explicitly contradicts what Elijah has said here, by adding even more information to what we already knew about the hundred faithful prophets.

---

6. In v. 15, the text says that the widow acts "as Elijah said" (lit., "according to the word of Elijah"), but this specification appears to have been absent in the Hebrew manuscript that the Septuagint was translating; it doubtless was not part of the original text (see Hugo, *Les deux visages d'Élie*, 183–88).

> In sum, Elijah is not just zealous for the Lord: he also craves recognition and has an erroneous perception of his ministry. Interestingly, the narrator has chosen not to say this explicitly (*telling*) but instead has demonstrated it (*showing*), simply by reporting Elijah's words.

B. Round or Flat Character?

This is a very simple but helpful distinction: Certain characters are somewhat one-dimensional, or "flat": that is, they are defined by only one major personality trait. Other characters are "round"; that is, they are presented with a plurality of characteristics and are sometimes inwardly conflicted.

EXAMPLE 11.2c ▸ Eli (1 Samuel 2)

> In 1 Sam 2, the sons of Eli, Hophni and Phinehas, are characterized only by their corruption: they are flat characters. By contrast, their father's behavior is complicated and seems to reflect a conflicted personality: He reproaches his sons for their actions (vv. 22–25), and we know from elsewhere that he has served God for a long time. On the other hand, he lets Hophni and Phinehas do what they want, like many a parent who shows a certain weakness toward their children.

C. Identify the Levels of Knowledge

Another storytelling parameter with which the narrator can play is the characters' varying levels of knowledge. Some characters know more than others do, and this can vary with time or this situation can even be inverted. The same applies to the reader, who may know more or less than some characters do.

EXAMPLE 11.2d ▸ Genesis 42

> When the brothers of Joseph appear before him (Gen 42), he recognizes them but they do not recognize him. He takes advantage of this by submitting them to an interrogation in which he accuses them of being spies. In so doing, he helps them to change; and during this time, we, as readers, are "in the know" since the narrator has placed us on the same level of knowledge as Joseph.

| EXAMPLE 11.2e ▸ Job |

In the book of Job, the reader knows more than the main character: the reader learns right at the beginning what is happening, because the narrator has let the reader see behind the scenes in heaven. But Job suffers without knowing why.

| EXAMPLE 11.2f ▸ Judges 13 |

Manoah is slow to understand that he is dealing with a messenger of the Lord. His wife had taken note that the man in question had the appearance of such a messenger and has apprised her husband of this (Judg 13:6). But Manoah does not seem to take this into account. He needs the whole rest of the chapter before he is able to realize something that his wife has already long surmised. Furthermore, the narrator has indicated to the reader early on, in v. 3, that the man in question is a messenger from the Lord, and he repeats this several times as the story unfolds. The narrator also insists on Manoah's ignorance of this fact by mentioning it explicitly (v. 16).

| EXAMPLE 11.2g ▸ 2 Kings 6:8–23 |

Here again, 2 Kgs 6:8–23 will serve as an example. The characters in this account function on three levels: (1) *the kings:* of Aram and of Israel; (2) *the subordinates:* Elisha's servant and the Aramean soldiers; (3) *the man of God:* Elisha. The narrator plays with the difference in the levels of knowledge of these characters and of the reader.

For example, the king of Aram is ignorant of a fact that is told to the reader in v. 2: his war orders are related to his enemy (the king of Israel) by Elisha (v. 9). When he realizes that there are "leaks," the king of Aram still doesn't attain the reader's level of knowledge, since, as a politician, he is thinking of a human betrayal and searches for the "mole" among his advisers. The reader, on the other hand, already knows that it is the man of God who has obtained—no doubt miraculously—the information for the Israelite king.

As for the king of Israel, he is the involuntary and embarrassed beneficiary of Elisha's powers. He cannot be completely surprised by being offered information in this situation, since he regularly receives military intelligence and uses it to his advantage. But such tactical aid typically lets him fully play the part of a king. After all, this type of information is usually obtained by human means, such as espionage; since the main part of the action is achieved by the army on the orders of the sovereign, he can usually pride himself on the victories that result. This time, however, the prophetic informer brings him the enemy troops on a plate, circumventing the royal prerogative. What is more, Elisha succeeds in a feat that is impossible for the king: he conquers without a fight and without victims; he brings docile hostages into the capital, like a living tribute! Unnerved, the Israelite leader does not know what to do with this cumbersome present. There is no instruction manual, no military tradition for such a success. The fact that he is reduced to asking Elisha advice about these prisoners only serves to complete the revelation of his confusion. Even worse, the suggestion he makes ("shall I strike them?") is set aside by Elisha as being irrelevant.

Elisha's servant gets up early and discovers an army surrounding his city, Dothan (v. 15). In this period of Aramean aggression against Israel (v. 8), an attack on Dothan was certainly not inconceivable, since the site was of some strategic interest. The source of the servant's surprise is different. Since it is his master who keeps the king himself informed of the movements of the enemy army, he has every reason to believe that he is one of the safest men in the country! If Dothan was chosen as a target by the king of Aram during a secret council meeting such as the one described at the beginning of the passage, Elisha would have been able to predict it. Hence the servant's stupefaction at seeing his city surrounded by a powerful Aramean division. Had the master, knowing in advance about foreign attacks, not anticipated this "visit"? The fact that the servant makes this discovery early in the morning further accentuates his surprise. In an instant, the usual reference points and the daily security of this man vanish.

The Aramean soldiers, for their part, although a threatening force, are not in a better position. Yet the task assigned to these professional warriors seems relatively easy; they have sprung a surprise attack on a city that no doubt lacks a military garrison and that is perhaps not even fortified, so victory seems a foregone conclusion. But they come back down to earth with a thud: struck blind, they suddenly find themselves unable to fight, and they are even dependent on someone else in order to move around. They docilely follow Elisha like sheep to the slaughter. Ironically, the soldiers who were meant to bring Elisha back under close escort to the Aramean capital find themselves guided to the center of the Israelite kingdom, and it is their human "target" who is leading them there. Thus, the two categories of subordinates in this story (the servant of Elisha and the Aramean soldiers) undergo an experience of complete disorientation. Even more obvious is the similarity in the way in which the servant and the soldiers recover their sight, since the statements in vv. 17 and 20 are essentially identical.

Finally, Elisha is the only character never to be surprised. He glides above the whole account through his level of knowledge that is superior even to that of the reader, who did not predict the presence of a hidden army. More precisely, it is Elisha who, by his prayers, determines (as it were) the degrees of vision enjoyed by the other characters, whether asking for their sight to be restored or lost.

11.3 IDENTIFY ANY *MISE EN ABYME*

A *mise en abyme* is present when an element in a narrative constitutes a sort of "reduction mirror" of the whole account or of an aspect of the whole.[7] This element thus constitutes an implicit commentary on the text by the narrator; this could be thought of as the text's own "feedback" on itself, which can enable us to better understand what is important in the story.

EXAMPLE 11.3 ▸ 2 Kings 6:8–23

In 2 Kgs 6:8–23, the text presents kings in disarray, subordinates who are disorientated and even struck blind, and a prophet who easily dominates the situation. The blinding of the soldiers serves as a *mise en abyme* of the whole situation. This physical condition serves as an illustration of how the kings have lost their footing and an illustration of the spiritual blindness of Elisha's servant. If the Aramean king is disorientated, it is because he is ignorant of Elisha's power; if the king of Israel seems lost, it is because power has passed from the throne to the prophet. Similarly, the fear felt by Elisha's servant comes from the fact that he does not even begin to imagine the heavenly power that is standing ready around his master. In sum, all the story's characters except Elisha are victims of a form of blindness: each is blind to the true power surrounding the man of God. Thus, the narrator uses the *physical* blindness of certain characters to prompt the reader to analyze the attitudes of other characters in terms of their *spiritual* blindness.

---

7. It is difficult to provide a literal or word-for-word English translation of the French phrase "*mise en abyme*" (it would be something like "placing into abyss"). The French writer André Gide introduced a form of this expression, in an entry in his diary dated to 1893, to explain how he composed some of his own books, in which some characters experience on their own scale the overall topic of the story. He first takes as an analogy the consequence of the presence of a mirror in some paintings (for instance, *Las Meninas*, painted by Diego Velázquez in 1656): the mirror contains a smaller reproduction of the room in which the painted scene takes place. Then he finds a closer analogy in heraldry: a (smaller) coat of arms is sometimes represented on a coat of arms. He mentions "this process in a coat of arms that consists of placing, in the first, a second 'in abyss'" (my translation; André Gide, *Journal, 1889–1939*, Bibliothèque de la Pléiade 54 [Paris: Gallimard, 1948], 41: "ce procédé du blason qui consiste, dans le premier, à en mettre un second 'en abyme'"). Presumably, "abyss" refers here to the effect created by an infinite recursion (although this analogy rests on a mistake because, as a rule, the smaller coat of arms does not reproduce the coat of arms on which it is pictured).

11.4 STUDY TYPE-SCENES

Attentive readers of the narratives in the Hebrew Bible will notice the presence of so-called type-scenes, a term referring to the fact that the same type of episode sometimes occurs, and is told in a similar way, several times. One of the most obvious of these is the "meeting at the well" type-scene (for example, Isaac's servant and Rebecca in Gen 24; Jacob and Rachel in Gen 29): here, a man meets a future wife near what was evidently an important place for social life! Among the other principal type-scenes found in the Bible are the announcement to a barren woman that she will conceive; the epiphany in a field; the flight to the desert, where help is found; and the testament of the protagonist who dies. The point of studying such accounts as type-scenes lies in the fact that the authors follow more or less rigorously a normal pattern in the way they tell the story. Indeed, the *deviations* from this pattern are in some cases their authors' implicit means of drawing readers' attention to a certain aspect of the story.

EXAMPLE 11.4 ▸ Judges 13

Benjamin Johnson has studied the account of the announcement of Samson's birth as an instance of a type-scene.[8] This text can be compared to other scenes of the same type that are found in the Hebrew Bible: e.g., the announcements made to Sarah, to Rebecca, and to Hannah. Table 11.1, in which the left-hand column indicates the elements that are typically found in this type of account, is adapted from the table on p. 286 of Johnson's article.

Table 11.1: Birth Announcements in the Hebrew Bible

	Sarah (Gen 16–18; 21; 25)	Rebecca (Gen 25)	Manoah's wife (Judg 13)	Hannah (1 Sam 1–2)
Mention of sterility	X	X	X	X
Hope for a child	X	X		X
Announcement of the birth	X	X	X	X
Information about the child	X	X	X	X

---

8. Benjamin J. M. Johnson, "What Type of Son Is Samson? Reading Judges 13 as a Biblical Type-Scene," *JETS* 53 (2010): 269–86.

	Sarah (Gen 16–18; 21; 25)	Rebecca (Gen 25)	Manoah's wife (Judg 13)	Hannah (1 Sam 1–2)
Reaction	doubt (17:17–18; 18:12)	question about the twins, who are struggling (25:22)	nothing (wife); worry (Manoah)	gratitude (1:20, 28)
Birth	X	X	X	X
The name given to the child is linked to the circumstances of the birth	X	X		X
Prosperity of the child, who is watched over by God	X	X	X	X

A comparison of these accounts brings out three ways in which Judg 13 deviates from the normal pattern:

- The other accounts all specifically mention the future parents' hope for a child, but this element is absent here.

- All the other future mothers react to the birth announcement, but Samson's mother does not. That said, Rebecca's case is debatable, since it is not the fact of the birth that she reacts to but rather the movements of the twins in her womb. Nevertheless, the total absence of expression of emotion on the part of Manoah's wife is surprising. The father does not always react in this type of narrative, but it can be noted that Manoah is moved neither to joy, nor to doubt, nor to gratitude: he simply wonders how he should bring up this unexpected child.

- The child generally receives a name linked to the circumstances of his birth (or his conception), but Samson's name apparently has no link to these circumstances. Worse, it could be understood as a name given in homage to a sun-god (Shamash), though this is uncertain.

To sum up, Manoah and his wife demonstrate astonishing behavior as a couple (compared to what is reported in similar situations in the Hebrew Bible): no comment is made about their desire for a child; the text reports no reaction from either of them that is linked directly to the fact that they will be having a son; finally, when Samson is born, they give him a name that has no link to the situation. This is all the more intriguing when we consider the importance of having children in the context of ancient Israel (consider the case of Abraham, for example). The narrator hereby has given the reader a riddle to solve, and there must be a lesson hidden in this riddle. More will be revealed on this below when we consider this text again, but for the moment, two remarks can be made. On the one hand, *the attitude of the couple is a mirror image of that of the whole people*, since the text reports no reaction on their part to their being oppressed and no cry to God to deliver them (that is, stage [3] of the cyclical pattern we find in Judges is absent in this case). The behavior of the couple serves here as a *mise en abyme* of the general attitude of the people! This explains the apparently abrupt leap from the national context in Judg 13:1 to a "zoom-in" on a particular situation—in other words, the jump from the general plot (the fate of the Israelites) discussed in Example 11.1c above to the second, more specific plot noted there (a childless couple). Moreover, we also considered a third plot there, and this can serve as a clue for how we continue our research on this passage.

11.5 IDENTIFY DISCREPANCIES OR ANOMALIES

While discrepancies and anomalies do not belong to any specific category in the standard descriptions of narrative criticism's theoretical framework, I suggest that studying them can lead us to detect and understand strategies on the part of biblical writers (or narrators). It is difficult to delineate a systematic approach to searching for anomalies and other discrepancies in the text. The idea is simply to be attentive to the possible presence of such features.

EXAMPLE 11.5a ▸ Judges 13

In the dialogue between Manoah and the messenger of the Lord in Judg 13:8–18, the narrator draws the attention of the reader to a surprising fact: although it is Manoah who prays for the messenger to return, it is to his wife that the latter (re)appears; the text underlines that "her husband Manoah was not with her" (v. 9). In the dialogue that follows, almost every reply by the messenger is a way of turning Manoah down flat:

- To the question "Are you the man who spoke to this woman?" the messenger replies with one word in Hebrew: אָנִי ("It is I"; v. 11). Nothing too strange up to this point, but this answer is notably very brief.
- Manoah asks him what attitude he should have in regard to the child, but the messenger only repeats what he has already said to the woman, without even giving all the details, only mentioning "all that I said to her" (v. 13).
- Manoah invites the man to share a meal, but he refuses this hospitality, insisting that it is out of the question for him to eat Manoah's bread (v. 16). This would almost certainly be an affront in this cultural context.
- Lastly, Manoah asks the man's name, and the latter dodges the question (v. 18).

In such conditions, it is hard to see the point of the second appearance of the messenger. However, there is one thing that he says to Manoah without being asked: "if you want to prepare a burnt offering, then offer it to the LORD" (v. 16). In saying this, the messenger suggests that Manoah worship the Lord. Up until now, as we have seen, Manoah has not expressed any particular emotion about having a son; he has only worried about the duties that this means for him. Above all, he has never expressed gratitude to God. And when he does pray to the Lord, he starts directly with his own concern, asking that the messenger come back, and he makes no remark on the fact that God is giving him a son. In this context, it is understandable that the messenger *redirects Manoah to the Lord by suggesting that he worship him*. Manoah had passed directly from the stage "announcement of the birth of a son" to the stage "duties required," without going through the stage "joy and gratitude."

There is more. When the messenger makes this suggestion, Manoah does not act on it straightaway. He is still worried by something else: the mystery of the identity of this man, whose name he asks so that he may "honor" him when his words come true. Yet the climax occurs at the moment when Manoah understands who it is he is talking to. In line with the lack of distinction between the "messenger of the LORD" and the Lord himself in the Hebrew Bible, Manoah believes that he has talked to God face to face. (Although nothing suggests that Manoah understands the implication, this would mean that the one who told him to worship the Lord was none other than the Lord himself!) Ironically, the man in whom Manoah was interested more than he was in God, the man whom he desperately wanted to thank while offering the sacrifice, was God himself. Even the upward movement of the messenger, when he goes up in the flame, redirects Manoah to heaven and to the Lord.

> **EXAMPLE 11.5b ▸ 2 Kings 6:8–23**
>
> Second Kings 6:8–23 seems to deliberately make use of subtle discrepancies. On the one hand, what happens to the subordinate characters is asymmetrical. It is true that both Elisha's servant and the Aramean troops recover their sight, and in both cases, this recovery follows a prayer by the man of God. But unlike the soldiers, the Israelite had not been "struck" blind. This suggests that Elisha's servant's ignorance of the presence of a "heavenly army" is due to a sort of *permanent* blindness on his part. If he needed his eyes to be opened without having been "struck," it is because he was *already* blind to certain realities. But on another level, the aforementioned asymmetry and the fact that the "horses and chariots of fire" were invisible to everyone in the story (except Elisha) suggest that this form of blindness is nothing out of the ordinary: it is not a lack of vision on the same level as that experienced by the soldiers, since there is nothing strange in not seeing a "heavenly army." Indeed, the level of vision that results from Elisha's two requests that eyes be opened is not the same: his servant perceives a supernatural reality, whereas the Aramean soldiers' eyes are only opened to the world as it is normally accessible to sensory perception. In sum, the ignorance of Elisha's servant can be interpreted as blindness, but an *ordinary* blindness.

11.6 STUDY THE FOCALIZATIONS

A narrator can describe action through the eyes of a character or describe the character's feelings, thus giving the reader access to the character's inner life: this is a switch to *internal focalization*. During this focalization, the reader's perception is governed by that of the character. This can be a way of making the reader feel closer to the character. The formula "and behold" (וְהִנֵּה) often introduces an internal focalization. The same technique is used in cinematography, often to create empathy, but also, in some cases, to create a complete turnaround at the end of a film, when viewers understand that they have only seen reality through the mental filter of one character and that he or she was wrong.[9] By contrast, if a scene is described as if by an outside observer, this is an example of *external focalization*. And if the reader is looking down from even higher—as the narrator provides details about an even larger context than the scene being described—this is called *zero focalization*. Of course, a narrative can pass freely from one focalization to another.

---

9. Think, for example, of the schizophrenia experienced by the protagonist played by Russell Crowe in the 2001 film *A Beautiful Mind*. The film makes viewers see and hear, as if they were real, the imaginary characters and voices that only this character perceives.

> **EXAMPLE 11.6** ▸ **2 Kings 6:8–23**
>
> In 2 Kgs 6:8–23, the play on perspectives that the narrator employs seems to draw the reader closer to the subordinate characters. Verses 15 and 20 make use of the formula "and behold" (וְהִנֵּה), which places the reader for a moment in the mind of Elisha's servant when he discovers that an Aramean force has surrounded the town he is in (v. 15), then in the mind of the soldiers when they realize that they are in Samaria (v. 20). As for the kings in this story, there is simply a brief description of the emotional state of the Syrian king in v. 11—an example of a rapid *internal focalization*.

11.7 IDENTIFY THE PRESENCE OF IRONY, DOUBLE MEANINGS, AND MISUNDERSTANDINGS

Two categories can be distinguished here: verbal irony (which is generated by the use of a word) and situational irony (for example, the reversal of a situation or the revelation of a situation's ridiculousness). "Double meanings" also appear in the mouth of biblical characters, and misunderstandings can happen. Here the reader's insight and presence of mind are called into play!

> **EXAMPLE 11.7a** ▸ **Esther**
>
> The classic example of situational irony in the Hebrew Bible is found in the book of Esther, which contains several situational reversals. For example:
>
> - Haman plots against Mordecai but is forced to honor him precisely because the king follows Haman's own advice (Esth 6)! The king asks him, "What shall be done for the man whom the king wishes to honor?" (v. 6), and Haman recommends clothing such a man in a royal garment, giving him a horse that the king has ridden, and then honoring him by public proclamation. Haman is thinking about himself, but it is his enemy who benefits from his advice.
>
> - Haman prepares a gallows for Mordecai (Esth 5), but it is he himself who will be hanged—and on the very same gallows (Esth 7).

- A decree is issued that the Jews should be persecuted (Esth 3), but in the end it is a decree in their favor that prevails (Esth 8) and they obtain vengence on those who wanted them dead (Esth 9).

EXAMPLE 11.7b ▸ Jonah

Another ironic situation is found in the book of Jonah. While the prophet runs away from the Lord precisely because he does not want to proclaim the word of the Lord to a foreign people, it is his flight that leads the sailors (each of whom worshiped a different god [Jonah 1:5]) to start praying to the God of Israel (v. 14)! As Daniel Timmer has put it, "Jonah's anti-missionary activity has ironically resulted in the conversion of non-Israelites."[10] This result is all the more striking since Jonah introduces himself to the sailors in a way that emphasizes his piety: "I am a Hebrew . . . I worship the LORD" (v. 9); as it happens, however, it is the sailors who show themselves to be more "spiritual." Later, Jonah's attitude toward Nineveh shows that "Jonah wants to receive God's grace without being changed by it, and at the same time to snatch it away from those whose lives *are* in fact changed by it."[11]

11.8 LISTEN TO THE NARRATIVE VOICE

The term "narrative voice" is used to designate comments, whether explicit or otherwise, that the narrator sometimes slips into his account. In the Bible, such comments are all the more significant when they appear because on the whole they are rare; that is, biblical narrators generally proceed more discreetly, thus demanding reflection on the part of the reader.

EXAMPLE 11.8a ▸ Eli (1 Samuel 2)

We have already looked at 1 Sam 2 in Example 11.2c. Here we can observe that as soon as the narrator introduces the sons of Eli, he states that they are "scoundrels" (v. 12). The narrator could have stopped there, but he immediately adds an explanation, "they had no regard for the LORD" (1 Sam 2:12),

---

10. Daniel C. Timmer, *A Gracious and Compassionate God: Mission, Salvation and Spirituality in the Book of Jonah*, NSBT 26 (Downers Grove, IL: InterVarsity Press, 2011), 75.
11. Timmer, *A Gracious and Compassionate God*, 133.

and a little further on, he comments that "the sin of the young men was very great in the sight of the LORD, for they treated the offerings of the LORD with contempt" (v. 17).

EXAMPLE 11.8b ▸ The Schism between Israel and Judah (1 Kings 12)

In the account of the schism between Israel and Judah in 1 Kgs 12, the cause of this event appears to be the uncompromising attitude of Rehoboam. However, the narrator offers a theological analysis (which does not exclude the first): "the king did not listen to the people because it was a turn of affairs brought about by the LORD to fulfill his word that the LORD had spoken by Ahijah the Shilonite to Jeroboam son of Nebat" (v. 15).

EXAMPLE 11.8c ▸ The Murder of Uriah (2 Samuel 11)

In the account of the murder of Uriah found in 2 Sam 11, the text presents a litany of actions that David does, without the slightest comment from the narrator—until the very last verse of the passage, that is, where he simply comments, "the thing that David had done displeased the LORD" (v. 27). In this chapter, the narrator has carefully multiplied the idea "David did this" throughout the text, thus highlighting not only this character's responsibility for his actions toward Bathsheba and Uriah but also the tenacity with which he proceeds, as well as his (direct) personal implication in having set up the (indirect) assassination of Uriah. After the narrator presents this torrent of activities and after having, as it were, let David act without saying anything about what he has done, the narrator's laconic comment at the end is all the more striking.

EXERCISES FOR CHAPTER 11

Exercise A
Study the characters Nabal and his wife in 1 Sam 25.

Exercise B
Study the character Jehu in 2 Kgs 9–10. To what extent does the narrator approve of his behavior?

Exercise C
Study the irony and ambiguity of Hushai's speech in 2 Sam 16:16–17:5.

Exercise D
Describe the plot structure of the book of Ruth.

Exercise E
Describe the plot structure of the book of Esther.

CHAPTER 12

INTERTEXTUALITY

OVERVIEW

As the name suggests, intertextuality is about the relationship between texts. But this could mean a variety of things. Let's first consider the most basic situation, which is when text *A* quotes, refers to, or alludes to another text, *B*. In this case, *B* is termed an *intertext* of *A*; one can also say that *A* and *B* are *co-texts*. This happens frequently in the Hebrew Bible: intertextuality was a powerful tool in the hands of the biblical writers, so they used it abundantly. For the sake of simplicity, I will use the expression "intertextual link" as an umbrella term to designate all the possible ways—quotation, allusion, reuse, and so on—in which a text might relate to an earlier text. Studying such links presents several advantages for exegesis.

First, by referring to an earlier text, an author sometimes provides a key for interpreting his or her own composition. For instance, the source text may be used as an authoritative reference to support an idea, or it may provide an illustration for the point the author is making; conversely, the author may refer to the source text in order to counter ideas it contains or to provide an opposing argument to one found in the source text. Therefore, identifying an intertextual link and the purpose it serves can prove crucial for understanding the very logic of a text. In fact, we have already encountered such situations in various examples found in the preceding chapters.

Second, the use of a source text in another passage of the Hebrew Bible provides information on the former's reception—namely, the way later redactors interpreted, commented on, or developed it; how they applied it to a new context; or how it influenced them. It may also indicate that the biblical book in which the source text appears already enjoyed a certain degree of authority at the point in Israel's history when the later text was written. Scholars use the expression "inner-biblical exegesis" to underline the fact that within the Hebrew Bible, certain authors are already, in a sense, doing exegesis of earlier biblical texts (see the sidebar "Inner-Biblical Exegesis" below). For example, Jer 25:11 declares that there will be seventy years of Babylonian domination over Judah; in the second half of the fourth century BCE, the Chronicler *interpreted* this as the time that was needed "until the land had made up for its Sabbaths" (2 Chr 36:21), an idea found in Lev 26:34–35.

Third, the fact that text *A* refers to text *B* implies that *A* was written after *B*, thus providing a valuable *relative dating*. This is actually one of the most frequently used methods for dating texts in diachronic studies, as we have already seen in the second chapter on compositional criticism (Section 4.3e: "Literary Dependence"). In such a situation, scholars generally say that *A* is "literarily *dependent* on" *B*. This is not a very helpful way to speak, however, since this wording certainly does not do justice to the active and often sophisticated ways in which redactors used earlier texts. But experience proves that scholars are sometimes incorrigible when it comes to their terminology, even when different terms would be more helpful!

Inner-Biblical Exegesis

The seminal publication in this area is Michael Fishbane's book *Biblical Interpretation in Ancient Israel* (Oxford: Clarendon, 1985), which has renewed scholarly interest in the various ways that redactors of *biblical* texts during the Second Temple period referred to, used, and interpreted earlier *biblical* texts. The expression "inner-biblical exegesis" captures the essence of this phenomenon.

Note that this expression has the disadvantage of presupposing the existence of the Hebrew Bible as a well-delimited corpus, which is incongruous with the fact that most scholars consider that the canon was not closed before the first century CE or even later. Strictly speaking, therefore, referring to "the Hebrew Bible" is anachronistic for earlier periods (though more limited collections of books may have already served as provisional "canons"). In addition, the phenomenon is obviously not restricted to the books that happened to become a part of the Hebrew Bible.[1] Some degree of anachronism is unavoidable in the current discussion, however, and it is already present whenever one speaks of a "biblical text" in the context of the first millennium BCE. Thus, what is important here is to be aware that the phrase inner-biblical exegesis and similar expressions concern the retrospective viewpoint of the exegete, and that scribes of the last centuries BCE were not thinking in these terms but rather were using discrete, earlier literary works (albeit ones that were possibly sometimes already part of a small collection, such as the Pentateuch).

---

1. On this subject and more generally, see Eva Mroczek, *The Literary Imagination in Jewish Antiquity* (New York: Oxford University Press, 2016).

A less restrictive, and more sophisticated, approach to intertextuality—one that approaches the phenomenon from the point of view of literary theory—consists of studying all the possible ways in which texts relate to each other, irrespective of possible intentional references and/or irrespective of the direction of a given reference. In this broader sense, one may find connections, correspondences or echoes, and similarities and differences between texts that may or may not have been written in light of each other. While the more restrictive approach described above is mostly concerned with the work of the *authors*, this broader perspective is mainly oriented toward the *reader*. But this approach also takes seriously the fluid circulation of ideas and traditions in societies, as well as the *de facto* presence of "networks" of ideas and motifs in literature. To put it another way, "no text is an island."[2] After all, during the last two millennia, readers of the Hebrew Bible have often found parallels and correspondences between texts without taking into account the *prima facie* relative dating of these texts, let alone the relative dating for them that has been proposed by biblical scholars. Besides, since it is often not possible to determine the direction of dependence, even when working within an author-oriented approach we are frequently left simply with the fact that a link exists between texts, without being able to draw diachronic conclusions from it. In such situations, exploring the connections from a purely synchronic perspective may represent a way forward.

To take a very simple illustration, both Nahum and Jonah discuss the fate of Nineveh but in very different ways: Nahum announces and rejoices over the destruction of the city, whereas Jonah tells a story in which God spares Nineveh from a similar fate. It is possible that Jonah was written as a counterpoint to Nahum, but that is difficult to prove. However, regardless of this possible intentionality, and even regardless of the relative dating of these two books, one can consider them to be "in dialogue" or "in conversation" with each other. Or, if you prefer, one can *put them* into dialogue with each other and compare their perspectives. Actually, at some point in antiquity, these books came to be included in the same small corpus that scholars call "the Book of the Twelve" (a.k.a. the Minor Prophets). Their very presence together in this collection invites the reader to put them into dialogue. As a matter of fact, most scholars consider that the "compiler" of the Twelve edited the books it contains to create further connections between them.

There is an additional reason that can make the broader approach to intertextuality relevant to some readers. Those who approach the Hebrew Bible in the context of religious belief generally consider that it constitutes a canon of authoritative texts (in Judaism) or is the first part of the canon (in Christianity). In such a perspective, the co-presence of books in the same set of authoritative writings invites the reader to find correspondences between them; he or she will want to hear what these various

---

2. This statement is from Peter D. Miscall, quoted in the very helpful article by Geoffrey D. Miller, "Intertextuality in Old Testament Research," *CurBR* 9 (2011): 283–309 (see 287 for the quotation). I borrow the designations "author-oriented approach" and "reader-oriented approach" from Miller.

authoritative voices have to say about the same subject. Thus, for example, rabbinic exegesis identifies echoes and reverberations between networks of verses scattered throughout the whole Hebrew Bible. In this perspective, the literary context of a verse is the whole Hebrew Bible. In fact, several religious traditions consider these books to have been written under the inspiration of the same God, who is regarded, in a way, as the ultimate "author" of the Bible (see, e.g., the Catholic document *Dei verbum* and traditional Protestant dogmatics).

12.1 THE AUTHOR-ORIENTED APPROACH: METHOD

In the framework of the author-oriented approach, the first issue is to be able to *detect* the presence of an intertextual link. However, just because you have detected an intertextual link between the text you are studying (*A*) and another text (*B*), this does not necessarily mean that *A* is interacting with *B*; it could be the other way around. In other words, you need to determine the direction of dependence between them. And once you have done this, it is important to go further and analyze the *purpose* of the intertextual link and its *results*, which may concern synchronic aspects of the text (literary effects) or diachronic aspects of it (relative dating). To sum up, here are the main steps to follow:

Ⓐ Detect an intertextual link (or several such links).

Ⓑ Determine the direction of dependence.

Ⓒ Determine the purpose of the intertextual link and the diachronic and synchronic consequences.

Let's review these steps in more detail.

A. Detect an Intertextual Link (or Several Such Links)

The easiest situation occurs when the text you are studying quotes a text with an explicit reference to it. For example, Jer 26:18 contains a quotation from Mic 3:12 after the following introduction: "Micah of Moresheth, who prophesied during the days of King Hezekiah of Judah, said to all the people of Judah." Similarly, in Joel 2:32 [3:5] we read that "in Mount Zion and in Jerusalem there shall be those who escape, *as the* Lord *has said.*" This last phrase alludes to the fact that the same assertion about survivors in Jerusalem has already been made elsewhere, and indeed in Obad 17 we read that "on Mount Zion there shall be those who escape."

But this kind of phenomenon is very rare. Moreover, most of the explicit references of this kind that we find in the Hebrew Bible concern works that are lost (assuming they really existed), such as "the book of Jashar" (Josh 10:13; 2 Sam 1:18), the royal annals (1 Kgs 11:41; 14:19; etc.), and prophetic works (2 Chr 32:32). Or, reference is made to a work that is not easily identified: for example, is "the book of the law of Moses" (2 Kgs 14:6), or "the book of Moses" (2 Chr 25:4), a reference to a version of Deuteronomy or to something else?

Again, these are exceptions. Most of the time, the text contains no such explicit indication of an intertextual link, so you have to detect it yourself. Of course, you are not the first to try, and you can use the following three kinds of resources as a shortcut:

- The **cross-references provided in a study Bible**, that is, in footnotes or in the margins. Note, however, that these cross-references are not meant to be exhaustive and that they generally include both intertextual links proper and passages that happen to use similar expressions or themes (which is more relevant to the reader-oriented approach to intertextuality).

- **Exegetical commentaries**, although it should be noted that commentators typically mention only what in their view are the most convincing links.

- **Articles or monographs** dedicated to the study of the intertextuality of a passage or of a section of a book. Table 12.1 takes Isaiah as an example.

Table 12.1: Monographs on Intertextuality in Isaiah

Isaiah 24–27	J. Todd Hibbard, *Intertextuality in Isaiah 24–27: The Reuse and Evocation of Earlier Texts and Traditions*, FAT 2.16 (Tübingen: Mohr Siebeck, 2006).
Isaiah 40–55	Patricia T. Willey, *Remember the Former Things: The Recollection of Previous Texts in Second Isaiah*, SBLDS 161 (Atlanta: SBL Press, 2011).
Isaiah 40–55 and Job	JiSeong James Kwon, *Scribal Culture and Intertextuality: Literary and Historical Relationships between Job and Deutero-Isaiah*, FAT 2.85 (Tübingen: Mohr Siebeck, 2016).
Isaiah 40–66	Benjamin D. Sommer, *A Prophet Reads Scripture: Allusion in Isaiah 40–66* (Stanford: Stanford University Press, 1998).

The intertextual links you will find in these resources may be incomplete or debatable. They may be helpful as a first step, to clear the ground, but it is necessary to critically assess these author's proposals to determine which of them you find really well grounded and to search for other possible links.

How should you proceed if you want to find other possible links? It may well be that your knowledge of the Bible and other ancient literature will lead you to think of other possible intertexts. But you can also focus on some striking or important expressions and do a **concordance search** with a printed concordance or, better, with software such as Accordance or Logos, which enable you to search not only for a word but also for combinations of words.

Once you have found a candidate for an intertext, you need to ascertain whether there is indeed an intertextual link. It is not enough to find elements common to the texts; you must also demonstrate that the author of one text has made use of the other. With this aim in mind, here is a list of **criteria** that correspond to various ways in which two texts *A* and *B* may relate to one another; of course, a combination of criteria enhances the likelihood that there is an intertextual link.[3]

- *A* and *B* **share verbal elements** (this is by far the most frequent situation).
- *A* and *B* make use of the **same motifs or images**.
- *A* and *B* **share a common theme**.
- The **storyline** of *B* is **modeled** on that of *A*, or a **character** in *B* is **modeled** on one in *A*.
- *A* and *B* are **parallel within a structure**.

When using these criteria, especially the first three, the goal is to determine whether the presence of the same or similar elements is due to borrowing or is coincidental. The probability that there is an intertextual link increases if:

- there is an **accumulation** of shared elements, especially if they are concentrated within a limited passage
- in the case of verbal elements, the two texts share **long phrases** or **whole sentences**
- the shared elements appear **in the same order**
- the shared elements are **relatively rare** in the Hebrew Bible (the more common a word is in Hebrew, the less its presence in *A* and *B* is significant, and vice versa)

B. Determine the Direction of Dependence

Once you have convincingly established that an intertextual relationship exists between two texts *A* and *B*, you need to determine the direction of dependence. The following criteria are helpful to make sure that it is *A* that is dependent on *B*, rather than the other way around:[4]

---

3. Some of these criteria are discussed in Miller, "Intertextuality in Old Testament Research."
4. This list takes up some of the criteria noted by David Carr and adds others (see David M. Carr, "Method in Determination of Direction of Dependence: An Empirical Test of Criteria Applied to

- An element in *B* is **developed** in *A*.
- An element in *B* is **specified** in *A*.
- An element in *B* has been **adapted to the new context** in *A*.
- In *A*, an element from *B* is **entangled** with other elements, so that it is unlikely that *B* extracted it from *A*, whereas it is likely that *A* took it up and combined it with new elements.
- *A* **combines** two elements that are distinct in *B*.
- *A* contains **a response to, a note of disagreement with, or a reversal of** an idea found in *B*.
- *A* contains an **unexpected** or **incongruous** element that is, by contrast, at home in *B* (and that thus resembles a **remnant** of *B*).
- A shared element is **indispensable** to the logic or story of *B* but not to *A*.
- *A* contains **a plus that fills a gap** in *B*.
- We know by other means that *A* is **later** than *B*.

A number of these criteria could be reversed. For instance, it may be difficult to decide whether an element from *B* has been developed in *A*, or whether *B* has abridged an element from *A*. Likewise, it can hard to discern whether it is *A* that constitutes a response to *B*, or vice versa, when the response is based on a subtle allusion. In such cases, it is important to explore the opposite scenarios and determine if one is more compelling than the other.

The last criterion in the list above points to the possible entanglement that can occur between intertextual study and compositional criticism. It is worth noting that in some cases, *A* is originally dependent on *B*, but later on during the compositional history, *B* was, in turn, edited in light of *A*—that is, reshaped in order to resemble *A* more closely (as we saw in chapter 6, this is called the "boomerang phenomenon"). In such a complicated situation, the influence was, in the end, bidirectional, although the first movement was in one direction.

On the other hand, intertextual links between two texts that belong to *the same book* are sometimes simply due to the work of the same author (or redactor). In this case, while the author certainly wrote one text after the other, there is no point in trying to determine the order in which they were written. However, there may be a synchronic direction to discern, in the sense that the author may have designed one text to echo the other—generally in a sequential reading.

Therefore, "direction of dependence" can designate two different situations that are not always easy to distinguish:

Exodus 34,11–26 and Its Parallels," in *Gottes Volk am Sinai: Untersuchungen zu Ex 32–34 und Dtn 9–10*, ed. Matthias Köckert and Erhard Blum, VWGT 18 [Gütersloh: Gütersloher Verlagshaus, 2011], 107–40).

- The contents and internal logic of *A* presuppose *B* (synchronic approach).
- *A* was written later than *B* and in light of *B* (diachronic approach).

C. Determine the Purpose of the Intertextual Link and the Diachronic and Synchronic Consequences

Among the many possible forms this step might take, an interesting question to reflect on is whether the purpose of the intertextual link is to make the reader recall the first text when reading the new one, or instead to create a new, completely autonomous text, without allusion to the earlier text. Thus, the books of Chronicles are a rewriting of Samuel and Kings, but they are meant to be read on their own, as an autonomous work. At the same time, the redactors sometimes presuppose that the reader has some prior knowledge of details that are conveyed only in Samuel or Kings.

To use modern analogies, the scenario in the book and movie *Bridget Jones's Diary* is loosely based on the novel *Pride and Prejudice* (the classic by Jane Austen) and can be considered a modernization of it. But many people read or watch it without realizing this (as I did: I needed my wife to explain this to me); awareness of the connection is not required in order to understand the story. Likewise, the novel *Ulysses*, by James Joyce, is based on the famous Homeric work the *Odyssey*, but it can be read on its own. Here, however, the title hints at the intertext.

D. Examples

The examples below are designed to illustrate various possible situations, and they all involve a combination of criteria, which will be explicitly indicated.

EXAMPLE 12.1a ▸ Zechariah 2:1–13 [5–17]

Criteria for detecting the intertextuality: same language, same theme

Criterion for determining the direction of dependence: **A combines two elements that are distinct in B**

In Zechariah's third vision (2:1–13 [5–17]), the Lord announces that he will intervene against the nations who "plundered" his people (v. 8 [12]) during the exilic period and, above all, that he will return to live in Jerusalem (vv. 10–11 [14–15]). The oracle ends as follows:

> Be silent, all flesh, before the LORD,
> for he has roused himself from his holy dwelling.

A concordance search shows several possible parallels to expressions found in this verse:

- A call to silence can be found in Judg 3:19; Amos 6:10; 8:3; Zeph 1:7; Hab 2:20.
- The idea that God has "roused himself" (or "awakened") is common to a whole series of passages that use the same Hebrew verb (Isa 42:13; 51:9; Pss 7:6 [7]; 35:23; 44:23 [24]; 59:4 [5]; 80:2 [3]).
- The expression "holy dwelling" or "holy habitation" (these translations render the same Hebrew phrase) appears in Deut 26:15; Jer 25:30; Ps 68:5 [6]; 2 Chr 30:27.

Thus far, it seems impossible to say if Zechariah is alluding to a specific text or is simply using standard expressions. Close inspection of these potential intertexts reveals, however, that Hab 2:20 contains a number of connections with Zech 2:13 [17] (see Table 12.2): both use the order "Be silent!" (הַס), the phrase "holy temple" in Hab 2:20 is synonymous with "holy dwelling" in Zech 2:13 [17] (both contain the word קָדְשׁוֹ), and "all the earth" in Hab 2:20 is the equivalent of "all flesh" in Zech 2:13 [17]. Interestingly, the order of the statement being made is reversed in Zech 2:13 [17] relative to Hab 2:20, which is an instance of Seidel's law (see the sidebar "Inverted Quotations, or Seidel's Law" below). Moreover, the immediately preceding verse in Habakkuk mocks idols by evoking an artisan who says in vain to a silent stone, "Rouse yourself [עוּרִי]!"; the same verb is used about the Lord in Zech 2:13 [17] ("he has roused himself" [נֵעוֹר]). Therefore, Zech 2:13 [17] combines elements from Hab 2:19–20, thus indicating the direction of dependence, a conclusion that is in line with the general relative dating of these two books (though they may contain later additions).

Table 12.2: Habakkuk 2 and Zechariah 2

Habakkuk 2:19–20	Zechariah 2:13 [17]
Alas for you who say to the wood, "Wake up!" to silent stone, "**Rouse yourself** [עוּרִי]!" Can it teach? See, it is gold and silver plated, and there is no breath in it at all.	
But the **Lord** is in **his holy** *temple*; וַיהוָה בְּהֵיכַל קָדְשׁוֹ	**Be silent**, *all flesh*, **before the Lord**, הַס כָּל־בָּשָׂר מִפְּנֵי יְהוָה
Let *all the earth* **keep silence before** him הַס מִפָּנָיו כָּל־הָאָרֶץ	for **he has roused himself** from **his** *holy* dwelling כִּי נֵעוֹר מִמְּעוֹן קָדְשׁוֹ

On the level of substance, in the time of Habakkuk—i.e., at the end of the seventh century, shortly before the exile—God *was present in* his temple (a static description). By contrast, in the time when Zechariah's visions are situated—the year 519—the Lord *comes out of* his heavenly temple to intervene on behalf of his people (a dynamic image). Furthermore, the fact that God awakes creates a contrast—one that is no doubt deliberate—with the idols who, according to the intertext (Hab 2:19), cannot do so.

Inverted Quotations, or Seidel's Law

An interesting phenomenon has been noted by Moshe Seidel: when a text A quotes or reuses an earlier passage B, it sometimes presents elements from B in reverse order. Exegetes sometimes speak of this as "inverted quotation."[5] Unfortunately, this phenomenon does not help to determine the direction of dependence, since the inversion could have happened in either direction—unless one sequence appears more "natural" than the other. Nevertheless, such an inversion is a feature that may corroborate the existence of an intertextual link.

EXAMPLE 12.1b ▸ Lamentations and Isaiah 40–55

Criteria for detecting the intertextuality: same language, same theme

Criterion for determining the direction of dependence: **A responds to B**

The book of Lamentations was written not long after the fall of Jerusalem, which occurred in 587/586 BCE. The first chapter mourns the fate of Lady Zion, that is, Jerusalem personified as a woman. No fewer than five times do we read, "she has no one to comfort her," or a similar formula:

"she has no one to comfort her" (אֵין־לָהּ מְנַחֵם; v. 2)

"with none to comfort her" (אֵין מְנַחֵם לָהּ; v. 9)

"for a comforter is far from me" (כִּי־רָחַק מִמֶּנִּי מְנַחֵם; v. 16)

---

5. Pancratius C. Beentjes, "Inverted Quotations in the Bible: A Neglected Stylistic Pattern," *Bib* 63 (1982): 506–23.

"there is no one to comfort her" (אֵין מְנַחֵם לָהּ; v. 17)

"with no one to comfort me" (אֵין מְנַחֵם לִי; v. 21).

Against this background, it is striking that Deutero-Isaiah (Isa 40–55), which most scholars believe was also written in the exilic period, begins with the following statement: "Comfort, O comfort [נַחֲמוּ נַחֲמוּ] my people, says your God. Speak tenderly to Jerusalem, and cry to her that she has served her term, that her penalty is paid" (Isa 40:1–2). The consolation of Jerusalem constitutes a theme that recurs later in this corpus, in statements such as "the LORD has comforted [נִחַם] his people" (49:13) and "the LORD will comfort [נִחַם] Zion" (51:3; see also 51:12; 52:9). It seems that Deutero-Isaiah deliberately echoes Lamentations' complaint by saying that, at last, "there is somebody to comfort her," and that this somebody is the Lord.

In this case, the lexical connection is limited to a verb (נחם), but the thematic connection is strong, and it is linked to the same historical context.[6]

EXAMPLE 12.1c ▸ Hosea 10:1–8, Isaiah 5:2–7, and Ezekiel 15:1–6; 17; 19:10–14

Criteria for detecting the intertextuality: same language, same (rare) image

Criterion for determining the direction of dependence: relative dating of the texts

Hosea (10:1–8), Isaiah (5:2–7), and Ezekiel (15:1–6; 17:1–24; 19:10–14) all make use of the image of a vineyard to describe the people of God. This is a relatively rare metaphor, and it is plausible (albeit not proven) that one of the redactors of Isaiah found this image in Hosea and reused it, and that, in turn, one of the redactors of Ezekiel did the same. This presupposes the traditional relative dating of the passages in question, though it could be argued that Hos 10:1–8, for instance, was written after Isa 5:2–7.[7]

---

6. On the intertextuality between Deutero-Isaiah and Lamentations, see Lena-Sofia Tiemeyer, *For the Comfort of Zion: The Geographical and Theological Location of Isaiah 40–55*, VTSup 139 (Leiden: Brill, 2011), 347–61.

7. Hosea 10:1–8 may come from Hosea himself (Hans Walter Wolff, *Hosea: A Commentary on the Book of the Prophet Hosea*, Hermeneia [Minneapolis: Fortress, 1974], xxiii, 173), and Isa 5:1–7 may come from Isaiah himself (Hugh G. M. Williamson, *Isaiah 1–27*, vol. 1, *Commentary on Isaiah 1–5*, ICC [London: T&T Clark, 2006], 330–31).

EXAMPLE 12.1d ▸ Isaiah 4:2–6 and Exodus

Criteria for detecting the intertextuality: same language, same theme

Criterion for determining the direction of dependence: presence of an element that is unexpected in the new context but typical in the source text

In Isa 4:2–6, the prophet depicts the "eschatological" Mount Zion as a place where the inhabitants of the purified Jerusalem will assemble in the presence of God, using the following specific image:

> Then the LORD will create over the whole site of Mount Zion and over its places of assembly *a cloud by day and smoke and the shining of a flaming fire by night* [עָנָן יוֹמָם וְעָשָׁן וְנֹגַהּ אֵשׁ לֶהָבָה לָיְלָה]. (v. 5)

This phrase recalls Exod 13:21–22: while the Hebrews were leaving Egypt,

> the LORD went in front of them *in a pillar of cloud by day* [יוֹמָם בְּעַמּוּד עָנָן], to lead them along the way, and *in a pillar of fire by night* [וְלַיְלָה בְּעַמּוּד אֵשׁ], to give them light . . . neither *the pillar of cloud by day nor the pillar of fire by night* [עַמּוּד הֶעָנָן יוֹמָם וְעַמּוּד הָאֵשׁ לָיְלָה] left its place in front of the people.

Here, the criterion of lexical similarity is interesting, but it is striking that the expressions are not exactly the same; for instance, the word "pillar" (עַמּוּד) does not appear in Isa 4:5. Nevertheless, both texts clearly evoke a similar *situation* with the same motif: God uses a cloud by day and a fire by night to lead his people. Moreover, it is evident that this motif is integral to the Exodus narrative and clearly related to its narrative context (see Exod 14:19–20, 24; 16:10; 33:9–10), whereas it is a bit unexpected in Isaiah; thus, it is the latter that borrowed it from Exodus. On the level of substance, this allusion in Isa 4:2–6 subtly presents a link between the "eschatological" Mount Zion and the exodus.

EXAMPLE 12.1e ▸ Isaiah 42 and 49

Criteria for detecting the intertextuality: same language, same theme

Direction of dependence: unclear

Scholars often identify in Isa 40–55 four specific oracles that describe a mysterious "servant" (42:1–13; 49:1–12; 50:4–11; 52:13–53:12). In the case of the first two passages, this thematic unity is reinforced by shared and synonymous expressions (see Table 12.3). The accumulation of these makes it clear that there is an intertextual relationship between these two passages.

Table 12.3: The Servant in Isaiah 42 and 49

Isaiah 42	Isaiah 49
"Here is **my servant**, whom I uphold, my chosen, *in whom my soul delights*" (v. 1)	"he said to me, 'You are **my servant**, Israel, *in whom I will be glorified.*'" (v. 3)
"the **coastlands** wait for his teaching" (v. 4)	"Listen to me, O **coastlands**" (v. 1)
"**I have given you as a covenant to the people,** a light to the nations" (v. 6)	"**I will give you as a light to the nations**" (v. 6) "**I have kept you and given you as a covenant to the people**" (v. 8)
"to **bring out the prisoners** from the dungeon, from the prison *those who sit in* **darkness**" (v. 7)	"saying to the **prisoners**, "Come out," to *those who are in* **darkness**, 'Show yourselves.'" (v. 9)

What about the direction of dependence? This seems difficult to determine, and some scholars believe that both passages are multilayered.[8] It may be that the influence was bidirectional.

At any rate, an interesting difference should be noted. While Isa 42 is related in the third-person singular, Isa 49 is written in the first-person singular. On a synchronic reading, therefore, one may say that while Isa 42 contains a description by God of his servant and the latter's mission, Isa 49 constitutes an appropriation by the servant of this commission.

EXAMPLE 12.1f   ▸   1 Kings 19 and Exodus 32–34

Criteria for detecting the intertextuality: same language, similar storyline

Criterion for determining the direction of dependence: presence of an element that is unexpected in the new context but typical in the source text

In 1 Kgs 19, Elijah feels depressed: despite his victory at Mount Carmel, which eliminates most of the prophets of Baal (1 Kgs 18), Jezebel's threat (18:1) means both that his religious reform will have little effect in Samaria and that he is in danger. So Elijah runs away; and the journey that he will make and the experience that he will undergo strongly recall an episode in the account of Moses' life:

---

8. Goldingay and Payne, *Commentary on Isaiah 44:24–55:13*, 211.

- In both cases, the events in question occur after the people have just undergone, at the instigation of a servant of God, a vigorous "reform" from their idolatry (Exod 32; 1 Kgs 18).

- Just as the people are fed miraculously by God in the desert for forty years, Elijah is fed by an angel so that he can survive during his journey in the desert for forty days.

- Like Moses (Exod 33:21), Elijah finds himself on a mountain, in a cave (1 Kgs 19:9), and the text of Kings makes sure to specify that this is Mount Horeb (v. 8), which establishes an obvious parallel.

- Both Moses and Elijah are beneficiaries of an exceptional theophany in which God "passes" before them and reveals something about himself (Exod 34:6; 1 Kgs 19:11). In Exod 34, this revelation is explicit: God himself proclaims his attributes (that he is merciful, slow to anger, etc.; Exod 34:6). In 1 Kgs 19, the revelation is implicit: the narrator states that God is not in the violent elements that pass before Elijah (the storm, earthquake, and fire); but when there is a "sound of sheer silence," the text does not state that God is not in it.

It is thus clear that a parallel is implicitly drawn between Moses and Elijah. While Elijah's journey to Horeb is quite unexpected, Moses' similar journey fits well in the narrative of Exodus, so the direction of dependence is also clear.

What is the *effect* of this comparison? On the one hand, it is positive for the characterization of Elijah, since he benefits from a theophany similar to the one that was given to Moses. On the other hand, the intertextual connection encourages the reader to compare the attitudes of these two leaders—and it turns out that they do not react in the same way when the people disappoint them. Despite the golden calf episode, Moses refuses God's proposal that he start a new people from Moses alone (Exod 32:9–14), even though he is the only one who did not give himself over to idolatry. By contrast, Elijah abandons his country, denounces to God the people who have betrayed the covenant, and sets himself up as the only faithful one (1 Kgs 19:10, 14)—though the text points to the existence of hundreds of prophets of the Lord (1 Kgs 18:4) and the Lord tells Elijah that he has kept for himself "seven thousand in Israel, all the knees that have not bowed to Baal" (19:18). In this sense, the comparison is unfavorable toward Elijah: it points to the fact that he has an incorrect understanding of the people's situation and his own. Furthermore, the motive for his despair is the fact that he is "no better than [his] ancestors" (19:4); in other words, he focuses his evaluation of the situation on his own achievements, a self-centered approach.

> **EXAMPLE 12.1g** ▸ Genesis 1 and 8–9

Criteria for detecting the intertextuality: same language, same storyline

No diachronic direction of dependence (same author), but A pictures a renewal of the situation in B

The account of the retreat of the flood waters in Gen 8–9 makes use of many expressions from the first creation account (Gen 1:1–2:3) and presents them in the same sequence (see Table 12.4). Since Gen 1 and the relevant verses in Gen 8–9 belong to the Priestly writing (P) (see the sidebar "Juxtaposition, Conflation, and Supplementation" in chapter 4), we are likely dealing with the work of the same redactor here. Thus, in studying the echoes of Gen 1 in Gen 8–9, there is little point in speaking, in diachronic terms, of a direction of dependence, except to note that this redactor wanted Gen 8–9 to echo Gen 1 rather than the other way around. The purpose of this echoing is to present the end of the flood and what follows as *a renewal of the creation*.

Table 12.4: Creation and Its Renewal in Genesis 1 and 8–9

Creation in Genesis 1	Renewal of the Creation in Genesis 8–9
"darkness covered the face of the deep, while a wind from God swept over the face of the waters" (1:2)	"God made a wind blow over the earth, . . . the fountains of the deep and the windows of the heavens were closed" (8:1–2)
"let the dry land appear" (1:9)	"the tops of the mountains appeared" (8:5)
"birds," "creeping things," "wild animals of the earth" (1:20–25)	"birds and animals and every creeping thing that creeps on the earth" (8:17–19)
Human beings as the "image of God" (1:26–27)	Human beings as the image of God (9:6)
God blesses them and says to them, "Be fruitful and multiply and fill the earth and subdue it and have dominion over the fish of the sea . . ." (1:28)	God blesses Noah and his sons and says to them, "Be fruitful and multiply and fill the earth. The fear and dread of you shall rest on every animal of the earth . . ." (9:1–2)
God tells the human beings what they can eat (1:29)	God tells the human beings what they can eat (9:3)

| EXAMPLE 12.1h | Genesis 3–4 and 9 |

Criterion for detecting the intertextuality: the storyline of A recapitulates the storyline of B

Criterion for determining the direction of dependence: A combines and recapitulates elements of B

The account of Noah's drunkenness that immediately follows the flood story combines aspects of Gen 3 and 4 (see Table 12.5). For one thing, Noah plays the role of a "new Adam." Then the story recapitulates, in a condensed form, the problems that were spread over two generations, that of Adam and that of his sons.

Because Gen 9 combines elements from Gen 3 and 4, it presupposes them. The traditional Documentary Hypothesis regards all these texts as belonging to the Yahwist (J). If you reason in the framework of this hypothesis, then the situation regarding direction of dependence is the same here as in the preceding example, but this time within J (rather than P). If you do not accept the existence of J, other possibilities exist, including Gen 9 being later than Gen 3–4.

What is the purpose of these intertextual connections? The point seems to be to show that after the flood, and in spite of the "reset" it represents, humanity still goes through the same steps as it has before, with a mixture of cultural development and problems.

Table 12.5: Adam and His Sons, Noah and His Sons

Adam in Genesis 3, Cain and Abel in Genesis 4	Noah and His Sons in Genesis 9
"the Lord God formed man from the dust of the ground" (2:7)	Noah becomes a "man of the soil" (9:20)
"the Lord God planted a garden in Eden, in the east, and there he put the man . . . to till it and keep it" (2:8, 15)	Noah "was the first to plant a vineyard" (9:20)
"she took of its fruit and ate, . . . he ate" (3:6)	"He drank some of the wine" (9:21)
Adam and Eve are embarrassed by their nakedness	Noah's nakedness is problematic (9:22–23)
They make loincloths for themselves (3:7) God dresses them in garments of skin (3:21)	Shem and Japheth cover their father with a garment (9:23)

"the eyes of both were opened, and they knew that they were naked" (3:7)	"When Noah awoke from his wine and knew what his youngest son had done to him, . . ." (9:24)
Cain is cursed (4:11)	Canaan is cursed (9:25)

EXAMPLE 12.1i ▶ Isaiah 2:1–4 and 4:2–6

Criteria for detecting the intertextuality: same language, same theme, parallels within a literary structure

Direction of dependence: not pertinent

We have already seen that when Isa 4:2–6 describes the Lord dwelling among his people on the purified Mount Zion, this alludes to his presence among his people during their flight from Egypt (v. 5 // Exod 13:21–22). Isaiah 4:2–6 is parallel, within a concentric structure comprising Isa 1–5, to another oracle that also concerns Mount Zion (2:1–4):

   A Oracles against Judah and Jerusalem (1:1–31)

      B *Mount Zion* (2:1–4)

         C The humiliation of humans and of the people of Judah (2:5–3:12)

            D The Lord comes in judgment (3:13–15)

         C′ The humiliation of the women of Jerusalem (3:16–4:1)

      B′ *Mount Zion* (4:2–6)

   A′ Oracles against Judah (5:1–30)

Isaiah 2:1–4 describes Mount Zion as the place of origin of the Torah (which can mean either "instruction" or "law"), depicting the mountain as attracting all the nations who decide to come and learn the "ways of the Lord."

In this instance, the intertextual link has been created by a compiler who made 2:1–4 and 4:2–6 parallels in an overall structure, thus representing a special situation. In terms of language, these passages share little significant vocabulary beyond "mountain" and "Zion." Therefore, the question of literary dependence is not pertinent here.

Rather, the parallelism creates a fuller picture. We read in these two passages about two complementary aspects of the eschatological Mount Zion that echo two aspects of Mount Sinai: the latter was both the point at which the people arrived after the exodus (a journey in which they were accompanied by God's presence) (B′) and the place where the law was given (B). In a word, the eschatological Mount Zion serves as a sort of new Mount Sinai.

> **EXAMPLE 12.1j** ▸ **Exodus 20:24 and Deuteronomy 12:13–14**

Criteria for detecting the intertextuality: shared language, same theme

Criteria for determining the direction of dependence: reversal, adaptation to a new context

The so-called Covenant Code, which is found in Exod 20:22–23:33, opens with instructions about worship and in particular about the place where sacrifices must be offered in order to be legitimate:

> You need make for me only an altar of earth and sacrifice on it your burnt offerings [עֹלֹתֶיךָ] and your offerings of well-being, your sheep and your oxen; in every place where I cause my name to be remembered [בְּכָל־הַמָּקוֹם אֲשֶׁר אַזְכִּיר אֶת־שְׁמִי] I will come to you and bless you. (Exod 20:24)

The Deuteronomic Code (Deut 12–26) opens with a law on the same subject, but it is radically different. The principle involved is repeated several times in Deut 12; vv. 13–14 can be taken as an illustration:

> Take care that you do not offer your burnt offerings [עֹלֹתֶיךָ] at any place you happen to see [בְּכָל־מָקוֹם אֲשֶׁר תִּרְאֶה]. But only at the place that the Lord will choose [כִּי אִם־בַּמָּקוֹם אֲשֶׁר־יִבְחַר יְהוָה] in one of your tribes—there you shall offer your burnt offerings [עֹלֹתֶיךָ], and there you shall do everything I command you. (Deut 12:13–14)

Whereas the Covenant Code allows for the building and use of altars in various places in the country, the Deuteronomic Code restricts the possibility for this activity to one place (thus promoting cult centralization). Therefore, these texts take radically different stances on a matter that was crucial in ancient Israelite society. They also share some language, especially in their variations on the syntactical construction "place that" (מָקוֹם אֲשֶׁר): there is an echo between "in every place where" (בְּכָל־הַמָּקוֹם אֲשֶׁר) in Exod 20 and the expressions "(not) in any place that" (בְּכָל־מָקוֹם אֲשֶׁר) and "only at the place that" (כִּי אִם־בַּמָּקוֹם אֲשֶׁר) in Deut 12. Bernard Levinson argues that Deut 12:14 reverses the elements of Exod 20:24 (a case of "inverted quotation"):[9]

> "[A] you shall sacrifice upon it your burnt offerings ... [B] in every place where ..." (Exod 20:24)

> "[B'] in the place which ... [A'] you shall offer your burnt offerings" (Deut 12:14)

---

9. Bernard M. Levinson, *Deuteronomy and the Hermeneutics of Legal Innovation* (New York: Oxford University Press, 1998), 35.

These thematic and formal elements, together with the fact that the rest of both codes often deal with similar topics, indicate that Exod 20:23–24 and Deut 12:13–14 do not just happen to treat the same subject independently; there is an intertextual link between them.

What about the direction of dependence? Two reasons lead most scholars to conclude that the altar law in Deut 12 is a modification of the altar law in Exod 20, and more generally that the Deuteronomic Code is a rewriting of the Covenant Code.

First, it is clear, both from biblical texts and from archaeology, that worship sites existed in various places in Israel and Judah during most or all of the monarchic period. The idea of cult centralization seems to have been a relatively late innovation, one that (in light of 2 Kgs 23) scholars generally situate in the time of Josiah; others, however, believe that it had earlier roots in the time of Hezekiah, while still others doubt the historicity of the cult reforms the texts attribute to both kings. The point is that, in contrast to the reality of a multiplicity of worship sites (a situation referred to in Exod 20), cult centralization is a secondary idea (promoted by Deut 12).

Second, a number of laws in the rest of the Deuteronomic Code can be read as an *adaptation* of laws from the Covenant Code to the new context marked by centralization. What remains a subject of debate among scholars is whether the Deuteronomic Code was meant to replace (and displace) the Covenant Code, as Levinson argues, or to stand alongside it as an updated supplement, as Hindy Najman thinks.[10]

12.2 THE READER-ORIENTED APPROACH: METHOD AND EXAMPLES

Let us now turn to the other approach to intertextuality. In a sense, the method in the reader-oriented approach seems less demanding than in the author-oriented one, because you do not need to establish that there was an intention to create a connection between two texts. Rather, you simply have to find some common trait(s) they share that will serve as a basis for setting the texts in dialogue with each other. Likewise, you do not have to determine a direction of dependence, though you may want to explore what happens when one reads the texts in a certain sequence. However, while in the reader-oriented approach you do not have the same burden of proof as in the author-oriented approach, you do need to be more creative in exploring the potentialities of the conversation you are initiating. Here are the steps you can follow:

---

10. Levinson, *Deuteronomy and the Hermeneutics of Legal Innovation*, 144–57; Najman, *Seconding Sinai*, 22–46.

Ⓐ Find some common trait(s) the texts share.

Ⓑ *[optional]* Choose a direction of reading.

Ⓒ Determine the outcomes of the dialogue.

Let's look at some examples:

EXAMPLE 12.2a ▸ Nahum and Jonah

We have already seen, in the introduction to this chapter, that Nahum and Jonah both deal with the fate of Nineveh and can thus be compared to each other. The prophet Nahum seems to await the destruction of the city as just retribution from the Lord; similarly, the book of Jonah features a prophet who does not want the Lord to spare the city from destruction. But the latter book is a satire that ridicules this attitude. At the same time, the situation is not exactly the same in the two books, since there is no question in Nahum that Nineveh might be willing to repent of her treatment of other nations. Or perhaps it is the very fact that such a possibility is not raised that is telling. What is certain is that allowing these two books to enter into a dialogue with each other immediately raises some interesting questions about what God wants, and what we want, to happen to oppressive powers.

Both books also contain statements about the Lord that include the same expression: in Jonah 4:2, the prophet says, "I knew that you are a God gracious and merciful, *slow to anger* [אֶרֶךְ אַפַּיִם], abounding in steadfast love, and relenting from punishment"; and Nah 1:3 declares that "the Lord is *slow to anger* [אֶרֶךְ אַפַּיִם] but great in power, and the Lord will by no means clear the guilty." A major difference here is that only Jonah mentions the Lord's mercifulness and reluctance to punish, whereas Nahum mitigates this notion by immediately adding that the Lord will not "clear the guilty."

There is more. As Hyun Chul Paul Kim notes, Jonah 4:2 is very similar to Joel 2:13, which states that "the Lord . . . is *gracious and merciful, slow to anger, abounding in steadfast love*, and *relenting from punishment*." And Nah 1:2–3 can be compared to the so-called "credo formula" that one finds in Exod 34:6–7:

> The Lord, the Lord,
> a God *merciful and gracious, slow to anger,*
> and *abounding in steadfast love* and faithfulness,
> keeping steadfast love for the thousandth generation,
> forgiving iniquity and transgression and sin,
> yet *by no means clearing the guilty*.

Micah 7:18–20 can also be brought into the conversation:

> Who is a God like you, pardoning iniquity
> and passing over the transgression
> of the remnant of his possession?
> He does not retain his anger forever
> because he delights in showing steadfast love.

The sequence in which one reads these texts creates different sorts of echoes. As Kim notes:

> If we employ a sequential reading of these books, Jonah reacts to Joel, whereas Nahum reacts to Micah and other preceding books. But if we follow the order of the LXX, both Jonah and Nahum are addressing Micah and Joel; in consequence, Jonah and Nahum, put right next to each other, are in dialogue. In either canonical order, the mutual comparison between Jonah and Nahum becomes legitimate by this common formula [viz., Exod 34:6–7].[11]

EXAMPLE 12.2b ▸ Deuteronomy 23:3 [4] and Nehemiah 9–10

Deuteronomy contains the following prohibition concerning who has the right to gain access to Israelite worship: "No Ammonite or Moabite shall come into the assembly of the LORD even to the tenth generation. None of their descendants shall come into the assembly of the LORD forever" (Deut 23:3 [4]). But this verse does not exhaust all that the Hebrew Bible has to say on these neighbors of Israel. The book of Ruth is entirely dedicated to the conversion and "redemption" of a Moabitess who will from then on belong to God's people and who will even become an ancestor of King David!

Ruth can also be put into dialogue with Ezra-Nehemiah, especially the story in which some Judeans repudiate their wives because of their foreign origins (Neh 9–10). By contrast, the book of Ruth implicitly praises Boaz, a man from Bethlehem, for marrying Ruth, a foreign woman. Some scholars go so far as to argue that Ruth was written as a reply to Ezra-Nehemiah. This cannot be proven, but regardless of whether or not it is the case, it is worth comparing these two perspectives.

---

11. Hyun Chul Paul Kim, "Jonah Read Intertextually," *JBL* 126 (2007): 497–528, with quotation on 509.

> **EXAMPLE 12.2c ▸ Ruth**
>
> Depending on the textual (and religious) tradition one follows, the book of Ruth is located in different places in the sequence of books of the Bible. In the Septuagint (see, notably, Codex Vaticanus), Ruth appears right after Judges. This makes sense, since the very first verse of Ruth situates its story "in the days when the judges ruled."
>
> In the Jewish canon, however, Ruth is part of a set of five books called the Megilloth, and it often appears right after Proverbs (e.g., in the Leningrad Codex). The latter book ends with a poem praising the "woman of strength" (אֵשֶׁת־חַיִל), which is translated as "capable wife" in the NRSVue and in the NJPS (Prov 31:10). Against this background, it is fascinating to see that Boaz tells Ruth that she is a "capable wife" (אֵשֶׁת־חַיִל) in Ruth 3:11 ("worthy woman" in the NRSVue, but this is the same Hebrew expression as in Prov 31:10). This creates an echo from Proverbs to Ruth.

Exercises for Chapter 12

Exercise A

In Song 7:10 [11], the Shulammite states: "I am my beloved's, and *his desire is for me* [וְעָלַי תְּשׁוּקָתוֹ]." Two verses in another biblical book have clauses that are very similar to the italicized clause here, and it may be that one of these verses in particular has an intertextual link to this verse from Song of Songs. Find this verse. In your view, is there a genuine intertextual link? If so, what is the direction of dependence, and what is the purpose of this link?

Exercise B

It is not difficult to find allusions to the exodus in Isa 11:11–16. Draw up a list of these allusions. Do they create intertextual links with particular passages in the book of Exodus? If so, what is the direction of dependence, and what is the purpose of these links?

Exercise C

In Joel 3:10 [4:10], we read: "Beat your plowshares into swords and your pruning hooks into spears." There are two other passages in the Bible that contain comparable statements about plowshares/swords and hooks/spears, though the idea in those texts is not the same as it is here. Find them and determine whether it is possible to speak of intertextual links between these passages and Joel 3:10 [4:10]. If it is, what would be the direction of dependence, and what would be the purpose of both the allusions and the changes the alluding texts have made to the source text?

Exercise D

Generally speaking, the book of Joel is filled with intertextual links connecting it to passages in other biblical books. Draw up a list of these links. Do you find it more likely that these books have all borrowed expressions from Joel or that Joel has collected them from earlier writings? What conclusions would you draw in terms of the relative dating of these books?

Exercise E

Find allusions in 2 Chr 20 to passages from Exodus. What is the direction of dependence, and what is the purpose of these intertextual links?

Exercise F

The books of Esther and Judith tell stories of women confronted with imperial structures. Put these books into dialogue with each other by comparing the attitudes of these two characters—especially the ones these books highlight and perhaps encourage.

PART THREE

THE READER IN FRONT OF THE TEXT

CHAPTER 13

RECEPTION

OVERVIEW

The term "reception" refers to the ways in which the text has been read, interpreted, represented (in images or music, for instance), or otherwise used through the centuries—or, conversely, how the text has influenced people. It is a truism to say that the Bible has had a huge influence over world history during the last two millennia and that it has been subjected to innumerable interpretations. But this does not mean that all biblical scholars are fully aware of the ramifications of this fact for exegesis. They are numerous and can directly impact one's undertakings.

First, exploring the reception history of a text allows you to give credit to interpreters from past centuries who put forward a given interpretation well before modern commentators rediscovered it. Indeed, many exegetes today propose hypotheses without realizing that they were already defended centuries ago, by Jewish exegetes or by the church fathers. The study of reception also enables you to discover interpretations that are now forgotten. To make things even more complicated (and also more interesting), we are influenced by past interpretations, even when we are under the illusion of starting over. The false idea of the complete newness of our own ideas, combined with a disdain for past interpretations, constitutes what Régis Burnet calls the "double illusion of the *tabula rasa*."[1]

Second, as Burnet has also demonstrated with regard to the New Testament, taking into account past interpretations, especially those from the remote past, broadens our perspective. Studying a text's reception history may thus help us to take a step back, identify prejudices in interpretations that are well received today, and find out about the origins of these prejudices and correct them.[2]

---

1. Régis Burnet, *Exegesis and History of Reception: Reading the New Testament Today with the Readers of the Past*, WUNT 455 (Tübingen: Mohr Siebeck, 2021), 25–36.
2. Burnet, *Exegesis and History of Reception*, 75–99.

Third, the study of reception often reveals that the interpretation of a text has changed over the centuries on the basis of the varying concerns, beliefs, and preconceptions of the interpreters. This correlation hints at the *historicity of interpretation*, that is, its *situatedness*. And this, in turn, points to our own hermeneutical situatedness. Whether we realize it or not, we think and interpret within a paradigm—i.e., a cultural, intellectual, and often religious framework—that is specific to our time. Moreover, we make personal use of this paradigm in light of our individual experience.

Fourth, reception is not just about the "posterity" of the texts; it is linked to their very nature. The reception history of the books that comprise the Hebrew Bible did not start when the canon was closed. Within the Hebrew Bible itself, we already find instances of reception of biblical passages. For example, we saw in the previous chapter that the famous declaration of the Lord about himself in Exod 34:6–7 ("The Lord, the Lord, a God *merciful and gracious, slow to anger* . . .") is reused in a number of the Minor Prophets (Jonah 4:2; Nah 1:2–3; etc.). What we have previously called "inner-biblical exegesis" can also be seen as a reception phenomenon. To take another example, Chronicles is basically a rewriting of Samuel and Kings. In addition, textual criticism and compositional criticism show that even within a pericope, you may find interpretive additions or other changes. In fact, interpretation belongs to the very nature of the Bible. Reception starts within the biblical texts themselves.

Indeed, it would be misguided to think of interpretation as a task that is purely "exterior" to the text. A neat distinction between a self-contained text and its inherent meaning, on the one hand, and its interpretation on the other, proves to be an illusion. The development of hermeneutical studies, especially since the mid-twentieth century, has made it increasingly clear that texts are "open" and require the participation of the reader. No narrative tells the reader everything that happens in the story, for instance. The reader has to supply details: he or she has to imagine what happened between two events. For example, as readers, we must infer that a character has moved from one place to another because a new scene situates this character in a different place; we have to imagine why a character behaves in a certain way; and so forth. As Umberto Eco has pointed out, all narratives contain many gaps like these that require the participation of the reader[3]—and this is only the most obvious situation. Biblical texts, like all texts, are also filled with equivocal statements, and the reader, whether he or she is aware of it or not, constantly makes decisions about the meaning of such statements. To put it another way, texts inherently contain some degree of indetermination. This is partly due to the fact that human language is always, to some degree, indeterminate, and also partly due to the fact that writers enjoy playing on words and using double entendres. We have encountered examples of indetermination when examining Song 2:8–17 (Example 10.4c).

Because the reader has to participate, he or she cannot avoid projecting presuppositions onto the text. In fact, the reader always comes to the text with his or her

---

3. Umberto Eco, *The Role of the Reader: Explorations in the Semiotics of Texts* (Bloomington: Indiana University Press, 1979).

own preconceptions and prejudices. Hans-Georg Gadamer has shown that this inevitable reality should not be seen as a misfortune to be fought against in a tireless war against prejudice, but as an opportunity. Preconceptions are not only inevitable, they are necessary to interpretation, in the same way that many people cannot read a text without glasses. This is a cognitive reality. You have to start somewhere; you come to the text with preconceived ideas and assumptions. For example, when we open a Bible to Isa 19, it is natural to think that this chapter is an "oracle *against* Egypt" because it appears in a section (Isa 13–23) that is traditionally called "oracles against the nations." The first half of the chapter confirms this idea, but then, when we read positive pronouncements about Egypt in the second half, we have to revise our conclusion; in the end, this chapter looks like an "oracle *about* a nation." What matters is being able to revise our preconceptions by confronting them with the text.

Needless to say, the literature relevant to the study of the reception of the Hebrew Bible stretches over vast periods, not to mention the Bible's reception in music, the visual arts, and other fields. The main challenge here is to know where to look for information. Accordingly, this chapter will provide you with tips and will indicate resources to help you find your way through the maze of reception history.

Before doing so, however, it should be noted that the reception history of the Hebrew Bible includes texts that have a special authority for religious readers. Thus, for Christians, the New Testament is not just one corpus among others in the reception history; it is the second part of the biblical canon. Similarly, in Judaism the Talmud has a very high degree of authority. For Jews and Christians, the reception of a biblical text within the biblical canon has a special status; hence the notion of *canonical interpretation*. Since my desire is that this handbook will be useful for readers of any persuasion—Jewish or Christian or anything else, religious or not—I have decided not to include a separate discussion on canonical interpretation that would privilege one corpus (e.g., the New Testament) over another, but rather to discuss reception as an overarching category. If the biblical canon has a special importance for you, you will easily be able to take this into account, and to do so according to the particular way in which you define the canon.

In what follows, I will assume that you are studying a single passage in the Hebrew Bible. If you are considering the reception of a figure (e.g., Solomon), you may have to study the reception of the *passages* (plural) in which he or she appears. In addition, given the limited framework of this handbook, I will focus on reception of the biblical text in literature, even though—as already noted—reception history encompasses music, the visual arts, and so forth as well.

Here are some steps you can follow:

> ❶ CONSULT PUBLICATIONS THAT PROVIDE **OVERVIEWS OF THE RECEPTION HISTORY** OF THE HEBREW BIBLE PASSAGE YOU ARE STUDYING.
>
> ❷ CONSULT THE **SCRIPTURAL INDEX OF A CORPUS** TO FIND OUT WHETHER—AND IF SO, WHERE—THE HEBREW BIBLE PASSAGE IS USED IN THAT CORPUS.

❸ **READ** THE RELEVANT TEXTS IN THE RECEPTION CORPUS; **CHECK WHETHER THE HEBREW BIBLE PASSAGE IS REALLY USED** IN THEM, AND **SELECT THE MOST IMPORTANT CASES**.

❹ FOR EACH EXAMPLE, CHECK THE **FORM OF THE HEBREW BIBLE PASSAGE THAT THE INTERPRETING TEXT HAS USED** (FOR INSTANCE, DOES THE INTERPRETER READ OR QUOTE THE MT, THE LXX, OR ANOTHER TEXT?).

❺ DETERMINE WHAT **KIND OF USE** THE INTERPRETING TEXT HAS MADE OF THE HEBREW BIBLE PASSAGE (DOES IT SERVE AS A PROOF TEXT, AS AN ILLUSTRATION, ETC.?).

❻ **CONSIDER THE USE AGAINST THE BACKDROP OF PAST AND CONTEMPORARY INTERPRETATIONS**, WHICH MAY HELP YOU CONTEXTUALIZE THIS USE AND (POSSIBLY) ASSESS ITS DEGREE OF ORIGINALITY.

I will now review these steps, providing useful bibliographical resources along the way; then, in this chapter's final section, I will provide a pair of detailed examples.

13.1 CONSULT OVERVIEWS OF THE RECEPTION HISTORY

Nowadays, a variety of publications exist that survey the reception history of a passage or a figure. Of course, these works only give a general panorama that you will have to refine if you want to carry out a more detailed study.

A. Chapter-by-Chapter Surveys

The Blackwell Bible Commentaries (BBC) series provides, for each chapter of a biblical book, a survey of the reception history. For instance:

- John F. A. Sawyer, *Isaiah through the Centuries*, BBC (Hoboken, NJ: Wiley-Blackwell, 2018).

Some commentaries in other series may include sections about reception history. For example:

- Carol A. Newsom, with Brennan W. Breed, *Daniel*, OTL (Louisville: Westminster John Knox, 2014).

B. Studies of the Use of the Hebrew Bible in New Testament Books

Some resources take New Testament books as their starting point and examine any quotations of or allusions to texts from the Hebrew Bible that they contain. The following book contains chapters on each New Testament book:

- G. K. Beale and D. A. Carson, eds., *Commentary on the New Testament Use of the Old Testament* (Grand Rapids: Baker Academic, 2007).

Similarly, the New Testament and the Scriptures of Israel series includes collections of essays on the use of the Hebrew Bible in New Testament books. For instance:

- Maarten J. J. Menken and Steven Moyise, eds., *The Psalms in the New Testament*, NTSI (London: T&T Clark, 2004).

C. Anthologies

The following series offers, for each biblical book, a sort of pericope-by-pericope commentary made up of selections of texts of the church fathers (in English translation):

- ACCS = Ancient Christian Commentary on Scripture (general editor: Thomas C. Oden) (Downers Grove, IL: InterVarsity Press).

For medieval Christian interpreters:

- BMT = The Bible in Medieval Tradition (general editors: H. Lawrence Bond, Philip Krey, and Thomas Ryan) (Grand Rapids: Eerdmans).

For the Reformers:

- RCS = Reformation Commentary on Scripture (general editor: Timothy F. George) (Downers Grove, IL: InterVarsity Press).

D. Survey the Reception History of a Passage or Figure

Some collected volumes are dedicated to an interdisciplinary overview of the interpretation of a text through the ages. This is the aim of the series Themes in Biblical Narrative. Here is an example of a book on the reception of a specific text:

- George H. van Kooten, ed., *The Creation of Heaven and Earth: Reinterpretations of Genesis 1 in the Context of Judaism, Ancient Philosophy, Christianity, and Modern Physics*, TBN 8 (Leiden: Brill, 2005).

Here is an example of a book dealing with a biblical figure:

- George H. van Kooten and Jacques van Ruiten, eds., *The Prestige of the Pagan Prophet Balaam in Judaism, Early Christianity and Islam*, TBN 11 (Leiden: Brill, 2008).

E. Encyclopedia

In addition to the usual information that one finds in an encyclopedia, the following ambitious work provides surveys of the reception history of each biblical book, and of the most important biblical characters, in Judaism, Christianity, Islam, the visual arts, and music:

- EBR = Hans-Josef Klauck et al., eds., *Encyclopedia of the Bible and Its Reception* (Berlin: de Gruyter, 2009–).

F. Study Bible

The project *BEST = Bible in Its Traditions, which is being developed both online and in printed volumes, offers translations of the main textual witnesses and detailed notes on a large variety of topics (e.g., philology, textual criticism, narrative criticism), including the reception history of the text. Some volumes are in French (the acronymn BEST derives from the French title of the series, La Bible en ses traditions), but the following one exists in English:

- Eugen J. Pentiuc, Gad Barnea, Étienne Méténier, Łukasz Popko, et al., *Hosea: The Word of the Lord Happened to Hosea*, BEST 3 (Leuven: Peeters, 2017).

G. Others

Finally, the following collected volume includes a large variety of chapters, some offering a general view of the reception of biblical books, others concentrating on the text's reception in ancient periods (for example, the reception of Genesis in Gnosticism) or in modern periods (for example, the use of the Bible in the songs of Bob Dylan):

- Michael Lieb, Emma Mason, Jonathan Roberts, and Christopher Rowland, eds., *The Oxford Handbook of the Reception History of the Bible* (Oxford: Oxford University Press, 2011).

13.2 CONSULT THE SCRIPTURAL INDEX OF A CORPUS

While indexes are not the most enjoyable parts of books, they prove very helpful if you want to find the places where a passage from the Hebrew Bible is quoted or alluded to in a specific corpus. Such corpora may include books in the Hebrew Bible that are later than the one in which your passage appears, Second Temple literature, the New Testament, rabbinic literature, the writings of the church fathers, the writings of medieval Jewish and Christian interpreters, Muslim interpretations, and more.

A. Second Temple Literature

The following book is extremely helpful, since it enables you to check, for each book of the Hebrew Bible, which verses are quoted or alluded to, and where, in Second Temple literature (including the Dead Sea Scrolls):

- Armin Lange and Matthias Weigold, *Biblical Quotations and Allusions in Second Temple Jewish Literature*, JAJSup 5 (Göttingen: Vandenhoeck & Ruprecht, 2011). This book also contains indexes that list, for each Second Temple text, the quotations and allusions it contains, in the order in which they occur in it—thus providing you with a list of all the references to Hebrew Bible passages in, say, Jubilees.

B. New Testament

The two main critical editions of the New Testament contain an index called "*Loci citati vel allegati*" that lists quotations of and allusions to texts from the Hebrew Bible:

- NA28 (i.e., Nestle-Aland, 28th edition) = Barbara and Kurt Aland, Johannes Karavidopoulos, Carlo M. Martini, and Bruce M. Metzger, eds., *Novum Testamentum Graece*, 28th ed. (Stuttgart: Deutsche Bibelgesellschaft, 2012).

- UBS5 (i.e., United Bible Societies, 5th edition) = Barbara and Kurt Aland, Johannes Karavidopoulos, Carlo M. Martini, and Bruce M. Metzger, eds., *The Greek New Testament*, 5th ed. (Stuttgart: Deutsche Bibelgesellschaft, 2014).

C. Church Fathers

Patristic literature contains innumerable quotations of and allusions to the Hebrew Bible. The following index is very helpful:

- Centre d'analyse et de documentation patristique, *Biblia Patristica: Index des citations et allusions bibliques dans la littérature patristique*, 7 vols. (Paris: Editions du CNRS, 1986–2000). Now replaced by an online version: *Biblindex.

Another helpful resource (if you read French) is the series "La Bible d'Alexandrie" (Paris: Cerf). It is an annotated translation of the books of the Septuagint, and the notes contain much information about patristic reception of the texts.

D. Apocryphal Literature

The following book contains lists of apocryphal texts that are inspired by particular biblical figures. Specifically, it provides an inventory of the Jewish and Christian apocryphal texts and classifies them according to the figure(s) from the Hebrew Bible they evoke or with whom they are connected in some way (for example, the chapter on Abraham, Isaac, and Jacob includes works like the *Testament of Abraham* and the *Apocryphon of Loth*):

- Jean-Claude Haelewyck, *Clavis Apocryphorum Veteris Testamenti*, Corpus Christianorum (Turnhout: Brepols, 1998).

E. Rabbinic Literature

Like the patristic corpus, rabbinic literature contains innumerable references to the Hebrew Bible, which makes the following resource very helpful:

- Caleb T. Friedeman, ed., *A Scripture Index to Rabbinic Literature* (Peabody, MA: Hendrickson Academic, 2021).

To get an idea of the various ways in which a biblical episode was elaborated in ancient Jewish traditions, you can also consult the following work. It follows the sequence of the biblical chronology and combines Jewish traditions in a continuous paraphrase and synthesis. While this combination may be confusing, the notes at the end of each volume provide references to the texts containing the relevant Jewish traditions that were combined in the continuous paraphrase:

- Louis Ginzberg, *Legends of the Jews*, trans. Henrietta Szold and Paul Radin, 2nd ed., 2 vols. (Philadelphia: Jewish Publication Society of America, 2003; original German edition, in seven volumes, 1909–38).

13.3 READ THE TEXTS AND CHECK WHETHER THE HEBREW BIBLE PASSAGE IS REALLY USED IN THEM

While the indexes mentioned above are very helpful, works of this kind may include references to places in which it is *possible*, but not certain, that the Hebrew Bible passage in view has been used. Therefore, you need to check this by reading the relevant sections of the works in question. In cases where it is difficult to determine whether there is indeed an allusion, you can have recourse to the same criteria that are helpful for studying intertextuality (see chapter 12).

For discussions of the criteria scholars use to make sure that a New Testament text is in fact alluding to a Hebrew Bible passage, see:

- David Allen, "The Use of Criteria: The State of the Question," in *Methodology in the Use of the Old Testament in the New: Context and Criteria*, ed. David Allen and Steve Smith, LNTS 579 (London: T&T Clark, 2019), 129–41.

- Steve Smith, "The Use of Criteria: A Proposal from Relevance Theory," in *Methodology in the Use of the Old Testament in the New: Context and Criteria*, ed. David Allen and Steve Smith, LNTS 579 (London: T&T Clark, 2019), 142–54.

Now, the practical question is: where can I find a good translation or edition of the literary work that (perhaps) refers to the part of the Hebrew Bible I am studying? Here are a few recommendations:

A. Second Temple Literature as a Whole

In the following excellent volumes, you will find translations of most of the Jewish literary works written during the Second Temple period. The introductions are also very helpful, and they provide bibliographical references for editions and studies:

- Louis H. Feldman, James L. Kugel, and Lawrence H. Schiffman, eds., *Outside the Bible: Ancient Jewish Writings Related to Scripture*, 3 vols. (Philadelphia: Jewish Publication Society of America, 2013).

The work just cited only contains excerpts of some of the writings of Philo and Josephus (which are voluminous). For complete translations (with commentary) of the writings of these two authors, see:

- Steve Mason, ed., *Flavius Josephus: Translation and Commentary*, 10 vols. (Leiden: Brill, 1999–). Most of the volumes have already been published.

- Philo of Alexandria Commentary Series (general editor: Gregory E. Sterling) (Leiden: Brill, 2001–).

The website *Sefaria: A Living Library of Torah is a treasure that contains many translations and transcriptions of works from the Second Temple period (and later periods too).

B. The (Nonbiblical) Dead Sea Scrolls in Particular

- Florentino García Martínez and Eibert J. C. Tigchelaar, *The Dead Sea Scrolls Study Edition*, 2 vols. (Leiden: Brill, 1997–98). A bilingual edition of the nonbiblical scrolls.

- Florentino García Martínez, *The Dead Sea Scrolls Translated: The Qumran Texts in English*, trans. Wilfred G. E. Watson (Leiden: Brill, 1994). A one-volume English translation of the nonbiblical scrolls.

- Donald W. Parry and Emanuel Tov, eds., *The Dead Sea Scrolls Reader*, 6 vols. (Leiden: Brill, 2004–5). A bilingual edition of the nonbiblical scrolls, grouped according to literary genre.

C. Rabbinic Literature and Medieval Jewish Interpreters

The website *Sefaria: A Living Library of Torah contains translations of rabbinic interpreters (the Talmud, midrashim, etc.) and medieval interpreters. The website *Online Responsa Project, which has been developed by Bar-Ilan University, provides the Hebrew text of (notably) the Talmud and early Jewish commentaries.

The *Miqra'ot Gedolot* (often called the "Rabbinic Bible") combines the commentaries (or questions) of the most prominent medieval interpreters: Abarbanel, Rashi, Rashbam, Ibn Ezra, Nahmanides, and Kimhi. For the Pentateuch, an English translation exists:

- Michael Carasik, *The Commentator's Bible: The Rubin JPS Miqra'ot Gedolot*, 5 vols. (Philadelphia: Jewish Publication Society of America, 2005–18).

In the JPS Bible Commentary series, some volumes take rabbinic and medieval Jewish interpreters into account more than others; a notable example of a volume that does so is:

- Michael Fishbane, *Song of Songs: The Traditional Hebrew Text with the New JPS Translation*, JPS Bible Commentary (Philadelphia: Jewish Publication Society of America, 2015).

D. Church Fathers

The website *Early Christian Writings contains English translations of the works of many church fathers, as does the website *Christian Classics Ethereal Library, which also includes later Christian authors. These sites are particularly popular among students, as they provide free and easily accessible translations. Be careful, however: most of the translations date back to the nineteenth century and are of uneven quality. It is better to consult the more recent translations found in the following series:

- Oxford Early Christian Texts (Oxford: Clarendon).
- Ancient Christian Writers Series (New York: Paulist).
- The Fathers of the Church (Washington, DC: Catholic University of America Press).

- Library of Christian Classics (London: SCM).

- Loeb Classical Library (Cambridge, MA: Harvard University Press). This is the standard series providing Greek or Latin texts with English translation; it includes only a few Christian authors.

- Message of the Fathers of the Church (Collegeville, MN: Liturgical Press). Provides a selection of important passages on various themes.

- Sources chrétiennes (Paris: Cerf). The most important collection of editions and translations in a modern language (French), comprising over six hundred volumes.

13.4 CHECK THE FORM OF THE HEBREW BIBLE PASSAGE THAT THE INTERPRETING TEXT HAS USED

As we saw in chapter 2, differences between the textual witnesses of the Hebrew Bible can prompt different interpretations. Therefore, it is important to know which form of the text the interpreter you are reading used. For instance, most church fathers quote the Septuagint. Therefore, you should not refer to the MT, but to the Septuagint, to understand their interpretations of the text. Conversely, Jewish interpreters used the MT.

13.5 DETERMINE WHAT KIND OF USE THE INTERPRETING TEXT HAS MADE OF THE HEBREW BIBLE PASSAGE

To analyze a literary work's use of the Hebrew Bible, you need to ask a number of questions. In particular, you may ask:

- Is the source text the starting point for a new reflection, or is it used to support a preexisting argument or to illustrate a point?

- Is the idea contained in the source text accepted or debated in the quoting or alluding text?

- Does the interpreter refer only to the source text he is quoting or alluding to, or does he also allude to this source text's literary context?

13.6 CONSIDER THE USE AGAINST THE BACKDROP OF PAST AND CONTEMPORARY INTERPRETATIONS

This step may entail two different tasks:

- Situate the interpretation within the context of **interpretive methods** that were in use at the time when the quoting or alluding text was written. This may help you understand the reasoning that underlies the analysis of the text.
- Situate the interpretation in the history of **interpretive traditions**. This may help you determine whether the author is putting forth an original view or is merely taking up an existing interpretation.

To find out about the interpretive methods that were in use in a given period, you can read an introduction devoted to that period. For example, if you are examining the reception of a Hebrew Bible passage in the Dead Sea Scrolls, it is worth learning more about the modes of interpretation that were practiced when they were written; to do so, you can turn to the following book:

- Matthias Henze, ed., *A Companion to Biblical Interpretation in Early Judaism* (Grand Rapids: Eerdmans, 2012). Includes chapters on inner-biblical exegesis, rewritten Scripture, Qumran literature, apocalyptic literature and testaments, wisdom literature, and Hellenistic Judaism.

If you want to learn more about the Jewish interpretation of the Hebrew Bible in the midrashim, see:

- Jacob Neusner and Alan J. Avery-Peck, eds., *Encyclopedia of Midrash: Biblical Interpretation in Formative Judaism*, 2 vols. (Leiden: Brill, 2005).

To take another illustration, during the Middle Ages, both Jews and Christians interpreted the Bible through the lenses of four "senses" (although some of them focused on one sense). In Judaism, these were *peshat* (the plain sense, based on grammar and context), *remez* (personal, spiritual, or philosophical signification), *derash* (the communal and theological signification in the context of the whole Hebrew Bible), and *sod* (metaphysical and mystical import). The widely used acronym PaRDeS (pronounced *par-**dase***) helps one remember these steps. For their part, medieval Christians distinguished between literal, allegorical, tropological (i.e., moral), and anagogical (i.e., mystical) senses. If you are studying the reception of a Hebrew Bible passage in the writings of medieval exegetes, you may find it helpful to learn more about these categories.

A general resource that covers all the periods of biblical interpretation is the series *New Cambridge History of the Bible*:

- James Carleton Paget and Joachim Schafer, eds., *New Cambridge History of the Bible*, vol. 1, *From 600 to 1450* (Cambridge: Cambridge University Press, 2012).

- Richard Marsden and E. Ann Matter, eds., *New Cambridge History of the Bible*, vol. 2, *From the Beginnings to 600* (Cambridge: Cambridge University Press, 2013).

- Euan Cameron, ed., *New Cambridge History of the Bible*, vol. 3, *From 1450 to 1750* (Cambridge: Cambridge University Press, 2016).

- John Riches, ed., *New Cambridge History of the Bible*, vol. 4, *From 1750 to the Present* (Cambridge: Cambridge University Press, 2015).

It should be noted that the three volumes of the old version of this series (the *Cambridge History of the Bible*)—which were published in the 1970s and edited, respectively, by Peter R. Ackroyd and Christopher F. Evans, Geoffrey W. H. Lampe, and Stanley L. Greenslade—can still be useful, especially in the large syntheses they contain.

The following works are also commendable:

- Henning Graf Reventlow, *History of Biblical Interpretation*, 4 vols., RBS 50, 61, 62, 63 (Atlanta: SBL Press, 2009–10).

- Magne Sæbø, ed., *Hebrew Bible / Old Testament: The History of Its Interpretation*, 3 vols. (Göttingen: Vandenhoeck & Ruprecht, 1996–2015).

Finding out about the interpretations that were available in a given period is more difficult, since the answer to this depends on the passage you are studying. For this, you can use the resources mentioned in section 13.1 above.

13.7 EXAMPLES

For this chapter, it makes more sense to provide a few extended examples that encompass a variety of receptions, rather than many limited examples. The two case studies examined below illustrate different situations.

EXAMPLE 13.7a ▸ Some Jewish and Christian Interpretations of Song of Songs 2:8–17

We have already examined Song 2:8–17 from different perspectives in the preceding chapters. In this passage, the beloved comes to the home of the woman he loves and invites her to go outside. He highlights the return of the spring and the associated rebirth of nature. Let's have a look at the reception of this passage in Jewish and Christian interpretation.

Second Temple Literature

By looking at Lange and Weigold's index of quotations and allusions, we can see that there is no reference to Song 2 in Second Temple literature.[4]

New Testament

The index *Loci citati vel allegati* in the *Novum Testamentum Graece* does not refer to any verse in Song 2:8–17. We could stop the investigation here, but a quick search in a library catalogue or a search engine reveals that an article by Peter Tomson (published after the latest edition of the *Novum Testamentum Graece*) deals with allusions to Song of Songs in the New Testament.[5] Tomson points out two possible allusions to verses from our passage:

- In Mark 13:28–29, Jesus says: "From the fig tree learn its lesson: as soon as its branch becomes tender and puts forth its leaves, you know that summer is near. So also, when you see these things taking place, you know that he is near, at the very gates." Could the reference to the fig and to the summer that is near be an allusion to Song 2:10–13? This is possible, but Jesus could also be using standard imagery.

- In Rev 3:20, Jesus says: "Listen! I am standing at the door, knocking; if you hear my voice and open the door, I will come in and eat with you, and you with me." The situation is reminiscent of that of the beloved asking the woman to come in Song 2:8–17, and it is noteworthy that Rev 21:2 likens the church to a bride and Jesus to her husband. However, apart from the "voice" (φωνή) mentioned in Rev 3:20, this verse shares little language with Song 2:8–17. In addition, Jesus is offering to come in, whereas the beloved in Song 2 is asking the woman to come out. The image of somebody standing at a door and knocking is commonplace, so it does not necessarily come from Song of Songs.

In sum, these passages may reuse images from Song 2, but this is very uncertain.

---

4. Armin Lange and Matthias Weigold, *Biblical Quotations and Allusions in Second Temple Jewish Literature*, JAJSup 5 (Göttingen: Vandenhoeck & Ruprecht, 2011), 184.

5. Peter Tomson, "The Song of Songs in the Teachings of Jesus and the Development of the Exposition on the Song," *NTS* 61 (2015): 429–94.

Ancient Jewish Interpreters

Let us turn now to ancient Jewish reception. We are fortunate enough to have Michael Fishbane's commentary on Song of Songs in the JPS Bible Commentary series, which devotes a good deal of space to this subject. As Fishbane explains in his introduction and in an excursus, he follows the traditional Jewish distinction between four senses of the Bible: *peshat*, *derash*, *remez*, and *sod*. His comments on *peshat* correspond to philological analysis, while the other senses are infused with past Jewish interpretations and therefore are more relevant for my present purpose.

While it is not possible here to do justice to the richness of Jewish interpretations of this passage, I will try to give a small idea of this by focusing on the text's main motifs: the invitation of the beloved to the woman to come out (Song 2:10) and the return of the spring (2:11–13).

With regard to the call to "arise" and "come," Fishbane observes:[6]

- *Derash:* This corresponds to the calls given by Moses and Aaron to the Hebrew slaves (71).

- *Remez:* "The soul is called to arise and follow: to ascend to a higher level and come away" (71).

- *Sod:* "The soul is bidden to ascend to its spiritual possibilities . . . and, like Abraham, to go forth to a new beginning" (71).

And with regard to the return of the spring:

- *Derash:* The end of the winter corresponds to the end of the Israelites' bondage in Egypt, and the blossoms represent Moses and Aaron. Amazingly enough, the Jewish interpreters echo two different analyses of the word זָמִיר, which can mean "song" or "pruning" (see Example 10.1b). Some interpreters think of a song of salvation, while others read "pruning" and relate this action to "the 'cutting off' of Egyptian idolatry" (73).

- *Remez:* The imagery of nature is read as a figure for the development of the soul, especially its growth (73).

- *Sod:* The time has come for "a new spiritual reality" (73).

As just indicated, Jewish readings of this part of Song 2 have both considered the spiritual journey of the soul (*remez* and *sod*) and viewed this text as a sort of historical allegory concerning the Hebrews at the time of the exodus (*derash*).

---

6. Michael Fishbane, *Song of Songs: The Traditional Hebrew Text with the New JPS Translation*, JPS Bible Commentary (Philadelphia: Jewish Publication Society of America, 2015), with quotations from 71–75.

Church Fathers

Turning to patristic interpretation, let us first consult a publication that provides an overview of interpretations by the church fathers. In the introduction of the pertinent volume in the series ACCS, we learn that only one interpreter, Theodore of Mopsuestia (360–429), opted exclusively for a literal interpretation of Song of Songs, which he read as an account of Solomon's marriage with Pharaoh's daughter. All the other fathers favored (sometimes in addition to a literal interpretation) an allegorical reading, interpreting the lover as representing Christ and the woman as representing either the soul of the Christian, the church, or Mary (often in combination).[7]

The same volume provides excerpts of patristic commentaries and an overview of their interpretations of Song 2:8–17:

> The Word of God came leaping over the mountains and bounding over the hills, present already but not yet (Cyril of Alexandria, Ambrose, Jerome). . . . The winter is not past (Origen, Gregory of Elvira). This is signified by the approach of the stag and the voice of the dove (Ambrose, Theodoret of Cyr), signified also by the advent of the gospel (Jerome) and the coming of Christ (Cyril of Alexandria). . . . But we should beware the little foxes in the vineyard who plot against the church (Apostolic Constitutions, Gregory of Elvira, Bede), and we must refute them as heretics (Theodoret of Cyr, Augustine). . . . The shadows have receded (Ambrose), the Lord has risen (Aponius), useless antiquity is terminated, spiritual meaning has been revealed (Augustine), heavenly heights are accessible (Cyril of Alexandria).[8]

We can see here the allegorical interpretation whereby the church is the woman of Song 2:8–17, since its enemies, the "heretics," are the little foxes of Song 2:15.

Now, it might be interesting to read in depth, and continuously, the interpretation of a well-chosen church father, rather than just brief excerpts and overviews. The introduction of the volume explains that Origen's interpretation of Song of Songs was very influential; it also mentions that Gregory of Nyssa wrote homilies of deep value. A quick search shows that an English translation of and commentary on these homilies was published a few years ago.[9] It turns out that Gregory of Nyssa insists on the "mystical" reading, whereby the woman represents the soul of the believer. In his fifth homily, he reads in Song 2:8–17 a story in which Christ wants to attract the soul:

---

7. J. Robert Wright, ed., *Proverbs, Ecclesiastes, Song of Solomon*, ACCS 9 (Downers Grove, IL: InterVarsity Press, 2005), xxv–xxvi.

8. Wright, *Proverbs, Ecclesiastes, Song of Solomon*, 317.

9. Richard A. Norris Jr., trans., *Gregory of Nyssa: Homilies on the Song of Songs*, WGRW 13 (Atlanta: SBL Press, 2012).

We see, then, that the Bride is being led by the Word through the ascents of virtue up to the heights, just as if she were climbing stairs. To this Bride the Lord first of all sends in, through the prophetic windows and the law's lattices, the ray of the commandments and summons her to draw near to the light and to become beautiful once, in the light, she has been given the shape of the dove. . . .

[The Lord] draws her towards participation in the transcendent Beauty. The result is that it seems to her that desire increases in proportion to her progress toward that Light which eternally shines out and at the same time her ascent is just beginning, on account of the transcendence of the good things, which are always beyond her. This is why he says once again to the awakened soul, *Rise up*, and to the soul that is coming, *Come!*

For to the one who has risen up in this manner there will never be wanting an up-rising without end; nor for one who runs to the Lord will opportunity for the divine race be used up. . . .

So it is, then, that the bride is commanded, dove though she was in her former achievements, to become nothing less than a dove again by being transformed for the better; and if this comes to pass, the Word, when next he uses the word dove, will again refer to what lies beyond this. For he says, *Come for yourself, my dove, to the shelter of the rock, close by the wall.*[10]

In this passage, we can see that Gregory of Nyssa offers an original interpretation of this biblical text: the soul is supposed to spiritually "ascend" in a never-ending journey. The introduction to the volume explains that this is a peculiar doctrine of Gregory's called *epektasis* (from ἐπεκτεινόμενος in Phil 3:13, the idea being that of "going forward"). In his view, the Christian life should be an unending ascent, a path of constant spiritual progress. It is fascinating to see that this idea of an ascent of the soul echoes some Jewish interpretations (see above).

Moreover, Gregory of Nyssa has filled in a gap in the text. Song of Songs 2 does not say whether the woman has consented to come out of her home to be with the beloved. Gregory made a decision here; this is a typical case where the text is open due to indetermination and the reader has to participate. Furthermore, Gregory's interpretation largely rests on repetitions in the text of Song of Songs: the repetition of "rise up!", "come!", and "dove." According to Gregory, even when the dove/soul has risen and come, she receives the same commandments, because the journey is never-ending. Even though she was already a dove, she is called to become a dove again. But the

---

10. *Gregory of Nyssa: Homilies on the Song of Songs* (trans. Norris), 171, 173.

> repetition of "dove" is only present in the LXX, where this word appears three times (in vv. 10, 13, 14). In the MT, it appears only once (in v. 14). This is an interesting case where the textual basis has prompted an interpreter to reinforce his personal interpretation.

EXAMPLE 13.7b ▸ The Fate of the Tower of Babel in Ancient Jewish Reception

The story of the tower of Babel (Gen 11:1–9) has enthralled readers throughout the centuries, notably because it evokes a mysterious giant tower and because it mentions a "division" of a unique language into many. In this example, I will focus on the fate of the tower.[11] You may have seen the famous paintings by Pieter Bruegel, dating to 1563 and 1564, in which the tower is still under construction. This is the kind of picture that most people have in mind when they think of this tower, because God supposedly stopped its construction and it was left unfinished. This, at least, is the most widespread interpretation of the text. If you look into the reception of this story among ancient Jewish interpreters, however, you will find that their opinions about the fate of the tower were actually divided on this point. To find out about this, you need to look for ancient Jewish texts that refer to this story, and to do so, you can look into the scriptural indexes cited above and then consult translations of the relevant texts. In what follows, I will summarize the results of my own (non-exhaustive) investigation by mentioning a few examples that reveal four different stances regarding the fate of the tower of Babel.

First, some literary works unambiguously state that the people ceased to build both the city and the tower. This is the case in Jubilees (10:24): "And the Lord went down and we went down with him. And we saw the city and the tower which the sons of men had built. And He mixed up their tongues, and, therefore, one did not hear another's word. And so they ceased to build the city and the tower."[12]

Likewise, the *Book of Biblical Antiquities* (*Liber antiquitatum biblicarum*), written not long after the destruction of the Second Temple, presupposes

---

11. This example draws on Matthieu Richelle, "Was the Tower of Babel Really Left Unfinished? Genesis 11:6 in Light of Hebrew Syntax, the Septuagint, and Jewish Reception," *Semitica* 63 (2021): 125–39. Some of the same observations, and the same conclusion about the Hebrew syntax of Gen 11:5, had already been made independently by David S. Vanderhooft, "Babylon as Cosmopolis in Israelite Texts and Achaemenid Architecture," *HeBAI* 9 (2020): 41–61, esp. 43–50. For other aspects of the reception of this story, see Philip M. Sherman, *Babel's Tower Translated: Genesis 11 and Ancient Jewish Interpretation* (Leiden: Brill, 2013).

12. James L. Kugel, "Jubilees," in *Outside the Bible: Ancient Jewish Writings Related to Scripture*, ed. Louis H. Feldman, James L. Kugel, and Lawrence H. Schiffman (Philadelphia: Jewish Publication Society of America, 2013), 332.

that the tower was unfinished because God intervened when the builders had just begun the construction:

> When the people inhabiting the earth *had begun to build the tower*, God divided up their languages and changed their appearances, and so they did not recognize each other nor did they understand each other's language. And so, when the builders would order their assistants to bring bricks, those would bring water; and if they requested water, they would bring straw. Thus, their plan was broken, and they stopped building the city.[13]

Second, Philo of Alexandria also defends, in *De confusione linguarum*, the notion that the tower was left unfinished, but he notes that Gen 11 contains a paradox. On the one hand, v. 5 indicates that the builders finished building the city and the tower, because, according to Philo, the last verb in the sentence points to a past event (which could be rendered in English as "built/had built"). On the other hand, v. 8 says that they did not complete the work. It is "scientific" arguments that nevertheless lead Philo to conclude that the building work had not been completed: first, it is unthinkable that something erected on earth could touch the heavens; second, even if they had been able to achieve this, the builders would have been consumed by the ether.[14]

Third, some other works do not contain any hint that the tower was left unfinished. This is the case, for example, in the story as it is retold by Josephus in his *Jewish Antiquities* (1.118):

> And they built a tower omitting nothing of zeal nor showing hesitancy in doing their work. And, owing to the great number of laborers, it reached a height more swiftly than anyone might have expected. However, its thickness was so strong that its height appeared smaller to those who saw it. It was built of baked brick bound together with bitumen, in order that it might not collapse. Seeing them thus out of their mind, God decided not to obliterate them utterly because they had not even been brought to their senses by those who had first perished, but he cast them in factional strife by causing them to speak various languages and causing them not to understand themselves owing to the variety of languages.[15]

---

13. Howard Jacobson, *A Commentary on Pseudo-Philo's* Liber Antiquitatum Biblicarum: *With Latin Text and English Translation* (Leiden: Brill, 1996) 1:101 (emphasis mine).

14. Philo, *De confusione linguarum*, with introduction, translation, and notes by J. G. Kahn, OPA 13 (Paris: Cerf, 1963), 129–31 (§§155–158). For a discussion, see Sherman, *Babel's Tower Translated*, 266–68.

15. Steve Mason, ed., *Flavius Josephus: Translation and Commentary*, vol. 3, *Judean Antiquities 1–4*, translation and commentary by L. H. Feldman (Leiden: Brill, 2000), 41.

No mention is made here that the building was interrupted; in fact, reading Josephus's narrative without any preconceptions actually gives the impression that the tower was completed.

Fourth, some later works mention the view, held by some sages, that the tower *was* completed. Thus we read in *Genesis Rabbah* (which dates to around the fifth century CE):

> R. Judan said: The tower they built, but they did not build the city. An objection is raised: But it is written: *And the Lord came down to see the city and the tower* (ib. 5)? Read what follows, he replied: *And they left off to build the city* (ib. 8), the tower, however, not being mentioned. R. Ḥiyya b. Abba said: A third of this tower which they built sank [into the earth], a third was burnt, while a third is still standing.[16]

The statement by Rabbi Ḥiyya ben Abba here is interesting, because it would be quite strange to talk about the three thirds of an unfinished tower. But Rabbi Judan's assertion is explicit and clear. It is based on the absence of the mention of the tower in v. 8.

Midrash Tanhuma—which is often dated to the ninth century CE, though some would prefer a date closer to the middle of the first millennium CE—should also be noted. Like *Genesis Rabbah*, it mentions Rabbi Hiyya ben Abba's description of the three thirds of the tower. But the most striking statement is the following: "Had He not permitted them to build the tower, they would have claimed: 'If we had built the tower, we would have ascended and waged war against Him.' Therefore, He allowed them to erect the tower. After that, He looked down upon them and scattered them."[17]

Here the very logic of the argument requires that the tower was completed: if its construction had been interrupted, then the humans could still object, "If we had built the tower entirely, we would have ascended and waged war against Him."

To sum up, the ancient Jewish reception of the story of Babel is more variegated than we might have expected. This prompts us to go back to the exegesis of Gen 11:1–9 and wonder if the widely received interpretation, according to which the tower was left unfinished, is correct. After all, if Jewish interpreters assumed the opposite, it may be because the Hebrew text of Genesis lent itself to such a reading, or because of textual variants.

Let's first check the textual witnesses of Gen 11—for instance, by looking at the BHQ edition. As a matter of fact, we have already seen, in Example 2.4a, that there is a variant in v. 8; the Septuagint and the Samaritan

---

16. Harry Freedman and Maurice Simon, ed., *Midrash Rabbah* (London: Soncino, 1939), 1:307. (The notation "*ib.*" in this quotation stands for "Gen 11.")

17. *Midrash Tanhuma*, Noach, Siman 18. Translation by Samuel A. Berman, available on the website *Sefaria.

Pentateuch have a plus: "They ceased building the city *and the tower*." This plus makes it clear that the construction of the tower was interrupted. Interestingly, the last sentence in the passage of Jubilees quoted above reproduces this expanded form of v. 8. So, the redactor of Jubilees may have had a Hebrew text of Genesis that contained this plus. Here the textual basis may have influenced the reception. In fact, because most church fathers read the Septuagint, they unanimously believed that the building of the tower of Babel had been stopped.

By contrast, the interpreters who believed that the construction was completed likely did not have this plus in their text of Genesis. That said, we have seen that for Philo, Gen 11:5 implied that the tower had been completed because the last verb in the verse referred to a past event. Philo read biblical texts in Greek, generally in the Septuagint, which here has:

καὶ κατέβη κύριος ἰδεῖν τὴν πόλιν καὶ τὸν πύργον,
ὃν ᾠκοδόμησαν οἱ υἱοὶ τῶν ἀνθρώπων.

And the Lord came down to see the city and the tower,
that the men had built. (NETS)

The aorist is often used as a pluperfect in the LXX, especially in relative clauses,[18] hence the pluperfect ("had built," for ᾠκοδόμησαν) in the translation just quoted.

Let us now go back to the Hebrew text:

וַיֵּרֶד יְהוָה לִרְאֹת אֶת־הָעִיר וְאֶת־הַמִּגְדָּל אֲשֶׁר בָּנוּ בְּנֵי הָאָדָם׃

The LORD came down to see the city and the tower,
which mortals *had built*. (NRSVue)

A look at Biblical Hebrew grammars shows that the use of a *qatal* form in a relative clause indicates anteriority with regard to the timeline of the narrative.[19] Hence the pluperfect used to render בָּנוּ in the NRSVue.

Now, while the antecedent of the relative clause obviously includes "the tower," it does not necessarily include "the city." A possible understanding would be the following: "The Lord came down to see the city, and the tower that the men had built." Here the comma is used to show that only "the tower" is the antecedent of the relative clause; that is, in Hebrew, only הַמִּגְדָּל is the antecedent of אֲשֶׁר בָּנוּ בְּנֵי הָאָדָם. Therefore, *the Hebrew text of Gen 11:5 could be read as implying that the tower had been completed*. In fact, this is how several ancient translators understood the text, notably the Septuagint (quoted above), where the relative pronoun ὅν, which is singular,

---

18. Takamitsu Muraoka, *A Syntax of Septuagint Greek* (Leuven: Peeters, 2016), 271–72.
19. For more details, see Richelle, "Was the Tower of Babel Really Left Unfinished?"

refers to τὸν πύργον only (in my view, the comma is misplaced in the NETS translation).[20] I would even argue that this is the best reading of Gen 11:5.[21]

In the end, exploring the ancient Jewish reception of Gen 11:1–9 may lead us to challenge what has become the most widely received interpretation of the story in modern times.

Exercises for Chapter 13

Exercise A

Study the reception of Ps 2:7 in the New Testament.

Exercise B

Study the reception of Gen 6:1–4 in Second Temple literature and in the New Testament.

Exercise C

Summarize the interpretation of Gen 12:10–20 that Origen gives in his *Homilies on Genesis*, and explain what method of interpretation he is using.

Exercise D

Summarize and compare the interpretations of Rashi, Ibn Ezra, Nahmanides, and Kimhi on the statement in Gen 2:7 that the Lord breathed the "breath of life" into the man. (Remember that their commentaries are quoted in the *Miqra'ot Gedolot*; see above.) Do their comments belong to *peshat*, *remez*, *derash*, or *sod*?

---

20. The same is true of the Vulgate (*descendit autem Dominus ut videret civitatem et turrem quam aedificabant filii Adam*), where the relative pronoun *quam* refers back to *turrem* only.

21. Richelle, "Was the Tower of Babel Really Left Unfinished?" I am not the first scholar to argue this: see my article for further references, and also already Vanderhooft, "Babylon as Cosmopolis in Israelite Texts and Achaemenid Architecture," 47–50.

CHAPTER 14
FEMINIST AND GENDER STUDIES

OVERVIEW

Feminist and gender studies is a dynamic field that may prove intimidating for beginners, due to its vastness and complexity. Historically, feminism precedes gender studies, which stemmed from the former and extends the scope of the discussion. There is a clear overlap between feminism and gender studies, but also differences of perspective, both in terms of the issues that are emphasized and the concepts that are used. These two fields are often dealt with together, whether because feminist studies now integrates insights from gender studies or because feminist interpretation is sometimes subsumed under the realm of gender studies. For the sake of convenience, this chapter will deal with both approaches while trying to respect their different points of emphasis.

Jennifer Koosed defines feminism as follows:

> Feminism is a philosophy, a political movement, a field of intellectual inquiry, and a worldview. In its essence, feminism is the belief that women and men are equal, and feminism is the movement to create a world of equal treatment and equal opportunity.

But she also notes that

> there is no single definition of feminism that has a wide consensus because people have different views about what constitutes sexist oppression, the origins of sexism, and the best methods of dismantling that sexism. As a movement that is rooted in women's experience, it necessarily encompasses as many definitions as there are women's experiences. Feminism, then, is an umbrella term that covers a range of perspectives about gender justice for women and men.[1]

---

1. Jennifer L. Koosed, *Reading the Bible as a Feminist*, BRP (Leiden: Brill, 2017), 4.

This variety is reflected in the many and various ways in which feminist scholars scrutinize the Hebrew Bible. Far from trying to cover all the possible aspects of the subject (see the sidebar "For Further Reading" below for book-length discussions), my aim in this chapter is to introduce you to the basic tasks that most feminist interpreters assign to themselves when exegeting a biblical text.

As a matter of fact, there is no such thing as "*the* feminist *method* for studying the Bible." Feminist interpretation—as Francisco Lozada says of postcolonial interpretation (the subject of chapter 15), liberation hermeneutics, and cultural studies—"is not a method per se but rather an ideological orientation toward the text and the reader or the reading communities,"[2] and this orientation is inspired by a philosophy (to use Koosed's word). To put it another way, feminist interpretation is defined by its aims rather than by a unique methodology. This does not mean, however, that "feminists lack a method"; on the contrary, this means that *a large array of exegetical methods can be used for feminist aims*. For instance, some scholars use narrative criticism to analyze how male characters act toward female characters. Others have recourse to the historical method in order to contextualize the ways in which legal texts presuppose or prescribe a different treatment of women compared to men. These methods are not feminist in themselves, but they can be employed with feminist intentions.[3]

Therefore, let us begin by delving into these intentions. The most urgent task of feminist interpretation is the critique of *patriarchy*, which basically designates all forms of male domination (although it originally described the nature of a society characterized by the domination of the father in the family sphere). While the term patriarchy is especially appropriate for describing the concrete expressions of male domination in society, *andocentrism* characterizes the bias of a discourse (often inscribed in a text) that privileges the perspective of men and that serves their interests. As a result, strictly speaking, feminist interpretation scrutinizes the biblical text for its possible androcentrism, which may reflect the patriarchal society of ancient Israel and/or the patriarchal mindset of the text's redactors. In practice, there is some degree of flexibility in the use of this terminology.

A recurring debate among feminist biblical scholars involves, on the one hand, those who believe that the patriarchy or androcentrism they find in the texts is an essential part of the message of these texts and, on the other hand, those who chalk up this patriarchy or androcentrism to the prevalent mindset that existed in ancient Israel and the related modes of expression. According to those on the former side of the debate, the biblical redactors actively endorse and even foster patriarchy; gender construction cannot be separated from their discourse. According to those on the latter side, such a charge is, at least partially, anachronistic; it misses the heart of the

---

2. Francisco Lozada Jr., *Toward a Latino/a Biblical Interpretation*, RBS 91 (Atlanta: SBL Press, 2017), 38.

3. This paragraph and others in this chapter owe much to Laura Quick, whom I thank warmly for her help.

message of the texts, which—even when it is expressed in androcentric terms because the redactors were historically situated in a patriarchal context—is not intrinsically patriarchal. For instance, most feminist interpreters take issue with the sexual metaphors in the prophetic books that characterize Israel as a woman who fornicates or prostitutes herself. An exception is Alice Keefe, who argues that in the book of Hosea, such gendered figures of speech operate at the level of expression rather than at the level of substance. In her view, the use of sexual metaphors is a reflection of the social dimensions of sexuality in ancient Israel.[4] Thus a debate exists as to whether one should locate the patriarchal ideology in the message of the text or in its historically situated form. That being said, it seems fair to also say that few feminists would deny that the Hebrew Bible is deeply infused with androcentrism.

In a related way, a number of feminist scholars argue that the Hebrew Bible also contains elements of non-patriarchal discourse. Phyllis Trible famously introduced the phrase "non-patriarchal principle," a reality she saw at work in the Hebrew Bible, and others have found expressions of this non-patriarchal, or even anti-patriarchal, dynamic in various texts. For instance, a number of female characters are celebrated; some "female qualities" are (more or less implicitly) praised; sexist stereotypes are overturned as women are given roles that are unexpected in the hierarchies of a patriarchal framework. Within a literature that predominantly reflects a patriarchal organization of society, this represents an interesting countercurrent that is of prime interest for feminist studies. That being said, a number of scholars find a degree of ambivalence here, for at least two reasons. First, they argue that the celebration of female characters is often tied to a narrow understanding of femininity, or even to an essentialist view of femininity. Proverbs 31:10–31, for example, celebrates a female figure, but only insofar as she fits into the social role that is expected from "active women" in a patriarchal society. And yet, this passage, like the rest of Prov 31, is ascribed to a woman (see v. 1)! A possible reason why this female author celebrates the woman of Prov 31:10–31 in the terms she does is that women in ancient Israel had to internalize the constraints of a patriarchal society, or had to adapt to it. This illustration may give an idea of the complexity of the situation. Second, it remains to be seen whether, when certain powerful female characters are celebrated (by men), this is done in order to overturn stereotypes or rather to illustrate the dangers of letting women take control. (We will return to this issue in Example 14.2a below.)

Feminist interpreters are further interested in the ways in which androcentrism (along with male domination in biblical studies) has impacted the history of interpretation and resulted not only in biased exegesis but also in the marginalization of female interpreters. Another relevant area of inquiry is the impact of androcentric interpretation on society, since the Hebrew Bible has historically been used (and is still used today) to marginalize and oppress women.

---

4. Alice A. Keefe, *Woman's Body and the Social Body in Hosea* (Sheffield: Sheffield Academic, 2001).

A last facet of feminist interpretation appears in yet another task that feminist scholars often undertake, namely, engaging in a reconstructive reading of the text. Concretely, this can entail rediscovering marginal female characters in biblical narratives; retelling the story from the point of view of such characters; engaging with narratives, oracles, or poetry from the vantage point of a contemporary situation; and also revisiting "traditional" exegetical matters such as authorship, by exploring the hypothesis that women wrote some biblical books.

At this juncture, it is important to make a distinction between two different kinds of feminist reading. On the one hand, some feminists adopt a *historical* perspective in order to uncover the situation and status of women in ancient Israel and to call out patriarchal attitudes and androcentric discourses. These scholars focus on the situation of women in the *past* and do not try to "rehabilitate" the biblical text. On the other hand, a number of those who adopt the approach to reconstructive reading just mentioned prefer to reinterpret the text precisely in order to "rehabilitate" it and to make it more palatable to modern readers. In so doing, these scholars focus on the *present* reception of the Hebrew Bible. This second approach is especially relevant for a *theologically* oriented reading and for some religious communities. The difference between these two approaches is sometimes related to diverging views among feminists on the authority of the Bible (see the sidebar "A Typology of Feminist Views on Biblical Authority").

Because the intentions behind these two approaches are very different, misunderstandings sometimes occur. Typically, some proponents of the historical approach accuse some practitioners of reconstructive reading of minimizing—or even of "whitewashing"—the problems contained in the text. Yet proponents of reconstructive reading do not necessarily deny the historical problems; rather, they focus on attempting to transcend them. Conversely, practitioners of reconstructive reading may sometimes feel like the historical approach is merely a negative task that results only in grief. In reality, engaging with the problems of the past (which are still very much present today) may have a therapeutic function for readers who have suffered from oppression, discrimination, or sexual abuse; it can also help prevent the recurrence of past problems and the use of the Bible to oppress women, as well as raise awareness of the issues.[5] Moreover, both approaches can be combined: a lucid historical analysis can serve as a basis for a reinterpretation of the text.

In sum, as Gloria Schaab writes, the "overall framework" of "feminist methodologies" generally "includes the basic elements of critique, retrieval, and (re)construction."[6] As we have just seen, critique concerns both the text and its interpreters.

---

5. Amy Kalmanofsky, "How Feminist Biblical Scholarship Can Heal Victims of Sexual Violation," in *Sexual Violence and Sacred Texts*, ed. Amy Kalmanofsky (Eugene, OR: Wipf & Stock, 2020), 15.

6. Gloria L. Schaab, "Feminist Theological Methodology: Toward a Kaleidoscopic Model," *TS* 62 (2001): 341–65 (with quotation on 357).

For Further Reading

The following books provided seminal analyses of biblical texts (mostly narratives) from a feminist point of view and have therefore become classics in the field. In spite of the criticism they have sometimes attracted from some other feminists, they remain interesting conversation partners:

- Phyllis Trible, *God and the Rhetoric of Sexuality* (Philadelphia: Fortress, 1978).
- Phyllis Trible, *Texts of Terror: Literary-Feminist Readings of Biblical Narratives* (Philadelphia: Fortress, 1984).
- J. Cheryl Exum, *Fragmented Women: Feminist (Sub)versions of Biblical Narratives* (JSOTSup 163; Sheffield: Sheffield Academic, 1993).
- Esther Fuchs, *Sexual Politics in the Biblical Narrative: Reading the Hebrew Bible as a Woman* (JSOTSup 310; London: Sheffield Academic, 2003).

The following books are good examples of up-to-date discussions:

- Amy Kalmanofsky, *Gender-Play in the Hebrew Bible: The Ways the Bible Challenges Its Gender Norms* (New York: Routledge, 2017).
- Rhiannon Graybill, *Texts after Terror: Rape, Sexual Violence, and the Hebrew Bible* (New York: Oxford University Press, 2021).

A set of collected volumes edited by Athalya Brenner explores different sections of the Hebrew Bible from a feminist point of view; for instance:

- *A Feminist Companion to Genesis*, FCB 2 (Sheffield: Sheffield Academic, 1997).

A second series is now being published; see, for instance:

- *A Feminist Companion to Genesis*, FCB (second series) 1 (Sheffield: Sheffield Academic, 1998).

The following one-volume commentary on the Bible is written by feminist scholars and views the text through the lens of the situation of women:

- Carol A. Newsom, Sharon H. Ringe, and Jacqueline E. Lapsley, eds., *Women's Bible Commentary*, 3rd ed. (Louisville: Westminster John Knox, 2012).

The following publications provide helpful surveys of the history of and variety of approaches in the field of feminist studies:

- Luise Schottroff, Silvia Schroer, and Marie-Theres Wacker, *Feminist Interpretation: The Bible in Women's Perspective* (Minneapolis: Fortress,

1998), Parts 1 and 2 (Part 3 concerns the New Testament and Early Christianity).

- Eryl W. Davies, *The Dissenting Reader: Feminist Approaches to the Hebrew Bible* (Aldershot: Ashgate, 2003).
- Esther Fuchs, *Feminist Theory and the Bible: Interrogating the Sources* (London: Lexington Books, 2016), esp. chapters 1 to 3.
- Jennifer L. Koosed, *Reading the Bible as a Feminist*, BRP (Leiden: Brill, 2017).

To get an idea of how globalization, neoliberalism, digital media cultures, and intersectional perspectives have impacted the field, see the large array of essays in the following handbook:

- Susanne Scholz, ed., *The Oxford Handbook of Feminist Approaches to the Hebrew Bible* (New York: Oxford University Press, 2021).

For a detailed introduction to the study of masculinity, see:

- Peter-Ben Smit, *Masculinity and the Bible: Survey, Models, and Perspectives*, BRP (Leiden: Brill, 2017).

For an introduction to womanist studies, see:

- Nyasha Junior, *An Introduction to Womanist Biblical Interpretation* (Louisville: Westminster John Knox, 2015).

Finally, the following book is an important general resource:

- Julia O'Brien, ed., *The Oxford Encyclopedia of the Bible and Gender Studies*, 2 vols. (New York: Oxford University Press, 2014).

As feminist studies developed during the last two decades of the twentieth century, a number of its limitations became increasingly apparent. For instance, the focus on women meant that masculinity was not scrutinized in the texts. More importantly, the concept of gender has come to the fore. Here again, Koosed provides a helpful definition:

> In stark contrast to sex, gender is a culturally constructed and historically variable set of beliefs about what constitutes proper behavior for males and females, as well as what it means to be masculine or feminine.[7]

The basic tenet of gender studies is that gender is a socio-cultural construct rather than a product of biology.[8] The belief that some characteristics are inherent to males

---

7. Koosed, *Reading the Bible as a Feminist*, 4.
8. In recent years, this notion has become the subject of controversy in the public arena (especially in the United States, but also in Europe), even though it is well received in academia. In

or females due to biology is called *essentialism*. Therefore, scholars who study the Hebrew Bible from the point of view of gender studies scrutinize the text for elements that either support essentialism or contribute to a specific construction of gender identity.

Thus, in recent years, scholars have increasingly paid attention to the ways the Hebrew Bible constructs or conveys certain understandings of masculinity. A key concept here is "hegemonic masculinity," which Susan Haddox defines as follows:

> It expresses the idea that masculinity is usually tightly entwined with power; thus studying masculinity involves analyzing the competing power structures in a given society. Hegemonic masculinity is the specific gender construction that is dominant in cultural and political power structures.[9]

Haddox has generated a list of "typical components of hegemonic masculinity": military might, bodily integrity (i.e., the ability to defend oneself from physical assault, rape, or corporal punishment), honor, virility, provisioning ("a man's ability to provide for his household"), and spatiality ("the exterior or public space" being conceived of as "the domain of men," as opposed to the interior, the house, which is regarded as the realm of women). She has further provided a helpful survey of recent studies that explore the ways in which parts of the Hebrew Bible (the Deuteronomistic History, the Prophets, the Torah, and the Writings) construct norms of masculinity or challenge such norms.[10]

In a word, in the same way that feminist interpretation scrutinizes the Hebrew Bible for androcentrism or challenges to patriarchy, gender studies scrutinizes it for the construction or deconstruction of gender ideology.

Feminist and gender studies continue to develop and take new forms. A relatively recent trend consists of *intersectional studies*, which takes into account the entanglement of gender, class, and race domination. For instance, a new field emerged

---

particular, because gender studies calls into question the traditional "order of things," those who believe that this order is based on the Bible and who infer it to be God-given are typically not attracted to this approach. As a result, while many students in theology or biblical studies find gender studies to be liberating, some who come from a conservative background find it difficult to square this approach with their religious beliefs, or they are tempted to ignore it altogether. If you find yourself in this situation, perhaps an aspect of the Hebrew Bible that gender studies has contributed to rediscovering may help you to find interest in this approach. Indeed, recent exegetical works have shown that a number of biblical texts themselves challenge the stereotypes that some believe to be based on the Bible. As we will see later (Examples 14.2a and 14.2c), some traditional "qualities," roles, and behaviors that are often deemed appropriate to males or females are overturned in some narratives, which show that they are not predetermined by biology. This is not the same as saying that the Hebrew Bible supports the major tenets of gender studies, but it is something to start with.

9. Susan E. Haddox, "Masculinity Studies of the Hebrew Bible: The First Two Decades," *CurBR* 14 (2016): 179.

10. Haddox, "Masculinity Studies of the Hebrew Bible," 188–200.

in the 1980s, *womanist biblical interpretation*, which focuses on the specific situation of Black women (including, but not limited to, African American women).[11] *Queer studies* does the same, today, with regard to people of various sexual orientations.

> ### A Typology of Feminist Views on Biblical Authority
>
> Feminist and gender studies often lead believing scholars to rethink their conception of biblical authority. Carolyn Osiek has offered a helpful typology of scholarly reactions to this challenge:[12]
>
> - The *rejectionist* gives up on the Hebrew Bible as authoritative because it is judged to be irredeemably infused with patriarchy.
>
> - The *loyalist* assumes that the Hebrew Bible, seen as the Word of God, cannot be wrong, including on matters of gender. Therefore, the loyalist either blames exegetes for having wrongly ascribed androcentric views to the writers of the Hebrew Bible (believing these exegetes must have misinterpreted the text by projecting their own views onto it) or accepts and internalizes the patriarchal order while lamenting the ways in which males have abused what the loyalist regards as their legitimate authority.
>
> - The *revisionist* believes that the theological message of the text can be extracted from its "patriarchal mold," which means that the biblical tradition can be redeemed by reformation.
>
> - The *sublimationist* looks for "the eternal feminine in biblical symbolism" in order to glorify it. Concretely, this means focusing on important female symbols (e.g., Israel as the bride of God).
>
> - The *liberationist* considers that the thrust of the biblical message, and the main objective of religion, is human liberation. A scholar working from this perspective focuses on passages that foster this liberation and does not regard those texts that are irredeemably compromised by the patriarchal agenda as conveying divine revelation.

---

11. Womanist and feminist studies are often regarded as closely related ("feminist/womanist studies"). That said, Nyasha Junior argues that they are two distinct fields (*An Introduction to Womanist Biblical Interpretation* [Louisville: Westminster John Knox, 2015], 118–23).

12. Carolyn Osiek, "The Feminist and the Bible: Hermeneutical Alternatives," *HTS* 53 (1997): 956–68.

Summing up the different tasks that we have discussed above, the following directions can be suggested for analyzing a biblical passage from the perspective of feminist and gender studies:

❶ SCRUTINIZE THE TEXT FOR **GENDER IDEOLOGY** (WHETHER PATRIARCHAL ELEMENTS OR CONSTRUCTION OF GENDER NORMS).

❷ SCRUTINIZE THE TEXT FOR **DECONSTRUCTION OF GENDER IDEOLOGY** (WHETHER ANTI-PATRIARCHAL ELEMENTS OR DECONSTRUCTION OF GENDER NORMS).

❸ SCRUTINIZE THE **INTERPRETATION HISTORY**.

❹ ENGAGE IN **RECONSTRUCTIVE READING**.

Let me stress the fact that these are four different possible *directions* of study, not successive *steps* that you need to follow. When studying a text, you may move through all these tasks together, but you do not have to. Some feminist publications engage in one of these tasks only.

14.1 SCRUTINIZE THE TEXT FOR GENDER IDEOLOGY

Typically, feminist scholars scrutinize the text for elements of **patriarchal ideology**, including:

- **androcentric representations of women** (whether based on biases, stereotypes, or derogatory characterizations of female characters)
- elements of discourse, notably **literary features or tropes** (e.g., metaphors) that are based on patriarchal representations of women, even when they are not directed to women; a special case would be:
- **male language about God** that contains or creates patriarchal representations of the deity, or that is preponderant in a biblical book
- mentions or depictions of **violence against women**, sometimes with approval or justification of it
- **silences** in the text; this can involve:
    - passages in which sexist oppression is not named or seems minimized
    - the absence (or marginalization) of female characters in a passage

In addition, gender studies attends to the various ways in which biblical texts construct or endorse **gender norms and gendered roles** (that is, ones that the redactors deem appropriate to femininity and masculinity). To this end, scholars scrutinize the text for:

- gendered representations that construct or endorse **forms of femininity and masculinity** (for instance, expressions of hegemonic masculinity)
- ancient **gendered conventions**, which a socio-archaeological approach can help recover; this can lead one to revisit the interpretation of (for instance) the behavior of a character
- implicit or explicit elements that **normalize, legitimize, or delegitimize** behaviors and traits of characters that are regarded as appropriate or not for gender roles
- legitimation or delegitimation of forms of sexuality

EXAMPLE 14.1a ▸ **Isaiah 3:12**

Isaiah 3:1–12 describes a situation in which Judah is deprived of its "elite" (warriors, soldiers, judges, prophets, diviners, elders, etc.). As a result, Yhwh says: "And I will make youths their princes, and children shall rule over them" (v. 4). But he also says (v. 12):

> My people—children are their oppressors,
> and women rule over them.
> O my people, your leaders mislead you,
> and confuse the course of your paths.

If this translation is correct,[13] the question arises of what is wrong, according to the redactor of this verse, with women ruling over Judah. The most likely explanation seems to be that the redactor mocks the actual rulers of Jerusalem by depicting them as women, the underlying idea being that women are not fit to govern. By doing so, the redactor implicitly relies on a stereotype: women as weak or spineless, for instance. The same kind of stereotype seems to lie behind Isa 19:16: "On that day the Egyptians will be like women and tremble with fear before the hand that the Lord of hosts raises against them." This passage ties fear to femininity and mocks the Egyptians for exhibiting the former.

As Susannah Rees observes, the underlying idea behind the statement in Isa 3:12 that children and women rule the people is that this constitutes

---

13. This translation of v. 12 is that of the original NRSV. Some commentators emend the text and read the first half of this verse differently, without any mention of women (see, e.g., H. G. M. Williamson, *Isaiah 1–5*, 261–62, and compare the 2022 updated edition of the NRSV, the NRSVue). The point here is not to decide what the best translation is in this particular case, but simply to use an existing translation to illustrate what feminist interpretation is.

"the inversion of normative world order," which "is a popular trope that is used to depict a chaotic world both in the Hebrew Bible and in the prophetic literature of the ancient Near East and Mediterranean more widely."[14] Rees demonstrates that this motif underlies the entirety of Isa 3, resurfacing in the passage about the "daughters of Zion" (vv. 16–24). Here we read an indictment followed by the announcement of a punishment:

> The LORD said:
> Because the daughters of Zion are haughty
> and walk with outstretched necks,
> glancing wantonly with their eyes,
> mincing along as they go,
> tinkling with their feet;
> the Lord will afflict with scabs
> the heads of the daughters of Zion,
> and the LORD will lay bare their scalps and heads.
>
> On that day the Lord will take away the finery of the anklets, the headbands, and the crescents; the pendants, the bracelets, and the scarfs; the headdresses, the armlets, the sashes, the perfume boxes, and the amulets; the signet rings and nose rings; the festal robes, the mantles, the cloaks, and the handbags; the garments of gauze, the linen garments, the turbans, and the veils.
>
> Instead of perfume there will be a stench;
> and instead of a sash, a rope;
> and instead of well-styled hair, baldness;
> and instead of a rich robe, a binding of sackcloth;
> instead of beauty, shame.

It is customary to read the list of dress items in vv. 18–23 as typically feminine and for modern translations (including the NRSVue, just quoted) to render the numerous Hebrew hapax legomena in this list accordingly. However, Rees has shown that this list actually mixes two different kinds of items. Some correspond to female-coded dress; that is, they are typical of what gendered norms in ancient Israel (or at least in the mind of the redactor of this passage) expected women to wear. Others, however, are actually mentioned in other parts of the Hebrew Bible as worn by men; what is more, they connote *male power*, because they are worn by male rulers and are symbols of their elevated functions. The rhetorical function of this

---

14. Susannah Rees, "'Women Rule Over Them': Dressing for an Inverted World in Isaiah 3," in *Dress Hermeneutics and the Hebrew Bible: "Let Your Garments Always Be Bright,"* ed. Antonios Finitsis, LHBOTS 724 (London: T&T Clark, 2022), 155–86 (with quotation on 169). I thank Laura Quick for directing my attention to this article, and Susannah Rees for allowing me to read the proofs.

surprising mixture is perfectly in line with the trope of inversion that runs through Isa 3 and that was mentioned above. As Rees observes,

> The passage concerning the dress of the Daughters of Zion fits into a broader pattern in Isaiah 3, which is concerned with women taking power, subverting social structures, and filling the power vacuum left after the removal of the male ruling class from Judah and Jerusalem.

Seen in this light, the rhetorical effect and the underlying message are clear:

> Items of dress that are socially coded as female and are elsewhere associated with subservience, commodification, and female labor are, therefore, ironically inverted by their inclusion in an assemblage of dress alongside royal insignia and other items of dress coded with an elite, male status and constitutive of political power, dominance, and leadership. The image evoked is thus one of total confusion and chaos. By literally assuming the mantle of male leadership, the Daughters of Zion represent another element of the inverted natural order in Isaiah 3 and the moral and social collapse it reflects.[15]

Rees's analysis represents a good illustration of how paying attention to gendered codes (here, in the realm of dress) can shed new light on little-understood passages and can prompt new interpretations.

EXAMPLE 14.1b ▸ Mothers in the Hebrew Bible

The Hebrew Bible valorizes motherhood. A number of women are praised for the efforts they make to get pregnant and for the care and compassion they have for their children. Moreover, Cheryl Exum has noted that the actions of mothers are often decisive at key moments in the history of Israel—for instance, for the fulfillment of the promises to the patriarchs in Genesis, which occurs through the chosen line, or to save Moses at the beginning of Exodus. While all this happens within the framework of patriarchy, the narratives ascribe a striking degree of importance to these women.[16]

On the other hand, however, Esther Fuchs argues that mothers are "implicitly or explicitly praised not despite but because of the Bible's patriarchal policy."[17] In other words, these women are valorized not for themselves, and their qualities (including their ability to procreate) are highlighted not

---

15. Rees, "Women Rule Over Them," 185–86.
16. J. Cheryl Exum, " 'Mother in Israel': A Familiar Figure Reconsidered," in *Feminist Interpretation of the Bible*, ed. Letty M. Russell (Philadelphia: Westminster, 1985), 73–85.
17. Esther Fuchs, *Sexual Politics in the Biblical Narrative: Reading the Hebrew Bible as a Woman*, JSOTSup 310 (London: Sheffield Academic, 2003), 47.

for themselves, but rather because they serve the interests of the patriarchal structure of society and thus of men. For example, if a good deal of attention is given to "barren women" who succeed in becoming pregnant, it is because this warrants the continuation of the patrilineal succession.[18] Fuchs insightfully notes that patriarchy "has little to gain from a total negation of women. It has much more to gain from valorizing the contribution of mothers to the patriarchal system."[19]

Fuchs's insights can be supplemented by an interesting comment made by Melody Knowles, who notes that when the Bible praises the ability of women to procreate and the care they show for their children, this is double-edged. She aptly captures the difficulty when she writes:

> Although womb and birthing imagery might allow a woman to relate to or read her own life into the God of the Psalms (or complicate a too-easy identification of God as male), female attributes and affinities cannot be confined to what is biologically sex-specific. Further, naming and associating behaviors (e.g., compassion) as feminine runs the danger of composing an essentialized femininity that conforms to socially prescribed behaviors and attributes—reifying "feminine" into a construction that constricts women instead of understanding it as a cultural performance.[20]

EXAMPLE 14.1c ▸ Jeremiah 13:22, 26

In Jer 13:20–27, the prophet addresses a female interlocutor who is presumably the personified city of Jerusalem. After alluding to an invasion from the "north" (v. 20), he accuses Jerusalem of adultery (v. 21) and describes a scene of sexual humiliation and violence (v. 22):

> And if you say in your heart,
> "Why have these things come upon me?"
> it is for the greatness of your iniquity
> that your skirts are lifted up
> and you are violated.

---

18. It should be noted that some biblical writers seem to have believed that only women could be barren, which, in retrospect, sounds unfair toward them, since we know that infertility can affect both men and women. But a consequence is that these biblical writers valorize the role played by women in God's design, inasmuch as this design entailed a succession of generations.

19. Fuchs, *Sexual Politics in the Biblical Narrative*, 47.

20. Melody D. Knowles, "Feminist Interpretation of the Psalms," in *The Oxford Handbook of the Psalms*, ed. William P. Brown (New York: Oxford University Press, 2014), 426.

The motif of "having the skirts lifted up (lit., uncovered)" (נִגְלוּ שׁוּלַיִךְ) means public humiliation by exhibition of the female private parts. The expression translated "you are violated" is literally "your heels are violated" (נֶחְמְסוּ עֲקֵבָיִךְ); most commentators believe that the word "heels" is, like "feet" in other passages (e.g., Exod 4:25; Isa 6:2; 7:20), a euphemism for the genitals. Accordingly, v. 22 refers to rape.[21]

Yhwh then makes it clear that all of this is a punishment that he has orchestrated because of Jerusalem's "prostitutions" (v. 25–27), which is a figure of speech for describing idolatry. In v. 26, Yhwh goes as far as to say:

> I myself will lift up your skirts over your face,
> and your shame will be seen.

According to a number of scholars, Yhwh is announcing here that he will himself sexually abuse personified Jerusalem. Alternatively, some commentators translate the first verb in v. 26 (חָשַׂפְתִּי) in the past tense ("I myself lifted up") and think that Yhwh is referring back to what was described in v. 22. In other words, in v. 26, Yhwh explains that it was he who supervised the rape of Jerusalem by other men.

Obviously, the notion that the husband Yhwh punishes his wife (personified Jerusalem) for being adulterous by having her raped by her lovers, and perhaps also by raping her (according to a possible interpretation of v. 26), makes this passage deeply offensive to modern readers. Feminist interpretation attends to this kind of problem and insists on naming what is depicted as rape; in addition, it questions the underlying representation of God's behavior toward humans.

14.2 SCRUTINIZE THE TEXT FOR DECONSTRUCTION OF GENDER IDEOLOGY

Feminist interpreters may also look for possible elements of **anti-patriarchy** in the text. Here, I use the term anti-patriarchy in the broadest possible sense; it can include a positive stance toward women or a notable valorization of women, insofar as this runs contrary to the dominant patriarchal framework of Israelite society. Anti-patriarchy can take several forms:

---

21. For the sake of completeness, it should be noted that another view exists: see Łukasz Popko, "What Has Happened with Jerusalem in Jer 13:26?" *RB* 117 (2010): 510–27.

- **valorization** of female characters

- **literary features or tropes** based on a positive view of women even though they are not applied to women; a specific case would be:

- **female language about God**

Gender studies extends this query by paying attention to ways in which the Hebrew Bible **deconstructs or challenges stereotypes and gender norms**. In particular, scholars look for:

- characters whose **role or behavior deviates from what would be expected** from women or men in a patriarchal framework

- (implicit) **critique of hegemonic masculinity**

EXAMPLE 14.2a ▸ Proverbs 31

As already noted in the introduction to this chapter, the poem in Prov 31:10–31 that praises the "valiant woman" is still based on the patriarchal assumption that women must fulfill certain roles in society. Her activities are clearly regarded as serving the interests of her husband, and notably, they are praised because they honor him. The fact that this presentation of the ideal woman is expressed only in terms of how her activities benefit her husband could be explained by the fact that the poem is presented as an instruction given by a mother to her son (v. 1): this mother is thinking of his best interests. Nevertheless, it is still striking that the women is regarded as basically serving him.

Yet it is possible to refine this remark by noting that the situation is more subtle than this. As Al Wolters has noticed, some of the imagery used to describe this woman is borrowed from heroic poetry (which usually praises men), and some of the terms in this passage even draw on language that elsewhere connotes activities like war and hunting, which are normally reserved for descriptions of men.[22] For instance, let us consider vv. 11 and 15:

> The heart of her husband trusts in her,
> and he will have no lack of gain.
> She rises while it is still night
> and provides food for her household
> and tasks for her female servants.

---

22. Al Wolters, "Proverbs XXXI 10–31 as Heroic Hymn: A Form-Critical Analysis," *VT* 38 (1988): 446–57, esp. 453–55.

The Hebrew term translated by "gain" in v. 11 (שָׁלָל) usually means "plunder." Likewise, the word rendered by "food" in v. 15 (טֶרֶף) usually means "prey."

In fact, the expression "capable woman" (אֵשֶׁת־חַיִל), literally "woman of might," seems to be modeled on the expression אִישׁ־חַיִל, literally "man of might," a phrase that designates valiant warriors (e.g., 2 Sam 24:9; 11:16 for the plural).

In sum, the portrayal of the woman who is praised in Prov 31:10–31 does not conform to what one might expect to be the gender role ascribed to women by the biblical authors. Although this passage belongs to the paradigm of androcentric representation of the social order, it subtly challenges some stereotypes. Or is it perhaps that we modern scholars tend to ascribe too narrow a view of gendered representations to the biblical writers and that this is why we are surprised when we find some of their works more subtle than we expected? This question will be the subject of an exercise at the end of this chapter!

EXAMPLE 14.2b ▸ Isaiah 42:14; 49:15

The second half of the book of Isaiah contains a number of metaphors that liken God to a woman, more precisely to a mother.[23] A good example occurs in 42:14:

> For a long time I have held my peace;
> I have kept still and restrained myself;
> now I will cry out like a woman in labor;
> I will gasp and pant.

The literary context makes it clear that in this verse God is speaking of his long-felt desire to intervene on behalf of his people, who are suffering from the Babylonian exile. The use of a simile in which God likens himself to "a woman in labor" is all the more striking because the preceding verse compares God to a warrior.

Another instance is found in Isa 49:15:

> Can a woman forget her nursing child
> or show no compassion for the child of her womb?
> Even these might forget,
> yet I will not forget you.

In the first half of the verse, it is a mother's care for her little child that is praised; she can't forget her baby. In the second half, God claims that he

---

23. Mayer I. Gruber, "The Motherhood of God in Second Isaiah," *RB* 90 (1986): 351–59.

will not forget Israel. By setting these two claims side by side, the redactor implicitly compares God's care for his people to a woman's care for her child. As a result, the redactor also implicitly compares God to a mother. Now, while this comparison is based on an appreciation of a mother's feeling, one could consider it to still be relying on a stereotyped view of mothers. Nevertheless, it is striking that this passage dares to use female language to speak about God.[24]

EXAMPLE 14.2c ▸ Judges

The book of Judges is very interesting to study from the perspective of gender. On the one hand, it deconstructs some stereotypes about gender roles by depicting reversals in the traditional hierarchies. As a judge and a prophet (Judg 4), Deborah exercises functions that are almost exclusively reserved for men in the Hebrew Bible.[25] By contrast, Barak, whom God commands to fight against the Canaanites (according to Deborah's oracle; 4:6–7), proves weak; he refuses to go to the battlefield unless Deborah accompanies him. She replies: "I will surely go with you; nevertheless, the road on which you are going will not lead to your glory, for the LORD will sell Sisera into the hand of a woman" (v. 9). Later on, Yael kills Sisera by thrusting a peg into his head (v. 21), a violent act that has few parallels in women's actions in the Bible. One of these few cases occurs in Judg 9:53, where an anonymous woman of Thebez drops an upper millstone on Abimelech's head so that it crushes his skull. Tellingly, Abimelech asks a young man to kill him lest people say, "A woman killed him" (v. 54). Another interesting case occurs in the deuterocanonical book of Judith: the main character, Judith, decapitates Holofernes. Such violence is normally the preserve of men in the biblical text. To that extent, Judges subverts the expected gender roles of women in a patriarchal world.

Moreover, some women in Judges are clearly depicted as more intelligent than their husbands. In the story where a messenger of the Lord announces the birth of Samson, the future parents differ in their reactions. Manoah, the future father, does not really know how to react, and his attitude when the messenger comes back is out of sync with the situation. When this messenger ascends in a flame, Manoah fears that he and his wife

---

24. It should be noted that this approach has recently been challenged by David J. A. Clines, "Alleged Female Language about the Deity in the Hebrew Bible," *JBL* 140 (2021): 229–49.

25. The Hebrew Bible designates a limited number of women as prophetesses: Miriam (Exod 15:20), Huldah (2 Kgs 22:14; 2 Chr 34:22), the unnamed "wife" of Isaiah (Isa 8:3), the false prophetess Noadiah (Neh 6:14), and the "daughters of your people" who prophesy (Ezek 13:17–23).

will die because he reckons that they have seen God (13:22), but she proves to be more perceptive: she reasons that if God had intended to kill them, he would not have accepted their offerings and have made the announcement he made to them (13:23).[26] Likewise, Manoah's son Samson, a mighty man who seems to embody hegemonic masculinity, is manipulated by Delilah, who manages to deprive him of his strength by cutting his hair (16:4–22). Like Barak, Samson's masculinity (according to a patriarchal understanding of masculinity) is compromised.

Yet on the other hand, Amy Kalmanofsky argues that the redactors of Judges highlight exceptional women not for their own sake but to illustrate a period of instability and social chaos in the history of Israel.[27] In her view, the implicit message carried by these narratives is that chaos happens when women control and overpower men—in other words, that "in a world in which men submit to the authority of women, men do not submit directly to God's authority."[28] Accordingly, although the book of Judges depicts characters whose behavior challenges traditional gender hierarchies, it does so in order to advocate the restoration of the latter. The narratives do show that masculinity does not consist of a fixed set of characteristics but rather is a "constructed identity." Nevertheless, in Kalmanofsky's judgment, they do this in order to show that masculinity can be endangered.

The end of the book of Judges depicts a sort of civil war and provides an explanation by criticizing the period of the judges: "In those days there was no king in Israel; all the people did what was right in their own eyes" (21:25). Ultimately, the book prepares for the establishment of "a new system of male authority, the monarchy."[29]

---

26. See chapter 11 for more details. For another interpretation, see Amy Kalmanofsky, *Gender-Play in the Hebrew Bible: The Ways the Bible Challenges Its Gender Norms* (New York: Routledge, 2017), 81: she thinks that Manoah's wife's reasoning is logical but that she is not entirely right since God could have retracted his prophecy. In Kalmanofsky's view, the couple does not die because the revelation was indirect: it is a messenger of God who appeared to them, not God himself. This is a good point, but I tend to think that the narrator highlights the validity of Manoah's wife's reasoning, notably by making it the "last word" in this story.

27. We also saw in Example 6.2a that the status of women deteriorates as the book of Judges progresses.

28. See Kalmanofsky, *Gender-Play in the Hebrew Bible*, 68–94 (with quotation on 71).

29. Kalmanofsky, *Gender-Play in the Hebrew Bible*, 90.

14.3 SCRUTINIZE THE INTERPRETATION HISTORY

Typically, feminist scholars seek to:

(A) expose **androcentric biases** in past or current interpretation (hence providing a metacommentary); these can include:

- bias toward **exegesis that condemns women or misinterprets them**
- minimization or justification of **violence toward women**
- **biased translations**; this includes, but is not limited to, the lack of use of gender-inclusive language; in particular, it concerns translation choices that conceal verbal violence toward women that is present in the text

(B) expose the historical **impact** of patriarchal interpretation on **society**

(C) recover **forgotten voices of female interpreters** that have been marginalized.

With regard to this last task, the following book is helpful:

- Marion Ann Taylor and Agnes Choi, *Handbook of Women Biblical Interpreters: A Historical and Biographical Guide* (Grand Rapids: Baker Academic, 2012).

Gender studies extends the scope of this inquiry by raising exactly the same questions about the ways in which interpretation history has been influenced by gender norms (or by the lack of understanding of ancient construction of gender), has impacted society, and has led to the marginalization of some interpreters.

It would not be accurate to state that the commentators and theologians of past centuries have been entirely indifferent to the fate of female characters, but they have reacted to this in various ways. Through a series of case studies, the following book shows how some earlier interpreters struggled with various texts:

- John L. Thompson, *Writing the Wrongs: Women of the Old Testament among Biblical Commentators from Philo through the Reformation*, OSHT (New York: Oxford University Press, 2001).

EXAMPLE 14.3a ▸ 2 Samuel 11

In 2 Sam 11, David watches Bathsheba bathing and has her come to the palace in order to sleep with her. Then he makes sure that her husband, Uriah, dies in a battle so that he (David) can take her as his wife.

A number of readers throughout the centuries, and some biblical scholars still today, argue that Bathsheba acted in order to entice David, that is, by intentionally exhibiting her body. She could not have been ignorant of the fact that she would be seen, the argument goes. Some go so far as to imagine that she did this in order to bear a royal child. On the other hand, many scholars blame David, who acted as a voyeur (v. 2) and then had intercourse with Bathsheba without her consent (v. 4)—that is, raped her.[30] Perhaps the most intriguing question is whether the narrator has left a gap in the story as regards Bathsheba's intentions when she went bathing, or whether the narrator himself (or herself) hints at one of the two aforementioned possibilities (Bathsheba as "innocent" or "guilty" of seduction, so to speak). Space constraints prevent a full discussion here, but it is worth briefly exploring the following three options:

Scenario 1: If the narrator has left a gap in the story with regard to Bathsheba's intentions, then a feminist metacommentary may ask whether it is a patriarchal mindset that has tilted some scholars' interpretation toward the notion that Bathsheba acted as a seducer, since (in this hypothesis) this conclusion is not based on any suggestion made by the text. This mindset may have led some exegetes to arbitrarily prefer this interpretation, or to misinterpret some details of the text in a way that favors it. Of course, there is a risk of imputing motives here, and other factors may have influenced interpreters who have held this view, but feminist scholars may well ask these questions.

Scenario 2: If the narrator suggests that Bathsheba had no intention of seducing David, feminist commentators could still take issue with the absence of explicit condemnation of David's behavior toward Bathsheba. Admittedly, David's attitude is condemned in general terms at the end of the story (11:27) and then in a parable told by the prophet Nathan (ch. 12). But while David is clearly criticized for taking the wife of another man, and for having her husband killed, it is not clear at all that this blame extends to David's behavior toward Bathsheba as it is narrated in 11:1–5. In fact, this does not seem to be the case. In Nathan's parable, it is a lamb that stands for Bathsheba; the lamb is slaughtered, but it is doubtful that in the mind of an ancient Israelite (who would be used to the sacrificial system) the motif of the death of a lamb was meant to elicit much compassion for the animal. Moreover, the imagery transforms the sufferings of a human into the

---

30. For a brief overview of the two main camps of interpretation, see Anne Létourneau, "Beauty, Bath and Beyond: Framing Bathsheba as a Royal Fantasy in 2 Sam 11,1–5," *SJOT* 32 (2018): 72–91, esp. 74–75. The representations of the scene in movies are also revealing; see Kristine Henriksen Garroway, "Was Bathsheba the Original Bridget Jones? A New Look at Bathsheba on Screen and in Biblical Scholarship," *Nashim: A Journal of Jewish Women's Studies & Gender Issues* 24 (2013): 53–73. Scholars debate whether David's action can be called rape; for recent discussion, see Rhiannon Graybill, *Texts after Terror: Rape, Sexual Violence, and the Hebrew Bible* (New York: Oxford University Press, 2021), 58–84, esp. 63–65.

(unproblematized) sufferings of an animal, and thus downplays the issue. It seems safe to say that Bathsheba's sufferings are not really represented in Nathan's parable.

Scenario 3: Finally, according to J. Cheryl Exum, the narrator *insinuates* that Bathsheba "asked for it" by allowing herself to be seen bathing. Thus, Exum sees here a typical male strategy of blaming the victim, which relies on "a fundamental patriarchal strategy for exercising social control over women," insofar as "using woman's fear of male violence as a means of regulating female behavior is one of patriarchy's most powerful weapons."[31]

We will come back to this issue in Example 14.4b.

EXAMPLE 14.3b ▸ Genesis 4:1

After giving birth to her elder son, Cain, Eve exclaims: "I have produced a man with the help of the Lord" (Gen 4:1). Or so we read in the NRSVue. This translation is actually debated, because the Hebrew preposition rendered here by "with the help of" (namely, אֶת) could also mean "like." Hence, for instance, the NET Bible translation (2nd ed.) reads, "I have created a man just as the Lord did!" Yet another possibility would be "along with."[32] At any rate, some feminist scholars suspect that the preference for "with the help of" in a number of modern versions reflects an androcentric perspective.[33] This translation suggests that Eve needed the help of God to "create" Cain, whereas this notion does not seem present in the Hebrew text at all. While it cannot be ruled out that a number of translators were simply not familiar with the two rarer meanings of the preposition mentioned above,[34] both of these meanings are listed in the well-known lexicon BDB. Interestingly, this lexicon itself suggests translating "with the help of" in Gen 4:1 and in a couple of other passages, but only after the mention "exceptionally," which supports the hypothesis that this rendering is an *ad hoc* proposal made for reasons other than purely philological ones.

---

31. J. Cheryl Exum, *Fragmented Women: Feminist (Sub)version of Biblical Narratives*, JSOTSup 163 (Sheffield: Sheffield Academic, 1993), 188–90, esp. 189. To go further in this debate, see Létourneau's nuanced discussion, where she argues that "beauty is used as a narrative device in 2 Sam 11 to sexualize Bathsheba's character and displays intimacy with this elite woman as royal entitlement" ("Beauty, Bath and Beyond," 86).

32. See David M. Carr, *Genesis 1–11*, IECOT (Stuttgart: Kohlhammer, 2021), 149, who notes an analogous usage in 1 Chr 2:18 ("Caleb son of Hezron fathered sons with his wife Azubah").

33. For this and other examples, see Silvia Schroer, "Feminist Hermeneutics and the First Testament," in Luise Schottroff, Silvia Schroer, and Marie-Theres Wacker, *Feminist Interpretation: The Bible in Women's Perspective* (Minneapolis: Fortress, 1998), 85–101, esp. 92–94.

34. One could also imagine that avoiding "like Yhwh" or "with Yhwh" is due to theological misgivings.

> **EXAMPLE 14.3c ▸ Cosmetics in Esther and Ruth**
>
> A number of modern interpreters of the book of Ruth believe that it depicts the eponymous character alluring Boaz. Before the book's central scene, which takes place in ch. 3, Naomi, Ruth's mother-in-law, tells her: "Now wash and anoint yourself, and put on your best clothes" (Ruth 3:3). In addition to doing this, Ruth uncovers Boaz's feet and lays down by his side (3:7). Some commentators interpret Ruth's use of cosmetic oil and nice clothes as meant to enhance her beauty and consider the mention of Boaz's feet to point, by way of euphemism, to sexual activity, since in some passages "feet" (sg. רֶגֶל) serves as a covert allusion to the genitals.
>
> However, based on a new analysis of the use of cosmetics in ancient Israel, Laura Quick has put forward a different interpretation: Ruth is not expressing her sexual availability, but her *availability for marriage*. First, Naomi tells her to bathe because, as a recent widow, she had probably abstained from washing and applying oil to herself during her time of mourning (cf. 2 Sam 14:2). Because she now wants to marry, this period has come to an end. The use of oil in Ruth contrasts with its use in other passages, especially in Esther, where beauty is explicitly indicated as the aim of applying oil to oneself.
>
> Second, the garment she wears (שִׂמְלָה) is also mentioned when David ceases mourning in 2 Sam 12:20; like Ruth, he bathes, applies oil to himself, and wears a שִׂמְלָה. It is only due to the "seduction" interpretation that the NRSVue renders this word in Ruth 3:3 as "best clothes." Third, the writer does not employ the word רֶגֶל, but מַרְגְּלוֹת, to designate Boaz's feet (Ruth 3:4, 7, 8, 14); Quick suggests that this author may have deliberately avoided the former term. Indeed, by uncovering Boaz's feet, Ruth alludes to the levirate law (or some version of it), according to which Boaz should marry the wife of his relative's widow: she wanted to "remind him of the levirate obligation, where the removal of the sandal signifies the termination of the obligation." Ruth's objective was "a change in the perception of her from widow to potential bride."[35]
>
> Like Rees's new interpretation of Isa 3:16–24, Quick's analysis of Ruth 3 is based on a careful study of an aspect of ancient Israelite life (and of the Hebrew Bible) that had previously received little consideration by scholars.[36]

---

35. Laura Quick, *Dress, Adornment, and the Body in the Hebrew Bible* (Oxford: Oxford University Press, 2021), 151–80 (with quotation on 170).

36. Sara Parks argues that taking into account aspects of the Bible that have been neglected by "mainstream scholarship" (which some call "malestream scholarship"), especially the status of women, has the potential to benefit everyone, including those engaged in historical study of the Bible ("'The Brooten Phenomenon': Moving Women from the Margins in Second-Temple and New Testament Scholarship," *The Bible and Critical Theory* 15 [2019]: 46–64.)

14.4 ENGAGE IN RECONSTRUCTIVE READING

In order to reappropriate a text for modern readers, feminist scholars can:

- **Ⓐ** rediscover **marginal female characters**
- **Ⓑ** **retell the story** from a **woman's point of view**, or from the point of view of a marginalized female character
- **Ⓒ** explore the hypothesis of **female authorship** of biblical passages as well as whole books

A possible hint of female authorship is an accumulation in a passage or book of female imagery (maternal tropes) and interests.

As noted in the introduction to this chapter, some feminists raise the question of whether reconstructive reading does not sometimes amount to a "rehabilitation" of the biblical text to make it palatable to modern readers. Or, perhaps better, they wonder whether this is done on legitimate grounds or just for the convenience of modern readers, or out of "apologetic" concerns. Rhiannon Graybill thus notes a tendency to look for "happy endings" in studies of rape stories in the Hebrew Bible; this can take several forms:

- "a way of reading that finds something positive or redemptive even in the ruins of tragedy—for example, arguing that the voices of rape victims speak across texts and time to demand justice"
- "retelling the story in a way that 'saves' its rape victim, whether by imagining her as a willing partner ... or by describing her as resisting and even fighting back"
- "the catharsis of a sad story well told—we read the story, we feel sadness, and we rest contented in that judgment"

By contrast, Graybill advocates "unhappy reading," which "holds space for ambiguity, ambivalence, and non-resolution."[37]

Therefore, it is important to keep in mind the fact that feminists react in different ways to reconstructive reading—or practice it in different ways.

EXAMPLE 14.4a ▸ 2 Kings 11

Upon the death of Ahaziah—who reigns over Judah for one year (2 Kgs 8:26)—his mother, Athaliah, has the entire royal line massacred (2 Kgs 11:1). This is a classic move, in the ancient Near East, for a ruler who accedes to

---

37. Graybill, *Texts after Terror*, 4.

the throne and wants to prevent any danger of a coup designed to (re)install a member of the dynastic line. The rest of the story confirms that for all practical purposes, Athaliah reigns over Judah. Verse 3 even mentions that Joash, who has escaped the massacre, lives hidden in the temple for "six years . . . while Athaliah reigned over the land." In sum, everything indicates that Athaliah was effectively queen of Judah for years.

And yet, the text conspicuously avoids stating this explicitly. The verb "reigned" in the verse just quoted is a participle (מֹלֶכֶת) that appears discreetly in a circumstantial clause; nowhere does the text use the title "queen" or "ruler" to designate Athaliah. What is more, Athaliah's reign is not integrated into the regnal (and chronological) framework of the books of Kings; the reader does not find here the formulaic indications that systematically introduce a reign and close the section concerning it. Clearly, in the eyes of the redactors of the books of Kings, Athaliah does not count as a queen of Judah—at least, they do not want the reader to regard her as such.

Now, it may be asked whether Athaliah's reign is glossed over because *(a)* she is a woman (patriarchal prejudice), or *(b)* because she defended the cult of Baal[38] (religious motive), or *(c)* because she belongs to the family of the infamous Ahab, a king of the Northern Kingdom who is strongly criticized in Kings (political reason). Or is it due to a combination of these motives? It should be noted that the two last factors, *(b)* and *(c)*, did not lead the redactors of Kings to deny the rank of king to male characters. Indeed, they deny this rank neither to sovereigns of the Northern Kingdom like Ahab, nor to Ahaziah, son of Joram, who reigned over the Southern Kingdom and who was a relative of Ahab (2 Kgs 8:25–27). Therefore, it is not just the idea of a relative of Ahab reigning over Judah that made the redactors of Kings regard Athaliah as illegitimate. One cannot help noticing a difference of treatment when it comes to the sole female ruler of Judah.

In addition, a consequence of this is that a reader of the books of Kings may well get the impression that only men ever reigned over Judah and Israel. Because these books helped shape the political imagination of readers of the Bible throughout the centuries, especially in Christianity, one may suspect that this has played a role in the exclusion of women from political roles. A feminist interpretation of 2 Kgs 11 will want to reinstate Athaliah to her full rank of queen, so to speak, thus restoring her political dignity and acknowledging her historical role.

---

38. This is implicit in the fact that Athaliah's adversaries, led by a priest of Yhwh, destroy Baal's temple as soon as they have killed her (v. 18).

EXAMPLE 14.4b ▸ 2 Samuel 11

Let us consider again the story of David and Bathsheba in 2 Sam 11 by discussing a recent interpretation that focuses on Bathsheba's point of view. Rhiannon Graybill argues that while the narrator implicitly characterizes Bathsheba as a victim and David as a sexual predator (one of the views mentioned in Example 14.3a), this is not the best way to analyze the situation. Victimization creates a risk of flattening, by essentializing Bathsheba's status as a victim and stripping her own agency from her. Graybill prefers to say that Bathsheba is "perempted" by the narrative and by David—meaning that her own sexual subjectivity is disqualified and thus immediately removed from consideration by the narrator, and by David. The absence of information about what she wants is part of the "fuzziness" that characterizes this story of rape (and other such stories in the Hebrew Bible); exactly what happens, and what the woman thinks and feels, is not described. Thinking in terms of a victim only also reduces the full extent of the harm: Bathsheba is not only abused, she is also limited in her autonomy and her own sexual subjectivity. In a word, ceasing to read the text through the lens of victimization allows the reader to realize that the question of what Bathsheba wants, experiences, thinks, and feels is silenced.[39]

EXAMPLE 14.4c ▸ Isaiah 40–55

A recent trend in the exegesis of Isa 40–55 argues that its author might have been a woman. This runs contrary to the overtones of the traditional appellation "Second Isaiah," which suggests that the redactor responsible for chs. 40–55 was like a new Isaiah and thus yet another male prophet. The hints in this text pointing to possible female authorship are its accumulation of female metaphors, its interest in childbirth, and the fact that it likens Yhwh himself to a woman. A variant of this hypothesis posits that at least a number of the redactors involved in an "Isaianic school" were female prophets.[40] Interestingly, First Isaiah (the traditional designation of Isa 1–39) already mentions a female prophet (Isa 8:3).

---

39. Graybill, *Texts after Terror*, 58–84.

40. Sharon Moughtin-Mumby, "Feminist/Womanist Readings of Isaiah," in *The Oxford Handbook of Isaiah*, ed. Lena-Sofia Tiemeyer (New York: Oxford University Press, 2020), 610–11.

Exercises for Chapter 14

Exercise A

Write a feminist interpretation of Ezek 16.

Exercise B

Examine Deut 32:18 and the similes this verse contains, and analyze them from a feminist point of view.

Exercise C

In Example 14.2a, we saw that although Prov 31:10–31 seems to fit an androcentric view of society, it also praises a woman in terms that challenge stereotypes; this subtle combination surprises modern interpreters. A question was then raised: is it because we modern scholars tend to ascribe too narrow a view of gendered representations to the biblical writers that we are surprised when we find some of their works to be more subtle than we expected?

What do you think? (In the context of a classroom discussion, this could lead to a debate between two students or groups of students, some defending a positive answer to the question just raised, others defending a negative answer.)

Exercise D

(This exercise requires a knowledge of Hebrew.) In Gen 2:18, God says, "It is not good that the man should be alone," and he then announces that he will create a new being to solve this problem (the rest of the story shows that this being is Eve). The Hebrew expression that designates this being is עֵזֶר כְּנֶגְדּוֹ. Here is a selection of modern translations of this expression:

> "a helper as his partner" (NRSVue)
> "a fitting helper for him" (NJPS)
> "a helper" (New Jerusalem Bible)
> "a companion for him who corresponds to him" (NET Bible, 2nd ed.)
> "a helper that is perfect for him" (Common English Bible)

From the point of view of feminist interpretation, the most important question is whether the Hebrew expression עֵזֶר כְּנֶגְדּוֹ carries an overtone of subordination or of equality. To answer this question, one must attend to two issues. First, what is the meaning of the word translated by "helper" or "companion" here (עֵזֶר), and does it bear connotations of subservience? In English, "helper" may suggest the latter, but is the same the case in Hebrew? Second, does the accompanying phrase כְּנֶגְדּוֹ—which is translated in various ways above (e.g., "fitting for him" or "perfect for him")—imply equal rank or a relationship of partnership, or something else? These two issues are debated.

On the one hand, Phyllis Trible argues that the word typically translated by "helper" (עֵזֶר) does not imply inferiority, since God himself is sometimes presented as the "helper" of Israel (e.g., Ps 118:13). It is unlikely that a redactor would have used this word to speak about God if it implied any kind of inferiority. On the contrary, the Hebrew word might suggest some degree of superiority, insofar as it is the person who benefits from help who is in need of it and the "helper" is the one able to provide it. In addition, Trible argues that the accompanying phrase כְּנֶגְדּוֹ implies equality or mutuality; it would even serve to "temper" the connotation of superiority carried by "helper" (עֵזֶר).[41]

On the other hand, David Clines, who confesses that he initially adopted Trible's analysis because he "wanted it to be true," has reviewed the biblical occurrences of the Hebrew word here that is typically translated as "helper" (עֵזֶר) and has concluded that

> being a helper is not a Hebrew way of being an equal. Helping is the same the world over. Phyllis Trible was right when she affirmed that it is a "relational" term that carried no implications about the respective statuses of the helper and the helpee. She was wrong, I think, when she argued that, because God is often said to be a "helper", the term itself has acquired connotations of superiority. Whether the helper is a superior or not will depend entirely on other factors, extrinsic to the relationship constituted by the act of helping.[42]

In order to form your own opinion, review the selection of occurrences explored by David Clines in his study (Josh 10:33; 1 Kgs 20:16; Isa 30:7; 1 Chr 12:21[22]; 2 Chr 18:31–32; 28:23; Pss 30:10[11]; 109:26; 118:13). You can also read Clines's comments on these verses. In your view, who is right, Trible or Clines? How would you translate the Hebrew expression? Do you think that this verse conveys a helpful or problematic view of women?

Exercise E

It has been suggested that Song of Songs was written by a woman. What aspects of the text could support this hypothesis?

---

41. Phyllis Trible, *God and the Rhetoric of Sexuality* (Philadelphia: Fortress, 1978), 88–90.
42. David J. A. Clines, *What Does Eve Do to Help? and Other Readerly Questions to the Old Testament*, JSOTSup 94 (Sheffield: JSOT Press, 1990), 25–48, esp. 32.

CHAPTER 15
POSTCOLONIAL CRITICISM

OVERVIEW

Postcolonial studies includes a large array of approaches and perspectives. Yet they all have at heart a critical examination of the many ways *colonial* structures and ideologies have shaped, and are still influencing, human history, societies, and lives. In fact, the same concern extends to various forms of past and present *imperialism*. Hence the development of "imperial studies" as a distinct field, although it is also possible to examine imperial situations in the framework of postcolonial studies,[1] as I will do in this chapter for the sake of convenience.

The relevance of such approaches for the Hebrew Bible is a direct consequence of the circumstances of its making. Most of the Hebrew Bible was written when empires dominated Israel and Judah, either as hegemonic powers with political, economic, and cultural influence over the Levant; or as suzerains in vassal relationships; or as empires into which the territories of Israel or Judah had been incorporated.

Postcolonial studies is interested in strategies of *domination* and instances of *resistance*. When it comes to literature, the first question is how colonial or imperial ideologies have influenced the writers and how this is reflected in their texts, either in overt apology or endorsement of these structures and their assumptions, or in veiled, often subconscious, manners. In addition, postcolonial readings seek to expose how texts have served to enforce or reinforce structures of domination, which can occur either when a text's own ideological contents are in line with these or when readers misuse the text. But other texts have served as vehicles for expressing resistance and have encouraged liberation movements, and practitioners of postcolonial studies mine literature, including the Hebrew Bible, for such voices.

---

1. Steed Vernyl Davidson, *Writing/Reading the Bible in Postcolonial Perspective*, BRP 2.3 (Leiden: Brill, 2017), 9.

On the other hand, postcolonial studies has pointed out that colonial or imperial situations created *liminality*, an in-between space where people reacted and interacted in various ways, and where cultural exchanges, and changes, took place. Some subalterns (people dominated by others within a colonial structure) accepted and internalized the representation of themselves imposed by the colonizers; others resisted. But Homi Bhabha has shown that subtler situations could occur. The encounters between different cultures led to *hybridity*: transcultural realities emerged, for instance on the level of language (creolization) or culture. Moreover, Bhabha has highlighted *mimicry*, which occurs when subalterns take up or imitate features of the colonizers (how they dress, behave, speak, etc.) or that the colonizers have imposed upon them, seemingly accepting them but doing so with mockery. Admittedly, the concepts of hybridity and mimicry have been criticized.[2] They may tend to overstate the mutuality of the relationships between colonizers and subalterns, as well as the subversive power of mimicry, and thus downplay the asymmetrical character of colonial situations. While it is important to keep in mind such limitations, these concepts remain essential to postcolonial studies.

It is also crucial to realize that hybridity and mimicry are often marked by *ambivalence*. Taking up features of a colonial structure in order to mock it still entails accepting some of its assumptions and thinking within the framework of imperial power. Being alert to such ambivalence requires taking a step back to adopt a more critical perspective on a situation.

Besides these caveats, two main criticisms have been raised against postcolonial studies. First, it is mostly text-based, focusing on literary productions, at the risk of neglecting many concrete situations in which subalterns may have found themselves that are not documented in writings. In the case of ancient societies, this is virtually inevitable, although archaeology sometimes yields information on the effects that imperialism had on the practical life of the inhabitants of Israel and Judah. Second, some practitioners of postcolonial studies run the risk of essentializing "the West," "Europe," or "the Enlightenment," regarding them as monolithic realities or transcendental categories, and relying on, or developing, simplistic views of complicated historical processes.

Still, the limits of postcolonial studies and the possible abuses by some of its proponents do not change the fact that these studies shed new light on biblical texts and yield crucial insights that could not be obtained by other exegetical approaches. They have unveiled aspects and readings of the Hebrew Bible that were neglected or altogether ignored by exegetes living in the seats of empires or former empires. Rasiah Sugirtharajah, a leading voice on the subject, has helpfully identified the three main tasks of postcolonial studies as it relates to the Bible, and we will attend to each of these in this chapter:[3]

---

2. Davidson, *Writing/Reading the Bible in Postcolonial Perspective*, 22–23.
3. Rasiah S. Sugirtharajah, *The Bible and the Third World: Precolonial, Colonial and Postcolonial Encounters* (Cambridge: Cambridge University Press, 2001), 250–57.

❶ "SCRUTIN[IZE] . . . BIBLICAL DOCUMENTS FOR THEIR **COLONIAL ENTANGLE-MENTS**."[4] THAT IS, DETECT IN THE BIBLE INFLUENCES OF, AFFINITIES WITH, OR ENDORSEMENTS OF COLONIAL STRUCTURES.

❷ "ENGAGE IN **RECONSTRUCTIVE [POSTCOLONIAL] READING** OF BIBLICAL TEXTS," WHICH CAN TAKE SEVERAL FORMS: "POSTCOLONIAL READING WILL REREAD BIBLICAL TEXTS FROM THE PERSPECTIVE OF **POSTCOLONIAL CONCERNS** SUCH AS LIBERATION STRUGGLES OF THE PAST AND PRESENT; IT WILL BE SENSITIVE TO **SUBALTERN AND FEMININE ELEMENTS** EMBEDDED IN THE TEXTS; IT WILL INTERACT WITH AND REFLECT ON **POSTCOLONIAL CIRCUMSTANCES** SUCH AS HYBRIDITY, FRAGMENTATION, DETERRITORIALIZATION, AND HYPHENATED, DOUBLE OR MULTIPLE IDENTITIES."[5]

❸ "**INTERROGATE BOTH COLONIAL AND METROPOLITAN INTERPRETATIONS**."[6] THIS ENTAILS UNVEILING THE WAYS IN WHICH COLONIAL IDEOLOGIES HAVE **INFLUENCED THE INTERPRETATION** OF THE TEXTS BY WESTERN EXEGETES AND IN WHICH THE LATTER HAVE **USED THE TEXTS** TO ENFORCE OR REINFORCE COLONIAL STRUCTURES.

15.1 SCRUTINIZE THE TEXT FOR COLONIAL ENTANGLEMENTS

This first task of postcolonial criticism of the Hebrew Bible stems from the idea that the biblical writers—who lived and thought in a world where monarchy was the standard form of political structure and empires were a permanent reality (in spite of the changing actors)—did not question but accepted the assumptions and norms of imperial structure. Steed Vernyl Davidson writes: "While a clear denunciation of specific empires can be noted in the Bible, no sustained critique against the structure of empire as a form of rule can be noted in the Bible as a whole. At best, the Bible advocates the destruction of evil empires, so they can be replaced by more benign expressions of similarly imperialistic rule."[7]

Thus, postcolonial analysis will seek to unveil the various ways in which biblical texts presuppose or implicitly accept the structure of empire as the normal form of rule, and what the consequences of this are. But it is also interested in exposing cases where the redactors do more than that and actively endorse imperialism. At this juncture, one could object that pointing out the limitations of the political thinking of an-

---

4. Sugirtharajah, *The Bible and the Third World*, 251 (with bold formatting added).
5. Sugirtharajah, *The Bible and the Third World*, 252–53 (with bold formatting added).
6. Sugirtharajah, *The Bible and the Third World*, 255 (with bold formatting added).
7. Davidson, *Writing/Reading the Bible in Postcolonial Perspective*, 36.

cient redactors may border on anachronistic value judgement, if one reproaches them for not exhibiting modern insights. However, the point is not to assess the subjective merits or demerits of the redactors, but to examine the possible objective affinities of the texts with certain power configurations, regardless of whether it would have been possible to "think outside the box" and criticize these configurations at that time.

> **EXAMPLE 15.1a ▸ Royal Psalms**
>
> Kingship is a recurrent theme in the Psalms. A number of these poems exalt the Lord as king (e.g., Pss 47; 93–99). This allows the psalmist to highlight the Lord's might, his control over nature or historical events, and his care for the people of Israel. At the same time, one may wonder whether this figurative manner of speaking of the Lord does not carry representations or connotations that are questionable. To use the language of CMT (Conceptual Metaphor Theory, on which see chapter 10), one may want to study the metaphor THE LORD IS KING and examine the aspects that are transferred from the source domain (kingship) to the Lord. In light of royal ideology in the ancient Near East, the source domain may contain ideas such as domination, supremacy, arbitrary ruling, abuse of power, etc. Are such aspects "mapped" onto the target domain, that is, the Lord (and his relationship with human beings)? Do they color the way he is evoked in the Psalms, or the way they describe how he interacts with nature or human beings?

> **EXAMPLE 15.1b ▸ Deuteronomy**
>
> The book of Deuteronomy is basically modeled on the vassal treaties that empires (e.g., Egypt or Assyria) concluded with smaller kingdoms (e.g., Ugarit, Aram-Damascus, Israel, or Judah). This is apparent in the overall structure of Deuteronomy, which echoes the typical successive sections of such a treaty; notably, this explains why the book includes and devotes so much time to the dire consequences that will result in the event of betrayal (see the curses and blessings in Deut 28). While some scholars believe that Deuteronomy was inspired by Hittite treaties from the Late Bronze Age, most think that it is based on Neo-Assyrian treaties from the Iron Age.
>
> The point is that Deuteronomy transposes the vassal relationship between kings (and their kingdoms) onto the relationship between the Lord and the people of Israel. This daring literary device has significant implications. It entails representing the relationship between the Lord and his people as based on a contractual, even legal, arrangement. This can be interpreted positively, as a clearly defined relationship with mutual commitments. But

it can also be regarded as a quite formal view of this relationship, one in which, in addition, faithfulness may be inspired by the fear of punishment (the curses) and interest in rewards (the blessings). Above all, this literary construction ascribes to the Lord a role equivalent to that of an ancient Near Eastern suzerain, which may carry a number of negative connotations. This echoes the preceding example, except that vassal relationship points to a specific subcategory of kings: those powerful enough to be suzerains, whose prime qualities were generally not benevolence and kindness but the aptitude for ruthless domination.

In sum, by taking up the notion of vassalship and the literary form of the vassal treaty, the redactors of Deuteronomy appropriated ancient Near Eastern representations that are typically imperialistic in the very manner in which they conceptualized the Lord and his relationship with his people. This created opportunities but also theological limitations.

Resources on Postcolonial Readings of the Hebrew Bible

For a survey of research history (up to 2009), see:

- Bradley L. Crowell, "Postcolonial Studies and the Hebrew Bible," *CurBR* 7 (2009): 217–44.

For thematic introductions, notably about the interplay between postcolonial criticism and other approaches (e.g., ecology, feminist studies), see:

- R. S. Sugirtharajah, ed., *The Oxford Handbook of Postcolonial Biblical Criticism* (Oxford: Oxford University Press, 2020).

For collections of discussions on biblical books, see:

- R. S. Sugirtharajah, ed., *The Postcolonial Biblical Reader* (Malden, MA: Blackwell, 2006). Includes chapters on Esther, Judith, Ruth, Dan 1, and 2 Kgs 24–25, and a variety of other chapters (involving both theoretical discussions and the application of postcolonial criticism to specific situations).

- Hemchand Gossai, ed., *Postcolonial Commentary and the Old Testament* (London: T&T Clark, 2018). With chapters on Exodus, Leviticus, Numbers, Deuteronomy, Judges, Wisdom of Solomon, 1 Kings, 1 Chronicles, Nehemiah, Esther, Psalms, Isa 1–39, Jeremiah, Lamentations, Jonah, and Nahum.

The following book is very helpful for getting acquainted with the successive imperial contexts in which the biblical books were written, the associated ideologies and metanarratives, and their reflections in the texts:

- Leo Perdue and Warren Carter, *Israel and Empire: A Postcolonial History of Israel and Early Judaism,* ed. Coleman A. Baker (London: Bloomsbury T&T Clark, 2015).

15.2 ENGAGE IN RECONSTRUCTIVE READING

Based on Sugirtharajah's comments that were quoted in the introduction to this chapter, this task can involve the following:

A reading the text **from the viewpoint of subaltern and marginalized** peoples and individuals and in light of their struggles

B identifying **situations** in the text that are relevant for postcolonial analysis: imperial rule over Israel or Judah; annexation of these territories within an empire; life in diaspora; multiple identities (e.g., being a Judean and a subject of the Persian empire); etc.

C looking for different kinds of **constructive reactions and interactions**—notably resistance, hybridity, and mimicry

EXAMPLE 15.2a › Isaiah 10:5–34

The prophet Isaiah lived at a time (second half of the eighth century and first half of the seventh century BCE) when the Neo-Assyrian empire was expanding westward. This empire annexed the kingdom of Israel ca. 720 BCE. About twenty years later, the Assyrian army ravaged the kingdom of Judah and came close to taking the capital, Jerusalem. It is no exaggeration to say that how to react in the face of Assyrian imperialistic policy represented the great question of the time, both for the Judean king and his counselors and for prophets, like Isaiah, who intervened in the debate. First Isaiah (Isa 1–39) is full of texts that deal with this geopolitical situation, and commentators have noticed that a number of these texts betray a good knowledge of Assyrian ideology and propaganda. What is more, some oracles turn this propaganda onto its head, thus being instances of resistance through mimicry.[8]

A good example of this phenomenon is Isa 10:5–34. Scholars have pointed out that numerous motifs and expressions in Isa 10:5–34 echo motifs and expressions found in Neo-Assyrian inscriptions.[9] Table 15.1 presents a selection of these echoes in vv. 5–15,[10] with brief comments; some concern topoi found in texts of various Assyrian kings, and others have especially striking parallels in texts from Sargon II and Sennacherib, the kings who were on the throne in the last two decades of the eighth century BCE.

Table 15.1: Selected Echoes of Neo-Assyrian texts in Isaiah 10:5–15

Isaiah 10:5–15	Neo-Assyrian Texts	Comment
"Woe to Assyria, the rod of my anger—the club in their hands is my fury!" (v. 5)	Assyrian kings hold a rod (or staff or scepter) as a symbol of their kingship, but also as a weapon that helps them conquer territories and punish enemies.	Isaiah turns the Assyrian imagery on its head: it is not the king of Assyria who uses a staff given by Assyrian gods to strike Judah; rather, Yhwh uses the king of Assyria as a staff to punish Judah (hence, Yhwh is in control of events).
"Against a godless nation I send him, and against the people of my wrath I command him, to take spoil and seize plunder" (v. 6)	Assyrian kings claim to be sent by their gods to extend the territory of the Assyrian empire.	Yhwh claims to be the one who sends the Assyrian king to punish Judah and plunder it.

---

8. For a recent study, see Shawn Zelig Aster, *Reflections of Empire in Isaiah 1–39: Responses to Assyrian Ideology*, ANEM 19 (Atlanta: SBL Press, 2017). See also the helpful survey in D. N. Prenmath, "The Empire and First Isaiah," in *Postcolonial Commentary and the Old Testament*, ed. Hemchand Gossai (London: T&T Clark, 2018), 240–58.

9. William R. Gallagher, *Sennacherib's Campaign to Judah: New Studies*, SHCANE 18 (Leiden: Brill, 1999), 78–83 (for vv. 13–14); Aster, *Reflections of Empire in Isaiah 1–39*, 181–234 (for the entirety of ch. 10).

10. Most scholars ascribe these verses to Isaiah himself, except for vv. 10–12; see the discussion in Hugh G. M. Williamson, *Isaiah 1–27*, vol. 2, *Commentary on Isaiah 6–12*, ICC (London: T&T Clark, 2018), 495–501.

"to take spoil and seize plunder." (v. 6)	Spoiling and plundering are routinely mentioned in Assyrian reports of military campaigns.	Isaiah seems well acquainted with these Assyrian policies.
"For he says: 'Are not my commanders all kings?'" (v. 8)	In vassalized countries that rebel, Assyrian kings often replace kings with their own officers.	
"For he says: 'By the strength of my hand I have done it, and by my wisdom, for I have understanding;" (v. 13)	Sargon II and Sennacherib claim that their "hands" have captured cities. They boast of their "wisdom" and of their knowledge or understanding.	Isaiah seems to be well acquainted with Assyrian boasting language.
"I have removed the boundaries of peoples and have plundered their treasures; like a bull I have brought down those who sat on thrones." (v. 13)	Sargon II and Sennacherib claim to "enlarge the border" of Assyria or add territories to it. Sennacherib claims to move "like a bull" during attacks on the enemy.	Assyria had annexed some territories in Israel ca. 734–732, and the rest of Israel ca. 720. Because of Assyrian involvement in the southern Levant, Judah lost control of some territories to the west, even before the invasion of 701 BCE.
"My hand has found, like a nest, the wealth of the peoples, and as one gathers eggs that have been forsaken, so I have gathered all the earth, and there was none that moved a wing or opened its mouth or chirped." (v. 14)	The enemy is often represented as a bird in a cage in Assyrian accounts of battles or sieges. Sennacherib uses the image of a nest.	Again, Isaiah seems well acquainted with Assyrian imagery as used in royal inscriptions.

After criticizing Assyria's ideology and claims in vv. 5–15, the chapter turns to the announcement of Yhwh's intervention against Assyria (vv. 16–34). As Aster notes, what makes Isa 10 special, compared to other texts in First Isaiah that deal with Assyria, is the fact that it does not react to Assyrian ideology by promising that Yhwh *will protect Judah*. Rather, this passage states that Yhwh *will punish Assyria* for its "arrogance in rivalling and disobeying God." What we read in Isa 10:5–34 is "the portrayal of a clash between two rivals who each claim primacy over the other."[11] While other passages in First Isaiah respond to Assyrian claims of supremacy with claims that Yhwh is the supreme sovereign, Isa 10:5–34 construes Assyrian expansionist ideology as a threat to Yhwh's sovereignty: "Assyria's actions have brought into the open the contest between God and Assyria."[12] Aster calls this contest a "clash of titans."[13]

EXAMPLE 15.2b ▸ Deuteronomy

Let us consider Deuteronomy again. Insofar as its redactors reused Assyrian categories when creating their own, unprecedented kind of theological document, one that is embedded in a Judean theology, Deuteronomy qualifies as an impressive result of hybridity. Could we go further and say that Deuteronomy involves mimicry? In other words, does it contain polemics against Assyria? This is a debated issue in current exegesis. Some argue that Deut 13 and 28 borrow specifically from Esarhaddon's Succession Treaty in order to criticize Assyrian oppression.[14] This does not mean that the redactors of these chapters called into question the imperalistic structure per se, but that they implicitly criticized Neo-Assyrian rule over their country. However, Carly Crouch argues that Deuteronomy does not contain the recognizable signals that would ensure that its audience would perceive allusions to Esarhaddon's Succession Treaty, or even to the Assyrian tradition; the similarities are too imprecise and occasional for that.[15]

EXAMPLE 15.2c ▸ Esther

The story of Esther is saturated with references to the imperial structures of Persia. But the narrative does not voice any criticism of these structures, and it does not include characters that call them into question but rather characters who end up surviving by using some of the mechanisms of the empire. Indeed, it is thanks to an imperial edict that the Jews are able to preemptively kill their adversaries, thereby using the very ploy that would have

---

11. Aster, *Reflections of Empire in Isaiah 1–39*, 174.
12. Aster, *Reflections of Empire in Isaiah 1–39*, 181.
13. Aster, *Reflections of Empire in Isaiah 1–39*, 173.
14. Bernard M. Levinson and Jeffrey Stackert, "Between the Covenant Code and Esarhaddon's Succession Treaty: Deuteronomy 13 and the Composition of Deuteronomy," *JAJ* 3 (2012): 123–40.
15. Carly L. Crouch, *Israel and the Assyrians: Deuteronomy, the Succession Treaty of Esarhaddon, and the Nature of Subversion*, ANEM 8 (Atlanta: SBL Press, 2014).

led them to the same fate. Esther succeeds in turning an imperial device against her enemies; she participates in the system and benefits from her position in it. The narrative is about *a reversal in the situation*, not *a subversion of the system*.

This is why Sugirtharajah notes that "the narrative as such does not question the Persian tributary system which sustains the empire, but aspires to survival or, at best, some degree of survival within the system. Before the text can be mined for its liberative potential, for example in the person of Vashti, its hegemonic assumptions have to be exposed."[16] In this connection, Sugirtharajah mentions the hierarchical system culminating with the king, the pervasive patriarchy, the wealth of the royal palace, and the absence of regard for the conditions of people who do not belong to the elite. He also writes that "in the name of struggle for national survival of the Jewish people, the narrative deprivileges the question of gender oppression and exploitation." Finally, "the book encourages largely a strategy of assimilation, endorses conformity and has little relevance for liberative purposes."[17]

These considerations may need some qualifications, however. Some commentators have pointed out that while the text never explicitly criticizes the imperial structure, its descriptions of the behavior of some characters, and of the machinery of the court, are full of sarcasm.[18] Thus, ch. 1 describes the wealth and pomp of the empire in such grandiose terms, and tells of banquets of such gargantuan proportions, that the attentive reader wonders: is this a very serious and deferential description, or a comical description told, tongue-in-cheek, by a narrator who wants the reader to perceive how extravagant and ridiculous the empire is? In addition, it turns out that for all his spectacularly macho behavior, King Ahasuerus, the most powerful man in the empire, needs to take advice from his sages to know how to deal with Vashti when she refuses to comply and come to the banquet (1:10–13). Moreover, the text explains that the imperial machinery requires the king to have recourse to an imperial edict, proclaimed in all the empire, to resolve this marital problem. Within the patriarchal framework and the related prejudices of this ancient society, the way he publicizes his inability to address this marital challenge is, again, ridiculous. Generally speaking, the text insists so much on the irrevocable character of the imperial edicts (8:8) that it seems to insinuate that the men are prisoners of the system they have created.

None of this amounts to a political challenge that would lead to subverting the imperial structure, but the book seems more critical of this structure than may appear at first sight, even though this criticism remains implicit.

---

16. Sugirtharajah, *The Bible and the Third World*, 251.
17. Sugirtharajah, *The Bible and the Third World*, 252.
18. Frederic W. Bush, *Ruth, Esther*, WBC 9 (Dallas: Word, 1996), 314–16.

> To this extent, the narrative includes some aspects that come close to mimicry, with all the ambivalence that this entails.
>
> In the end, this example illustrates the difficulty posed by biblical narratives that describe situations without taking an explicit stance on them, which is often the case. The challenge for critical readings is to determine whether this is because the text accepts the assumptions of an ideology or because the redactors chose to resort to veiled criticism. To detect the latter may require a close reading informed by the resources of narrative analysis.

Encultured and Cross-Textual Readings

Yet another kind of postcolonial interpretation of the Hebrew Bible involves reading a text in relation to a concrete, modern postcolonial situation. Bradley Crowell notes that this is done in at least two different ways:

- **"Encultured reading"**: An author who belongs to an oppressed society interprets the text in light of his or her experience, highlighting aspects that have been neglected in past exegesis; or, conversely, this author uses the biblical text to address issues proper to his or her postcolonial context.

- **"Cross-textual reading,"** which consists of putting a biblical text into dialogue with an indigenous narrative, with potential insights for both texts.

For examples and further references, see:

- Bradley L. Crowell, "Postcolonial Studies and the Hebrew Bible," *CurBR* 7 (2009): 227–33.

An important example of postcolonial interpretation situated in specific cultural contexts is African exegesis, on which see:

- Gerald O. West, "African Biblical Scholarship as Post-Colonial, Tri-Polar, and a Site-of-Struggle," in *Present and Future of Biblical Studies: Celebrating 25 Years of Brill's Biblical Interpretation*, ed. Tat-siong Benny Liew, BIS 161 (Leiden: Brill, 2018), 240–73.

- Musa W. Dube, Andrew M. Mbuvi, and Dora R. Mbuwayesango, eds., *Postcolonial Perspectives in African Biblical Interpretations*, GPBS 13 (Atlanta: SBL, 2012).

15.3 SCRUTINIZE THE RECEPTION HISTORY

This task involves scrutinizing the reception history of a text to determine possible colonial entanglements in the text or how colonial ideologies have influenced its interpretation. Here chapter 13 may give you direction for where to look.

> **EXAMPLE 15.3** ▸ **Genesis 9:23–26**
>
> In Gen 9, after the flood narrative, we read of a surprising episode during which Noah becomes drunk and undresses himself. One of his sons, Ham, sees him naked, whereas his two other sons "walked backward and covered the nakedness of their father; their faces were turned away, and they did not see their father's nakedness." (v. 23). Then we read the following: "When Noah awoke from his wine and knew what his youngest son had done to him, he said, 'Cursed be Canaan; lowest of slaves shall he be to his brothers.' He also said, 'Blessed by the Lord my God be Shem, and let Canaan be his slave'" (vv. 24–26).
>
> Surprisingly, Noah curses Canaan for an action that was the fault of Canaan's father, Ham. Scholars propose several explanations: Ham's involvement is a secondary phenomenon due to a later compositional layer; a redactor wanted to avoid the idea that a curse affected people who had been blessed by God (9:1); Noah punished the son of Ham because the latter had sinned against him as his son.[19]
>
> At any rate, the reception history shows that many readers throughout the centuries have focused on Ham, who was widely regarded as the ancestor of Africans and of Black people in general, in connection with a particular interpretation of the table of nations found in Gen 10.
>
> The story in Gen 9:23–26 was used in Europe to justify the intercontinental slave trade (and slavery within Europe as well), and then extensively in America, from the eighteenth century onward, to justify Black slavery.[20] Some of the antislavery authors also shared this idea, but they pointed out

---

19. Markus Witte, "Ham," *EBR* 11, cols. 63–64.
20. Robin Blackburn, "The Old Word Background to European Colonial Slavery," *The William and Mary Quarterly* 54 (1997): 65–102; Stephen R. Haynes, *Noah's Curse: The Biblical Justification for Slavery* (New York: Oxford University Press, 2002); David M. Goldenberg, *The Curse of Ham: Race and Slavery in Early Judaism, Christianity, and Islam* (Princeton: Princeton University Press, 2003); Goldenberg, *Black and Slave: The Origins and History of the Curse of Ham*, SBR 10 (Berlin: de Gruyter, 2017).

> the great achievements of Egypt and Ethiopia. The link between skin color and slavery, in connection with this story of Genesis, was already made much earlier in some Muslim sources.
>
> From whatever angle you look at it, this is an absurd interpretation, but it has played a role in the immense tragedy of white domination for centuries.

Exercises for Chapter 15

Exercise A

Find references to the exodus in two African American spirituals.

Exercise B

The setting of the narratives at the heart of the book of Daniel—especially those in chs. 1 through 6—is the Babylonian and Persian courts. Scrutinize these chapters and mine them for entanglements with empire or criticism of it.

Exercise C

Explain how Nahum can be read as a case of resistance literature against Assyrian domination. To this end, briefly summarize the historical context, point out situations mentioned or alluded to in the book that criticize Assyria's behavior toward people it subjugated, and explain how this book may have helped Judeans.

Exercise D

Read Isa 2:5–22 and find echoes of Neo-Assyrian ideology and propaganda. As a help, you may use exegetical commentaries and Shawn Aster's monograph *Reflections of Empire in Isaiah 1–39* (which has been made available as an open-access resource by the publisher, SBL Press, on its website). Do you find resistance and/or mimicry in this biblical passage?

Exercise E

Find a historical example from centuries past of the use of the book of Joshua to justify the colonization of a country.

BIBLIOGRAPHY

Abegg, Martin G., Jr., with James E. Bowley and Edward Cook. *The Dead Sea Scrolls Concordance*. 3 vols. Leiden: Brill, 2003–10.
Abegg, Martin, Jr., Peter Flint, and Eugene Ulrich. *The Dead Sea Scrolls Bible*. New York: HarperCollins, 1999.
Abel, Félix-Marie Abel. *Géographie de la Palestine*. 2 vols. Ebib. Paris: Gabalda, 1967.
Adams, Russell B., ed. *Jordan: An Archaeological Reader*. London: Equinox, 2008.
Aharoni, Yohanan. *The Land of the Bible: A Historical Geography*. Philadelphia: Westminster, 1979.
Aḥituv, Shmuel. *Echoes from the Past: Hebrew and Cognate Inscriptions from the Biblical Period*. Jerusalem: Carta, 2008.
Aitken, James T., ed. *The T&T Clark Companion to the Septuagint*. London: T&T Clark, 2015.
Albertson, R. G. "Job and Ancient Near Eastern Wisdom Literature." Pages 213–30 in *Scripture in Context*, vol. 2, *More Essays on the Comparative Method*. Edited by William W. Hallo, James C. Moyer, and Leo G. Perdue. Winona Lake, IN: Eisenbrauns, 1983.
Allen, David. "The Use of Criteria: The State of the Question." Pages 129–41 in *Methodology in the Use of the Old Testament in the New: Context and Criteria*. Edited by David Allen and Steve Smith. LNTS 579. London: T&T Clark, 2019.
Allen, James P. *The Ancient Egyptian Pyramid Texts*. WAW 38. Atlanta: SBL Press, 2015.
Alonso Schökel, Luis. *A Manual of Hebrew Poetics*. SubBi 11. Rome: Pontifical Biblical Institute, 2000.
Alter, Robert. *The Art of Biblical Narrative*. 2nd ed. New York: Basic Books, 2011.
———. *The Art of Biblical Poetry*. 2nd ed. New York: Basic Books, 2011.
Amit, Yairah. *Reading Biblical Narratives: Literary Criticism and the Hebrew Bible*. Minneapolis: Fortress, 2001.
Annus, Amar, and Alan Lenzi. *Ludlul bēl nēmeqi: The Standard Babylonian Poem of the Righteous Sufferer*. SAACT 7. Helsinki: Neo-Assyrian Text Corpus Project, 2010.
Arie, Eran. "Reconsidering the Iron Age II Strata at Tel Dan: Archaeological and Historical Implications." *TA* 35 (2008): 6–64.

Arnold, Bill T., and Richard S. Hess, eds. *Ancient Israel's History: An Introduction to Issues and Sources*. Grand Rapids: Baker Academic, 2014.

Arnold, Bill T., and Brian E. Beyer. *Readings from the Ancient Near East: Primary Sources for Old Testament Study*. Grand Rapids: Baker Academic, 2002.

Arnold, Bill T., and John H. Choi. *A Guide to Biblical Hebrew Syntax*. 2nd ed. Cambridge: Cambridge University Press, 2018.

Arnold, Bill T., and Brent A. Strawn, eds. *The World around the Old Testament: The People and Places of the Ancient Near East*. Grand Rapids: Baker Academic, 2016.

Assis, Elie. *Flashes of Fire: A Literary Analysis of the Song of Songs*. LHBOTS 503. London: T&T Clark, 2009.

Assmann, Jan. *Cultural Memory and Early Civilization: Writing, Remembrance, and Political Imagination*. New York: Cambridge University Press, 2012; original German edition, 2007.

Aster, Shawn Zelig. *Reflections of Empire in Isaiah 1–39: Responses to Assyrian Ideology*. ANEM 19. Atlanta: SBL Press, 2017.

Avi-Yonah, Michael. *The Holy Land from the Persian to the Arab Conquests, 536 B.C. to A.D. 640: A Historical Geography*. Rev. ed. Grand Rapids: Baker, 1977.

Baden, Joel S. *The Composition of the Pentateuch: Renewing the Documentary Hypothesis*. AYBRL. New Haven: Yale University Press, 2012.

Baden, Joel S., and Jeffrey Stackert, eds. *The Oxford Handbook of the Pentateuch*. New York: Oxford University Press, 2021.

Baker, David W. "Leviticus 1–7 and the Punic Tariffs: A Form-Critical Comparison." *ZAW* 99 (1987): 188–97.

Balentine, Samuel L., ed. *The Oxford Handbook of Ritual and Worship in the Hebrew Bible*. New York: Oxford University Press, 2020.

Baly, Denis. *Geography of the Bible: A Study in Historical Geography*. New York: Harper & Brothers, 1957.

Barmash, Pamela, ed. *The Oxford Handbook of Biblical Law*. New York: Oxford University Press, 2019.

Bar-On (Gesundheit), Shimon. "The Three Festival Calendars in Exodus XXIII 14–19 and XXXIV 18–26." *VT* 48 (1998): 161–95.

Barrera, Julio Trebolle. *Centena in libros Samuelis et Regum: Variantes textuales y composición literaria en los libros de Samuel y Reyes*. TECC. Madrid: Instituto de Filología, 1989.

Barr, James. *Comparative Philology and the Text of the Old Testament*. 2nd ed. Winona Lake, IN: Eisenbrauns, 1987.

Barthélemy, Dominique. *Critique textuelle de l'Ancien Testament*. 4 vols. OBO 50. Fribourg: Éditions Universitaires; Göttingen: Vandenhoeck & Ruprecht, 1982–2005.

Baruchi-Unna, Amitai. "The Story of Hezekiah's Prayer." *JSOT* 39 (2015): 281–97.

Bauks, Michaela. *Die Welt am Anfang: Zum Verhaltnis von Vorwelt und Weltentstehung in Gen 1 und in der altorientalischen Literatur*. WMANT 74. Neukirchen-Vluyn: Neukirchener Verlag, 1997.

Beale, G. K., and D. A. Carson, eds. *Commentary on the New Testament Use of the Old Testament*. Grand Rapids: Baker Academic, 2007.

Beentjes, Pancratius C. "Inverted Quotations in the Bible: A Neglected Stylistic Pattern." *Bib* 63 (1982): 506–23.

Beeston, Alfred Felix Landon, Mahmud Ali Ghul, and Walter W. Müller. *Dictionnaire sabéen (anglais – français – arabe)*. Louvain-la-Neuve: Peeters; Beyrouth: Librairie du Liban, 1982.

Bekins, Peter. *Inscriptions from the World of the Bible: A Reader and Introduction to Old Northwest Semitic*. Peabody, MA: Hendrickson Academic, 2020.

Ben-Dov, Meir. *Carta's Illustrated History of Jerusalem*. 2nd ed. Jerusalem: Carta, 2006.

Benner, Drayton C., Andrew Zulker, James R. Covington, and H. H. Hardy II. *The Hebrew Old Testament, Reader's Edition*. Wheaton, IL: Crossway, 2020.

Ben-Yehuda, Eliezer. *Dictionary and Thesaurus of the Hebrew Language*. 8 vols. New York: Yoseloff, 1960. [Hebrew]

Berlin, Adele. *The Dynamics of Biblical Parallelism*. Rev. ed. Grand Rapids: Eerdmans; Dearborn, MI: Dove Booksellers, 2008.

Biella, Joan Copeland. *Dictionary of Old South Arabic: Sabaean Dialect*. HSS 25. Chico, CA: Scholars Press, 1982.

Biran, Avraham. *Biblical Dan*. Jerusalem: Israel Exploration Society, 1994.

Blackburn, Robin. "The Old World Background to European Colonial Slavery." *The William and Mary Quarterly* 54 (1997): 65–102.

Blair, Thom, ed. *Hebrew-English Interlinear ESV Old Testament: Biblia Hebraica Stuttgartensia (BHS) and English Standard Version (ESV)*. Wheaton, IL: Crossway, 2014.

Blenkinsopp, Joseph. *Isaiah 1–39: A New Translation with Introduction and Commentary*. AB 19. New York: Doubleday, 2000.

Blum, Erhard, and Kristin Weingart. "The Joseph Story: Diaspora Novella or North-Israelite Narrative?" *ZAW* 129 (2017): 501–21.

Borowski, Oded. *Agriculture in Iron Age Israel*. Winona Lake, IN: Eisenbrauns, 1987.

———. *Daily Life in Biblical Times*. Atlanta: SBL Press, 2003.

Bott, Travis J. "Praise and Metonymy in the Psalms." Pages 131–46 in *The Oxford Handbook of the Psalms*. Edited by William P. Brown. New York: Oxford University Press, 2014.

Braun, Joachim. *Music in Ancient Israel/Palestine: Archaeological, Written, and Comparative Sources*. Translated by Douglas W. Stott. Grand Rapids: Eerdmans, 2002; original German edition, 1999.

Brenner, Athalya. *A Feminist Companion to Genesis*. FCB 2. Sheffield: Sheffield Academic, 1997.

———. *A Feminist Companion to Genesis*. FCB (second series) 1. Sheffield: Sheffield Academic, 1998.

Briant, Pierre. *From Cyrus to Alexander: A History of the Persian Empire*. Translated by Peter T. Daniels. Winona Lake, IN: Eisenbrauns, 2002.

Brooke, Alan England, Norman McLean, and Henry St. John Thackeray. *The Old Testament in Greek*. 9 vols. Cambridge: Cambridge University Press, 1906–40.

Brosius, Maria. *A History of Ancient Persia: The Achaemenid Empire*. BHAW. Hoboken, NJ: Wiley-Blackwell, 2021.

Brotzman, Ellis R. *Old Testament Textual Criticism: A Practical Introduction*. Grand Rapids: Baker, 1994.

Brown, A. Philip, II, and Bryan W. Smith. *A Reader's Hebrew Bible*. Grand Rapids: Zondervan, 2008.

Bryce, Glendon E. *A Legacy of Wisdom: The Egyptian Contribution to the Wisdom of Israel*. Lewisburg, PA: Bucknell University Press, 1979.

Bryce, Trevor. *The Kingdom of the Hittites*. 2nd ed. Oxford: Clarendon, 2005.

Burnet, Régis. *Exegesis and History of Reception: Reading the New Testament Today with the Readers of the Past*. WUNT 455. Tübingen: Mohr Siebeck, 2021.

Butterworth, Mike. *Structure and the Book of Zechariah*. JSOTSup 130. Sheffield: JSOT Press, 1992.

Cameron, Euan, ed. *New Cambridge History of the Bible*, vol. 3, *From 1450 to 1750*. Cambridge: Cambridge University Press, 2016.

Carasik, Michael. *The Commentator's Bible: The Rubin JPS Miqra'ot Gedolot*. 5 vols. Philadelphia: Jewish Publication Society of America, 2005–18.

Carleton Paget, James, and Joachim Schafer, eds. *New Cambridge History of the Bible*, vol. 1, *From 600 to 1450*. Cambridge: Cambridge University Press, 2012.

Carr, David M. *The Formation of Genesis 1–11: Biblical and Other Precursors*. New York: Oxford University Press, 2020.

———. *The Formation of the Hebrew Bible*. New York: Oxford University Press, 2011.

———. *Genesis 1–11*. IECOT. Stuttgart: Kohlhammer, 2021.

———. "Method in Determination of Direction of Dependence: An Empirical Test of Criteria Applied to Exodus 34,11–26 and Its Parallels." Pages 107–40 in *Gottes Volk am Sinai: Untersuchungen zu Ex 32–34 und Dtn 9–10*. Edited by Matthias Köckert and Erhard Blum. VWGT 18. Gütersloh: Gütersloher Verlagshaus, 2011.

Centre d'analyse et de documentation patristique. *Biblia Patristica: Index des citations et allusions bibliques dans la littérature patristique*. 7 vols. Paris: Editions du CNRS, 1986–2000.

Chike, Julian. "The Literary Development of MT 1Kgs 8:1–11 in Light of the Septuagint." *Textus* 28 (2019): 45–66.

Clifford, Richard J. *Creation Accounts in the Ancient Near East and in the Bible*. CBQMS 26. Washington, DC: Catholic Biblical Association, 1994.

Clines, David J. A. "Alleged Female Language about the Deity in the Hebrew Bible." *JBL* 140 (2021): 229–49.

———. *What Does Eve Do to Help? and Other Readerly Questions to the Old Testament*. JSOTSup 94. Sheffield: JSOT Press, 1990.

Cogan, Mordechai. *1 Kings: A New Translation and Commentary*. AB 10. New York: Doubleday, 2001.

Cohen, David. *Dictionnaire des racines sémitiques ou attestées dans les langues sémitiques*. Paris: Mouton, 1970–.

Cohen, Mark E. *The Canonical Lamentations of Ancient Mesopotamia*. Potomac, MD: Capital Decisions, 1988.

Collins, Billie Jean. *The Hittites and Their World*. ABS 7. Atlanta: SBL Press, 2007.

Coogan, Michael D. *A Reader of Ancient Near Eastern Texts: Sources for the Study of the Old Testament*. New York: Oxford University Press, 2013.

Crouch, Carly L. *Israel and the Assyrians: Deuteronomy, the Succession Treaty of Esarhaddon, and the Nature of Subversion*. ANEM 8. Atlanta: SBL Press, 2014.

Crowell, Bradley L. *Edom at the Edge of Empire: A Social and Political History*. ABS 29. Atlanta: SBL Press, 2021.

———. "Postcolonial Studies and the Hebrew Bible." *CurBR* 7 (2009): 217–44.

Curtis, Adrian. *Oxford Bible Atlas*. Oxford: Oxford University Press, 2007.

Dalley, Stephanie. *Myths from Mesopotamia: Creation, the Flood, Gilgamesh, and Others*. Oxford: Oxford University Press, 1989.

Davidson, Steed Vernyl. *Writing/Reading the Bible in Postcolonial Perspective*. BRP 2.3. Leiden: Brill, 2017.

Davies, Eryl W. *The Dissenting Reader: Feminist Approaches to the Hebrew Bible*. Aldershot: Ashgate, 2003.

Davies, Graham I. *Ancient Hebrew Inscriptions: Corpus and Concordance*. 2 vols. Cambridge: Cambridge University Press, 1991–2004.

———. *A Critical and Exegetical Commentary on Exodus 1–18*, vol. 2, *Commentary on Exodus 11–18*. ICC. London: T&T Clark, 2020.

Davis, Andrew R. *Tel Dan in Its Northern Cultic Context*. ABS 10. Atlanta: SBL Press, 2013.

Day, John. "Foreign Semitic Influence on the Wisdom of Israel and Its Appropriation in the Book of Proverbs." Pages 55–70 in *Wisdom in Ancient Israel: Essays in Honour of J. A. Emerton*. Edited by John Day, Robert P. Gordon, and Hugh G. M. Williamson. Cambridge: Cambridge University Press, 1998.

De Hulster, Izaak J. *Iconographic Exegesis and Third Isaiah*. FAT 2.36. Tübingen: Mohr Siebeck, 2009.

De Hulster, Izaak J., Brent A. Strawn, and Ryan P. Bonfiglio, eds. *Iconographic Exegesis of the Hebrew Bible/Old Testament: An Introduction to Its Method and Practice*. Göttingen: Vandenhoeck & Ruprecht, 2015.

De Joode, Johan. *Metaphorical Landscapes and the Theology of the Book of Job: An Analysis of Job's Spatial Metaphors*. VTSup 179. Leiden: Brill, 2019.

Dever, William G. *Beyond the Texts: An Archaeological Portrait of Ancient Israel and Judah*. Atlanta: SBL Press, 2017.

———. *The Lives of Ordinary People in Ancient Israel: Where Archaeology and the Bible Intersect*. Grand Rapids: Eerdmans, 2012.

Doak, Brian R. *Ancient Israel's Neighbors*. EBS. Oxford: Oxford University Press, 2020.

Dobbs-Allsopp, F. W. *On Biblical Poetry*. New York: Oxford University Press, 2015.

Dobbs-Allsopp, F. W., J. J. M. Roberts, Choon-Leong Seow, and Richard E. Whitaker. *Hebrew Inscriptions: Texts from the Biblical Period of the Monarchy with Concordance*. New Haven: Yale University Press, 2005.

Driver, Samuel Rolles. *An Introduction to the Literature of the Old Testament*. 2nd ed. New York: Scribner's Sons, 1914.

Dube, Musa W., Andrew M. Mbuvi, and Dora R. Mbuwayesango, eds. *Postcolonial Perspectives in African Biblical Interpretations*. GPBS 13. Atlanta: SBL, 2012.

Eco, Umberto. *The Role of the Reader: Explorations in the Semiotics of Texts*. Bloomington: Indiana University Press, 1979.

Edelman, Diana. "Hezekiah's Alleged Centralization." *JSOT* 32 (2008): 395–434.

Ego, Beate, Armin Lange, Hermann Lichtenberger, and Kristin De Troyer. *Biblia Qumranica*, vol. 3B, *Minor Prophets*. Leiden: Brill, 2005.

Elayi, Josette. *The History of Phoenicia*. Atlanta: Lockwood Press, 2015.

———. *Sennacherib, King of Assyria*. ABS 24. Atlanta: SBL Press, 2018.

Elitzur, Yoel. *Ancient Place Names in the Holy Land: Preservation and History*. Jerusalem: Magnes, 2004.

Elliger, Karl, and Wilhelm Rudolph, eds. *Biblia Hebraica Stuttgartensia*. 5th ed. Edited by Adrian Schenker. Stuttgart: Deutsche Bibelgesellschaft, 1997.

Etz, Donald V. "The Numbers of Genesis V 3–31: A Suggested Conversion and Its Implications." *VT* 43 (1993): 171–89.

Even-Shoshan, Abraham, ed. *A New Concordance of the Bible*. Jerusalem: Kiryat Sefer, 1989.

Exum, J. Cheryl. *Fragmented Women: Feminist (Sub)versions of Biblical Narratives*. JSOTSup 163. Sheffield: Sheffield Academic, 1993.

———. "'Mother in Israel': A Familiar Figure Reconsidered." Pages 73–85 in *Feminist Interpretation of the Bible*. Edited by Letty M. Russell. Philadelphia: Westminster, 1985.

Faust, Avraham. *The Archaeology of Israelite Society in Iron Age II*. Winona Lake, IN: Eisenbrauns, 2012.

———. "Israelite Temples: Where Was Israelite Cult [*sic*] Not Practiced, and Why." *Religions* 10 (2019): Article 106 (online).

Feder, Yitzhaq. *Blood Expiation in Hittite and Biblical Ritual: Origins, Context, and Meaning*. WAWsup 2. Atlanta: SBL Press, 2011.

Feldman, Louis H., James L. Kugel, and Lawrence H. Schiffman, eds. *Outside the Bible: Ancient Jewish Writings Related to Scripture*. 3 vols. Philadelphia: Jewish Publication Society of America, 2013.

Ferris, Paul W., Jr. *The Genre of Communal Lament in the Bible and the Ancient Near East*. SBLDS 127. Atlanta: Scholars Press, 1992.

Fewell, Danna Nolan, ed. *The Oxford Handbook of Biblical Narrative*. New York: Oxford University Press, 2016.

Field, Frederick. *Origenis Hexaplorum quae supersunt sive veterum interpretum graecorum in totum Vetus Testamentum fragmenta*. 2 vols. London: Clarendon, 1875.

Finkelstein, Israel, and Neil Asher Silberman. *The Bible Unearthed: Archaeology's New Vision of Ancient Israel and the Origins of Its Sacred Texts*. New York: Touchstone, 2002.

Fishbane, Michael. *Biblical Interpretation in Ancient Israel*. Oxford: Clarendon, 1985.

———. *Song of Songs: The Traditional Hebrew Text with the New JPS Translation*. JPS Bible Commentary. Philadelphia: Jewish Publication Society of America, 2015.

Fokkelman, J. P. *Major Poems of the Hebrew Bible: At the Interface of Prosody and Structural Analysis*. 4 vols. SSN 37, 41, 43, 47. Assen: Van Gorcum, 1998–2004.

———. *Narrative Art and Poetry in the Books of Samuel: A Full Interpretation Based on Stylistic and Structural Analyses*. 4 vols. SSN 20, 23, 27, 31. Assen: Van Gorcum, 1981–93.

———. *Narrative Art in Genesis: Specimens of Stylistic and Structural Analysis*. 2nd ed. BS 12. Sheffield: JSOT Press, 1991; repr., Eugene, OR: Wipf & Stock, 2004.

———. *Reading Biblical Narrative: An Introductory Guide*. Translated by Ineke Smit. Louisville: Westminster John Knox, 2000.

———. *Reading Biblical Poetry: An Introductory Guide*. Translated by Ineke Smit. Louisville: Westminster John Knox, 2001.

Foster, John L. *Hymns, Prayers, and Songs: An Anthology of Ancient Egyptian Lyric Poetry*. WAW 8. Atlanta: SBL Press, 1995.

Fox, Michael V. "From Amenemope to Proverbs: Editorial Art in Proverbs 22,17–23,11." *ZAW* 126 (2014): 76–91.

———. *The Song of Songs and Ancient Egyptian Love Songs*. Madison: University of Wisconsin Press, 1985.

Frankel, David. *The Murmuring Stories of the Priestly School: A Retrieval of Ancient Sacerdotal Lore*. VTSup 89. Leiden: Brill, 2002.

Freedman, Henry, and Maurice Simon, ed. *Midrash Rabbah*. London: Soncino, 1939.

Freeman-Grenville, G. S. P., Rupert L. Chapman III, and Joan E. Taylor. *The Onomasticon by Eusebius of Caesarea: Palestine in the Fourth Century A.D.* Jerusalem: Carta, 2003.

Fried, Lisbeth S. "The High Places (*bāmôt*) and the Reforms of Hezekiah and Josiah: An Archaeological Investigation." *JAOS* 122 (2002): 437–65.

Friedeman, Caleb T., ed. *A Scripture Index to Rabbinic Literature*. Peabody, MA: Hendrickson Academic, 2021.

Frood, Elizabeth. *Biographical Texts from Ramessid Egypt*. WAW 26. Atlanta: SBL Press, 2007.

Fu, Janling, Cynthia Shafer-Elliott, and Carol Meyers, eds. *The T&T Clark Handbook of Food in the Hebrew Bible and Ancient Israel*. London: T&T Clark, 2021.

Fuchs, Esther. *Feminist Theory and the Bible: Interrogating the Sources*. London: Lexington Books, 2016.

———. *Sexual Politics in the Biblical Narrative: Reading the Hebrew Bible as a Woman*. JSOTSup 310. London: Sheffield Academic, 2003.

Gallagher, William R. *Sennacherib's Campaign to Judah: New Studies*. SHCANE 18. Leiden: Brill, 1999.

Ganor, Saar, and Igor Kreimerman. "An Eighth-Century B.C.E. Gate Shrine at Tel Lachish." *BASOR* 381 (2019): 211–36.

Garr, W. Randall. "The Qinah: A Study of Poetic Meter, Syntax, and Style." *ZAW* 95 (1983): 54–75.

Garroway, Kristine Henriksen. "Was Bathsheba the Original Bridget Jones? A New Look at Bathsheba on Screen and in Biblical Scholarship." *Nashim: A Journal of Jewish Women's Studies & Gender Issues* 24 (2013): 53–73.

Gasquet, Francis Aidan, et al. *Biblia Sacra iuxta Latinam Vulgatam versionem*. 18 vols. Rome: Libreria Editrice Vaticana, 1926–96.

Gaß, Erasmus. *Die Moabiter: Geschichte und Kultur eines ostjordanischen Volkes im 1. Jahrtausend v. Chr.* ADPV 38. Wiesbaden: Harrassowitz, 2009.

———. *Ortsnamen des Richterbuchs in historischer und redaktioneller Perspektive.* ADPV 3. Wiesbaden: Harrassowitz, 2005.

———. "Topographical Considerations and Redaction Criticism in 2 Kings 3." *JBL* 128 (2009): 65–84.

Gault, Brian P. *Body as Lanscape, Love as Intoxication*. AIL 36. Atlanta: SBL Press, 2019.

Geoghegan, Jeffrey C. "'Until this Day' and the Preexilic Redaction of the Deuteronomistic History." *JBL* 122 (2003): 201–27.

Gertz, Jan Christian, Angelika Berlejung, Konrad Schmid, and Markus Witte. *T&T Clark Handbook of the Old Testament: An Introduction to the Literature, Religion and History of the Old Testament*. New York: T&T Clark, 2012; original German (3rd) edition, 2008.

Gesenius, Wilhelm. *Hebräisches und Aramäisches Handwörterbuch über das Alte Testament*. 18th ed. 6 vols. Berlin: Springer, 1987–2010.

Gide, André. *Journal, 1889–1939*. Bibliothèque de la Pléiade 54. Paris: Gallimard, 1948.

Ginzberg, Louis. *Legends of the Jews*. Translated by Henrietta Szold and Paul Radin. 2nd ed. 2 vols. Philadelphia: Jewish Publication Society of America, 2003.

Glassner, Jean-Jacques. *Mesopotamian Chronicles*. WAW 19. Atlanta: SBL Press, 2004.

Gogel, Sandra. *A Grammar of Epigraphic Hebrew*. RBS 23. Atlanta: Scholars Press, 1998.

Goldenberg, David M. *Black and Slave: The Origins and History of the Curse of Ham*. SBR 10. Berlin: de Gruyter, 2017.

———. *The Curse of Ham: Race and Slavery in Early Judaism, Christianity, and Islam*. Princeton: Princeton University Press, 2003.

Goldingay, John, and David Payne. *A Critical and Exegetical Commentary on Isaiah 40–55*, vol. 2, *Commentary on Isaiah 44:24–55:13*. ICC. London: T&T Clark, 2006.

Gossai, Hemchand, ed. *Postcolonial Commentary and the Old Testament*. London: T&T Clark, 2018.

Grabbe, Lester L. *Ancient Israel: What Do We Know and How Do We Know It?* London: T&T Clark, 2007.

———. *A History of the Jews and Judaism in the Second Temple Period*. 4 vols. LSTS. London: T&T Clark, 2004–21.

Graybill, Rhiannon. *Texts after Terror: Rape, Sexual Violence, and the Hebrew Bible*. New York: Oxford University Press, 2021.

Gruber, Mayer I. "The Motherhood of God in Second Isaiah." *RB* 90 (1986): 351–59.

Guillaume, Philippe, and Ernst-Axel Knauf. *A History of Biblical Israel: The Fate of the Tribes and Kingdoms from Merenptah to Bar Kochba*. WANEM. Sheffield: Equinox, 2016.

Gunn, David M., and Danna Nolan Fewell. *Narrative in the Hebrew Bible*. New York: Oxford University Press, 1993.

Haddox, Susan E. "Masculinity Studies of the Hebrew Bible: The First Two Decades." *CurBR* 14 (2016): 176–206.

Haelewyck, Jean-Claude. *Clavis Apocryphorum Veteris Testamenti*. Corpus Christianorum. Turnhout: Brepols, 1998.

Haupt, Paul, ed. *The Sacred Books of the Old Testament: A Critical Edition of the Hebrew Text Printed in Colors, with Notes*. Leipzig: Hinrichs, 1893–1904.

Haynes, Stephen R. *Noah's Curse: The Biblical Justification for Slavery*. New York: Oxford University Press, 2002.

Hays, Christopher B. *Hidden Riches: A Sourcebook for the Comparative Study of the Hebrew Bible and Ancient Near East*. Louisville: Westminster John Knox, 2014.

Hendel, Ronald. "The Exodus as Cultural Memory: Egyptian Bondage and the Song of the Sea." Pages 65–77 in *Israel's Exodus in Transdisciplinary Perspective: Text, Archaeology, and Geoscience*. Edited by Thomas E. Levy, Thomas Schneider, and William H. C. Propp. Cham: Springer, 2015.

———. *Remembering Abraham: Culture, Memory, and History in the Hebrew Bible*. New York: Oxford University Press, 2005.

———. *Steps to a New Edition of the Hebrew Bible*. TCSt 10. Atlanta: SBL Press, 2016.

Henze, Matthias, ed. *A Companion to Biblical Interpretation in Early Judaism*. Grand Rapids: Eerdmans, 2012.

Herzog, Ze'ev. "The Fortress Mound at Tel Arad: An Interim Report." *TA* 29 (2002): 3–109.

———. "Perspectives on Southern Israel's Cult Centralization: Arad and Beer-Sheba." Pages 169–99 in *One God – One Cult – One Nation: Archaeological and Biblical Perspectives*. Edited by Reinhard G. Kratz and Hermann Spieckermann. BZAW 405. Berlin: de Gruyter, 2010.

Hess, Richard S. "The Genealogies of Genesis 1–11 and Comparative Literature." *Bib* 70 (1989): 241–54. Reprinted in pages 58–72 of *I Studied Inscriptions from before the Flood: Ancient Near Eastern, Literary, and Linguistic Approaches to Genesis 1–11*. Edited by Richard Hess and David T. Tsumura. Winona Lake, IN: Eisenbrauns, 1994.

Hibbard, J. Todd. *Intertextuality in Isaiah 24–27: The Reuse and Evocation of Earlier Texts and Traditions*. FAT 2.16. Tübingen: Mohr Siebeck, 2006.

Hoffmeier, James K. "The Structure of Joshua 1–11 and the Annals of Thutmose III." Pages 165–79 in *Faith, Tradition, and History*. Edited by Alan R. Millard, James K. Hoffmeier, and David W. Baker. Winona Lake, IN: Eisenbrauns, 1994.

Hoffner, Harry A., Jr. *Letters from the Hittite Kingdom*. WAW 15. Atlanta: SBL Press, 2009.

Hoftijzer, Jacob, and Gerrit van der Kooij. *Aramaic Texts from Deir 'Alla*. Leiden: Brill, 1976.

———, eds. *The Balaam Text from Deir 'Alla Re-Evaluated*. Leiden: Brill, 1991.

Hugo, Philippe. *Les deux visages d'Élie: Texte massorétique et Septante dans l'histoire la plus ancienne du texte de 1 Rois 17–18*. OBO 217. Göttingen: Vandenhoeck & Ruprecht, 2006.

Hurvitz, Avi. *A Concise Lexicon of Late Biblical Hebrew: Linguistic Innovations in the Writings of the Second Temple Period*. VTSup 160. Leiden: Brill, 2014.

Jacobson, Howard. *A Commentary on Pseudo-Philo's* Liber Antiquitatum Biblicarum: *With Latin Text and English Translation*. Leiden: Brill, 1996.

Japhet, Sara. *The Ideology of the Book of Chronicles and Its Place in Biblical Thought*. Winona Lake, IN: Eisenbrauns, 2009.

Jastrow, Marcus. *A Dictionary of the Targumim, the Talmud Babli and Yerushalmi, and the Midrashic Literature*. 2 vols. New York: Title Publishing, 1943.

Johnson, Benjamin J. M. "What Type of Son Is Samson? Reading Judges 13 as a Biblical Type-Scene." *JETS* 53 (2010): 269–86.

Junior, Nyasha. *An Introduction to Womanist Biblical Interpretation*. Louisville: Westminster John Knox, 2015.

Kalmanofsky, Amy. *Gender-Play in the Hebrew Bible: The Ways the Bible Challenges Its Gender Norms*. New York: Routledge, 2017.

———. "How Feminist Biblical Scholarship Can Heal Victims of Sexual Violation." Pages 9–30 in *Sexual Violence and Sacred Texts*. Edited by Amy Kalmanofsky. Eugene, OR: Wipf & Stock, 2020.

Keefe, Alice A. *Woman's Body and the Social Body in Hosea*. Sheffield: Sheffield Academic, 2001.

Kelley, Page H., Daniel S. Mynatt, and Timothy G. Crawford. *The Masorah of* Biblia Hebraica Stuttgartensia: *Introduction and Annotated Glossary*. Grand Rapids: Eerdmans, 1998.

Kahn, Dan'el. *Sennacherib's Campaign Against Judah: A Source Analysis of Isaiah 36–37*. SOTSMS. Cambridge: Cambridge University Press, 2020.

Kallai, Zecharia. *Historical Geography of the Bible*. Jerusalem: Magnes, 1986.

Kartveit, Magnar. "The Date of II Reg 17,24–41." *ZAW* 126 (2014): 31–44.

Keel, Othmar. *Orte und Landschaften der Bibel: Ein Handbuch und Studien-Reiseführer zum Heiligen Land*. 2 vols. Göttingen: Vandenhoeck & Ruprecht, 1982–84.

———. *The Song of Songs: A Continental Commentary*. Minneapolis: Fortress, 1994.

———. *The Symbolism of the Biblical World: Ancient Near Eastern Iconography and the Book of Psalms*. Translated by T. J. Hallett. Winona Lake, IN: Eisenbrauns, 1997.

Keel, Othmar, and Christoph Uehlinger. *Gods, Goddesses, and Images of God in Ancient Israel*. Translated by Thomas H. Trapp. Minneapolis: Fortress, 1998.

Khan, Geoffrey, et al. *The Oxford Grammar of Biblical Hebrew (based on Gesenius' Hebrew Grammar)*. Oxford: Oxford University Press, forthcoming.

Kim, Hyun Chul Paul. "Jonah Read Intertextually." *JBL* 126 (2007): 497–528.

King, Philip J., and Lawrence E. Stager. *Life in Biblical Israel*. LAI. Louisville: Westminster John Knox, 2001.

Kisilevitz, Shua, and Oded Lipschits. "Tel Moẓa: An Economic and Cultic Center from the Iron Age II (First Temple Period)." Pages 295–312 in *The Mega Project at Motza (Moẓa): The Neolithic and Later Occupations up to the 20th Century*. Edited by Hamoudi Khalaily, Amit Re'em, Jacob Vardi, and Ianir Milevski. Jerusalem: Israel Antiquities Authority, 2020.

Kitchen, Kenneth A. *On the Reliability of the Old Testament*. Grand Rapids: Eerdmans, 2003.

Kitchen, Kenneth A., and Paul J. N. Lawrence. *Treaty, Law and Covenant in the Ancient Near East*. 3 vols. Wiesbaden: Harrassowitz, 2012.

Klein, Ernest. *A Comprehensive Etymological Dictionary of the Hebrew Language for Readers of English*. Jerusalem: Carta, 1987.

Kline, Jonathan G. *Allusive Soundplay in the Hebrew Bible*. AIL 28. Atlanta: SBL Press, 2016.

Klingbeil, Martin. *Yahweh Fighting from Heaven: God as Warrior and as God of Heaven in the Hebrew Psalter and Ancient Near Eastern Iconography*. OBO 169. Göttingen: Vandenhoeck & Ruprecht, 1999.

Knohl, Israel. *The Sanctuary of Silence: The Priestly Torah and the Holiness School*. Minneapolis: Fortress, 1995.

Knowles, Melody D. "Feminist Interpretation of the Psalms." Pages 424–36 in *The Oxford Handbook of the Psalms*. Edited by William P. Brown. New York: Oxford University Press, 2014.

Kohlenberger, John R., III. *The Interlinear NIV Hebrew-English Old Testament*. Grand Rapids: Zondervan, 1993.

Koopmans, William T. *Haggai*. HCOT. Leuven: Peeters, 2017.

Koosed, Jennifer L. *Reading the Bible as a Feminist*. BRP. Leiden: Brill, 2017.

Korpel, Marjo C. A., and Johannes C. de Moor. *The Structure of Classical Hebrew Poetry: Isaiah 40–55*. OTS 41. Leiden: Brill, 1998.

Krahmalkov, Charles R. *Phoenician-Punic Dictionary*. Leuven: Peeters, 2000.

Kratz, Reinhard G. *The Composition of the Narrative Books of the Old Testament*. Translated by John Bowden. New York: T&T Clark, 2005; original German edition, 2000.

———. *Historical and Biblical Israel: The History, Tradition, and Archives of Israel and Judah*. Translated by Paul Michael Kurtz. New York: Oxford University Press, 2015; original German edition, 2013.

Kraus, Wolfgang, and Martin Karrer. *Septuaginta Deutsch: Das griechische Alte Testament in deutscher Übersetzung*. Stuttgart: Deutsche Bibelgesellschaft, 2009.

Kugel, James L. "Jubilees." Pages 272–465 in *Outside the Bible: Ancient Jewish Writings Related to Scripture*. Edited by Louis H. Feldman, James L. Kugel, and Lawrence H. Schiffman. Philadelphia: Jewish Publication Society of America, 2013.

Kuhrt, Amélie. *The Ancient Near East c. 3000–330 BCE*. 2 vols. RHAW. London: Routledge, 1995.

Kwon, JiSeong James. *Scribal Culture and Intertextuality: Literary and Historical Relationships between Job and Deutero-Isaiah*. FAT 2.85. Tübingen: Mohr Siebeck, 2016.

Kvangig, Helge S. *Primeval History: Babylonian, Biblical, and Enochic; An Intertextual Reading*. JSJSup 149. Leiden: Brill, 2011.

Labuschagne, Casper J. "The Life Spans of the Patriarchs." Pages 121–27 in *New Avenues in the Study of the Old Testament*. Edited by Adam S. van der Woude. OTS 25. Leiden: Brill, 1989.

Lakoff, George, and Mark Johnson. *Metaphors We Live By*. Chicago: University of Chicago Press, 1980.

Lambert, Wilfred G. *Babylonian Wisdom Literature*. Oxford: Clarendon, 1960.

Lane, Edward William. *An Arabic-English Lexicon*. 8 vols. London: Williams & Norgate, 1863–93.

Lange, Armin, and Matthias Weigold. *Biblical Quotations and Allusions in Second Temple Jewish Literature*. JAJSup 5. Göttingen: Vandenhoeck & Ruprecht, 2011.

Lanier, Gregory R., and William A. Ross, eds. *Septuaginta: A Reader's Edition*. 2 vols. Peabody, MA: Hendrickson; Stuttgart: Deutsche Bibelgesellschaft, 2018.

Launderville, Dale. "Ezekiel's Cherub: A Promising Symbol or a Dangerous Idol?" *CBQ* 65 (2004): 165–83.

Lee, Jongkyung. *A Redactional Study of Isaiah 13–23*. OTRM. Oxford: Oxford University Press, 2018.

Lee, Lydia. "The Tyrian King in MT and LXX Ezekiel 28:12b–15." *Religions* 12 (2021): Article 91 (online).

Lenzi, Alan, ed. *Reading Akkadian Prayers and Hymns: An Introduction*. ANEM 3. Atlanta: SBL Press, 2011.

Leslau, Wolf. *Comparative Dictionary of Ge'ez (Classical Ethiopic): Ge'ez-English/English-Ge'ez; With an Index of Semitic Roots*. Wiesbaden: Harrassowitz, 1987.

———. *Concise Dictionary of Ge'ez (Classical Ethiopic)*. Wiesbaden: Harrassowitz, 1989.

Létourneau, Anne. "Beauty, Bath and Beyond: Framing Bathsheba as a Royal Fantasy in 2 Sam 11,1–5." *SJOT* 32 (2018): 72–91.

Levinson, Bernard M. *Deuteronomy and the Hermeneutics of Legal Innovation*. New York: Oxford University Press, 1998.

Levinson, Bernard M., and Jeffrey Stackert. "Between the Covenant Code and Esarhaddon's Succession Treaty: Deuteronomy 13 and the Composition of Deuteronomy." *JAJ* 3 (2012): 123–40.

Lieb, Michael, Emma Mason, Jonathan Roberts, and Christopher Rowland, eds. *The Oxford Handbook of the Reception History of the Bible*. Oxford: Oxford University Press, 2011.

Lindenberger, James M. *Ancient Aramaic and Hebrew Letters*. 2nd ed. WAW 4. Atlanta: Scholars Press, 2003.

Lipiński, Edward. *The Aramaeans: Their Ancient History, Culture, Religion*. OLA 100. Leuven: Peeters, 2000.

———. *On the Skirts of Canaan in the Iron Age: Historical and Topographical Researches*. OLA 153. Leuven: Peeters, 2006.

Liraz, Elad. "A Second Cult Room at the Lachish Gate?" *NEA* 81 (2018): 269–75.

Lisowsky, Gerhard. *Konkordanz zum Hebräischen Alten Testament*. 2nd ed. Stuttgart: Württembergische Bibelanstalt, 1958.

Liverani, Mario. *Israel's History and the History of Israel*. Translated by Chiara Peri and Philip R. Davies. London: Equinox, 2009; original Italian edition, 2003.

Longman, Tremper, III. *Fictional Akkadian Autobiography: A Generic and Comparative Study*. Winona Lake, IN: Eisenbrauns, 1991.

Lozada, Francisco, Jr. *Toward a Latino/a Biblical Interpretation*. RBS 91. Atlanta: SBL Press, 2017.

Luciani, Dider. *Sainteté et pardon: Structure littéraire du Lévitique*. 2 vols. BETL 185A–B. Leuven: Peeters, 2005.

Lundbom, Jack R. *Jeremiah 1–20: A New Translation with Introduction and Commentary*. AB 21A. New York: Doubleday, 1999.

Lust, Johan, Erik Eynikel, and Katrin Hauspie. *A Greek-English Lexicon of the Septuagint*. 2nd ed. Stuttgart: Deutsche Bibelgesellschaft, 2003.

Macchi, Jean-Daniel. *Esther*. IECOT. Stuttgart: Kohlhammer, 2018.

MacDonald, Nathan. *What Did the Ancient Israelites Eat? Diet in Biblical Times*. Grand Rapids: Eerdmans, 2008.

Macintosh, Andrew A. *A Critical and Exegetical Commentary on Hosea*. ICC. Edinburgh: T&T Clark, 1997.

Marcos, Natalio Fernández, and José Ramón Busto Saiz. *El texto antioqueno de la Biblia griega*, vol. 1, *1–2 Samuel*. TECC. Madrid: Instituto de Filología del Consejo Superior de Investigaciones Científicas, 1989.

———. *El texto antioqueno de la Biblia griega*, vol. 2, *1–2 Reyes*. TECC. Madrid: Instituto de Filología del Consejo Superior de Investigaciones Científicas, 1992.

Marcus, David. *The Masorah of the Former Prophets in the Leningrad Codex*, vol. 5, *1 Kings*. Text and Studies 14. Piscataway, NJ: Gorgias, 2021.

Marsden, Richard, and E. Ann Matter, eds. *New Cambridge History of the Bible*, vol. 2, *From the Beginnings to 600*. Cambridge: Cambridge University Press, 2013.

Martin, Michael Wade. "Does Ancient Hebrew Poetry Have Meter?" *JBL* 140 (2021): 503–29.

Martínez, Florentino García. *The Dead Sea Scrolls Translated: The Qumran Texts in English*. Translated by Wilfred G. E. Watson. Leiden: Brill, 1994.

Martínez, Florentino García, and Eibert J. C. Tigchelaar. *The Dead Sea Scrolls Study Edition*. 2 vols. Leiden: Brill, 1997–98.

Mason, Steve, ed. *Flavius Josephus: Translation and Commentary*. 10 vols. Leiden: Brill, 1999–.

Matthews, Victor H. *The Cultural World of the Bible: An Illustrated Guide to Manners and Customs*. 4th ed. Grand Rapids: Baker Academic, 2015.

McCarthy, Carmel, ed. *Deuteronomy*. BHQ 5. Stuttgart: Deutsche Bibelgesellschaft, 2007.

McKenzie, Steven L. *1 Kings 16–2 Kings 16*. IECOT. Stuttgart: Kohlhammer, 2019.

Menken, Maarten J. J., and Steven Moyise, eds. *The Psalms in the New Testament*. NTSI. London: T&T Clark, 2004.

Meynet, Roland. *Rhetorical Analysis: An Introduction to Biblical Rhetoric*. LHBOTS. Sheffield: Sheffield Academic, 1998.

Michalowski, Piotr. *The Lamentation over the Destruction of Sumer and Ur*. MC 1. Winona Lake, IN: Eisenbrauns, 1989.

Milgrom, Jacob. "Concerning Jeremiah's Repudiation of Sacrifice." ZAW 89 (1977): 173–75.

Miller, Geoffrey D. "Intertextuality in Old Testament Research." *CurBR* 9 (2011): 283–309.

Miller, J. Maxwell, and John H. Hayes. *A History of Ancient Israel and Judah*. 2nd ed. Louisville: Westminster John Knox, 2006.

Mittmann, Siegfrid, and Götz Schmitt, eds. *Tübinger Bibelatlas*. Stuttgart: Deutsche Bibelgesellschaft, 2001.

Morrow, William S. "Treaties/Loyalty Oaths and Biblical Law." Pages 319–32 in *The Oxford Handbook of Biblical Law*. Edited by Pamela Barmash. New York: Oxford University Press, 2019.

Moscati, Sabatino. *An Introduction to the Comparative Grammar of the Semitic Languages: Phonology and Morphology*. PLO 6. Wiesbaden: Harrassowitz, 1980.

Moughtin-Mumby, Sharon. "Feminist/Womanist Readings of Isaiah." Pages 601–20 in *The Oxford Handbook of Isaiah*. Edited by Lena-Sofia Tiemeyer. New York: Oxford University Press, 2020.

Mroczek, Eva. *The Literary Imagination in Jewish Antiquity*. New York: Oxford University Press, 2016.

Muraoka, Takamitsu. *A Biblical Aramaic Reader: With an Outline Grammar*. 2nd ed. Leuven: Peeters, 2020.

———. *A Greek-English Lexicon of the Septuagint*. Leuven: Peeters, 2009.

———. *A Syntax of Septuagint Greek*. Leuven: Peeters, 2016.

Na'aman, Nadav. "New Light on Hezekiah's Second Prophetic Story (2 Kgs 19,9b–35)." *Bib* 81 (2000): 393–402.

Najman, Hindy. *Seconding Sinai: The Development of Mosaic Discourse in Second Temple Judaism*. JSJSup 77. Leiden: Brill, 2003.

Neujahr, Matthew. *Predicting the Past in the Ancient Near East: Mantic Historiography in Ancient Mesopotamia, Judah, and the Mediterranean World*. BJS 354. Providence, RI: Brown Judaic Studies, 2012.

Neusner, Jacob, and Alan J. Avery-Peck, eds. *Encyclopedia of Midrash: Biblical Interpretation in Formative Judaism*. 2 vols. Leiden: Brill, 2005.

Newsom, Carol A., with Brennan W. Breed. *Daniel*. OTL. Louisville: Westminster John Knox, 2014.

Newsom, Carol A., Sharon H. Ringe, and Jacqueline E. Lapsley, eds. *Women's Bible Commentary*. 3rd ed. Louisville: Westminster John Knox, 2012.

Nihan, Christophe. "L'analyse rédactionnelle." Pages 137–89 in *Manuel d'exégèse de l'Ancien Testament*. Edited by Michaela Bauks and Christophe Nihan. MdB 61. Geneva: Labor et Fides, 2008.

———. *From Priestly Torah to Pentateuch: A Study in the Composition of the Book of Leviticus*. FAT 2.25. Tübingen: Mohr Siebeck, 2007.

Nissinen, Martti. *Ancient Prophecy: Near Eastern, Biblical, and Greek Perspectives*. Oxford: Oxford University Press, 2017.

———. *Prophets and Prophecy in the Ancient Near East*. 2nd ed. WAW 12. Atlanta: SBL Press, 2019.

Noegel, Scott B. *"Wordplay" in Ancient Near Eastern Texts*. ANEM 26. Atlanta: SBL Press, 2021.

Noonan, Benjamin N. *Advances in the Study of Biblical Hebrew and Aramaic: New Insights for Reading the Old Testament*. Grand Rapids: Zondervan Academic, 2020.

Norris, Richard A., Jr., trans. *Gregory of Nyssa: Homilies on the Song of Songs*. WGRW 13. Atlanta: SBL Press, 2012.

Notley, R. Steven, and Ze'ev Safrai. *Eusebius, Onomasticon: A Triglott Edition with Notes and Commentary*. JCP 9. Leiden: Brill, 2004.

O'Brien, Julia, ed. *The Oxford Encyclopedia of the Bible and Gender Studies*. 2 vols. New York: Oxford University Press, 2014.

O'Connell, Robert H. *The Rhetoric of the Book of Judges*. Leiden: Brill, 1996.

Ofer, Yosef. *The Masorah on Scripture and Its Methods*. FSBP 7. Berlin: de Gruyter, 2019.

Olmo Lete, Gregorio del, and Joaquín Sanmartín. *A Dictionary of the Ugaritic Language in the Alphabetic Tradition*. Translated and edited by Wilfred G. E. Watson. 3rd ed. 2 vols. HdO 112. Brill: Leiden, 2015.

Oshima, Takayoshi. *Babylonian Poems of Pious Sufferers*. ORA 14. Tübingen: Mohr Siebeck, 2014.

Osiek, Carolyn. "The Feminist and the Bible: Hermeneutical Alternatives." *HTS* 53 (1997): 956–68.

Pakkala, Juha. *God's Word Omitted: Omissions in the Transmission of the Hebrew Bible*. FRLANT 251. Göttingen: Vandenhoeck & Ruprecht, 2013.

Pardee, Dennis. *Handbook of Ancient Hebrew Letters: A Study Edition*. SBLSBS 15. Atlanta: Scholars Press, 1982.

———. *Ritual and Cult at Ugarit*. WAW 10. Atlanta: SBL Press, 2002.

Parks, Sara. "'The Brooten Phenomenon': Moving Women from the Margins in Second-Temple and New Testament Scholarship." *The Bible and Critical Theory* 15 (2019): 46–64.

Parpola, Simo, and Kazuko Watanabe. *Neo-Assyrian Treaties and Loyalty Oaths*. SAAS 2. Helsinki: Helsinki University Press, 1988.

Parry, Donald W., and Emanuel Tov, eds. *The Dead Sea Scrolls Reader*. 6 vols. Leiden: Brill, 2004–5.

Patmore, Hector. *Adam, Satan, and the King of Tyre: The Interpretation of Ezekiel 28:11–19 in Late Antiquity*. JCI 20. Leiden: Brill, 2012.

Patron, Sylvie, ed. *Optional-Narrator Theory: Principles, Perspectives, Proposals*. Lincoln: University of Nebraska Press, 2021.

Payne Smith, Jessie, ed. *A Compendious Syriac Dictionary: Founded upon the Thesaurus Syriacus of R. Payne Smith*. Oxford: Clarendon, 1903; repr., Eugene, OR: Wipf & Stock, 1999.

Pentiuc, Eugen J., Gad Barnea, Étienne Méténier, Łukasz Popko, et al. *Hosea: The Word of the Lord Happened to Hosea*. BEST 3. Leuven: Peeters, 2017.

Perdue, Leo, and Warren Carter. *Israel and Empire: A Postcolonial History of Israel and Early Judaism*. Edited by Coleman A. Baker. London: Bloomsbury T&T Clark, 2015.

Philo. *De confusione linguarum*. Introduction, translation, and notes by J. G. Kahn. OPA 13. Paris: Cerf, 1963.

Popko, Łukasz. "What Has Happened with Jerusalem in Jer 13:26?" *RB* 117 (2010): 510–27.

Porten, Bezalel. *The Elephantine Papyri in English: Three Millennia of Cross-Cultural Continuity and Change*. 2nd ed. Atlanta: SBL Press, 2011.

Prenmath, D. N. "The Empire and First Isaiah." Pages 240–58 in *Postcolonial Commentary and the Old Testament*. Edited by Hemchand Gossai. London: T&T Clark, 2018.

Provan, Iain, V. Philips Long, and Tremper Longman III. *A Biblical History of Israel*. Louisville: Westminster John Knox, 2003.

Puech, Emile. "Le Cantique des Cantiques dans les manuscrits de Qumrân: 4Q106, 4Q107, 4Q108 et 6Q6." *RB* 123 (2016): 29–53.

Quick, Laura. *Dress, Adornment, and the Body in the Hebrew Bible*. Oxford: Oxford University Press, 2021.

Rahlfs, Alfred. *Septuaginta: Id est Vetus Testamentum graece iuxta LXX interpretes*. 2nd ed. Revised by Robert Hanhart. Stuttgart: Deutsche Bibelgesellschaft, 2006.

Rainey, Anson F., and R. Steven Notley. *The Sacred Bridge: Carta's Atlas of the Biblical World*. 2nd ed. Jerusalem: Carta, 2015.

Rees, Susannah. "'Women Rule Over Them': Dressing for an Inverted World in Isaiah 3." Pages 155–86 in *Dress Hermeneutics and the Hebrew Bible: "Let Your Garments Always Be Bright."* Edited by Antonios Finitsis. LHBOTS 724. London: T&T Clark, 2022.

Rendsburg, Gary A. *How the Bible Is Written*. Peabody, MA: Hendrickson, 2019.

Rendtorff, Rolf. *The Old Testament: An Introduction*. London: SCM Press, 1985.

Renkema, Johan. *Lamentations*. HCOT. Leuven: Peeters, 1998.

———. *Obadiah*. HCOT. Leuven: Peeters, 2003.

Renz, Johannes, and Wolfgang Röllig. *Handbuch der althebraïschen Epigraphik*. 3 vols. Darmstadt: Wissenschaftliche Buchgesellschaft, 1995.

Reventlow, Henning Graf. *History of Biblical Interpretation*. 4 vols. RBS 50, 61, 62, 63. Atlanta: SBL Press, 2009–10.

Reymond, Eric D. *Intermediate Biblical Hebrew Grammar: A Student's Guide to Phonology and Morphology*. RBS 89. Atlanta: SBL Press, 2018.

Richelle, Matthieu. "Jeremiah and Baruch." Pages 259–74 in *The Oxford Handbook of the Septuagint*. Edited by T. Michael Law and Alison Salvesen. Oxford: Oxford University Press, 2021.

———. "La pierre angulaire d'Ésaïe 28 à la lumière de l'oracle contre l'Égypte." *ZAW* 123 (2011): 437–40.

———. "Le portrait changeant du roi de Tyr (Ézéchiel 28) dans les traditions textuelles anciennes." Pages 113–25 in *Phéniciens d'Orient et d'Occident: Mélanges Josette Elayi*. Edited by André Lemaire. CIPOA 2. Paris: Maisonneuve, 2014.

———. "Literacy and Scribalism in Israel during the Iron Age (ca. 1200–586 BCE)." In *The Ancient Israelite World*. Edited by Kyle Keimer and George A. Pierce. RW. London: Routledge, forthcoming.

———. "Quel rôle a joué l'époque perse dans la diversification textuelle issue des livres des Rois?" *Transeuphratène* 50 (2018): 155–79.

———. "Reflections on the Model of Early Parallel Texts." In *Urtext – Fluidity – Convergence? The Quest for the Texts of the Hebrew Bible*. Edited by Jean-Sébastien Rey and Stefan Schorch. CBET. Leuven: Peeters, forthcoming.

———. "Un triptyque au coeur du livre de Michée (Mi 4–5)." *VT* 62 (2012): 232–47.

———. "Une cécité ordinaire: Analyse narrative de 2 R 6.8–23." *ThEv* 10 (2011): 1–13.

———. "Was the Tower of Babel Really Left Unfinished? Genesis 11:6 in Light of Hebrew Syntax, the Septuagint, and Jewish Reception." *Semitica* 63 (2021): 125–39.

Riches, John, ed. *New Cambridge History of the Bible*, vol. 4, *From 1750 to the Present*. Cambridge: Cambridge University Press, 2015.

Ricks, Stephen D. *Lexicon of Inscriptional Qatabanian*. StPohl 14. Rome: Pontifical Biblical Institute, 1989.

Roberts, J. J. M. *First Isaiah: A Commentary*. Hermeneia. Minneapolis: Fortress, 2015.

Roi, Micha. "1 Kings 19: A 'Departure on a Journey Story.'" *JSOT* 37 (2012): 25–44.

Römer, Thomas. "How 'Persian' or 'Hellenistic' is the Joseph Narrative?" Pages 35–53 in *The Joseph Story between Egypt and Israel*. Edited by Thomas Römer, Konrad Schmid, and Axel Bühler. ArchBib 5. Tübingen: Mohr Siebeck, 2021.

———. "The Joseph Story in the Book of Genesis: Pre-P or Post-P?" Pages 185–201 in *The Post-Priestly Pentateuch: New Perspectives on Its Redactional Development and Theological Profiles*. Edited by Federico Giuntoli and Konrad Schmid. FAT 101. Tübingen: Mohr Siebeck, 2015.

———. "The So-Called Deuteronomistic History and Its Theories of Composition." Pages 303–22 in *The Oxford Handbook of the Historical Books of the Hebrew Bible*. Edited by Brad E. Kelle and Brent A. Strawn. New York: Oxford University Press, 2020.

———. "The Strange Conversion of Naaman, Chief of the Aramaean Army." Pages 105–20 in *Research on Israel and Aram: Autonomy, Independence and Related Issues*. Edited by Angelika Berlejung and Aren M. Maeir. ORA 34. Tübingen: Mohr Siebeck, 2019.

Römer, Thomas, and Israel Finkelstein. "Comments on the Historical Background of the Abraham Narratives: Between 'Realia' and 'Exegetica.'" *HeBAI* 3 (2014): 3–23.

Römheld, Diethard. *Wege der Weisheit: Die Lehren Amenemopes und Proverbien 22.17–24.22*. BZAW 184. Berlin: de Gruyter, 1989.

Rosenthal, Franz. *A Grammar of Biblical Aramaic*. 7th ed. Wiesbaden: Harrassowitz, 2006.

Ross, William A., and W. Edward Glenny, eds. *The T&T Clark Handbook of Septuagint Research*. New York: T&T Clark, 2020.

Roth, Martha T. *Law Collections from Mesopotamia and Asia Minor*. 2nd ed. WAW 6. Atlanta: SBL Press, 1997.

Sader, Hélène. *The History and Archaeology of Phoenicia*. ABS 25. Atlanta: SBL Press, 2018.

Sæbø, Magne, ed. *Hebrew Bible / Old Testament: The History of Its Interpretation*. 3 vols. Göttingen: Vandenhoeck & Ruprecht, 1996–2015.

Salvesen, Alison, and T. Michael Law, eds. *The Oxford Handbook of the Septuagint*. Oxford: Oxford University Press, 2021.

Sawyer, John F. A. *Isaiah through the Centuries*. BBC. Hoboken, NJ: Wiley-Blackwell, 2018.

Schaab, Gloria L. "Feminist Theological Methodology: Toward a Kaleidoscopic Model." *TS* 62 (2001): 341–65.

Schenker, Adrian, ed. *Biblia Hebraica Quinta*. Stuttgart: Deutsche Bibelgesellschaft, 2004–.

Schipper, Bernd U. *A Concise History of Ancient Israel: From the Beginnings through the Hellenistic Era*. CSHB 11. University Park, PA: Eisenbrauns, 2019; original German edition, 2018.

———. *Proverbs 1–15: A Commentary*. Hermeneia. Minneapolis: Fortress, 2019.

Schmid, Konrad. "Die Datierung der Josephsgeschichte: Ein Gespräch mit Erhard Blum und Kristin Weingart." Pages 99–109 in *Eigensinn und Entstehung der Hebräischen Bibel: Erhard Blum zum siebzigsten Geburtstag*. Edited by Joachim J. Krause, Wolfgang Oswald, and Kristin Weingart. FAT 136. Tübingen: Mohr Siebeck, 2020.

———. *A Historical Theology of the Hebrew Bible*. Translated by Peter Altmann. Grand Rapids: Eerdmans, 2019; original German edition, 2018.

———. "How to Identify a Persian Period Text in the Pentateuch." Pages 101–18 in *On Dating Biblical Texts to the Persian Period: Discerning Criteria and Establishing Epochs*. Edited by Richard J. Bautch and Mark Lackowski. Tübingen: Mohr Siebeck, 2019.

———. "The Neo-Documentarian Manifesto: A Critical Reading." *JBL* 140 (2021): 461–79.

Scholz, Susanne, ed. *The Oxford Handbook of Feminist Approaches to the Hebrew Bible*. New York: Oxford University Press, 2021.

Schorch, Stefan, ed. *The Samaritan Pentateuch: A Critical Editio Maior*. Berlin: de Gruyter, 2018–.

Schottroff, Luise, Silvia Schroer, and Marie-Theres Wacker. *Feminist Interpretation: The Bible in Women's Perspective*. Minneapolis: Fortress, 1998.

Schroer, Silvia. "Feminist Hermeneutics and the First Testament." Pages 85–101 in *Feminist Interpretation: The Bible in Women's Perspective*. Edited by Luise Schottroff, Silvia Schroer, and Marie-Theres Wacker. Minneapolis: Fortress, 1998.

Schwiderski, Dirk. *Handbuch des nordwestsemitischen Briefformulars: Ein Beitrag zur Echtheitsfrage der aramäischen Briefe des Esrabuches*. BZAW 295. Berlin: de Gruyter, 2000.

Scott, William R. *A Simplified Guide to BHS: Critical Apparatus, Masora, Accents, Unusual Letters & Other Markings*. 4th ed. Richlands Hills, TX: BIBAL Press, 2007.

Sefati, Yitzhak. *Love Songs in Sumerian Literature: Critical Edition of the Dumuzi-Inanna Songs*. Ramat-Gan: Bar-Ilan University Press, 1998.

Seow, Choon-Leong. *Job 1–21: Interpretation and Commentary*. Illuminations. Grand Rapids: Eerdmans, 2013.

Shafer-Elliott, Cynthia. *Food in Ancient Judah: Domestic Cooking in the Time of the Hebrew Bible*. London: Equinox, 2013.

Shaw, Ian, ed. *The Oxford History of Ancient Egypt*. New York: Oxford University Press, 2000.

Sherman, Philip M. *Babel's Tower Translated: Genesis 11 and Ancient Jewish Interpretation*. Leiden: Brill, 2013.

Singer, Itamar. *Hittite Prayers*. WAW 11. Atlanta: SBL Press, 2002.

Ska, Jean-Louis. *Introduction to Reading the Pentateuch*. Translated by Pascale Dominique. Winona Lake, IN: Eisenbrauns, 2006.

———. *"Our Fathers Have Told Us": Introduction to the Analysis of Hebrew Narratives*. SubBi 13. Rome: Pontifical Biblical Institute, 2000.

Smit, Peter-Ben. *Masculinity and the Bible: Survey, Models, and Perspectives*. BRP. Leiden: Brill, 2017.

Smith, Steve. "The Use of Criteria: A Proposal from Relevance Theory." Pages 142–54 in *Methodology in the Use of the Old Testament in the New: Context and Criteria*. Edited by David Allen and Steve Smith. LNTS 579. London: T&T Clark, 2019.

Soggin, J. Alberto. *An Introduction to the History of Israel and Judah*. Translated by John Bowden. 3rd ed. London: SCM Press, 1999; original Italian edition, 1998.

Sokoloff, Michael. *A Syriac Lexicon: A Translation from Latin; Correction, Expansion, and Update of C. Brockelmann's Lexicon Syriacum*. Winona Lake, IN: Eisenbrauns; Piscataway, NJ: Gorgias, 2009.

Sommer, Benjamin D. "Dating Pentateuchal Texts and the Perils of Pseudo-Historicism." Pages 85–108 in *The Pentateuch: International Perspectives on Current Research*. Edited by Thomas B. Dozeman, Konrad Schmid, and Baruch J. Schwartz. FAT 78. Tübingen: Mohr Siebeck, 2011.

———. *A Prophet Reads Scripture: Allusion in Isaiah 40–66*. Stanford: Stanford University Press, 1998.

———. *Revelation and Authority: Sinai in Jewish Scripture and Tradition*. New Haven: Yale University Press, 2015.

Sparks, Kenton L. *Ancient Texts for the Study of the Hebrew Bible: A Guide to the Background Literature*. Grand Rapids: Baker Academic, 2017.

Spronk, Klaas. *Nahum*. HCOT. Kampen: Pharos, 1997.

Suriano, Matthew J. "A Place in the Dust: Text, Topography and a Toponymic Note on Micah 1:10–12a*." *VT* 60 (2010): 433–46.

Sternberg, Meir. *The Poetics of Biblical Narrative: Ideological Literature and the Drama of Reading*. Bloomington: Indiana University Press, 1987.

Stökl, Jonathan. *Prophecy in the Ancient Near East: A Philological and Sociological Comparison*. CHANE 56. Leiden: Brill, 2012.

Sugirtharajah, R. S. *The Bible and the Third World: Precolonial, Colonial and Postcolonial Encounters*. Cambridge: Cambridge University Press, 2001.

———, ed. *The Oxford Handbook of Postcolonial Biblical Criticism*. Oxford: Oxford University Press, 2020.

———, ed. *The Postcolonial Biblical Reader*. Malden, MA: Blackwell, 2006.

Svensson, Jan. *Towns and Toponyms in the Old Testament: With Special Emphasis on Joshua 14–21*. Stockholm: Almqvist & Wiksell, 1994.

Tal, Abraham, and Moshe Florentin. *The Pentateuch: The Samaritan Version and the Masoretic Version*. Tel Aviv: Haim Rubin Tel Aviv University Press, 2010. [Hebrew]

Talmon, Shemaryahu. "Textual Criticism: The Ancient Versions." Pages 383–418 in *Text and Canon of the Hebrew Bible: Collected Studies*. Winona Lake, IN: Eisenbrauns, 2010.

Talon, Philippe. *The Standard Babylonian Creation Myth Enūma Eliš*. SAATC 4. Helsinki: Neo-Assyrian Text Corpus Project, 2005.

Taylor, Bernard A. *Analytical Lexicon to the Septuagint*. Peabody, MA: Hendrickson; Stuttgart: Deutsche Bibelgesellschaft, 2009.

Taylor, Marion Ann, and Agnes Choi. *Handbook of Women Biblical Interpreters: A Historical and Biographical Guide*. Grand Rapids: Baker Academic, 2012.

Thomas, Benjamin D. *Hezekiah and the Compositional History of the Book of Kings*. FAT 2.63. Tübingen: Mohr Siebeck, 2014.

Thompson, John L. *Writing the Wrongs: Women of the Old Testament among Biblical Commentators from Philo through the Reformation*. OSHT. New York: Oxford University Press, 2001.

Tiemeyer, Lena-Sofia. *For the Comfort of Zion: The Geographical and Theological Location of Isaiah 40–55*. VTSup 139. Leiden: Brill, 2011.

———. "Prophecy as a Way of Cancelling Prophecy—the Strategic Uses of Foreknowledge." *ZAW* 117 (2005): 329–50.

Timmer, Daniel C. *A Gracious and Compassionate God: Mission, Salvation and Spirituality in the Book of Jonah*. NSBT 26. Downers Grove, IL: InterVarsity Press, 2011.

Tomson, Peter. "The Song of Songs in the Teachings of Jesus and the Development of the Exposition on the Song." *NTS* 61 (2015): 429–94.

Tov, Emanuel. *Textual Criticism of the Hebrew Bible*. 3rd ed. Minneapolis: Fortress, 2012.

Tov, Emanuel, and Eugene Ulrich. "(1.1.1) The Search for an Original Text." Pages 15–19 in vol. 1A of *Textual History of the Bible*. Edited by Armin Lange and Emanuel Tov. Leiden: Brill, 2016.

Trible, Phyllis. *God and the Rhetoric of Sexuality*. Philadelphia: Fortress, 1978.

———. *Texts of Terror: Literary-Feminist Readings of Biblical Narratives*. Philadelphia: Fortress, 1984.

Tyson, Craig W. *The Ammonites: Elites, Empires, and Sociopolitical Change (1000–500 BCE)*. London: Bloomsbury, 2014.

Ulrich, Eugene. *The Biblical Qumran Scrolls: Transcriptions and Textual Variants*. VTSup 134. Leiden: Brill, 2010.

———. "Deuteronomistically Inspired Scribal Insertions into the Developing Biblical Texts: 4QJudgª and 4QJerª." Pages 489–506 in *Houses Full of All Good Things: Essays in Memory of Timo Veijola*. Edited by Juha Pakkala and Martti Nissinen. Helsinki: Finnish Exegetical Society, 2008.

Ussishkin, David. "Was a 'Gate Shrine' Built at the Level III Inner City Gate of Lachish? A Response to Ganor and Kreimerman." *BASOR* 385 (2021): 153–70.

Vance, Donald R., George Athas, and Yael Avrahami. *Biblia Hebraica Stuttgartensia: A Reader's Edition*. Peabody, MA: Hendrickson; Stuttgart: Deutsche Bibelgesellschaft, 2014.

Vance, Donald R., George Athas, Yael Avrahami, and Jonathan G. Kline. *Biblical Aramaic: A Reader & Handbook*. Peabody, MA: Hendrickson, 2016.

Van De Mieroop, Marc. *A History of Ancient Egypt*. 2nd ed. BHAW. Hoboken, NJ: Wiley-Blackwell, 2021.

———. *A History of the Ancient Near East, ca. 3000–332 BC*. 3rd ed. BHAW. Malden, MA: Wiley-Blackwell, 2016.

Vanderhooft, David S. "Babylon as Cosmopolis in Israelite Texts and Achaemenid Architecture." *HeBAI* 9 (2020): 41–61.

Van der Lugt, Pieter. *Cantos and Strophes in Biblical Hebrew Poetry*. 3 vols. OTS 53, 57, 63. Leiden: Brill, 2006–14.

Van der Merwe, Christo H. J., Jacobus A. Naudé, and Jan H. Kroeze. *A Biblical Hebrew Reference Grammar*. 2nd ed. London: Bloomsbury, 2017.

Van Hecke, Pierre. "Are People Walking After or Before God? On the Metaphorical Use of הלך אחרי and הלך לפני." *OLP* 30 (1999): 37–71.

———. "Conceptual Blending: A Recent Approach to Metaphor. Illustrated with the Pastoral Metaphor in Hos 4,16." Pages 215–31 in *Metaphor in the Hebrew Bible*. Edited by Pierre van Hecke. BETL 187. Leuven: Peeters, 2005.

Van Kooten, George H., ed. *The Creation of Heaven and Earth: Re-interpretations of Genesis 1 in the Context of Judaism, Ancient Philosophy, Christianity, and Modern Physics*. TBN 8. Leiden: Brill, 2005.

Van Kooten, George H., and Jacques van Ruiten, eds. *The Prestige of the Pagan Prophet Balaam in Judaism, Early Christianity and Islam*. TBN 11. Leiden: Brill, 2008.

Van Seters, John. "Joshua's Campaign and Near Eastern Historiography." *SJOT* 2 (1990): 1–12.

Vayntrub, Jacqueline. *Beyond Orality: Biblical Poetry on Its Own Terms*. New York: Routledge, 2019.

Veyne, Paul. *Writing History: Essay on Epistemology*. Translated by Mina Moore-Rinvolucri. Middletown, CT: Wesleyan University Press, 1984.

Vogt, Ernst, ed. *A Lexicon of Biblical Aramaic: Clarified by Ancient Documents*. Translated and revised by James A. Fitzmyer. Rome: Gregorian and Biblical Press, 2011.

Walsh, Jerome T. *Style and Structure in Biblical Hebrew Narrative*. Collegeville, MN: Liturgical Press, 2001.

Watson, Wilfred G. E. *Classical Hebrew Poetry: A Guide to Its Techniques*. JSOTSup 26. Sheffield: JSOT Press, 1986.

———. *Traditional Techniques in Classical Hebrew Verse*. JSOTSup 170. Sheffield: JSOT Press, 1994.

———. "Verse Patterns in the Song of Songs." *JNSL* 21 (1995): 111–22.

Watson, Wilfred G. E., and Nicholas Wyatt, eds. *Handbook of Ugaritic Studies*. Leiden: Brill, 1999.

Weigl, Michael. *Die aramäischen Achikar-Sprüche aus Elephantine und die alttestamentliche Weisheitsliteratur*. BZAW 399. Berlin: de Gruyter, 2010.

Weinfeld, Moshe. *Deuteronomy and the Deuteronomistic School*. Oxford: Clarendon, 1972.

Wente, Edward F. *Letters from Ancient Egypt*. WAW 1. Atlanta: SBL Press, 1990.

West, Gerald O. "African Biblical Scholarship as Post-Colonial, Tri-Polar, and a Site-of-Struggle." Pp. 240–73 in *Present and Future of Biblical Studies: Celebrating 25 Years of Brill's Biblical Interpretation*. Edited by Tat-siong Benny Liew. BIS 161. Leiden: Brill, 2018.

Westbrook, Richard. *Studies in Biblical and Cuneiform Law*. CahRB 26. Paris: Gabalda, 1988.

Williamson, Hugh G. M. "History and Memory in the Prophets." Pages 133–48 in *The Oxford Handbook of the Prophets*. Edited by Carolyn J. Sharp. New York: Oxford University Press, 2016.

———. *Isaiah 1–27*, vol. 1, *Commentary on Isaiah 1–5*. ICC. London: T&T Clark, 2006.

———. *Isaiah 1–27*, vol. 2, *Commentary on Isaiah 6–12*. ICC. London: T&T Clark, 2018.

Wolff, Hans Walter. *Hosea: A Commentary on the Book of the Prophet Hosea*. Hermeneia. Minneapolis: Fortress, 1974.

Wolters, Al. "Proverbs XXXI 10–31 as Heroic Hymn: A Form-Critical Analysis." *VT* 38 (1988): 446–57.

Wong, Gregory T. K. *Compositional Strategy of the Book of Judges: An Inductive, Rhetorical Study*. VTSup 111. Leiden: Brill, 2006.

Wood, Alice. *Of Wings and Wheels: A Synthetic Study of the Biblical Cherubim*. BZAW 385. Berlin: de Gruyter, 2008.

Woolmer, Mark. *A Short History of the Phoenicians*. Rev. ed. London: Bloomsbury Academic, 2022.

Wright, J. Robert, ed. *Proverbs, Ecclesiastes, Song of Solomon*. ACCS 9. Downers Grove, IL: InterVarsity Press, 2005.

Wright, Paul H. *Holman Illustrated Guide to Biblical Geography: Reading the Land*. Nashville: Holman Reference, 2020.

Würthwein, Ernst. *Die Bücher der Könige: 1. Kön. 17 – 2. Kön. 25*. ATD 11.2. Göttingen: Vandenhoeck & Ruprecht, 1984.

———. *The Text of the Old Testament: An Introduction to the* Biblia Hebraica. Translated by Erroll F. Rhodes. Revised and expanded by Alexander Achilles Fischer. 3rd ed. Grand Rapids: Eerdmans, 2014.

Yamauchi, Edwin M., and Marvin R. Wilson, eds. *Dictionary of Daily Life in Biblical and Post-Biblical Antiquity*. 4 vols. Peabody, MA: Hendrickson, 2014–16.

Young, Dwight W. "The Influence of Babylonian Algebra on Longevity among the Antediluvians." *ZAW* 102 (1990): 321–25.

———. "A Mathematical Approach to Certain Dynastic Spans in the Sumerian King List." *JNES* 47 (1988): 123–29.

———. "On the Applications of Numbers from Babylonian Mathematics to Biblical Life Spans and Epochs." *ZAW* 100 (1988): 332–61.

Younger, K. Lawson. *Ancient Conquest Accounts: A Study in Ancient Near Eastern and Biblical History Writing*. JSOTSup 98. Sheffield: JSOT Press, 1990.

———. *A Political History of the Arameans: From the Origins to the End of Their Polities*. ABS 13. Atlanta: SBL Press, 2016.

Zakovitch, Yair. "The Book of the Covenant Interprets the Book of the Covenant: The 'Boomerang Phenomenon.'" Pages 59*–64* in *Texts, Temples, and Traditions: A Tribute to Menahem Haran*. Edited by Michael V. Fox et al. Winona Lake, IN: Eisenbrauns, 1996. [Hebrew]

Zevit, Ziony. *The Religions of Ancient Israel: A Synthesis of Parallactic Approaches*. London: Continuum, 2001.

INDEX OF BIBLICAL REFERENCES

Hebrew Bible / Old Testament

Genesis
1   82, 98, 103, 129, 153, 286
1–3   142, 146
1–11   130
1:1–2:3   98, 286
1:2   286
1:6   37
1:9   286
1:20–25   286
1:26–27   286
1:27   152
1:28   286
1:29   286
2   82, 98
2–3   71, 98, 103, 129, 164
2–4   165
2:2   73
2:4–3:24   98
2:7   82, 287, 318
2:8   287
2:15   287
2:17   32
2:18   344
3   72, 159–60, 164–65, 287
3–4   287
3:6   287
3:7   287–88
3:9   159
3:10   160
3:13   159
3:16   159
3:17   160
3:19   160
3:21   160, 287
3:24   160, 197
4   142, 146, 159–60, 164–65, 287
4:1   339
4:1–16   159
4:7   159
4:9   159–60

4:10   159
4:11   160, 288
4:12   160
4:13   160
4:14   160
4:15   160
4:16   160
4:26   100
5   130, 142, 146, 150–52
5:23   151
5:24   151
6–9   129, 142, 146, 151, 153
6:1–4   318
6:5–6   103
6:6   72
6:7aα   103
6:9–22   103
6:9–9:29   223
7:1–2   103
7:3b–5   103
7:6   103
7:7   103
7:10   103
7:11   103
7:12   103
7:13–16a   103
7:16b   103
7:17   103
7:18–21   103
7:22   103
7:23   103
7:24   103
8–9   286
8:1–2   286
8:1–2a   103
8:2b–3a   103
8:3b–5   103
8:5   286
8:6–12   103
8:9   286
8:13a   103
8:13b   103
8:14–19   103

8:17–19   286
8:20–22   103
9   287, 357
9:1   357
9:1–2   286
9:1–17   103
9:3   286
9:6   286
9:20   287
9:21   287
9:22–23   287
9:23   287, 357
9:23–26   357
9:24   288
9:24–26   357
9:25   288
10   130, 357
11   142, 146, 150–52, 315–16
11:1–9   33, 314, 316, 318
11:3   33
11:4   61
11:5   61, 314–18
11:8   52, 60–61, 315–17
11:9   33
11:28   108
11:31   108
12   165
12–25   165
12–50   129, 142
12:1–9   155
12:2   155
12:7   156
12:10–20   155, 318
14   105–6
14:17   105
14:18–20   105–6
14:21   105
15:7   108
15:13–15   100
16   131, 204
16–18   263
16:4   204
16:6   204

17:17–18   264
18:12   264
19:3–38   137
21   263
22   165
23   155
24   88, 107, 263
24:3   88
24:7   88
24:17   88
25   263–64
25:22   264
27:41–28:22   131
29   263
30:19   72
31:54   32
35:4   73
36   94
36:31   94
37–50   109
42   259
42:8   109
43:11   27–28
49   80
50:18   109

Exodus
1:1–6   100
2   101
2:11–4:17   131
2:18   101
3   90, 100
3:1   101
3:1–4:18   90, 100–101
3:13–16   101
4:1   90
4:10   90
4:19–20   101
4:25   332
4:26   101
6   90, 100
6:2   90, 100
6:2–7:7   90, 100–101
6:5–7   90
6:10–13   90
6:12–13   90
6:14–25   90–91, 100
6:26–30   90–91
6:28–7:7   90
6:30   90
12:1–3   102
12:1–13   102
12:1–28   102
12:14   102
12:14b–17   102
12:15–20   102–3
12:16a   102
12:17   102
12:21–23   102
12:24–28   102

12:34   102
13:3   19
13:21–22   283, 288
14   133
14:19–20   283
14:21   133
14:24   283
15   80, 133, 162
15:1   28
15:1–21   130, 133
15:2   27–28
15:4   133
15:5   133
15:8   133
15:20   335
15:22   162
15:22–23   162
15:22–27   161–62, 164
15:22–17:7   161
15:24   161–62
15:25   162
16   162
16:1   162
16:1–36   161, 164
16:2   162
16:3   161–62
16:4   162
16:4–5   162
16:8   162
16:10   283
16:11–18   162
17   162
17:1   162
17:1–7   161–62, 164
17:2   161–62
17:3   162
17:6   162
17:7   162
20   289–90
20–23   130
20:22–23:33   289
20:23–24   290
20:24   289
22:2–3 [1–2]   148
23   115
23:14–17   116
23:18   115
24:1–11   123
26:1   197
26:31   197
32   115, 284–85
32–33   115
32–34   284
32:4   115–16
32:8   115–16
32:9–14   285
33:9–10   283
33:21   285
34   115–16, 285
34:6   285

34:6–7   291–92, 298
34:11   115
34:11–26   115–16
34:17   116
34:18–20   116
34:22a   116
34:24   116
34:25   115
36:8   197
36:35   197
37:7–9   197

Leviticus
1–16   100, 130, 183
4:6   25
6:8–13 [1–6]   217
17–26   100, 102, 183
18   183
18:1   183
18:6–20   183
18:21   183
18:22–23   183
18:24–30   183
19:4   116
23   116
23:5–8   102
26:34–35   273

Numbers
16   123
20:1–13   161
22–24   89
22:20   89
22:20–21   89
22:21   89
22:22   89
22:22–35   89
22:31   89
22:35   89
24:3–4   89
28–29   116
31:16   89

Deuteronomy
4   119
4:40   115
5:25   118
6:6   115
12   190, 192, 289–90
12–26   289
12:3   88, 113
12:5   190
12:13–14   289–90
12:14   289
13   354
17:14   62
17:15   62
23:3 [4]   292
26:15   280
28   349, 354

28:36   62
32   80
32:18   344

Joshua
2–12   129
10:13   276
10:33   345
13:22   89
14–21   170

Judges
1:12–15   158
3:19   280
4   133, 335
4–5   133, 158
4:4   69
4:6–7   335
4:9   335
4:21   335
5   80, 130, 133
6   69–70, 78
6:1a   69
6:1b–6a   69
6:6b–7   69
6:7–11   69
6:7a   69
6:8–10   69, 76, 78
6:11   69
6:11–16   69
9:8–15   129
9:50–57   158
9:53   335
9:54   335
10:11–14   70
11   158
12:9   158
13   158, 253–55, 260, 263–65
13:1   254–55, 265
13:2   254, 256
13:3   254, 260
13:5   254–56
13:6   254, 256, 260
13:8–18   265
13:9   265
13:11   266
13:13   266
13:16   260, 266
13:18   266
13:20   256
13:22   336
13:23   336
13:24   256
16:4–22   336
17   158
17:6   111
17:21   111
18:1   111
18:20   111
19   159

19:1   111
20:1   173
20:2   36
21   159
21:25   111, 336

Ruth
3   340
3:3   340
3:4   340
3:7   340
3:8   340
3:11   293
3:14   340

1 Samuel
1–2   264
1:2   263
1:20   264
1:28   264
2   259, 269
2:1–10   130
2:12   269
2:17   270
2:22–25   259
3:14   31
3:20   173
4:4   197
13:21   179
14:38   36
16   176
24   166
25   166, 270
26   166

2 Samuel
1:18   276
2:18   243
6:2   197
6:14   106
6:18   106
7   16, 113
7:2   16
7:6–7   16
7:11   16
7:13   16
8:18   106
9:4–5   35
11   270, 337, 339, 343
11:1–5   338
11:2   338
11:4   338
11:16   334
11:27   270, 338
12   338
12:1–4   129
12:20   340
14:2   340
16:16–17:5   271
17:27   35

21–24   223
22   133
23:24–29   130
24:9   334
24:25   106

1 Kings
3:4   106
3:15   106
6:7–15   93
6:23–35   197
7:29   197
7:36   197
8   68, 106, 190
8:1–6   66–67
8:6   197
8:8   111
8:48   11
11:41   276
12   270
12:15   270
12:29–30   173
12:32–33   106
14:19   276
14:23   190
14:24   55
15:12   55
15:14   184
15:27   55
16:9–16   55
16:20   55
17   257–58
17:1   257–58
17:3   257
17:8   257
17:15   258
17:16   258
17:18   258
17:24   258
18   119, 132, 284–85
18:1   258, 284
18:4   285
18:13   258
18:22   258
18:28   204
18:36   94, 258
19   37, 131–32, 284–85
19:4   258, 285
19:8   285
19:8–18   94
19:9   285
19:10   258, 285
19:11   285
19:12   132
19:14   258, 285
19:15   132
19:15–18   132
19:18   132, 258, 285
20:16   345
22   121

22:1–38   121
22:4   121
22:7–8   121
22:15   251
22:23   251
22:28   72
22:46 [47]   55
22:47 [48]   120

2 Kings
1:9–16   35
3   120–21, 205
3:1–6   120
3:4–6   121–22
3:6   121
3:7   121
3:7–18   122
3:7–23   120
3:11   121
3:18   121–22, 251
3:19   122
3:20–24aα   122
3:24–27   120
3:24aβ   121
3:24aβ–27   121–22
3:24b   121
3:25   122
3:25aα   121–22
3:27   121–22, 251
4:38–41   165
4:42–44   165–66
5   119
5:1–19   119
5:6   18
5:15   119
5:17   119
5:17–18   119
6:2   260
6:8   261
6:8–23   255, 260, 262, 267–68
6:8a   255
6:8b–17   255
6:9   260
6:11   268
6:15   261, 268
6:17   261
6:18   255
6:19–23   255
6:20   261, 268
6:23   255
8   200
8:20   120
8:25–27   342
8:26   341
9   200
9–10   270
9:14   55
9:14–28   199
10   200
10:9   55

11   341–42
11:1   341
11:3   342
11:14   55
11:18   342
12:3 [4]   184
12:20 [21]   55
13:23   94
14:4   184
14:6   276
14:19   55
14:25   176
15   94
15:1–3   94
15:4   184
15:6–7   94
15:10   55
15:15   55
15:25   55
15:30   55
15:35   184
16:4   184, 190
17   70, 91
17:1   36
17:1–6   91
17:1–23   107
17:4   55
17:7–23   91
17:10   190
17:24   91
17:24–34   107
17:25–34a   91
17:33–34a   91–92
17:34–40   91
17:34–41   91
17:34b   91, 107
17:34b–40a   92, 107
17:40a   91
17:40b–41   92
17:41   107
18   113, 184
18–19   112, 201
18:4   184–85, 192
18:13   93, 112, 201
18:13–16   92–93
18:13–19:37   92, 112, 201
18:14–16   93, 112, 201–2
18:14–19:36   201
18:17–19a   201
18:17–35   92
18:17–19:9a   92–93, 112
18:17–19:37   92
18:20–25   184
18:22   184, 192
18:36–19:4   92
19:5–7   92
19:7   201
19:8–9a   92
19:9   202
19:9a   201

19:9b–13   92
19:9b–36   93, 112, 201
19:9b–37   92
19:12–13   112, 202
19:14–19   92
19:17–18   112
19:20–34   92
19:35–37   92
19:37   93, 112, 201
21   182
21:23   55
22–23   204
22:9   18
22:14   335
23   290
23:7   55
23:14   184–85
23:25   113
23:26–27   182
24   121
24–25   350
25   111, 121
25:9–18   111

1 Chronicles
1–9   130
2:18   339
12:8 [9]   243
12:21 [22]   345
15–16   138
21–22   138
23–26   138
28:8–9   138

2 Chronicles
5   68
7:14   182
12:5   138
18:31–32   345
20   294
20:2   172
20:17   172
25:4   276
28:23   345
30:27   280
32   201
32:32   276
33   182
33:1–10   182
33:11–13   182
33:11–19   182
33:15–17   182
34:22   335
36:21   273
36:22–23   138
36:23   88

Ezra
1:2   88
2   127

4–7   127
4:8–24   130
5–6   247
5:6–17   130
8   127
10   127

Nehemiah
1:4–5   88
2:4   88
2:20   88
6:14   335
9–10   292

Esther
1   355
1:10–13   355
3   269
3:12–13   135
5   268
6   268
6:6   268
7   268
8   269
8:8   355
9   269

Job
1–2   166
1:8   257
2:11   84
3   166
3–31   84
3–41   166
4–31   84
7:17   33–34
7:18   34
15:14   33–34
32   83–84
32–37   83–84
32:2–4   84
32:4   84
36:22–37:24   84
37   84
38–40   84
42   166
42:2   11
42:7–10   84

Psalms
1   130, 156, 207–8, 219, 249
1:1   219
1:1–2   156, 219
1:2   220
1:3   219
1:4   36, 219
1:5   156, 219–20
1:5–6   219
1:6   219
2   130, 156, 157, 207–8

2:7   156, 318
3   130
5   130
7:6 [7]   280
7:12 [13]   14
8   130, 208
8:4 [5]   33–34
9–10   130, 210
13   130
14:7   230
15:1–3   157
16:2   11–12
16:10   37
18   130, 133
18:2–16 [3–17]   133
18:7 [8]   133
18:8 [9]   133
18:10 [11]   197
19   130
20   130
21   130
22   130, 153
23   242
23:1   241
23:1–4   242
23:1b   241
23:3a   241
23:3b   241
25   130, 210
26   221
26–32   221
26:1   221
27   221
27:14   221
28   221
28:1   221
29   130, 221, 231, 237
29:1   237
29:1–2   231–33
29:2   237
29:3   232–33, 237
29:3–9   231
29:3a   232
29:4   231–33, 237
29:5   230–33, 237
29:6   232–33, 238
29:7   232–33, 238
29:8   232–33, 238
29:9   238
29:9a   232–33
29:9b   233
29:10   233, 238
29:11   233, 237–38
30   221
30:4   221
30:10 [11]   345
31   221
31:24   221
32   130, 221
32:5   221

33   130
34   130, 210
34:13 [14]   157
35:23   280
37   130, 210
37:3–4   228
37:16–17   157
40   130
44   130
44:23 [24]   280
45   130
46   130
47   130, 349
48   130
57   223
59:4 [5]   280
66   130
67   130
68:5 [6]   280
76   130
79   130
80   130
80:1 [2]   197
80:2 [3]   280
81:2 [3]   27
83   130
87   130, 134
89   130
92:2 [3]   230
92:5 [6]   228
93   238
93–99   130, 349
93:1a   238–40
93:1b   239
93:1b–2   239–40
93:1b–3   239
93:1b–5   239
93:2   239
93:3   229, 239–40
93:4   226, 239–40
93:5   239–40
93:5a   239
96   249
96:7–9   229
96:12b–13   230
98:5   27
100   130
103   130, 208
103:1   11
104   130, 153
105   166
106   166
109:26   345
110   130
111   130, 163–64, 210
111:3   163
111:4   163
111:5   163
112   130, 163–64, 210
112:3   163

112:4   163
112:6   163
112:9   163
117:1   226–27, 229
117:2   229
118:4   27
118:13   345
118:17–18   227–28
118:22   36
119   130, 210
124   130
129   130
132   130, 216
132:1–2   216
132:1–10   216
132:3–5   216
132:6–8   216
132:8   216
132:9   216–17
132:10   217
132:11–18   216
132:11a   216
132:11b–12   216
132:13–14   216
132:13–15   216
132:16   216–17
132:17–18   217
140:12 [13]   11
145   130, 210

Proverbs
1–9   131
1:1   75
1:22   221–22
1:22–23   222
1:22–33   221–22
1:24–28   222
1:24–31   222
1:24a   222
1:29   222
1:29–31   222
1:32   221–22
1:32–33   222
1:33   222
5:19   243
8   156
10–31   131
10:1   75, 228
14:7   228
19:8   228
25:1   75
30:1   75
30:15   228
31   321, 333
31:1   75, 321, 333
31:10   293
31:10–31   210, 321, 333–34, 344
31:11   333–34
31:15   333–34

Ecclesiastes
7:1–8   131
10:1–4   131
12:1–7   131

Song of Songs
2   64, 244, 310–11, 313
2:7   211
2:8   211–13, 243–44
2:8–9   212–13, 234, 244
2:8–9a   211
2:8–17   211–13, 234, 243–44, 248, 298, 309–10, 312
2:9   65, 243, 248
2:9a   211
2:10   212, 236, 311, 314
2:10–13   244, 310
2:10–14   211–13, 235
2:11   64
2:11–13   311
2:12   64, 212, 234–36, 244
2:12–14   64–65, 236
2:13   64, 212–13, 314
2:13b   236
2:14   65, 212, 234–36, 244, 314
2:14a   244
2:14b   244
2:15   212–13, 248, 312
2:16–17   212, 244, 248
2:17   64–65, 211–13, 243–44, 248
3:1   211
4:5   243–44
4:6   243
7:3 [4]   243–44
7:10 [11]   293

Isaiah
1–5   288
1–39   343, 350–51
1:1–31   288
2:1–4   288
2:1–5   85–86
2:5–22   358
2:5–3:12   288
3   329–30
3:1–12   328
3:4   328
3:8   230
3:12   328
3:13–15   288
3:16–24   329, 340
3:16–4:1   288
3:18–23   329
4:2–6   283, 288
4:5   283, 288
5:1–7   283
5:1–30   288
5:2–7   282
6:2   332
7:20   332

8:3   335, 343
9:1 [8:23]   177
10   353
10:5   352
10:5–15   352–53
10:5–34   351–54
10:6   352–53
10:8   353
10:13   353
10:14   353
10:16–34   353
10:27–34   177
11:11–16   293
12:2   27
13–21   137
13–23   97, 130, 299
14   130
14:1–2   97
14:32   97
15   172
16   172
16:1–5   97
17   87
17:1–6   87
17:7–8   87, 113
17:8   87–88
17:9–10   87
18:7   97
19   63, 97, 299
19:1–5   85
19:1–15   85
19:14   36
19:16   85, 328
19:16–17   86
19:16–25   85–86, 97
19:16a   86
19:18   64, 85–86
19:18–25   85–86
19:19   85
19:19–21   64, 85
19:21   85
19:23   85
19:23–25   86
19:24   85
19:25   63–64
22:15   19
22:16   20
23:15–18   97
24–27   88, 276
27:9   88
28   36
28:7–13   36
28:16   36
29:16   14
30:7   345
36–39   201
36:7   184
37–38   93
40–55   97, 119, 134, 276, 281–83, 343

Index of Biblical References

40–66   76, 80, 85, 276
40:1–2   282
40:7–8   58, 60
42   283–84
42:1   284
42:1–13   283
42:4   284
42:6   284
42:7   284
42:13   280
42:14   334
49   283–84
49:1   284
49:1–12   283
49:3   284
49:6   284
49:8   284
49:9   284
49:13   282
49:14–26   134, 249
49:15   334
50:4–11   283
51:3   282
51:9   280
51:12   282
52:9   282
52:13   25
52:13–53:12   283
52:14   25–26
52:14–15   25
52:15   25–26
53   25
53:3   27
55   134
55:1–10   134
57:5   190

Jeremiah
2:20   190
3:6   190
7:22   118
11:13   190
13:20   331
13:20–27   331
13:21   331
13:22   331–32
13:25–27   332
13:26   331–32
25:8–14   73
25:11   272
25:12   66
25:30   280
26:16–19   135
26:17–19   246
26:18   275
33:14–26   66
46–51   130, 137
48:28   244
50–51   111–12
50:10   111

50:15   111
51:11   111

Lamentations
1   210, 281
1–5   130
1:2   281
1:5b   234
1:9   281
1:16   281
1:17   282
1:21   282
2   210
3   210, 249
4   210

Ezekiel
1–3   130
4–5   130
6:13   190
8–11   130
10   197–98
13:17–23   335
15:1–6   282
16   344
16:59   11
17   282
17:1–24   282
19:10–14   282
26–28   169
26–29   195
26:1   195
26:7–12   195–96
26:19   169
27:32   169
28   72, 130
28:2   169
28:11–19   70
28:13   71
28:14   71–72
28:14–16   71
28:16   71
29:17   195
29:18   195
34:23–24   176
36   130
37:24   176
40–48   130, 156
40:1–4   156
41:1–2   156
41:3–4   156

Daniel
1   350
1–6   358
2   218–19
2–7   218
2:4b–7   218
2:18–19   88
2:37   88

2:44   88
3   218–19
4   218–19
5   218–19
6   218–19
7   218–19
11   130, 143, 147

Hosea
1–2   134
1–3   249
1:7   94, 96
3:5   96
4   83
4:5   96
4:15   96, 177
4:15–17   83
4:16   134
5:5   94, 96
6:11a   96
6:11b   96
9:4   96
10:1   134
10:1–8   282
10:11   96
11:8   177
11:10   96
12:1 [2]   96
12:2 [3]   83
12:3 [4]   96

Joel
1–2   134
2:13   291
2:32 [3:5]   275
3:2 [4:2]   177
3:10 [4:10]   293
3:12 [4:12]   177

Amos
1   137
1–2   137
1:3–5   214
1:3–2:16   213
1:6   53
1:6–8   214
1:9–10   214
1:11–12   214
1:13–15   214
2:1–3   214
2:4–5   214
2:6–16   214
5:23   27
5:25   118
6:10   280
6:12   35
6:12b–13   35
6:13   35
6:14   176
8:3   280
9:1   73

Obadiah
17   275

Jonah
1:5   269
1:9   88, 269
1:14   269
3:4   134
3:10   134
4:2   291, 298

Micah
1:1   176
1:10   175
1:10–15   175
1:14   176
3   134, 209–10
3:1   209
3:1–4   209–10
3:2   210
3:2–3   245–46
3:3   210
3:4   210
3:5   209
3:5–8   209
3:9   209–10
3:9–11   246
3:9–12   209–10
3:10   210
3:11–12   210
3:12   135, 246, 275
5   176
5:2 [1]   176
5:4 [3]   176
6   130
7:18–20   292

Nahum
1:2–3   291, 298
1:2–11   210
1:3   291
3:8   110–11
3   110–11, 224

Habakkuk
2   280
2:6b   209
2:6b–8   209
2:6b–20   209
2:9   209
2:9–11   209
2:12   209
2:12–14   209
2:15   209
2:15–17   209
2:18–20   209
2:19   209, 281
2:19–20   280
2:20   280

Zephaniah
1:7   280
3:6   36

Haggai
1:1–11   247
1:2–4   247
1:4   247
1:5   247
1:7   247
1:9   247
1:12–15   247
2:1–9   247
2:3   247
2:10–19   247
2:12   247
2:13   73, 247
2:19   247
2:20–23   247

Zechariah
1–9   130
2   280
2:1–13 [5–17]   279
2:8 [12]   279
2:10–11 [14–15]   279
2:13 [17]   280
4:2   57
10:4   36

Malachi
1:1   214
1:2   214
1:2–5   214
1:6   214
1:6–2:9   214
1:7–8   214
2:10–16   214
2:17–3:5   214
3:6–12   214
3:13–4:3 [3:13–21]   214
4:4–6 [3:22–24]   214

New Testament

Mark
12:10   36
13:28–29   310

Acts
2:27   37
4:11   36
13:33   156
13:35   37

Ephesians
2:20   36

Philippians
3:13   313

1 Peter
2:6   36

2 Peter
2:15   89

Jude
11   89

Revelation
2:14   89
3:20   310
21:2   310

About the Author

Matthieu Richelle (PhD, EPHE-Sorbonne; Habil, Université de Strasbourg) is Professor of Old Testament Exegesis at the Université catholique de Louvain, in Louvain-la-Neuve, Belgium. He is a former student of the École biblique et archéologique française de Jérusalem. He is involved in two major projects that are producing new editions of the biblical text: as lead editor of 1 Kings in the HBCE (The Hebrew Bible: A Critical Edition), and as a collaborating editor on the BHQ (*Biblia Hebraica Quinta*). The author of four books, sixty scholarly articles, and several dozen popular articles, Richelle has published extensively on the exegesis of the Hebrew Bible and ancient Semitic inscriptions. *Interpreting Israel's Scriptures* is the second of his books to be translated into English, after *The Bible and Archaeology* (also with Hendrickson).